Pioneers in Their Own Rights

by

Henry Poellnitz Johnston

(Author of *Little Acorns from the Mighty Oak*)

1

Published by THE FEATON PRESS

P. O. Box 7661

Birmingham, Ala.
35223

Printed by *Vulcan Printing & Lithographing Co.*

Birmingham, Ala.
35203

Dedicated

to

My Mother

ELOISE SIMMS WHITE JOHNSTON

who taught me to pray

and

the value of prayer

"If each of us can be helped by science

to live a hundred years,

what will it profit if our hates and fears,

our loneliness and our remorse

will not permit us to enjoy them?

What use is an extra year or two

to the man who 'kills' what time he has?"

.........Anonymous

People will not look

forward to posterity,

who never looked

backward to their ancestors.

...... *Edmund Burke*

By adverting to the dignity of this high
calling, our ancestors have turned a savage
wilderness into a glorious empire; and have
made the most extensive and the only honorable
conquests, not by destroying but by promoting
the wealth, the number, and the happiness of
the human race.

.... *Edmund Burke*

AUTHOR'S NOTES and EXPLANATIONS

ABBREVIATIONS:

    b................birth

    ca...............about the time of

    d................died

    m................married

    NFI..............no further information
                    available at this time

ADDENDUM (corrections and additions).....at end
    of book

FOOTNOTES...........sometimes as * or ** at bottom
    of page; sometimes numbered and placed at the
    end of the chapter.

                    THE AUTHOR,

                Henry Poellnitz Johnston

FOREWORD

When I was a child, Sunday afternoon visiting with our kinfolks came almost as regularly as the new week.

Our visits were not confined to my father's side of the family, though he was a devout family man. My Mother was close to her family too, so we visited both sides.

Over dusty roads, and sometimes over rain-soaked roads, we would leave home after Sunday dinner for an afternoon visit.

As vividly as yesterday, I remember an hour and a half ride to Marion to see my *White* relatives.....I make this same distance now in less than thirty minutes. Another time it was a visit to Newbern to see the *Whites*, or to Sugarville to see the *Phillips*. Some of those we visited along the way were just friends, so far as I knew, but with the writing of this book, I found some to have been married into the family or connected by marriage and, thus, they became a part of "our family"!

I guess everything one does in life must have a reason or a purpose......certainly our visitations were because of the closeness of family ties and the desire to keep a closer contact with our kin, and to "introduce the newer generation" to each other.

During these fast moving times of the middle twentieth century we have all been ALL too busy for much visitation and,as a result, families are.....and have been growing apart.

The writing of this book has behind it a purpose.......the purpose being to acquaint others with their own relatives....sort of an introduction to our neighbors who we never realized were also our kin. And, in working on this book that is exactly what has happened to me. Several people living right here in Birmingham who I have known for years have turned out to be either my blood kin, or kin by marriage.

Of course, the writing of a book with the magnitude and scope of *Pioneers In Their Own Rights* could never be accomplished by a single person. It must, through necessity, be a combined effort of several. Therefore, I confess that *Pioneers In Their Own Rights* is not MY book, but a combination of work and effort by many other people who have contributed.

The combined many years put into the gathering of the information of this book would well exceed a half century. To those tireless hours given by our kin in making this book possible, I must give thanks, and MANY thanks. I wish it were possible to mention each person individually, but that would be impossible.

It would be quite unfair, however, not to mention the years of work put in research by *Henry P. White*, now deceased, and by *Edna White Wood*, now deceased. The use of their material made the White line the easier.

Frances Underwood has spent hours in checking the Perry County Court House, in correspondence and in personal contacts. Without her, much of the documented information on those who were *Pioneers In Their Own Rights* in Perry County would have been impossible.

To *Frances Jeter Michaelcheck, Ethyle Edmonston Pritchett,* and *Florence Elliott Hillis* go thanks for helping in much information about the Whites of Weakley Co., Tennessee.

Under the chapter on *The Whites* we find that the children of Joshua White, with the exception of George M. White, moved to Weakley County. On one occasion George M. White and his first child, Martha (Matt), visited relatives in Weakley, and on one occasion Joshua Asbury White and his son, Garland, visited Uniontown. Since before the turn of the century there has been no correspondence or contacts between the Weakley County Whites and the Perry County Whites, to the best of my knowledge. A by-chance letter from Florence Elliott Hillis to Frances Underwood, Marion, which was turned over to me has again brought the families in contact with each other. And, thanks to *Mary Fisher Hunt Clement* of Oxford, Granville Co., N. C.

Mary Graves White, Lizzie White Woods, Mattie Brown Pou have helped in descendants of the George M. White line.

To *Cousin Nannie Turner White,* a native of Warren County, North Carolina, and now living in Birmingham, special thanks go for her efforts and the material she secured, which otherwise could never have been secured. I hope her material will introduce the younger Whites of Granville with the younger Whites of Warren.

My thanks go to *Mary Louise King, Mayfield Gattis* and *Lottie Morgan Bradford*, deceased, for their help in gathering information on the PHILLIPS family.

On the SIMMS side of the family, I wish to express my appreciation to Cousin *Emma Wheeler Poche* and *Lois Wheeler Maynard*.

Carl C. Morgan, Marshall M. Levis, Marion M. Frost, Adele Underwood, Walter West Underwood, Robert Bruce Underwood, John Tolliver Underwood, Katie Underwood, and many others were most helpful with the MORGAN descendants.

Lucile Dorroh Burton has been working for nearly thirty-five years collecting material on the DORROH line. Without her help the Dorroh material would have been quite insufficient. She has kept a keen interest in her family alive and has secured the help and cooperation of many in the family. To her... for her work and her interest.....I can never sufficiently express my gratitude.

I wish space permitted my mentioning others......I am grateful to all of them.

On the professional genealogical side, I should mention that documented material has been furnished from *Miss Eva Moore Fagan, Mrs. W. Fred Irwin, Mrs. David George, William Perry*

Johnson, Mrs. Lucille S. Hutt, Mrs. William Dabney Duke, and Miss Caroline Cunningham.

It must be remembered that much information, especially dates of birth, death and marriages in the more recent years have come from information furnished me by others; and there may be some conflicting dates.....there are possibly some deaths, births, and marriages that have transpired since the book was started and, therefore, are not included..... for any of these omissions, we ask your forgiveness. For all that is right and correct, we ask you to remember it is because of a combined effort of many.....if there are errors, I can only ask your indulgence.

To my regrets, you will find some missing information. In some instances, dates will be incomplete.....names will be lacking....lines of descent are concluded abruptly. For all this, we have sincere regrets, but it was impossible to include many of these because information was not sent.........after one, two and sometimes three requests! I hope those who have been omitted, because information was not available, will not be too critical...... experience from a former book has proved to me that the ones who failed to cooperate are usually one's severest critic.

This undertaking has been a real pleasure, though discouraging at times. But....... since its completion....it is, and has been a gratifying undertaking.

Henry Poellnitz Johnston

WILLS, COURT RECORDS

and

OLD LETTERS

CONTENTS

ALABAMA IN 1820

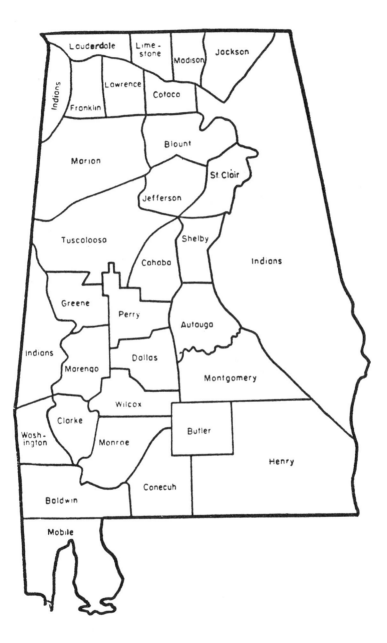

VIRTUS OMNIA VINCIT

White

Virtue Conquers All

The Whites

Daniel White was not the first white person in the colony of Virginia nor was he the first *White* to set foot on American soil.

But, we do find Daniel White thoroughly capable of being known as one of our *Pioneers In Their Own Rights*.

The first we hear of this ancestor, and it is not safe to assume he was our progenitor, was on the fourth day of September 1661 when he, a gentleman, secured 69 acres at a place called Round Hill, on the high-upper side of the Machotic River in Westmoreland County, Virginia, beginning at head line of land formerly belonging to Thomas Boyce, deceased, northwest to land formerly belonging to John Hillier, deceased. [1] And, we find that in Westmoreland County on March 5, 1664 Daniel White, with William Browne and William Boltrop received 744 acres of land (jointly) in the forest between the Potomac and the Rappahannock Rivers for the transportation of 15 people to the colony. [2]

At this point it might be interesting to note that Westmoreland County was formed from Northumberland County in 1653 and, in turn, Northumberland was formed from York in 1634. York was one of the original shires or counties in the Colony of Virginia, all of which were formed in 1634.....so we can easily see that Northumberland was formed only a short time after York County, and Westmoreland became a separate county nine years later.

The name *White* is English by origin and

is one of the more common names in America. It would be easy for any of us to guess that Smith was the most common name and then perhaps Jones, and Brown, but we would be slightly off base. Smith is the most common name, with Johnson in second place, followed by Williams, Jones in fourth and Brown in fifth place. And, *White* is in thirteenth place.... but this does not include the *Whytes*. [3] It is assumed that the name originally came as a descriptive noun meaning that the person was light in coloring or lighter than others in his coloring.

Other families whose names appear in the 216 most popular names in America and appear prominently in this book are: *Allen* with a rank of 24, *Phillips* 37, *Morgan* 51, *Cunningham* 147, and *Hopkins* 206. And, lest we forget, the author's own family name *Johnston* ranks 115.....though more often than not..... he is labeled *Johnson*, **which** is more than not acceptable to one of a Scotch descent.

One of the things that has puzzled me in the study of the *White* family is that the first of our line which we can document bears the name *Daniel*, yet we do not find this name occurring and reoccurring as is usually the case. In our family we find George and John most common names.

Early English tax records, census figures and church records show that *White* families, were anciently seated in the following locations: York, Berks, Kent, Cornwall, Devon, Dorestshire, Weymouth, Derby, Durham, Hants, Wainsborough and Hampshire in England. And, there were branches of the family in Scotland and Ireland.

And, the *Whites* came early to America. Many of them indeed were *Pioneers In Their Own Rights*. The first person bearing the name *White* in America is believed to be a George White who on Oct. 20, 1617 was pardoned by Governor Argell of the Colony of Virginia, for running away to the Indians with his arms and ammunition. [4] We have found nothing further on this George White.......

But, there was a land grant to a "Mr. George White, 'minister of the word of God', 200 acres lying northerly upon the river Nanzemond (present spelling Nansemond), and westernly upon a creek dividing said land from that of James Knot, and easterly upon a creek called the first creek, due for the transportation of four persons." This was in June of 1635. [5] So by the year 1635 we know there were, or had been, two George Whites in Virginia. This latter George is believed to be the same who matriculated on June 12, 1618 age 17, in Broadgates Hall, Oxford University.

We must remember that the first permanent white settlers came to America, landing at Jamestown May 14, 1607, thirteen years before the Pilgrims landed at Plymouth. There were three ships in the "convoy"; Susan Constant, Goodspeed, and Discovery. On these three ships were 100 men and 4 boys, no women. These colonizers were sent from London by a group of merchants known as the Virginia Company. Their purpose was search for treasure, to spread Christianity among the Indians, and to raise farm products that could not grow in England. The town and river, Jamestown and James River, were named in honor of their King, King James I of England, who had been James VI of Scotland.

From Jamestown, slowly but surely, with the passing of time the settlers moved westward......up the James River, up the Pamukey and Mattoponi Rivers, and then the Rappahannock and Potomac. And by 1634 enough settlers had come to that section between the Rappahannock and Potomac that Westmoreland County was carved from Northampton and we find our Daniel White.

From the first....it would seem he was a young man and prosperous, but by 1677 he had fallen into financial difficulties as seen from the following correspondence: [6]

"To ye sixth afermative

"Mr. Step: Mannering Warrant to Danniel Whitte:

"By virtue of a warrant by me received from ye Honble Gen^{ll} Tho: Goodwiche for ye impressing of all ye pvisions belonging to ye delinqüents & secureing of ye estates of all those y^t are fledd Till further ord^r from ye Right Honble Nathaniell Bacon, General of his Maj^{ts} forces in Virginia, and heareing y^t Coll. John Washingtons overseers are conveying of Corne, meat & Tobacco in a sloope or sloops over to Maryland and being myselfe at this instant goeing against ye Indians These are therefor in his Maj^{ts} name to will & require you Daniel White upon sight hereof immediately to goe to ye plantacon of ye s^d Washington by ye river side & cease & impress all ye corne & pvision, Tobacco, stocke or stocks y^t belong to ye s^d Washingtons either one y^t plantacon or one ye other plantacon called ye Round hills & to command ye overseer of both plantacons In his Maj^{ts} name not to suffer any corne, cattle, horses, mares, servants, or any other things to be conveyed away by any pson or psons till further order from ye Generall & to cease y^t sloope, or sloops y^t shall in any wise attempt ye take-ing pvision conveying of any p't or parssells of goods y^t either belong to the said Wash-ington or any other delinquent y^t str fleed fayle not hereof as you will answer ye con-trary at y^r utmost pill. Given under my hand this 21st of October, 1676.

Stephen Man^{r}ing

"This warrant was recorded June ye 19th,1677.

"Mr Daniell White 's Letter to Coll. Nich Spencer:

"S^r you forced me ye last court to give security to ye good behaviour for what I know not unlesse thereby I might be ye more awd to give my estate to Coll. Washington w^{sh} I have donne, or at least soe much of it as he was pleased to demand, or If he be not satisfied if he please to demand more I am ready to give it knoweing y^t there is Almighty pviden-ce y^t doth rule or govern all actions And y^t I may not (a word undecipherable) seeke my owne revenge, but rather say with Daniell ye Lord hath bidden him: who himselfe hath pmised by ye words of St.Paul to be the aven-ger of all such things And I did aske Coll. Washington to be there with me & not demand the rigger of s^d bonde in appeareing ye next co^{rt} because I am a poore man & labour hard for my liveing & ye neglect thereof is much damage to me & my children wch hee would not doe unlesse I would Right to you because you were please to tell me I was a contemner of

Authority and in not appeareing I might soe
be pved w^eh words you had noe reason   at   all
to speake because there hath never   bin y^e
least misdemeanor pved ag^t me by any pson in
this County though I have bin now a house--
keeper therein this 20 yeares neither have
you or any prson in authority ever seene any
such thing by me Although it may be some hon-
ourlicke (?) men whom I have not bin over
fond in adoring(not as they were magistrates)
but, as they were proud men & may inform you
as much, but their malice ought not to be believed for itt did sufficiently appeare ag^t
me in there life time, but it hath pleased
God to remove them & now feareing ye Devill
will alwayes be intrigueing ag^t me my request
to yor Hono^rs is to be pleased to Judge more
favourably than formerly you have done & Con-
sider I Labor hard & that ye yeare is more
then ordinary laborious & if I have no horse
4 or 5 dayes must needs much hinder my bus-
inesse & labour in travellinge & be pleased
to excuse my not appearing this Court without
urging any Contempt ag^t me soe y^t forfeiture
of my bond & I will attend ye next Court to
know further of your pleasure who am your servant,

Daniel White,

July ye 24th, 1677.

"This letter was recorded ye 29 Sept. 1677."

Thus we note from the above letter that
Daniel White had been a house keeper,other-
wise head of a household, for at least twenty
years and, thus, we may certainly assume him
to be no less than forty years old at the
writing of his letter in 1677, which would

make us assume him to be born sometime between 1630 and 1635. This could have easily
made him fit in the period when he could have
been a son of the Reverend George White, who
secured 200 acres of land on Nansemond River
in 1635.......though there is certainly nothing in our research to make us do more than
speculate, and do a bit of wishful thinking.

When reading the correspondence between
Stephen Mannering and Daniel White we ran
across the following confession from Mr. Mannering concerning his participation in the Na-
thanial Bacon Rebellion. Because of the historical factor of this rebellion, we think
this would be interesting to have in this
book:

"June ye 19th 1677, this warrant was
recorded:

"Stephen Man^{r}ing. Joseph Hardwick & Rich
Bartton, Rich: Donahan confession:

"Ifforasmuch as wee Stephen Man^{r}ing, Joseph Hardwick, Rich: Bartton, Rich: Donahan
have bin currently notoriously actors in y^e
late horrid rebellion sett on foot by Nathaniel Bacon Junr to ye great dishonor of God,
perturbacon of ye peace, wellfare & safety of
his Maj^{ts} Collony of Virginia & to evill ex-
ample of our fellow subjects within the same.
Wee ye said Stephen Man^{r}ring, Joseph Hardwick,
& Richard Barton, Richard Donnaham doe upon
our bended knees humbly, heartily & unfeignedly confesse & acknowledge the saide, trait-
erous & rebellious practises. Whereby wee
have rendered ourselves lyable to ye most severe punishm^t, but doe humbly crave & implor

mercy & pardon of God Almighty, the King's most excellent Maj^ty, His most sacred Maj^trs Governor & other inferior officers & all other our fellow subjects within this Collony for such our horrid, treasonable & rebellious practices, heartily & unfeignedly resolveing with ourselves & humbly begging assistance from God Almighty, never to perpetrate, attempt or consent to Y^e like,"

"This recognitr wee desire to bee Recorded this 19th of June 1677."

> *Joseph Hardwick*
> *Richard Barton*
> *Richard Donahan*
> *Stephen Manring*   [7]

The correspondence between Daniel White and Stephen Mannring reproduced above might leave the impression our ancestor might be more in trouble with the laws than in the good graces of the courts. For that reason I quote the following:

"Mr. Stephen Man^ring warrant to Daniel White:
"These are his Maj^ts name to Impower Mr Daniel White to take into his custody two young mares belonging to Jno. Griffin & them reserve till further order from Y^e Generall or Lt. Generall, or till such time that ye sd Griffin hath cleared himself trespasse committed against ye said

Lt Generall & y^t he shall   not   have anything
to   doe at ye plantacon of Coll. Spencer till
further order.   Given under my   hand this 6th
day of November, 1676."

Stephen Man^{r}ing.

The Colonel Washington mentioned   in the
correspondence was   the   great grandfather of
George, our first president, and   he   settled
in Westmoreland probably   very   soon after it
was formed from Northumberland. Colonel Richard Lee, the immigrant,settled in York County
in   1640   and between 1647 and 1651 had built
Cobbs Hall in   Northumberland   in that   part
which   became Westmoreland in   1653, and   we
must not forget   both of these   counties, Northumberland and Westmoreland, were   once   a
part of York.

The   Washington family should   be   quite
interesting to the readers of this book as we
find Captain Nicholas Martian,a French Hugue-
not,was born ca 1591 and came to Virginia before 1620 [8].   He was   in   the House of Burgess 1623 and 1631-2-3, and served as Justice
of   York from 1633   to   1657.   His   will   was
proved   in   York County April   24, 1657.   His
daughter,   Elizabeth, married   George   Reade,
who we shall discuss in more detail later....
pausing only to say that George White, grandson of Daniel White, married Susannah Read of
Westmoreland County.

We find   that   Mildred Read, daughter of
Elizabeth Martian   and   George   Read, married
Augustine   Warner, Jr.   and,   in   turn,their
daughter,   Mildred,married Lawrence Washington
son   of Col. John and father   of Augustine and
grandfather of Gen. George Washington.

But, let's not digress further from our
Daniel White: we have estimated him to have
been born about 1630/5 and he died in 1700.
His will was written the latter part of 1699
and was ordered recorded in Westmoreland
County, August 28, 1700. Mrs. Lucille S.
Hutt, Deputy Clerk of the Circuit Court of
Westmoreland County, wrote on Dec. 15, 1960
that: "I am enclosing the Order of proof for
Daniel White's will.......I do not understand
why the will is not recorded here after hav-
ing been ordered to be by the Court."

The Order from the Court granted his son
John White, to proceed with the probation of
the will as provided.

John White continued to live in Westmoreland County until his death early in 1750. We
find from a deed executed by John White that
his father, Daniel, had secured land as late
as 1694, six years before his death; and that
John White had secured for himself land near
Round Hill. This is documented by the following transaction recorded in Westmoreland County, Will and Deeds No. 9. page 35:

"Deed between John White of Washington
Parish, Westmoreland County, Virginia, planter, and George Blackman of same, on 19th of
March, 1739. That whereas, I, Daniel White,
late of the said parish planter, deceased,
father of the said John White, in his lifetime
did obtain a grant from the proprietors of
the Northern Neck bearing date of 21st day of
December, 1694, and was that tract of land in
the parish of Washington, County of Westmoreland, adjoining Anthony Beard, Thomas Bullock,
etc., land formerly belonging to Thomas Brice,

deceased. Said Daniel White in his lifetime did also obtain a patent for 69 acres being the place called Round Hills near to upper Machotick run, said patent bearing date of Spetember, 1661. The said Daniel White by his will dated 30th of December, 1699 among other things did advise to his son, John White, the two above patents of land and whereas Nathaniel Gray by his deed on 25th day of Mar.1714, did sell to John White land near Round Hills."

John White's age is unknown; in his will written Feb. 18, 1746 [10] he says he is 63 years old, or thereabouts, which make him to be born about 1683. Fortunately, we found a copy of his will, reproduced in its entirety under WILLS, COURT RECORDS, LETTERS...he mentions sons George, William; daughters Mary White, Ann Walker, Sarah Russell; grandchildren Elizabeth White and John White. He provided that George White was to inherit "all my land and plantation and my mill and all belonging to it provided he doth not sell it and if he should (sell) that, Brother and Sisters should have an equal parte."

His widow, Mary White (maiden name unknown) wrote her will Oct. 20, 1764. She died before Feb.26, 1765 when her will was probated in Westmoreland Co. [11] She speaks of Ann Porter,daughter of Sarah Russell;Mary White , daughter of Phillip White;and son,George White.

Phillip White and children are unmentioned in his father's will. In Mary White's will she leaves nothing to Phillip White: mentions daughters Mary and Ann Porter.Nothing is left daughters Sarah Russell, Ann Walker,or grandchildren John and Elizabeth. From John's will his son,William, apparently was unmarried at the time of his death. As William is not mentioned by his mother it may be he died without issue.

George White, after his marriage to Susannah Read, had the wander lust to move into newly developed lands and, thus, became another one of those *Pioneers In Their Own Rights*, for by 1764 he had moved to Lunenburg County, Virginia. But, George had no intention of disposing of the lands he had inherited from his father,so we find in Westmoreland County, Deeds and Wills Book 16, page 92, a deed of George White and Susannah, his wife, contents of which follows:

"Deed of George White and Susannah, his wife, of County of Mecklenburg, to William Porter, Sr. of Westmoreland for 17 pounds, 16 shillings, tract of land in Westmoreland County Parish of Cahle, on Head branch of Manokin run in Moniny Forrest, land given said George White by his father, John White, deceased by will and was leased by said George White to William Porter, Sr. for 99 years bearing date of November 5, 1764, recorded in Westmoreland County.

"Witnesses: - Joseph Lane, Spencer Gill, James Reynolds, James Smith, Nathaniel Pope, Daniel Walker, Will Read, Jr., Aaron Hardge."

While George White was holding onto his Westmoreland County property, inherited from his father with the understanding that he would not sell the property, we find that George White, of County Mecklenburg, Virginia did deed to Joseph Redman, Thomas Yeatman,and Gerrard McKing of the County of Richmond,Virginia the whole and sole estate belonging to "my wife, left her by her deceased father." This was signed and executed May 16,1768.[12]

We also find that a deed of George White

"of County Lunenburg,but late of Westmoreland Virginia" leases 100 acres of land on the branches of the Manocan Run. [13]

During this same period we find George White increasing his holdings in Mecklenburg County, and in Lunenburg County. On May 10, 1764 we find George White bought from Nathaniel Robertson and his wife, Elizabeth,of Lunenburg 374 acres of land for 150 pounds in the Parish of St. James on both sides of Mitchell's Creek beginning at a white oak on the county line. [14]And, a year later, we find that George White, with his wife, Susana, signed a deed to George Duncan stating "On this eighth day of May in the year of our Lord one thousand seven hundred and sixty--five between George White of the County of Mecklenburg and Parish of St. James, of the one part,and George Duncan of the same county and Parish, of the other part wit.said George White for and in consideration of the sum of 30 pounds current money of Virginia to said George Duncan bargain and release parcel of land lying in the Parish and being land said Duncan now lives on, 100 acres more or less bounded as follows: the beginning of Edmund Taylor corner, White Oak on the county line standing in his Mill Creek and running thence on his line across a ridge to a white oak.[15]

Though this was the first transaction where George White was disposing of land in Virginia, it was no indication that he was moving into Granville County, North Carolina this early for we find on September 26, 1778 that he purchased from Edmund Taylor 245 acres of land for 50 pounds. This property is described as "beginning at the said George White's red oak and running along his line to the said Charles Lewis "line to the road thence along the road to pointers on the said road on the Carolina line". [16]

From all indication George White retained title to his Mecklenburg County property until 1784 when he sold one portion to William Taylor amounting to 100 acres and on the same day sold 444 acres to Francis Williams, both gentlemen of Mecklenburg County. [17]

The homestead of George White, as above mentioned, was on the Virginia-North Carolina line. Whether he had actually secured property in North Carolina before the Revolution is not documented, but he did serve in the war from the State of North Carolina, according to North Carolina Colonial Records by Clark, Vol. 17, page 260.

As mentioned above, George White married in Westmoreland County Mary Susannah Read, the daughter of Coleman Read, whose will was proved in Westmoreland County on April 26, 1748. He mentions his wife as Ruth and two sons, Joseph and Richard, and one daughter, Mary Susannah, but does not mention her last name; so we are not sure she had married before his death or shortly after......but best records indicate she and George White did marry in 1748. He also mentions in his will three grandsons: Coleman Brown, Coleman Dunkin, and merely Hutt. A complete copy of the Coleman Read will can be found under *WILLS COURT RECORDS, and OLD LETTERS.*

The father of Coleman Read was Andrew Read, also of Westmoreland County. He mentions his son Coleman Read and son Andrew Read. Unfortunately, the will is not complete, or it might have revealed more, but what was available will be found under WILLS, COURT RECORDS, OLD LETTERS. His wife is not mentioned, so it is likely she pre-deceased him and since the will is filed in Book 2, Deeds and Wills of Westmoreland Court which contains documents between 1691-99, he had died before Daniel White.

It is quite unfortunate that we have not been able to document the father of Andrew Read. In my search of the Read family I found in the Virginia State Land Office, Richmond, Va. that Maj. George Read secured 500 acres in Northumberland between 1652-55; Thomas Read received 300 acres in Northumberland during the same period; Col. George Read (same as George above) received 2,000 acres in Westmoreland between 1655 and 1664; Andrew Read received 400 acres in Westmoreland between 1661-6. There should be little doubt that there was a definite family connection with these Reads and our Andrew.

I checked on George Read and through him traced the family back to Andrew Reade, whose will was proved in 1623. This Andrew Reade was from Faccombe, in the County of Southampton. Copying from the Virginia Historical Magazine we find "In 1584 Andrew Reade bought the manor of Linkenholt, Hampshire." His will was dated Oct. 7, 1619, with a codicil Nov. 15, 1621, and proved Oct. 24, 1623. He had daughters: Margaret, Mildred, Anne, and Mary and five sons: Henry, *Robert*, John, George, and Andrew.

Robert Reade married Mildred Windebanke and his will was written in 1626. We find he had, like his father, five sons: Andrew,William, Thomas, Robert and George.

The youngest son George came to Virginia in 1640 and was deputy secretary, James City Co. in 1649 a member of the House of Burgesses, and also a member from York County in 1652. He was confirmed Counsel of State in 1660 by Charles II of England and died in 1671. His surviving children were Robert, Francis, Thomas, Benjamin, Mildred--wife of Col. Augustin Warner, and Elizabeth--wife of Capt. Thomas Chesman.

The information concerning Andrew Reade came from Vol. XXVII, Virginia Quarterly, pages 303-4-5-6; and that on George Reade came from Vol. I, Tyler, page 248.

George Reade's will speaks of a grandson Andrew Read.

From this, we find Andrew Reade died in 1623. His grandson, George, son of Robert, died in 1671. Thus, we find our Andrew Read's will was proved between 1691 and 1699, and all of this adds up to the proper time lapse for our Andrew Read to have been the same Andrew Read spoken of as a grandson of George Read; and thus he *could have been* the son of Robert, Francis, Thomas or Benjamin Read. Unfortunately, many of the old records of York, Northumberland, and Westmoreland have been destroyed and documentation is impossible.

Laurence Washington married Mildred Read, a sister of the four Read brothers above mentioned. That would make Laurence and Mildred Read Washington's son, Augustine, a first cousin of the children of Robert, Francis, Thomas

and Benjamin Read; and if Andrew were the son
of one of these brothers,then Andrew Read and
George Washington, son of Augustine, were
cousins.

It is my sincere hope that what has been
above written about John Washington, Daniel
White,George Reade and their descendants will
create enough interest that others will join
with me in further research on these lines;
and, perhaps, some day we might be able to
document these possible connections.

But, now let's go back to our George
White and his wife, Susannah Read:

There were 10 known children of this
family. There might have been others who died
in infancy, leaving no information concerning
them. The children in their order were: Mary
who married a Mr. Meginess; Ruth (Ruthy) Read
who married Jesse Carter; John, who married
Agnes Mayfield...they moved to Warren County,
N. C.; William who married a Miss Bellair;
Coleman Read,who married first Celah Bradford
and second Polly Cole; Philip,who married Ann
Mann; Ann Read, who married Josiah Allen;
Garrot; Joshua, who married Rachel Allen; and
Joseph, who married Nancy Mann.

Following pages go into more detail as
to the *descendants of George White and Susannah Read.*

With the use of only a single name, we
continue through this book to find it quite
difficult to always document individuals. On
May 2,1768 a deed was executed between George
and John White on the one hand and John Bus-
bee, of Granville Co., on the other. This
deed is recorded in Granville County Book H,
page 412 and speaks of George and John White

as the sons of George White, Sr., of Mecklenburg. This, of course, gave several of the
very earlier researchers the idea that there
were two brothers, George and John White, who
came from eastern Virginia; and as one early
researcher wrote, "one brother settled in
Warren County, N. C. and the other in Granville. This one was George."

Who the George and John White were remains a mystery to me, but it is for certain
that *our* George White, who settled in Lunenburg and Mecklenburg and then Granville was
not the same George, for his father was John,
son of Daniel. The John who settled in Warr-
en Co., N. C. was the son of George White,
husband of Mary Susannah Read.

The 1788 **Tax** List for Granville Co.shows
quite a number of Whites in the county, namely: Coleman, George, John, Searl, and William Roads, all from Fort Creek District; Jonathan, Phillip, Sr., and Phillip, Jr. from
Oxford; Mark, Thomas, and Valentine from Epp-
ing Forest.

I have not been able to find any connection between Searl White and George White,and
I am not sure whether this William Roads
White and George's son, William, are one and
the same or not.

It is quite unlikely that the Oxford
Whites are related to George White, and I
feel sure there are no connections between
Mark, Thomas, and Valentine White and our
George. Years ago in searching for *Johnston*
information in Lanchester and Dauphin Coun-
ties, Pennsylvania, I ran across a Valentine
White and I suspect he is the same one we

now find in Granville. The Johnstons moved from Pennsylvania to what was Granville, then Orange, and today the old Johnston homesteads would stand in both Orange and Alamance.

We are inadequate in our knowledge of where the descendants of George White and Susannah Read lived. But, to the best of our knowledge, William eventually moved to middle Tennessee; John remained in Warren Co., and Coleman Read White and perhaps Phillip remained in Granville. We know Garrot disposed of his North Carolina lands and it is believed he moved to Tennessee. Joshua is known to have died in Granville and it is believed Joseph did likewise.

Descendants of Joshua White and his wife Rachel Allen seem to have developed the wander lust like their grandfather George, and they, in turn, became *Pioneers in Their Own Rights*.

George M. White, the oldest child, came the long journey from Granville to Perry County on horseback, accompanied only by a Negro slave known as *Reuben*. Why he came to Alabama when other members of his family moved to Weakley Co., Tennessee has always been an unknown secret.....just as George M. White never told anyone what the M. in his name stood for. When asked, he would only laugh and say, *"it was just 'M' or maybe it stands for Moses"*, and he died without anyone ever knowing for sure!

George M. White came to Perry Co. around 1835. Early records show that on July 9, 1836 he bought 80 acres of land in Section 23 in the present Walthall Beat, located some six or seven miles north of present day Uniontown off the old Marion Road, now State Road 183. This was bought from William G. Phillips of Dallas County. On June 24, 1840 he bought 520 acres from Francis M. Phillips of Dallas County. This land was in the Coffee Springs Community in the vicinity of Coffee Creek. The land was located on both sides of Federal Highway 80, about 3 or 4 miles east of Uniontown. It was here that he lived until after the birth of his first child, Aunt Mat who married James Brown......and as a child I remember Aunt Mat so affectionately. Sometime in 1846,or early 1847, he moved to Sugarville in Walthall Beat and he sold his Coffee Creek plantation. The Perry County tax records of 1856 show that in that year he owned 1,000 acres of land in that section of the county.

And, I am proud and happy that some of these holdings of George M. White in the Sugarville section are owned by my Mother,*Eloise Simms White Johnston.*

About a half mile south of Uniontown, just off the Freetown Road,was a little Coffee Spring Cumberland Church. Later the church was moved into Woodville, now Uniontown, and on Nov. 1, 1854 the *"meeting house lot was sold"*. The new church was to be known as the Uniontown Presbyterian Church. The White family has been active for generations in this church, as a matter of fact, since the Coffee

Spring church was first organized in 1848. *The Whites* have furnished many officers of the church, including deacons and elders.

As this book develops you will find that Cunninghams and Morgans are believed to have lived in Lunenburg and Mecklenburg counties in Virginia and then perhaps Granville and then in Laurens District, South Carolina..... so, it might be supposed that correspondence between these families and the Whites contin- ued and that through this correspondence George M.White chose his treck to Perry Coun- ty.

Other children of Joshua and Rachel Allen White moved to Weakley Co., Tennessee and, likewise, became *Pioneers in Their Own Rights*.

Mary Brown White married Ruben Edmonston and they were *Pioneers in Their Own Rights*, he being among the earliest settlers of Weak- ley Co. He first settled a few miles south of Dresden. His brother-in-law, John Brad- shaw, settled on Mud Creek. [18]

Archibald Edmonston,the father of Ruben, came from Todd Co.,Kentucky to Weakley County and settled on the North Obion River. James Hornbeck came a little later and settled be- tween Middle and South Forks of the Obion and also came William Hillis.

When the Edmonstons first came to Weak- ley, wild animals such as elks, bears, deer, panthers, wolves, wildcats and beavers were plentiful, according to Goodspeed, and he re- ports that the first year Ruben Edmonston lived there, that he and his brother-in-law,

John Bradshaw, killed 85 bears! Certainly, no one can dispute they were *Pioneers in Their Own Rights*. Joshua Asbury White came a little later and then came Nancy and her husband, Caleb Brasfield; then Philip, who married Eliza Hornbeck.

The James Hornbeck mentioned above was the father of Elliott D. Hornbeck. Elliott married Elizabeth White, daughter of Joshua Asbury White.

The William Hillis, above mentioned, is an ancestor of Russell Hillis, husband of Florence Elliott who has been so interested in this *White* manuscript.

Though we have made no attempt to make a comprehensive search of the Allen family, we did find that Samuel Allen and Mary McAllister were the parents of Rachel Allen who married Joshua White and Susanna Allen who married Robert Jeter, and this couple moved to Weakley Co., Tennessee. Robert Jeter's father was Samuel Jeter and his mother, Mary Dudley. Samuel had bought land on May 9,1764 on the waters of Flat Creek in Granville County and continued to purchase other lands until 1779.

The Allen family had several other children than Rachel and Susanna, among them being Zachariah, who became a Baptist minister and preached at Grassy Creek Baptist Church in northern Granville and later at Brassfield Church in southern Granville. William was another child and so was Garland, named for his uncle, Garland McAllister. It is believed that Garland A. White, son of Joshua Asbury

White, was Garland Allen.......named for his
uncle.

And, perhaps we could go on and on with
the Allen family, who had moved from Virginia
to Granville.......we would only enlarge this
work........and prove only that they were all
Pioneers in Their Own Rights.

Let's go back to George White and Mary
Susannah Read! Let's follow their children
and their children's children and bring ourselves up to the modern 1960s. Following the
FOOTNOTES, see *Descendants of George White
and Susannah Read.*

F O O T N O T E S

[1] Land Patents-Nugent. *"Cavalliers and
Pioneers,"* page 90.

[2] ibid., page 471.Both records were sworn
to as being correct, by Ida J. Lee, genealogist of Richmond, Va., May 13, 1954.

[3] Press release from the Veterans Administration used in article under title *Charlie
Rice's Punchbowl* in THIS WEEK MAGAZINE.

[4] *Virginia Quarterly,* Volume 15, page 401.

[5] *The Colonial Church of Virginia* by Rev.
Edward Lewis Goodwin.

[6] Copied from First Series of the *William
and Mary Quarterly,* Vol. 2, pages 43, 44, 46,
and 47.

[7] ibid., page 44.

[8] ibid., page 44.

[9] *Virginia Quarterly*, Volume IV, page 426.

[10] By the Gregorian Calendar.

[11] Deeds and Wills, Westmoreland Co., Va., Book 14, page 303

[12] Westmoreland Co., Rec. & Inv.No. 5, page 37.

[13] Westmoreland Co., Deeds and Wills No. 14 page 324.

[14] Lunenburg Co. Deeds and Wills Book 8 , page 54.

[15] Mecklenburg Co. Deed Book 1, page 60.

[16] Mecklenburg Co. Deed Book 5, page 341.

[17] The first of these transactions is recorded in Mecklenburg Co. Deed Book 6, page 368, and the second transaction was recorded in the same book, page 373.

[18] Goodspeed's *"History of Tennessee"*, Weakley Co., page 832.

Descendants of George White and Susannah Read

I   Mary   b   m   **Meginess**   NFI

II   Ruth (Ruthy) Read b   m
      Jesse Carter b   NFI

III   John b   1750 [1] d   1801
     m   1772 Agnes Mayfield b
     1775 d   1830   CHILDREN:

     A   Nancy b   1773 m   a
         Mr. Parker b   NFI

     B   Martha b   1776 m   a
         Mr. Jenkins b   NFI

     C   Ailcy b   1778 m   a
         Mr. Cole b   NFI

     D   Edmund b   1780 d
         1854 m FIRST Dec. 19, 1821 Mary Haygood
         b   d May 23, 1825   CHILD:

         1   William Wallace   [2] b May 23, 1825
            d Nov. 9, 1911 m Oct. 12, 1848
            Panthea Burwell Boyd b May 24, 1830
            d Feb. 6, 1912   CHILDREN: SEE
            SEPARATE LISTING under DESCENDANTS
            OF WILLIAM WALLACE WHITE AND PANTHEA
            BURWELL BOYD

         m   SECOND Sept. 7, 1833 Mary Williamson
         Hilliard b   1799 d   1878
         CHILD:

         2   Sally Agnes b   1834 d
            1891 m Oct. 17, 1855 Doctor William
            Coleman White (M.D.) [3] b Feb. 1,
            1827 d Nov. 27, 1903   CHILDREN:
            SEE SEPARATE LISTING under DESCEND-
            ANTS OF DOCTOR COLEMAN WHITE and
            SALLY AGNES WHITE

IV   William b   m   a Miss
     Bellair and moved to Tennessee   NFI

V   Coleman Read b March 9, 1765 d Sept. 7, 1835
     m FIRST March 12, 1786 Celah Bradford b
     March 18, 1767 d   1811 CHILDREN:

   A   Elizabeth b March 8, 1787 m
       Robert Allison b   NFI

   B   Mary (Polly) b Dec.   1789 m March
       20, 1811 John M. Vincent b   NFI

   C   John b Feb. 29, 1796 d April 5, 1865 m
       Nov. 30, 1825 Hixey Cole b Sept. 1, 1800
       d March 15, 1885. Both buried Banks
       Church burying ground.   CHILDREN:

       1   Doctor William Coleman b Feb. 1,
           1827 d Nov. 27, 1903 m Oct. 17,
           1855 Sally Agnes White b   1834
           d   1891 (See III D a on
           previous page.) CHILDREN: SEE
           SEPARATE LISTING under DESCENDANTS
           OF DOCTOR WILLIAM COLEMAN WHITE
           and SALLY AGNES WHITE

       2   Caroline Narcissus b Jan. 24, 1830
           d May 1, 1889 m Dec. 2, 1856
           Robert Longmire Hunt b July 24,
           1827 d April 1, 1883 CHILDREN:

           a   Victoria Coleman b November
               10, 1857 d July 12, 1912 m
               June 8, 1881 Romulus Bragg
               Parker b June 3, 1856
               CHILD:

    i   Robert Hunt b Feb. 15, 1892 d   m Nov. 28, 1925 Mrs. Rie Alston Williams Rand b   NFI

b   John Graham, M.D., b Jan. 5, 1861 d June 2, 1908 m June 1, 1887 Lorena P. Bobbitt b Dec. 7, 1862 d Dec. 21, 1949   NO ISSUE

c   Joseph Sidney b May 15, 1864 d July 14, 1906 m Jan. 8, 1890 Ann Milburn Gordon b Oct. 27, 1867 d Nov. 24, 1902 CHILDREN:

    i   Gordon b Nov. 8, 1890 d March 12, 1950 m Dec. 27, 1920 Margaret Ann Nail b   CHILDREN:

        (a)   Ada Milburn b Jan. 10, 1922 m Lee Hinshaw b July 31, 1915 Live Winston Salem, N.C.   CHILDREN:

            (i)   Ann Milburn b June 14, 1950

            (ii) Carol Hunt b Nov. 6, 1962

            (iii)David Scott b Dec. 31, 1954

        (b)   Margaret b June 21, 1923 m Philip L. Chapman b June 27, 1923 Live Winston Salem, N. C. CHILDREN:

            (i)   Gordon Hunt b Mar. 2, 1951

            (ii) Philip Vance b Nov. 15, 1952

(c) Joseph Graham b
July 10, 1924 m
Jane Tyson b Nov.
18, 1925 CHILDREN:

    (i) Jane Tyson b
       Mar. 20, 1957

    (ii) Joanna Graham
        b Sept. 13,
        1959

(d) James Sidney b Nov.
9, 1925 m Elizabeth
Dell Maxwell b Nov.
28, 1925 CHILDREN:

    (i) James Sidney II
       b Mar. 8, 1951

    (ii) Elizabeth Max-
        well b June 7,
        1954

    (iii)Gordon Raymond
        b Nov. 1958

(e) Elizabeth Ann b Nov.
24, 1929 m Luther
Bridges Lewis b
Sept. 29, 1929
CHILDREN:

    (i) Margaret b Nov.
       20, 1956

    (ii) John Luther b
        Dec. 26, 1960

(f) Robert Longmire b
June 25, 1933 m Lois
Spahn b Dec. 29,
1933 CHILDREN:

    (i) Mary Pagie b
       Oct. 19, 1959

    (ii) Susanne b Nov.
        28, 1960

          (iii) Robert Blake b
             Jan. 22, 1963

   ii   Mary Fisher b May 16,
        1894 m Jan. 14, 1936
        Amos Baxter Clement b
        March 7, 1891 d Aug. 19,
        1951   NO ISSUE

   iii   Victoria Caroline b July
        4, 1900 UNMARRIED

d   Robert Longmire b Oct. 27,
      1867 d Mar. 12, 1902 UNMARRIED

3   Mary Susannah b Feb. 6, 1833 d Apr.
    3, 1898 m Oct. 23, 1852 Rev. James
    Bell Floyd b Oct. 10, 1830 d Aug.
    1, 1915 Both buried Banks Church
    burying ground CHILDREN: SEE SEP-
    ARATE LISTING under DESCENDANTS OF
    MARY SUSANNAH WHITE and REV. JAMES
    BELL FLOYD

D   Ruth b Dec. 20, 1799 d   m Nov.
   2, 1819 John Crook b   NFI

E   Susannah b April 18, 1802 d   m
   Sept. 10, 1822 Lemuel McGehee b Jan. 30,
   1796 d Jan. 11, 1846 CHILDREN:

   1   J. Y. b Aug. 23, 1823 d Aug. 28,
      1902 m   Susan Cannady b
      1828 d   1907   NFI

   2   W.R. b   NFI

V m SECOND Sept. 26, 1812 Polly Cole b
   d Oct. 12, 1831   CHILDREN:

F   Haskey Ann Nelson b Sept. 18, 1813 d Dec.
   21, 1884 m Nov. 26, 1830 Elias Sanford
   Jenkins b July 16, 1808 d Sept. 27, 1875
   Both buried Weakley Co.Tenn. CHILDREN:
   SEE SEPARATE LISTING under DESCENDANTS
   OF HASKEY ANN NELSON WHITE and ELIAS
   SANFORD JENKINS

G   William George Vaughn b Aug. 3, 1818 d
    Sept. 21, 1881 Weakley Co.,Tenn. m Oct.
    5, 1836 Miranda V. Hester b   NFI
                                    [1]
H   Thomas Person b Apr. 15, 1819 d Jan. 22,
    1888 m Sept. 10, 1844 Rebecca W. Kittrell
    b Nov. 27, 1820 d Aug. 20, 1901 CHILDREN:
    SEE SEPARATE LISTING under DESCENDANTS
    OF THOMAS PERSON WHITE and REBECCA W.
    KITTRELL

I   Frances Long Jane b Dec. 18, 1821 d
    m Jan. 28, 1847 E. J. Looney b   after
    1813 d   1878 CHILD:

    1   Maby Coleman b April 12, 1855 d
         May 13, 1862

J   Sarah Coleman b Jan. 26, 1823 d June 11,
    1907 m FIRST Sept. 20, 1842 James W.
    Lyons b   d   NFI

    m SECOND   James B. Peace b Mar.
    29, 1810 d Aug. 18, 1876

VI Philip b   1768 d   m Feb. 7, 1797
    Ann Mann b   d   CHILDREN:

A   William Read b   1800 d   m
    1830 Franky Gill b   d
    CHILDREN:

    1   William Read II b   d young

[1] Granville Co. Book 14, page 258, June 6,1845
shows he gave power of attorney to his brother,
John White of Granville, to collect his interest
in the estate of William Kittrell (his father-in-
law), deceased, of Granville, Co. His mother-in-
law was the former Lucy Hayes. Thomas Person
White was shown as living in Weakley Co.,Tenn.

2   William Philo b   1836 d 1917
m Oct. 18, 1858 Nancy Mitchell b
July 1, 1837 d   1913 [1]

B   Holly D. b d m Jan. 4, 1919
Lemuel Mitchell b   d   NFI

C   Jacksey b ca 1800 d ca 1875 m Nov. 19,
1833 Guilford Dudley Sims, M.D., b 1789
d   1854 . Both buried Liberty
Cemetery, near Dresden, Tenn. CHILDREN:
SEE SEPARATE LISTING under DESCENDANTS
OF JACKSEY WHITE and DR. GUILFORD
DUDLEY SIMS

VII Ann Read b   d   m July 21, 1794
Josiah Allen b   d   CHILDREN:

A   Harriet b   m   Johnson M. Dunagan
b   NFI

B   Martha b   m John Barker b   NFI

C   Annie E. b   NFI

D   Mary I.

E   Samuel

F. Josiah L.

G   Charles W.

VIII Garrot b   d   NFI [2]

IX Joshua b   1775 d   1826 m Jan. 7,
1805 Rachel Allen b   d   CHILDREN:

[1] Marriage bonds show a Philo W. White m Sept.
7, 1858 Nancy Mitchell (Book 21, page 147, Nov.15,
1859 Elizabeth Buchanan of Warren Co.Ky. gave
power of attorney to Philo White to act in her behalf in the settling of the estate of Valentine
Mayfield)

[2] Granville Co. Deeds Book Q, page 529 shows
he sold his land on Beaverdam Creek to John Shad-
wick in 1802 and left N. C., but no indication as
to where he went.

A   George **M.** b April 17, 1807 d Nov. 9, 1866 m Aug. 22, 1844 Nancy McDavid Morgan b Aug. 2, 1823 d Oct. 25, 1908 Both buried Uniontown, Perry Co., Ala. CHILDREN: SEE SEPARATE LISTING under DESCENDANTS OF GEORGE M. WHITE and NANCY McDAVID MORGAN

B   Mary Brown b July 24, 1808 d July 24, 1874 m   Ruben Edmonston b Dec. 1, 1802 d Nov. 16, 1892 Both buried Liberty Church, near Dresden, Tenn. CHILDREN: SEE SEPARATE LISTING under DESCENDANTS OF MARY BROWN WHITE and RUBEN EDMONSTON

C   Joshua Asbury b Dec. 25, 1811 d June 10, 1883 m FIRST Jan. 7, 1832 Prudence Buchanan b   d Aug. 5, 1840 (age 30 on tombstone) CHILDREN: SEE SEPARATE LISTING under DESCENDANTS OF JOSHUA ASBURY WHITE and PRUDENCE BUCHANAN

      m SECOND   Prescilla Buchanan b ca 1814 [1] d   CHILDREN: SEE SEPARATE LISTING under DESCENDANTS OF JOSHUA ASBURY WHITE and PRESCILLA BUCHANAN

D   **Nancy A.**   b   1812   d   m Caleb Brasfield b   ca 1787 d   ca 1846 CHILD:

      1   Leonard b ca 1841 d   1885 m Elizabeth Annie Jeter b   d CHILDREN:

           a   Caleb Samuel b   1864 d   1895 m Jan. 5, 1888 K. A. Overton b   d   NO ISSUE

           b   William Dennis b   ca 1867 d ca 1921 m   Kate Virginia McKenzie b   d   NO ISSUE

           c   Leonard Coke b Nov. 29, 1869 d m Nannie Ward b Jan. 1, 1874 CHILDREN:

[1]   Prudence and Prescilla were sisters.

i   Mamie b Sept. 9 1895 m
Nov. 15, 1926 Selden
Maiden b   CHILD:

    (a)   William L. b Nov. 4,
    1926 m   Sarah
    Millirons b   NFI

d   Minnie b ca 1872 d   m
Chris Overton b ca 1855 d
ca 1926   CHILD:

    i   Bessie b ca 1893 Lives
    Greenfield, Tenn., m
    Mike Elam b ca 1890 d
    1961   CHILD:

        (a)   Felix b   m   Ann
        Pope b   NFI

e   George Jeter b ca 1874 d
before 1948 m Dec. 12, 1895
Ola Womble b   CHILD:

    i   Lyndell b   m
    Wildone Harris b   CHILD

    (a)   George b   NFI

f   Oscar (M.D.) b   ca 1879 NFI

g   E. Tansil b   ca 1879 d
m Dec. 6, 1899 Alba Swaim b
CHILDREN:

    i   Len Brock b   NFI

    ii   Stella May b   NFI

E   Philip W.   b   1815 [1] d   m
FIRST Aug. 27, 1846   **Eliza R. Hornbeck**
b   d   [2]   CHILDREN:

[1] This birth date from 1850 WEakley Co.Census,
but 1870 census shows him born 1810; either could
be possible.

[2] Name appears in 1850 Weakley Census, but not
in 1860 or 1870 census.

1   William b   1847   NFI

2   George E.

3   John E. b   1853   [1]

4   Mattie b   1855   [1]

E   m   SECOND Sept. 7, 1858 Nancy Mitchell
     [2]   b   d   CHILD:

5   Mollie b   1859   [1]

F   Deremay R. b   NFI

X   Joseph b   1777 d   1829 m Oct. 24,
     1799 Nancy Mann   b   d   CHILDREN:

A   Hixey D. b   d   1844   m
     George Winston b   d   ca 1866 (about
     97 yrs. old) CHILDREN: (had 4, but only
     2 are listed):

1   James N. b   NFI

2   John R. b Jan.   1840 d   m Oct.
     1867 Mary J. Baucom b   d
     (A physician & druggist) CHILDREN:

     a   Minnie C.   b   NFI

     b   Martha A.   b   NFI

     c   Nellie S.   NFI

     d   John S.   NFI

     e   George b   NFI

[1] These birth dates taken from ages shown in
the 1870 census, Weakley Co.Census.

[2] Granville Co. Marriage Records. Neither Eliza
nor Nancy show in the 1870 census; so both wives
must have been dead before 1870 census of Weakley
Co.

B   Eaton J. b   1802 d   1867 m May
     23, 1844 Mary Neely b   1805 d
     Lived in Weakley Co.,Tenn. CHILDREN:

     1   Joseph b   1834

     2   Mary b   1843

C   Tyson M. b   NFI

D   Ann Mann b May 22, 1807 d March 29,
     1872 m Feb. 28, 1827 Jordan D. Moss b
     Jan. 3, 1806 d Jan. 16, 1873 CHILDREN:

     1   Joseph Y. b   NFI

     2   Farah D. b April 9, 1830 d Oct.
          25, 1891   UNMARRIED

     3   Howell C.   NFI

     4   John R.

     5   Lucy F. m   Bailey   NFI

     6   Peter M.

     7   Louis H.

E   Fannie   NFI

F   John F.   NFI

F O O T N O T E S

[1] He was Capt. in Rev. Colonial Records of N.C.
Saunders, Vol. X, page 287; N.C. Rev. Army Accts.
Vol. VIII, page 40, Folio 3. Believe they were
married in Mecklenburg Co., Va.
[2] A Diary of Capt. William Wallace White has
been edited by his granddaughter Nannie Turner
White of Birmingham and her brother (now deceased)
published this splendid book. Over 10 years was
spent in compilation of this diary. He was Leonard Henderson White, buried in Elmwood,Birmingham.
[3] Son of John White, the third child of Coleman Read White, who in turn was the fifth child of
George White. See details under descendants of
Coleman Read White and Celah Bradford.

Descendants of William Wallace White and Panthea Burwell Boyd

I   Lewis Boyd b Nov. 4, 1849 d Dec. 10, 1929 m
        Oct. 31, 1877 Frances Erskine Henderson b Feb.
        10, 1854 d April 8, 1946 (92 yrs. old)
        CHILDREN:

    A   Panthea Boyd b Aug. 3, 1878 Vance Co.,
         N.C., d Dec. 31, 1930 m July 3, 1903
         John W. Mayfield   b Jan. 16, 1873 d
         Sept. 4, 1946   CHILDREN:

         1   John Weldon b June 8, 1904 m
                   Margaret Mills b July 4, 1907
            CHILD:

            a   Margaret Ann b Dec. 22, 1930
                 m Aug. 9, 1952 Merle Harring-
                 ton b Jan. 9, 1930   CHILDREN:

               i   Scott Mayfield b Oct. 20,
                   1953

               ii   David Merle b Nov. 19,
                   1958

         2   James Horace b June 22, 1906 m June
            16, 1921 Mildred Pruden Moore b
            NO ISSUE

         3   Frank Henderson (M.D.)   b June
            23, 1908 m Aug. 21, 1936 Queenee
            Jones b Sept. 24, 1910   CHILDREN:

            a   Sara Frances b March 25, 1938
                 m Aug. 20, 1960 William H.
                 Shreiver b   CHILDREN:

               i   Susan b Sept. 12, 1961

            b   Frank Henderson II b July 20,
                 1939 m Jan. 30, 1958 Judith
                 Rodabaugh b
               CHILDREN:

   i Deborah Frances b Sept. 25, 1958

   ii David Glen b Aug. 9, 1960

   iii Diana b July 20, 1962

  c Richard Glen b Sept. 24, 1941 UNMARRIED

  d Jeanne Victoria b July 13, 1945 UNMARRIED

4 Wallace Boyd b Aug. 14, 1910 m Alma Eaton Kimball b Feb. 27, 1910 CHILDREN:

  a Frank Boyd b July 13, 1943

  b John Allen b Apr. 14, 1946

  c Ruth Henderson b Nov. 3,

5 Lucy Turner b Aug. 20, 1912 m Samuel Trueblood Brown b CHILD:

  a Kay Trueblood b May 21, 1942 m   David Wayne Barrow b Nov. 15, 1940 NO ISSUE

6 Katherine Palmer b Aug. 28, 1917 m July 6, 1940 George E. Shorr b CHILDREN:

  a Joy Panthea b Aug. 2, 1943

  b Craig Mayfield b Aug. 8, 1947

B Nancy (Nannie) b May 9, 1880 UNMARRIED Living Birmingham, Ala. taught school in N. C. for 44 years

C Leonard Henderson b Mar. 1, 1882 d Aug. 22, 1962 Buried Elmwood Cemetery, Birmingham, m Aug. 25, 1908 Stella

Arnold b Jan.   1882. Lived Flowing W
Farm on Highway 5 south of Marion, Ala.
CHILDREN:

1   William Wallace III b July 3, 1909
     d April 18, 1955 Buried Elmwood,
     Birmingham, m Jan. 23, 1939 Alice
     Dutton b   d
     NO ISSUE

2   Eugenia Arnold b July 30, 1910 m
     Aug. 28, 1934 Thomas Jefferson
     Dickey b May 31, 1913 Living Flow-
     ing W. Ranch   CHILD:

     a   Leonard Henderson b July 2,
          1936 m Mar. 10 1961 Hilergard
          Ruth Bauer b * May 10, 1938
          NO ISSUE

3   Francis Erskine b Aug. 30, 1912 m
     Sept. 3, 1938 Molly Tyson b Feb.
     28, 1913   CHILDREN:

     a   Jane Tyson b Sept. 20, 1939 m
                    Thomas Nelson
          Fickling b May 29, 1936
          CHILDREN:

          i   Frances Erskine b Mar.
               22, 1960

          ii   Thomas Nelson II b Dec.
               15, 1962

     b   Mary Frances b Sept. 14, 1944
          m July 29, 1961 Timothy
          Flemming b Oct. 22, 1943
          CHILD:

          i   Molly b April 27, 1962

4   Claude Carlos b Aug. 11, 1915 m
     FIRST Aug. 27, 1936 Alva Dickey b
     Jan. 25, 1918   CHILDREN:

*   Born in Schorndorf West Germany.

a Claude Carlos II b Mar. 26,
1938 m Aug. 22, 1960 Frances
Bond b NO ISSUE

b Thomas Eugene b Apr. 24, 1941

c Louise Malone b Nov. 23, 1946

m SECOND March 25, 1961 Doris Dodd
b Dec. 5, 1933 CHILDREN:

d Elizabett Dodd b Mar. 18, 1962

e Scott Arnold b June 26, 1963

5 Leonard Henderson II b June 7, 1920
m Dec. 2, 1949 Margery Burland b
Aug. 6, 1921 CHILDREN:

a Monroe Fields b Jan. 15, 1942
(by former marriage)

b Linda (White) b Sept. 15, 1948
(by former marriage)

c Barbara Ann b Sept. 27, 1950

d Nancy Lynn b Mar. 5, 1954

e Leonard Henderson III b Mar.
9, 1959

6 Lewis Pierce b Mar. 26, 1925 m Dec.
30, 1950 Frieda Frances Rosa b Apr.
13, 1929 (Miss Alabama 1949)
CHILDREN:

a Karen Frances b Sept. 9, 1953

b Lewis Pierce II b Apr. 26,
1956

c Elizabeth Anne b Dec. 31, 1957

Lucy Ellen b Dec. 6, 1885 m Sept. 7,
1914 Albert W. Smith b June 17, 1886
Living Birmingham, Ala. CHILDREN:

    1   James Clemon b Nov. 7, 1915 d

    2   Lloyd Batre b Apr. 28, 1919 m Oct. 4, 1946 Evelyn Davis b
        CHILDREN:

        a   Terry Ann b Oct. 18, 1947

        b   Kenneth James b May 7, 1953

        c   Kathryn Leigh b June 12, 1954

E   Mary Alice b   d in infancy

II   Edmond b June 25, 1851 d Aug. 8, 1912
UNMARRIED

III   William Wallace II b May 28, 1853 d Jan. 12, 1869

IV   John Richard b Jan. 3, 1855 d Aug. 18, 1929 m Sept.   1893 Annie Catherine Adams b Jan. 17, 1871 d Aug. 11, 1921   CHILDREN:

A   Adams Boyd b Aug. 27, 1894   UNMARRIED

B   Nancye Elizabeth b Dec. 22, 1898
UNMARRIED

C   Cornelia Alice b Aug. 13, 1900 UNMARRIED
Living Raleigh, N. C.

V   Mary Ellen b July 1, 1857 d Feb. 15, 1929 m Oct. 31, 1877 John Cawthorn II b
d   CHILDREN:

A   Sarah Blount b Oct. 13, 1878 d
1903   UNMARRIED

B   Wallace White b May 19, 1881 d
1941 m Nanny Jerman Robinson b
d   NO ISSUE

C   John III b June 27, 1884 m
Rebecca Bullock b Sept. 12, 1888 d July 26, 1956   CHILDREN:

1   John IV (Jack) b Nov. 30, 1918 m
     April 9, 1947 Frances Mary Anne
     Millard b April 9, 1928 CHILDREN:

     a   John V b Mar. 19, 1948

     b   Patrick James b June 16, 1949

     c   William H. b July 18, 1952

     d   Joanne b Sept. 10, 1954

     e   Mathew Howard b April 16, 1959

2   Anne b Feb. 2, 1922 UNMARRIED

3   Walter Wallace b Aug. 1, 1924 m
     Sept. 12, 1950 Mazie Seargent b
     March 4,   CHILDREN:

     a   Rebecca Sue b Feb. 24, 1952

     b   Walter Wallace II b Feb. 2,
          1954

     c   Winnifred Jeane b Sept. 11,
          1957

     d   Susanne Carroll b Nov. 16,
          1959 d Nov. 16, 1959

4   Joel Watkins b July 7, 1926 m Nov.
     28, 1958 Winnifred Grace b
          CHILDREN:

     a   Robert John b Mar. 15, 1960

     b   Joel Williams b Oct. 31, 1962

     c   David Lester b June 15, 1963

D   Mary Howard b   d
          UNMARRIED

E   Panthea Boyd b April 27, 1895 m Oct. 22,
     1920 Malcolm Price Stewart b
     CHILDREN:

1   Ellen Clack b Jan. 9, 1922 m Aug. 3, 1951 Franklin Herbert Thompson b   CHILDREN:

a   Andrea Linda b Mar. 25, 1952

b   Franklin Herbert II b June 26, 1955

2   Panthea Boyd b Sept. 28, 1924 m April 3, 1943 Andrew Sampson Kenley b   CHILDREN:

a   Margaret Ellen b Oct. 29, 1946

b   Panthea Elizabeth b May 23, 1949

c   Paula Lynn b July 22, 1952

d   Andrew Stewart b Apr. 29, 1955

3   Malcolm Price II b Oct. 20, 1929 UNMARRIED

VI   Charles Mayfield b March 3, 1860 d Dec. 4, 1936 m Oct. 25, 1899 Sally Daniel Boyd b d   CHILDREN:

A   Charles Mayfield II b Sept. 22, 1900 m June 1925 Kate Bowen b CHILD:

1   Charles Mayfield III b Aug. 2, 1926 m   Sally Tarry b CHILDREN:

a   Charles Mayfield IV b May 9, 1957

b   Mary Tarry b Aug. 10, 1959

c   Alice Bowen b Dec. 7, 1961

B   William Wallace III b Feb. 22, 1902 UNMARRIED

C   Alice Boyd b July 26, 1904 m June 27, 1934 Fuller McDuffie b CHILD:

    a   Sarah Alice b Jan. 23, 1941 m Sept. Sept. 6, 1962 Lambert Paschal McLaurin II b   NO ISSUE

VII Sally Sims b March 7, 1863 d   1864

VIII Cornelia Alice b Oct. 31, 1864 d Nov. 10, 1957   UNMARRIED

IX   George Robinson b May 21, 1867 d July 13, 1928 m Oct. 26, 1905 Sally Palmer Mayfield b Jan. 9, 1876 d April 8, 1961 NO ISSUE

X   Wallace b May 28, 1870 d Dec. 21, 1932 m
            Annie Lee Harris b May 24, 1884 d Feb. 15, 1921   CHILDREN:

A   Mary Boyd b June 29, 1910 m April 1932 Charles Casimir Siegling b Feb. 25, 1908   CHILDREN:

    1   Annie Lee b Dec. 20, 1933 m Jan. 1956 Brantley Denmark Thomas II b Nov. 20, 1933   CHILDREN:

        a   Brantley Denmark III b Nov. 14 1956

        b   Elizabeth Tidwell b Oct. 18, 1958

        c   Rudolph Siegling b June 27, 1960

    2   Frances DeMars b July 28, 1935 m Oct.   1954 William Leighton Filson I b Jan. 16, 1930 CHILDREN:

        a   William Leighton II b Jan. 10, 1956

        b   Charles Siegling b Sept. 10, 1957

        c   Frances Siegling b Aug. 9, 1959

3   Charles Siegling II b Aug. 2, 1936

4   Mary Boyd b July 19, 1946 UNMARRIED

5   Kate Patrick b Aug. 4, 1949

B   Annie Lee b April 28, 1913 m July 13,
1932 Walter Robert Vaugham II b
CHILDREN:

1   Mary Elizabeth b April 3, 1933 m
June 5, 1954 Thomas Eugene Register
b   CHILDREN:

a   Thomas Eugene II b May 2, 1958

b   Robert Vaugham b Feb. 18, 1960

c   Mary Anne b Dec. 26, 1962

2   Walter Robert III b
UNMARRIED

3   Wallace White b Jan. 22, 1942 m
Sept. 28, 1963 Beverly Carol Copeland b   NO ISSUE

4   Sally Anne b Feb. 25, 1943 UNMARRIED

C   Sally Hill b Oct. 7, 1914 m FIRST
John Vickers b
NO ISSUE

m SECOND   Caldwell Westmoreland Nixon I b   CHILD:

1   Caldwell Westmoreland II b Nov. 14,
1943

XI   Henry Burwell b Aug. 31, 1872 d Dec. 28, 1951
m   1914 Sue Olivia Boyd b June 22,
1890   CHILDREN:

A   Henry Burwell II b Feb. 13, 1915 m Ethel
Newell b June 2, 1917   NO ISSUE

B   Edmund Watkins b Jan. 7, 1917 m
Minnie Lou Parkam b Dec. 14, 1911
NO ISSUE

C   Nathaniel Boyd b Oct. 29, 1919 m
        Nelle Jarvis b July 7, 1927
CHILDREN:

1   Nathaniel (Nat) Boyd II b Nov. 25,
    1950

2   Stephen Jarvis b July 27, 1952

3   Henry Burwell III b Aug. 16, 1957

D   William Wallace IV b March 24, 1930
    (twin) m   1956 Dixie Lee King b
             CHILD:

1   William Wallace V b Oct. 25, 1957

E   Walter Alston b March 24, 1930 (twin) m
        Rose Hayes Hawk b Nov.
    17, 1938   NO ISSUE

F O O T N O T E S

(see following page.)

48

   The following information on the descendants
of WILLIAM WALLACE WHITE and PANTHEA BURWELL BOYD
was furnished by Miss Nannie Turner White, of
Birmingham, Alabama.

   In order to simplify proper identification of
each individual with his position in the family, we
are listing the individual by the proper number in
the listing; in other words, I A 3 is the listing
for Frank Henderson Mayfield, et cetera.....

I A 3   Frank Henderson Mayfield, commissioned
         a Captain, M C, AFS, Aug. 8, 1942.Served
         at Percy Jones Army Hospital, Battle
         Creek, Mich. as Chief of Dept. of Neuro-
         surgery. Left the service in 1946 as
         Lt. Col., and received the Distinguished
         Service Medal.

I A 3 c   Richard Glen Mayfield, OC 3,Marine
         Corps at Quantico, Virginia

I C   Leonard Henderson White, Captain, Corps
         of Engineers in World War I. Published
         Diary of Capt. William Wallace White in
         collaboration with his sister Nannie
         Turner White.

I C 2 a   Leonard Henderson Dickey was com-
         missioned 2nd Lt. Army, Corps of Eng.
         March 13, 1959 Auburn University. Spent
         2 years in Germany. Re-called to active
         duty 1961, sent as advisor to Vietnam,
         received the Combat Infantry Badge, be-
         ing the first officer to receive this in
         Vietnam, made Captain in July 1963, help
         ed to construct the Le Bac Bridge(larg-
         est U.S. military bridge in Vietnam).

I D 1   James Clemon Smith, Lt. jg, Ensign and
         fighter pilot on Carrier HORNET, comm-
         issioned in 1941. Was aboard the HORNET
         when it picked up Jimmie Doolittle and
         his bombers on their mission to bomb
         Tokyo Apr. 18, 1942. Was "downed" after

Battle of Midway, and picked up by destroyer
Cunningham. Received special attention for
having made the 61,000th landing on the
"Saratoga". His squadron accounted for 96
Japanese planes. Was presumed lost after a
year and awarded the Purple Heart.

I D 2   Lloyd Batre Smith (1st Lt.) Proof Officer at Aberdeen Md., 1942. Served five years
in World War II.

IV   A   Adams Boyd White, served in war and was
carried in the Reserves until honorably discharged in April 1, 1953. Temporary rank was
Captain, permanent rank was 1st Lieut.

IV   B   Nancye Elizabeth White, poetess. Photo
cover of Feb. 1954 edition of *Scimitar and
Song* says of her: "attended Flora McDonald
College, Red Springs, N. C., and Peace College, Raleigh, N. C., A primary teacher..
....began writing rhymes and nature poems at
an early age. She has appeared in *The Anthology, Poetry Digest Annual, The Palbar Anthology of Verse and Golden Verse Anthology.*
The poetess has a 'light touch which has the
sweetness and sponteneity of children at play"

V C 1   John Cawthorn IV Served in World War II
1941-1945, was in 1st Inf. Division, in cam-
paigns in Algeria, French Morrocca, Tunisia,
Sicily, Normandy, NOrthern France, and Central Europe.

V C 3   Walter Wallace Cawthorn, Served in Navy
1944-1946. BS degree in Greek, University of
the South, Sewanee, Tenn. June 1950; BD June,
1951. Served as Rector; now Vicar, St. Lukes
and St. Peter's Church, St. Cloud, Florida.

V C 4   Joel Watkins Cawthorn. Served 1944-1946
Navy, Seaman, First Class. Was aboard the
USS Logic (Mine Sweeper) and USS Portsmouth
(Cruiser)

V E 1   Ellen Clack Stewart had duty in WAVES
from 1944-1946. Was at New River, Cherry Pt.
and Oak Grove, N. C., (marine bases); also
Norfolk, Va. Pharmacist mate, 3rd Class.

Her husband, Frank, also in Navy.

VI A 1 Charles Mayfield White III, served in Navy and Merchant Marine. Inducted 1943, discharged 1945. Served at Hawaii, Okinawa, and other Pacific posts. Discharged as Pharmacy Mate.

VI B William Wallace White. Has made several "around the world tours" by ship and by air. Has visited almost every independent country in the world. Served 3 terms in the N. C. State Senate 1937-'41 and '47.

VI C Alice White McDuffie, teacher of English in N. C. for 27 years; Coach of State Triangular Debates for 15 years; member of Delta Kappa Gamma. Active in NEA, NCEA, and Classroom Teachers Organization.

X C Sally Hill White Westmoreland, a poetess numerous poems and prose published including a piece in the *Charlotte Observer* about Pres. Kennedy's funeral. Also has sold rights to words for an anthem; recently set her own music to her own words. Studied with University of Chicago and University of Wisconsin. Is a Vice-Pres. of N. C. Poetry Society, a member of American Academy of Political and Social Science. A book club in Henderson gave a program of her poetry.

XI Sue Olivia Boyd White, served as Pres. of 15th Dist. of N. C. Home Demonstration Clubs, Pres. of Middleburg Garden Club, Sec. of Vance Co. Council of Garden Clubs, served 15 years on Middleburg School Committee. Was recently chosen Mother of the Year for Vance Co.

XI A Henry Burwell White, II inducted U.S. Navy in Oct.8,1943, discharged Dec. 1945 Served at Hawaii, Okinawa, and other Pacific posts. Discharged as Pharmacy Mate.

XI C Nathaniel Boyd White, inducted U. S. Navy in 1942, discharged June 1946. Served in Atlantic and Pacific fleets. Rank on discharge Lt. Sr. Grade.

XI   D   Dr. William Wallace White, inducted U.S. Air Force Oct. 5, 1957, discharged Oct. 5, 1959. Discharged as Captain of U.S. Air Force Medical Corps.

XI   E   Dr. Walter Alston White (dentist) inducted in Air Cadet Corps, U.S. Air Force Dec. 28 1952 Discharged Dec. 7, 1954 as an Airman 2nd Class.

Descendants of Doctor Coleman White and Sally Agnes White

I Edmund Thomas (M.D.) b May 25, 1858 d 1928
m 1883 Ida Pen Hunt b March 3, 1862 d
Oct. 5, 1933 Both buried Elmwood Cemetery,
Oxford, N. C. CHILDREN:

 A Helen Agnes b Aug. 1, 1884 d Oct. 5,
  1936 UNMARRIED

 B Edna Hilliard b Oct. 29, 1889 d Jan. 10,
  1956 m Jan. 25, 1928 James Robert Wood
  b 1875 d April 1944 NO ISSUE

 C Ida Hixey b May 27, 1894 m Oct. 9, 1920
  Ewing Smith b April 6, 1898 d June 22,
  1934 CHILD:

  1 Elizabeth b May 14, 1921 m FIRST
   Oct. 21, 1939 Samuel Frederick
   Lanier b Feb. 20, 1921 d Aug. 6,
   1948 CHILDREN:

   a Thomas Frederick (twin) b
    June 25, 1942

   b Helen Elizabeth (twin) b June
    25, 1942 m Sept. 1, 1962
    Stephen Edwin Knott b

   c Jerry White b Jan. 22, 1947

   m SECOND Oct. 19, 1952 David N. Hix
   b Jan. 12, 1905 (Supt. of Granville Co. Schools.)

II Mary Bella Lee b Aug. 7, 1863 d Feb. 2, 1923
m Dec. 9, 1885 Robert Harris b Aug. 1856 d
1918 CHILDREN:

 A Sallie (Sadie) Coleman b Sept. 27, 1886
  m June 12, 1912 Oscar Breedlove b Sept.
  5, 1884 NO ISSUE

 B Henry Grady b Jan. 14, 1890

C Graham Waverly b June 24, 1894 d Nov.
   25, 1941 m Sept. 19, 1920 Frances
   (Fannie) Worthington Taylor b   1899
   CHILD:

   1   Maria Kerr b Jan. 2, 1923 m Oct. 8,
        1948 Luther Davies Blackwell b
        1917 CHILDREN:

        a   Maria Kerr b May 3, 1949

        b   Katherine Lindsey b June 26,
             1952

D Carrie Susan b March 21, 1897 m June 3,
   1922 Ross Fizer b   CHILDREN:

   1   Della Lee b Oct. 13, 1923 m June 8,
        1946 Rev. Herbert M. Jamieson b
        CHILDREN:

        a   Herbert M. II b   1947

        b   Susan b   1949

        c   Barbara b   1956

   2   J. Ross II b   m   Frances
        CHILD:

        a   A girl   NFI

E Edmund White b April   1899 m Dec. 31,
   1920 Beatrice Wadé b   CHILDREN:

   1   Edmund White II b   NFI

   2   Robert Wade

   3   Charles Leon

III Caroline Coleman b Nov. 9, 1870 d Aug. 7,
     1895 m Oct. 18, 1892 S. H. Smith b   d
     CHILD:

A Wilbur White   b July 12, 1893 m
   FIRST   1919 Eileen McKinnedy Murray

   m SECOND Oct. 1936 Engela Kruger

IV   Laura Belle b   m Eugene Grissom
Morris b   1873   CHILDREN:

A   Sue Smith b Jan. 4, 1880 m Homer E.
Henson b   1875   NO ISSUE

B   Eugenia (Genie) b June 1, 1882 m Alexander Bobbit Jenkins b   1880 d June
3, 1957   CHILDREN:

    1   Edward Shore m Violet Burns b
      CHILDREN:

        a   Harold b   m Barbara Clay-
           ton b   CHILD:

           i   Curtis b   NFI

        b   David b   UNMARRIED

    2   Mary Belle b   m Howard Jones
      NO ISSUE

    3   Robert Eugene b   m Frances
      Cook b   CHILD:

        a   Patsy b   m John Clark
           b   CHILDREN:

           i   Cathrine b   NFI

           ii   Linda

           iii Mark

    4   Al Burnard b   m Edna Hadden
      b   NO ISSUE

    5   Irvin Lee b   m Grace Sadler
      b   CHILDREN:

        a   Linda b   NFI

        b   Sue

    6   Bessie Coleman b   m Carey
      Dorset b   CHILDREN:

        a   Roger b   NFI

b   Helen

7   William Alexander b   m Mildred Allen b   CHILDREN:

    a   Tim b   NFI

    b   Tommy b   NFI

C   Elizabeth Barnard (Bessie) b Feb. 10, 1887 m Willie D. Gooch b Nov. 5, 1883 CHILD:

    1   Margaret Elizabeth b April 29, 1921 m Otis Allen Jenkins b June 21, 1919   CHILD:

        a   Elizabeth Lola (Beth) b Apr. 19, 1954

V   Walter b   m Dora Mitchell b   CHILDREN:

A   Chester b   NFI

B   Ulys

C   Myrtle

D   Aubry

E   Sity

F   Grace

G   Vesper

H   NFI

*   See III A above: In a clipping from a Durham N.C. newspaper of Nov. 1, 1963, graveside services for Wilbur White Smith, 70, were announced, He had lived in Cape Town, South Africa, since 1917. His death was Sept. 26, 1963. He was the son of Simeon Hudson Smith and Carolina Coleman White Smith.

Descendants of Mary Susannah White and Rev. J.B. Floyd

I   Robert P. b Aug. 31, 1854 d Jan. 9, 1933 m
Jan. 13, 1880 Eugenia Chamblee b
d Nov. 24, 1927   CHILDREN:

    A   Ollie b   NFI

    B   Hattie b   m   Martin

    C   Charlie Victor b   m Minnie Balen-
tine b   CHILDREN: 5   NFI

    D   Una b   m   C. C. Williams b
CHILDREN: 7   NFI

II   Charles Nicholas b Apr. 14, 1859 d   1930
m Feb. 7,   Lucretia Mitchell b
d   CHILDREN:

    A   Pearl b   m   William Bragg b
CHILDREN:

        1   Louise b   UNMARRIED

        2   Evelyn b   m   NFI

    B   Elizabeth Lorenzo (Bessie) b   m
FIRST Mell York b   d
NO ISSUE

        m SECOND   Rev. W. G. Farrar b

    C   Jarvis b   d   UNMARRIED

    D   Mary Bell b   m   Graham Allen b
CHILDREN:

        1   Floyd b   m   CHILDREN: NFI

        2   Mable b m   CHILDREN:

            a   (girl)   m   NFI

            b   (girl)   m   NFI

        3   Alvis b   m   CHILDREN: NFI

III   Lavenia b Mar. 16, 1861 d Dec. 8, 1924 m Mar.
35, 1885 Lucius Fuller b May 11, 1850 d Jan.
19, 1899 CHILDREN:

A   Ida b   1887   UNMARRIED

B   James b   1888 m   1911 Lynda
Booker b   CHILDREN:

(3 girls, 1 boy)   NFI

C   Sudie b   1890 m   1911 W. D.
Fulcher b   CHILDREN:

(4 girls, 1 boy)   NFI

D   Ruth b   1892 m   R. L. Dixon b   1912
CHILDREN: (2 boys, 2 girls)   NFI

E   June Johnson b   1894 d   1896

F   Edwin b   1896 d   m   NO ISSUE

G   Lucius Johnson b   1898 d   1915

IV   John W. b Oct. 19, 1865 d Jan. 13, 1944 m
Jan. 18, 1893 Clara Lawrence b May 14, 1871
d May 6, 1932   CHILD:

A   Elizabeth b   UNMARRIED

V   Henry Coleman b Oct. 26, 1867 d Sept. 1944
m Nov. 28, 1894 Ada York b   d   1960
CHILDREN:

A   Edward b   1897 m FIRST   Annie Garner
b   d   1920   CHILD:

1   (girl) b and died 1920

m SECOND Eunice Blair b   CHILDREN:
(2 girls, NFI)

B   Ralph b   1901   m FIRST Elizabeth Man-
gum b   CHILDREN:
(A girl and a boy,   NFI)

m SECOND   NFI

VI   James Pleasant b   1870

VII   Carrie b   1872 d   1922 m   1895 Edgar Crews
b   1867 d   1948   CHILDREN:

A   Carlyle b   UNMARRIED

B   Rena b   m   Hazel Wheeler
      b   NO ISSUE

C   Reid b   m Frances Bullock b
      CHILDREN: NFI

VIII Frank Fuller b   1874 d   m   1900
Samuella Huffoker b   d   CHILD:

A   Carrie b   m   L. L. Montgomery
      b   CHILDREN:

      (2   NFI)

Descendants of Haskey Ann Nelson White and Elias Sanford Jenkins

I   Mary L. C. b May 5, 1832 d May 24, 1863 m
James A. Winston b   d Sept. 23, 1881
CHILD:

    A   Cicero A., b Jan. 16, 1859   NFI

II   Arabella Frances A. b July 27, 1834 d Dec.
12, 1865 m Oct. 1, 1853 William M. Elliott
b Dec. 13, 1828 d Dec. 7, 1884   CHILDREN:
                                          [1]
    A   Isaac Davis b Sept. 19, 1854 d Dec. 1,
1916 m FIRST Dec. 2, 1874 Paralee Jolly
b July 31, 1859 d Jan. 8, 1899CHILDREN:

        1   Mary Frances (Molly) b Sept. 25,
1875 d Oct. 10, 1958 m Nov. 23,
1890 William Walter House b Dec.16,
1869 d July 14, 1932   CHILDREN:

            a   Pauline b Dec. 23, 1893 d Nov.
21, 1895

            b   William (Bill)Jennings Bryan
b June 10, 1896 d Jan. 11,
1955   UNMARRIED

            c   Paralee b Jan. 11, 1899 m Dec..
1, 1930 Fayne Taylor b July
13, 1899 NO ISSUE Living
Dresden, Tenn. [2]

            d   Irene b Aug. 15, 1902 d Feb.
13, 1921   UNMARRIED

            e   Robert (Bob) Lee b Mar. 10,
1905 m June 20, 1935 Mary
White b Mar. 4, 1908 Living
Greenfield, Tenn. [2]

            f   D (Dee) b Jan. 23, 1907 m
July 18, 1939 Sarah Everette
b Jan.14, 1919 CHILDREN:

[1] He is buried East Side Cemetery, Martin,Weak-
ley Co.,Tenn.

[2] Weakley County, Tennessee

    i   Frances Ann b Mar. 15, 1941

    ii   Sally b Sept. 28, 1944

    iii   Everette Dee b Feb. 4, 1955

g   Martha b Feb. 14, 1909 m July 13, 1930 Jimmy Young b Apr. 20, 1907 Living Union City, Tenn., Obion Co. Tenn. CHILD:

    i   James Alexander b May 6, 1932 m Aug. 30, 1953 Faye Cloys b Mar. 4, 1935 CHILDREN:

        (a)   Michael Allen b July 18, 1954

        (b)   Janet Lee b Dec. 13, 1955

h   Mary Nell b July 15, 1912 m Sept. 19, 1938 William (Bill) Winfrey b Feb. 7, 1911 NO ISSUE

2   Leonidus Augustus b Jan. 2, 1877 d Jan. 3, 1948 m June 22, 1897 Pearl Blakemore b Sept. 30, 1878 d July 5, 1960 (Both buried East Side Cemetery, Martin, Weakley Co. Tenn.) CHILDREN:

a   A boy, b 1898 d 1898

b   Rebecca b July 15, 1899 d June 21, 1919 UNMARRIED

c   Pearlee b Jan. 28, 1905 m Aug. 30, 1924 Daniel Porter Henegar b Sept. 21, 1897 Living McMinnville, Tenn. CHILD:

    i   Thomas Lee b Aug. 18, 1929 UNMARRIED

d Edyth Mae b June 27, 1909 m Nov. 26, 1924 John Morris Davies b Mar. 10, 1906 Living McMinnville, Warren Co.,Tenn. CHILD:

 i Rebecca b Feb. 25, 1937 m June 14, 1958 Wallace Doyle Grissom, M.D. b Mar. 17, 1937 CHILD:

  (a) Cynthia (Cindy) Leigh b Nov. 18, 1962

e Florence Elizabeth b May 15, 1911 m Mar. 15, 1941,Martin, Tenn. Russell W. Hillis b Dec. 8, 1914 Living Knoxville,Tenn. CHILD:

 i Stephen Lee b Oct. 25, 1947

3 Eveline (Evy) b June 14, 1879 d Nov. 7, 1956 m May 30, 1900 L. Frank Frazier II b Dec. 31 ca 1876 CHILD:

a L. Frank III b July 18, 1909 d Aug. 25, 1958 m FIRST Lila Johnson b

 m SECOND Mary Norman b Aug. 8, 1913 CHILD:

 i Frank Norman b Jan. 26, 1942

4 Lena Bell b Jan. 28, 1884 Living Knoxville, Tenn. m Jan. 27, 1905 Talbert A. Lewis b Sept. 1, 1880 d Oct. 17, 1959 CHILDREN:

a Faye b Sept. 3, 1907 m Aug. 15, 1935 Guy S. Miles, PHD, b June 30, 1908 (Prof. of Eng. Univers. of Fla.) Living Gains ville, Fla.

b   Frances Elizabeth b Dec. 11, 1911 m Oct. 31, 1934 Dresden, Tenn. Leonard F. Hurley b Feb. 28, 1898 Living Knoxville,Tenn CHILDREN:

    i   Len b Oct. 31, 1935 UNMARRIED

    ii   Don b Mar. 4, 1937 m Sept. 5, 1959 Marie Andes b Feb. 25, 1939 CHILD:

        (a) Miles Patrick b April 9, 1962

    iii   Margaret Faye b July 15, 1942

5   Lora May b   d infancy, 18 months

6   William Abraham b Feb. 16, 1891 d Mar. 6, 1918 m Dec. 30, 1917 Lottie Mae Lavender   NO ISSUE

7   Infant, b & d Dec. 5, 1898

m SECOND Jan. 2, 1900 Blanche Medlin b Mar. 4, 1874 d Apr. 24, 1929 CHILDREN:

8   Annette b Oct. 12, 1901 UNMARRIED Living Dyer, Gibson Co.,Tenn.

9   James Vernon b May 23, 1906 d July 22, 1962 m   1929 Mary Jones b Apr. 15, 1910 Nashville, Tenn. CHILDREN:

    a   Dorothy Jane b April 12, 1930 m   Ronald A. Pettit b June 7, 1933 CHILDREN:

        i   David Allen b May 16, 1955

        ii   Karen Lynn b Jan. 3, 1957

       b   Miriam b Jan. 16, 1937
           UNMARRIED Living Nashville,
           Tenn.

       c   Rebekah Ruth b Oct. 19, 1940
           m Aug.   1962 Donald Warren
           b May 16, 1938 NO ISSUE

B   Adda b Oct. 22, 1856   NFI

C   Lora Ann b May 6, 1859 d Sept. 12,1885
     m Dec. 3, 1874 W. A. McClain b   NFI

III Mansfield Davis b Aug. 2, 1836 d Nov. 22,
     1862 (Lt. Col. Killed in Civil War.) UNMARR-
     IED

IV Ellozer Cecilia (Delia) b Dec. 11, 1838 d
    May 21, 1922 m Feb. 3, 1867 William M.
    Elliott b Dec. 13, 1828 d Dec. 7, 1884 [1]
    CHILDREN:

    A   Edward Thomas b Nov. 8, 1869 d Feb. 15,
       1938 m Oct. 26, 1904 Jane Nual Barber
       b April 14, 1881   CHILDREN:

       1   William b Jan. 3, 1913 UNMARRIED

       2   Vivian b Dec. 9, 1914 m Jan. 11,
           1950 Dossie Hicks b July 16, 1914
           CHILD:

           a   Edward Bell b Dec. 18, 1953

    B   Lizza Etta b Nov. 28, 1871 d Aug. 19,
       1872

    C   Georgia Vernorah b Aug. 4, 1873 d Jan.
       18, 1874

    D   Willie Emergene b July 30, 1875 d May
       12, 1941 m Oct. 5, 1894 R. H. Cobb b
       Oct. 3, 1870 d Oct. 29, 1957 CHILDREN:

       1   Junius Marvin b   d,6 weeks
           old

       2   Wayne Elliott b July 19, 1899 d
           May 23, 1958 UNMARRIED
[1] He married FIRST Arabella Frances A.Jenkins

3   Margaret Lola b Nov. 1, 1901 m
     FIRST April 16, 1921 John Green b

     m SECOND Nov. 30, 1934 Herchel
     Morris b Aug. 19, 1895 Living May-
     field, Ky.

E   James J. b Nov. 6, 1877 d Nov. 24, 1901
     m   Ella Weldon b Dec. 16, 1877
     d Nov. 20, 1906 CHILD:

     1   Gladys b March 6, 1899 Living Ven-
          tura, Calif. m   Buford B.
          Jenkins b June 8, 1891 CHILD:

          a   Virginia Elouise b Nov. 6,
               1924 m   Mark Jones b
               May 15, 1921 CHILD:

               i   Markland Gary b Dec. 1,
                    1944

F   Junious Markum b Oct. 11, 1881 d April
     9, 1952   UNMARRIED

V   Elizabeth Jane b Aug. 15, 1841 d July 14,
     1846 Weakley Co.,Tenn.

VI   Augustus Pauldin b June 22, 1843 d July 21,
     1846

VII William G. C. b June 15, 1846 d before
     1920 m FIRST Dec. 9, 1866 Emma S. Walker b
     CHILDREN:

A   P. D. b Jan. 2, 1869   NFI

B   M. Laura b May 27, 1871 d

C   Will F. b Mar. 31, 1874

D   Thomas Edd b Mar. 19, 1876 d   m
     CHILDREN: (3 boys, 1 girl....NFI)

E   Kathrine Drucilla b Aug. 19, 1878

     m   SECOND Mary Douglas Magee b Sept. 24,
     1864   CHILDREN:

F   Magnus Eustace b Aug. 2, 1881 d

G   Almus Royal b Nov. 24, 1883 d   m
CHILDREN: (2 girls.....NFI)

H   William Myrtie b Jan. 19, 1887 m
CHILD:

    1   A girl   NFI

I   Junious Maskey b Nov. 6, 1889   NFI

J   Buford B. b June 8, 1891 m
Gladys Jenkins b March 6, 1899 (cousins)
See IV

K   Gladys Blanch b April 26, 1894 Lives
Piggott, Ark., m   Buck Fitzgerald
b   CHILD:

    1   A girl   NFI

VIII Cicero b Sept. 22, 1848 d Jan. 7, 1856

IX Ducitius b Dec. 10, 1851 d Jan. 17, 1925 m
FIRST Nov. 7, 1871 Mary Etta Vincent b Oct.
31, 1854 d Dec. 17, 1872   CHILDREN:

A   Etta b Dec. 17, 1872 d   1943 m
CHILDREN:

    1   Mirtle b   NFI

    2   Gertie

    3   Ludie

    4   Fred

    5   Est--

m   SECOND May 3, 1875 Bessie Selmore
McClain b Aug. 4, 1852 d June 8, 1877
CHILDREN:

B   Georgia b April 10, 1875 d Aug. 10,
1956 m Millard Myrick b   CHILDREN:

    1   Mary Francis b Sept. 10, 1902
UNMARRIED

2 James McClain b Feb. 16, 1899 m
   CHILD:

   a Jack b   m   Lives
     La. CHILDREN: 2 NFI

m THIRD Ella Moss b July 9, 1856 d Sept.
1883 CHILDREN:

C Percie b April 22, 1882 m Feb. 9,
   1902 Oscar Hynds b July 1, 1880 d July
   16, 1947 CHILD:

   1 Ruth b Dec. 9, 1909 m April 11,
     1941 Earl McGraw b June 22, 1910
     CHILD:

     a Robert Earl b Nov. 9, 1942 m
       June 2, 1963 Barbara McManus
       b March 16, 1944

D Davis b April 8, 1884 d July   1884

m FOURTH   Narcissa Travis b July 19,
1868 d July 1, 1951 CHILDREN:

E Joseph Edward (Jodie) b Dec. 16, 1889 m
   FIRST Lena Cook b Aug. 11, 1894 d Jan.
   17, 1936 CHILDREN:

   1 Virselle b Oct. 29, 1914 m Howard
     Forrister

   2 Cathelene b Feb. 20, 1916 m Vince
     DeLucas

   3 Forest Lee b May 8, 1917 d

   4 Annie Laure b Nov. 22, 1914 d

   m SECOND Mrs. Bessie Cravens Cloar b
   Feb. 14   NFI

F William L. (JINKINS)[1] b April 10,1892
   m Sadie Bynum b June 15, 1899 CHILDREN:

[1] This family says the spelling is JINKINS and
the one giving this information to Mrs. F.E.Hillis

1 Rachel b Jan. 16, 1919 m Bonnie
Dalton b   CHILD:

 a Thomas Glenn b Sept. 3, 1949

2 Reba Dora b Aug. 22, 1921 m Harry
Hill b   CHILD:

 a Harriet Sue b Oct. 21,

3 James D. b July 9, 1924 m Katie
Rapier b   CHILDREN:

 a Kathy Marcella b NFI

 b James D.

 c Michael Franklin

4 William Harold b Oct. 9, 1925 m
Vivion Bow b   CHILDREN:

 a Wilma Mae

 b Keneth Wayne

5 Lowell b June 13, 1929 m Bonnie
Clark b   CHILDREN:

 a Bobby NFI

 b Tommie

 c David

6 Lora b June 13, 1929 m James
Bodkins b   d 1963
CHILDREN:

 a Paula NFI

 b James R.

 c Debra

 d Bonnie

 e Teresa

7   Junius Bynum b Sept. 14, 1930 m
     Barbara Redman b   CHILDREN

     a   Jeffery b   NFI

     b   Jennie b

8   Doris Ann b March 14, 1935   m
     Robert Flynn b   CHILDREN:

     a   Kieth b   NFI

     b   John Charles b

G   Bertie b Jan. 13, 1895 Living Union
     City, Tenn.   UNMARRIED

H   Kellie Davis b Feb. 4, 1897 m Oct. 29,
     1916 Virginia Leach b July 27, 1899
     CHILDREN:

     1   Bennell b Aug. 22, 1917 m   Duke
          Crews b   CHILD:

          a   Nancy

     2   Hellen b Oct. 22, 1921 m   Billy
          Lowe b   CHILDREN:

          a   Jimmie   NFI

          b   Patricia

     3   Davis Junius b March 29, 1924 m
          Mary Eliah

     4   Sarah Ruth b Sept. 4, 1931 m   Earl
          Hackerd b   CHILD:

          a   Janet Lynn   NFI

Descendants of Thomas Person White and Rebecca W. Kittrell

I   J. Jim b Sept. 27, 1846 d   1931, age
    85, m   Virginia Ann Dowd b
    d   CHILDREN:

    A   Frances (Fannie) Rebeccah b Aug.   1883
         Living Martin, Tenn. m   Bobby
         F. Hawks b   CHILDREN:

         1   Aubry b   NFI

         2   Aron H.

         3   Rovanell b   m   Fisher
              b

         4   Kinsie b   m   Jake
              Graves b

    B   Percy b June   1885 m FIRST   Jessie
         Glasgow b   d
         CHILDREN:

         1   Ewing b   NFI

         2   Earl

         3   Vida

         4   Fred

         m   SECOND   Mrs. Lora Hicks
         Olds b

    C   George Junius II b Oct. 20, 1887 m
         FIRST Dec. 24, 1912 Ollie Dismuke b
         CHILDREN:

         1   William Junius b   m
              Lorena Somerville b

         2   Margaret b   m
              Radford b

         3   Sue b   m
              Billingly b

    4   Joan Ann b   m
         Kemp b

    m SECOND Aug. 26, 1951 Mrs. Finch
    Higgs Harris b   NO ISSUE

D   Ruperd Dowd b   d   1963
    m   Kathleen Higgs b
    CHILDREN:

    1   Forest b   m
         Living Memphis, Tenn.   NFI

    2   Russell b   m
         Living Martin, Tenn.   NFI

    3   Eugene b   m
         Living Martin, Tenn.   NFI

    4   Buford b   (In Germany)

    5   Glen b   Living in Tex.

    6   Madge b   d   NFI

    7   Robert b   m   NFI

E   Blanch b   d   m
    Cacye Wright b   d
    CHILDREN:

    1   J. C.   b   NFI

    2   Bernard b   NFI

F   Vida b   d   NFI

G   Rice Pierce b   m   Mary
    Gunther b   Living
    Memphis, Tenn.   CHILDREN:

    1   Rice Pierce II b   m

    2   Mary Frances b   m

H   James Bell b   m   Lois
    Chance b   Living Martin, Tenn.
    CHILDREN:

```
        1      Edward Neal b          m
               Carolyn Davis b

        2      Virginia Mae b          m

        3      John Marvin          NFI

        4      James Bell II b

        5      Jane Ellen b

   I    Rass b                    NFI

II    John b              d          m
      Suckie McCall b                d
      CHILDREN:

      A    Mattie b              NFI

      B    Tom

      C    Gert

      D    Kathryn

      E    Ann Lou

      F    Hoyt

III   Antionette b        d          m
      Wesley Summers b        d      CHILDREN:

      A    William b        m          Bessie
           Glasgow b        NFI

      B    Jean b

      C    Myrtle

      D    Pinkie

      E    Bessie

IV    Pink b            d          m  Tom Jones b

V     Kat b            d          m  Tom Vaughn b

VI    "Bud" b          d young
```

(Above material furnished by Mrs. Florence Hillis)

Descendants of Jacksey White and Dr. Guilford Dudley Sims

I   William (Bill) V. b ca 1835 d   m
Pennie C. Winston b   ca 1838 CHILDREN:

    A   John William b ca 1858 d   m
        Mattie Bobbitt b   CHILDREN:

        1   Walter b   NFI

        2   Jess b

        3   Zera

        4   Clyde

        5   Wiley

        6   Pennie b   m   John
            W. Jones b   Live McKenzie,
            Tenn.

    B   Guildord Dudley b   Moved to
        Texas   NFI

    C   Kate b   d young

II   Ann E. b   1836 d   1863 m*
John W. Jeter b Jan. 12, 1831 d   1896
CHILDREN:

    A   William S. b   1854 d   1902
        m   Nannie Shannon b   1858
        d   1945   CHILD:

        1   Maud b   m   Barton
            b   Living Greenfield, Tenn.

    B   Ella Frances b   1857 d   1919
        m   Samuel Egbert Young   b
        1854   d   1928   CHILDREN:

        1   Imo Frances b   1878 d
            1957 m   William Jordan Jeter
            b   1875 d   1946
        CHILDREN:

            a   Claud Samuel b   m
                Maggie Nowell b   CHILD:
*   m date 1853

       i   Claudia Jean b Sept. 15, 1946

b   Ella Dale b   UNMARRIED

c   Paul b   m   Eula
E. McDaniel b   NO ISSUE

d   Mary Tennessee b   m
George Parker II b
CHILD:

       i   George III b July 20, 1950

e   Imo Frances b Oct. 1, 1918 m
Aug. 2, 1942 William Dooley
Michaelcheck b Sept. 11, 1917
CHILDREN:

       i   William Jeter b April 22, 1947

       ii   Sherry Joy b Sept. 8, 1952

2   Annie B. b   m   Caleb
Brasfield Higgs b
CHILDREN:

a   Willa Dean b   m
F. P. Wirth b   m

b   Alpheus b   NFI

c   Virginia b   NFI

3   John William b   m
Ivy Bailey b   CHILDREN:

a   Samuel b   NFI

b   James b

4   James b   UNMARRIED

5   Kate b   m   Egbert
Bullock b   CHILDREN:

           a   Carl Thomas b   NFI

           b   Benjamin b

      6   Earl b   m
           Lorene Finch b
           NO ISSUE
    C   Catherine b   m   Henry
         Finch b   CHILD:

      1   John b

IV   James Robert (Bob) b Sept. 24, 1846 d Oct.
     11, 1900 m March 16, 1869 Sallie Pointer b
     Aug. 2, 1846 d Dec. 10, 1917 Both buried in
     Arkansas.   NO ISSUE

V   Rufus Elbert Granville b Aug. 19, 1848 d
     1850

Descendants of George M. White and Nancy McDavid Morgan

I   Martha Jane b Oct. 2, 1845 Coffee Springs, Perry Co., Ala., d Jan. 2, 1920 m Sept. 20, 1870 James Joyner Brown b Dec. 26, 1845 Holly Hill, Charles City Co.,Va., d Jan. 5, 1912 CHILDREN: SEE SEPARATE LISTING

II   George Phillips b July 20, 1847 d June 17, 1929 m FIRST May 17, 1870 Mary Elizabeth Bailey b Nov. 2, 1850 d Jan. 22, 1902 CHILDREN: SEE SEPARATE LISTING

     m SECOND July 7, 1903 (Mrs.)Nannie Ezelle Bates b Feb. 23, 1877 d June 11, 1959 CHILDREN: SEE SEPARATE LISTING

III John Henry b May 17, 1849 d March 3, 1901 m Nov. 16, 1871 Ella Simms b Dec. 10, 1850 d April 2, 1937, buried Uniontown, Alabama CHILDREN: SEE SEPARATE LISTING

IV   Thomas Jefferson (M.D.) b Nov. 15, 1850 d March 25, 1887 m Dec. 16, 1875 Kate Shearen b June 22, 1857 d Oct. 3, 1943 CHILDREN: SEE SEPARATE LISTING

V   Samuel Dorroh b Feb. 16, 1852 d Aug. 4, 1855 near Uniontown.

VI   Charles Edward b Oct. 18, 1853 d Feb. 14,1869 in Uniontown.

VII Benjamin Franklin b Dec. 12, 1855 d July 1, 1866

VIII Robert Allen b Sept. 14, 1857 d April 15, 1925, Jackson, Miss. m Nov. 23, 1882 Mary Adelaide Brown b Dec. 20, 1858 Charles City Co.,Va., d July 4, 1945 Buried Uniontown,Ala. CHILDREN: SEE SEPARATE LISTING

IX   Mary Elizabeth b June 23, 1859 d Feb. 20,1869

X   Helen b Nov. 25, 1860 d Uniontown, Sept. 20, 1904 UNMARRIED

XI   Joseph Johnston b Nov. 2, 1862 d June 14, 1937 m FIRST Oct. 14, 1885 Virginia Randolph

Sherman b Feb. 9, 1865 Columbus, Miss., d
Jan. 2, 1888 Uniontown, Ala. CHILDREN:
SEE SEPARATE LISTING

m SECOND June 20, 1889 Grace Stewart
Triplitt b July 4, 1864 d 1950 CHILDREN:
SEE SEPARATE LISTING

XII James Walter b May 10, 1864 d Nov. 25, 1928
Buried Uniontown, Ala. UNMARRIED

XIII Alice Nancy b Jan. 12, 1866 d Jan. 18, 1956
m Oct. 28, 1891 Frank McCorkle b 1851 d May
24, 1924 CHILDREN: SEE SEPARATE LISTING

Descendants of Martha Jane White and James Joyner Brown

I   Junie b July 8, 1871 d March 7, 1877

II   Nannie b Aug. 30, 1872 d Oct. 18, 1877

III   Mary b July 18, 1874 d April 19, 1938
UNMARRIED

IV   George b April 24, 1876 d Sept. 28, 1876,
Faunsdale

V   Helen b Sept. 17, 1877 d Feb. 24, 1929 m
June 7, 1905 Marion Wheeler Moore b Aug. 2,
1874 d Nov. 24, 1925 CHILDREN:

    A   Helen White b Feb. 1, 1907, living
Canyon City, Tex. UNMARRIED

    B   Sara b Nov. 21, 1910 d Dec. 16, 1950 m
May 30, 1936 James Henry Sears b
CHILDREN:

        1   James Henry II b March 8, 1938

        2   Wheeler Moore b June 26, 1939 m
July 3, 1961 Sharan Lee Bohannon b
Oct. 12, 1939 CHILD:

           a   James Wheeler b Apr. 11, 1962

        3   Helen White b Aug. 15, 1944

VI   James b Feb. 19, 1879 d Dec. 12, 1932 m April
6, 1904 Louise Carr b Nov. 4, 1879 d Feb. 15,
1956 NO ISSUE

VII   Mattie b Dec. 25, 1880, living Uniontown, Ala
m June 5, 1901 Anderson Louis Pou b Sept. 11,
1872 d Jan. 16, 1943 CHILDREN:

    A   Martha Louise b March 21, 1902, living
Birmingham, m Sept. 4, 1928 Dr. Wallace
A. Clyde b Oct. 18, 1901 CHILDREN:

        1   Dr. Wallace A., II, b Nov. 7, 1929
living Cleveland, Ohio, m Aug. 21,
1953 Barbara Cleveland McLean b
June 27, 1930 CHILDREN:

a Martha Elizabeth b Jan. 9,
1957

b Susan Ann b Dec. 31, 1958

2 Martha Louise b July 11, 1936 d
Jan. 17, 1953

B Alice b Feb. 28, 1903, living Uniontown
Ala., m FIRST March 8, 1936 Victor
Quintus Prowell b April 5, 1873 d Nov.
30, 1948 NO ISSUE

m SECOND Feb. 1, 1958 Dr. Leslie Alexander Moseley b Aug. 5, 1890 NO ISSUE

C Dorothy b Oct. 3, 1906, living Uniontown
Ala., m June 3, 1931 John Scott McGuire
b Feb. 15, 1905 d July 10, 1954 CHILD:

1 Mary Alice b Feb. 22, 1941

VIII Alice b March 30, 1883 m Nov. 15, 1906 George
Edwin West b Jan. 25, 1882 CHILDREN:

A George Edwin II b Oct. 24, 1907 d Dec.
9, 1907

B Kathryn Marie b May 13, 1909, living
Longview, Tex. m June 3, 1938 Joseph
Phillips Goodwin b Sept. 18, 1909
CHILDREN:

1 Martha Alice b Sept. 24, 1942 m
Sept. 5, 1961 Lynn Allen Boatner
b Aug. 3, 1938

2 Emily Kathryn (Kay) b Sept. 18,
1946

C Martha White b Aug. 20, 1910, living
Longview, Tex. m June 3, 1931 Carroll
Otis Graves b Aug. 30, 1903 NO ISSUE

IX Albert Walter b July 15, 1884 d Nov. 27,
1910 UNMARRIED

Descendants of George Phillips White and Mary Elizabeth Bailey

I   Fannie Belle b March 22, 1872 d Sept. 22,
     1962 m May 24, 1893 [1] Isaac (Ike) Nelms
     Underwood b Nov. 20, 1863 d July 13, 1937
     CHILDREN:

     A   Infant son, b Sept. 15, 1894 d Oct. 17,
          1894

     B   Hugh White b Nov. 2, 1895 m Jan. 14,
          1916 Virginia Marguerite Griffin b Oct.
          28, 1900 CHILDREN:

          1   Hugh White II (D.D.S.) b June 10,
               1917 m Oct. 21, 1947 Ann Hamilton
               b Jan. 28, 1918. Living Selma,
               Ala. CHILDREN:

               a   Hugh White III b Sept. 3, 1948

               b   Robert Hamilton b Jan. 22,
                    1951 d Jan. 24, 1951

               c   Paul Stewart b Mar. 11, 1952

          2   William Edward b Dec. 11, 1919 [2]
               m FIRST Feb. 27, 1946 Doris Camille
               Rolfes b Aug. 19, 1928 CHILDREN:

               a   William Edward II b June 19,
                    1947 Norfolk, Va.

               b   Jefferson Gordon b Feb. 8,
                    1949, Groton, Conn.

               m SECOND May 26, 1956 Sophia Anne
               Duffey b

[1] Married in Friendship Presbyterian Church,
     Cunningham Beat, Perry County, Ala.

[2] Graduate of Annapolis, Commander, U.S.Navy.

C   Frances b April 21, 1899 Living Marion, Ala. UNMARRIED

D   Bettie Bailey b Aug. 1, 1906 m Feb. 24, 1951 Earl G. Cherry b July 3, 1921 NO ISSUE

II James Bailey b March 20, 1874 d Sept. 27, 1939 m April 17, 1901 Berta Benton Jones b Dec. 2, 1880 d May 6, 1951 Buried Centreville, Bibb Co., Ala. CHILDREN:

A   James Bailey II, Postmaster, b Aug. 8, 1905 m Feb. 24, 1933 Mozelle Phillips b Living Centreville, Ala. CHILD:

1   Sally Bert b Oct. 9, 1939 m June 17, 1957 Roy Edward Fitts II b CHILD:

a   Stephanie White b Sept. 2, 1958

B   Beulah Elizabeth b Feb. 15, 1910 m June 22, 1933 Brady Belcher b Living Centreville, Ala. NO ISSUE

C   George Phillips II, Attorney, b Aug. 4, 1915 m Nov. 28, 1952 Betty Ann Poag b Living Centreville, Ala. CHILDREN:

1   George Phillips III b March 31, 1954

2   Allison Elizabeth b Aug. 1, 1956

3   Rachel Stewart b March 12, 1958

III George Morgan b Nov. 29, 1876 Uniontown, Ala. d March 16, 1948 Columbus, Ga., m Sept. 26, 1900 Mary Elizabeth Roark [1] b June 17, 1878 d March 23, 1961 CHILDREN:

[1] Daughter of Richard H. and Elizabeth Moss Roark of Perry County, Alabama

A   George Morgan II b Oct. 30, 1901 d Oct. 19, 1907

B   James Bailey b May 30, 1903 Perry Co., m June 16, 1928 Helen Irene Keene b March 5, 1906 Portland, Tenn. Living Nashville, Tenn. CHILDREN:

    1   James Edward b Feb. 18, 1935 Nashville, Tenn., m Nov. 25, 1958 Sara Jo Wallen b Jan. 31, 1939 Murfreesboro, Tenn. CHILDREN:

        a   Sara Suzanne b Sept. 25, 1959 Murfreesboro, Tenn.

        b   James Edward b Jan. 13, 1962

    2   Helen Elizabeth b Sept. 16, 1942 Nashville, Tenn., m May 16, 1959 Pinkney Boyd Hester b Sept. 9, 1940 Trigg Co., Kentucky, CHILD:

        a   Wanette b Dec. 1961

C   Richard Freeman b Nov. 11, 1906 Perry Co., Ala. d Jan. 8, 1933 Columbus, Ga. m June 6, 1931 Hilda Jones b Oct. 4, 1912. Living Columbus, Ga. CHILD:

    1   Hilda Louise b March 22, 1932 Columbus, Ga. m Aug. 8, 1953 Maxwell Cole Murphy II, Major, U.S.A., b CHILDREN:

        a   Maxwell Cole III b July 11, 1954 Texas

        b   Geraldine Louise b April 16, 1956 West Point, N. Y.

        c   Jeffry Richard b Aug. 11, 1957, West Point, N.Y.

D   Robert Phillip b Sept. 28, 1908 m Aug. 31, 1935 Thurline Elizabeth Dunshee b June 17, 1911 CHILDREN:

1 Nancy Kay [1] b Feb. 24, 1934
Council Bluffs, Iowa, m June 4,
1957 Stanley Earl Elliott b CHILD:

    a   Linda Kay b May 2, 1958

2 Michael Morgan b March 10, 1937
Council Bluffs, Iowa [2]UNMARRIED

E Mary Elizabeth b Sept. 26, 1913 Perry
Co.,Ala., m Feb. 14, 1932 J. Edmond
Harrison II b July 27, 1911 Living
Columbus, Ga. CHILDREN:

1 Jane Bailey b July 3, 1938 Columbus
Ga. m June 15, 1957 Alvin Porte
Horne II b March 29, 1937 Living
Columbus, Ga. CHILDREN:

    a   Elizabeth (Beth) Jane b July
        1, 1958

    b   Jennifer Louise b Jan. 21,
        1960

    c   A son, name and date unavail-
        able

2 Richard Edmond b July 26, 1939 m
Jan. 14, 1959 Carol Coleman b
CHILD:

    a   A son, name and date unavail-
        able.

IV Hugh Lee b Aug. 25, 1878 d July 31, 1895

V Henry Phillips b July 19, 1881 d Nov. 13,
1925 m Oct. 20, 1910 Lucia Reynolds b April
13, 1890 d Nov. 18, 1957 NO ISSUE

[1] Daughter of wife by previous marriage.

[2] Graduate of TCU, Fort Worth,Tex.,Lt. USAF.

VI   John Gwin b Apr. 24, 1883 d May 10, 1956 m
      Apr. 26, 1905 Addie Poindexter Morgan [1]
      b Jan. 14, 1883 d July 13, 1951 CHILDREN:

A   John Morgan b Aug. 28, 1907, living
      Uniontown, Ala., m June 29, 1929 Kate
      Hope Irby b Dec. 16, 1910 CHILDREN:

      1   Pauline Hope b Oct. 13, 1933 m Oct.
           19, 1954 Charles Molton Williams
           b June 21, 1920 CHILDREN:

           a   Charles Molton II b Aug. 2,
                1955

           b   John Thomas Hunter b April 7,
                1957

           c   John White b May 20, 1960

           d   Kate Hope b July 16, 1963

      2   John Morgan II b Aug. 21, 1938

      3   Christopher Gwin b Jan. 28, 1944

B   Bettie Morgan b Sept. 16, 1914 UNMARRIED
      Living in Birmingham, Ala.

VII   Ruby (Jewel) b Oct. 17, 1885, living Boone,
      N.C., m Dec. 30, 1906 Elisha Ford King III
      (Civil Engineer) b May 4, 1880 d Nov. 26,
      1951 Boone, N.C. CHILDREN:

A   Elizabeth White b Mar. 22, 1913 m Aug.
      13, 1933 H. Cooker Triplett b Dec. 18,
      1911 CHILDREN:

      1   H. Cooker II (Budi) b July 15,1934
           m Nov. 1, 1957 Peggy Anne Klutz b
           Dec. 3, 1934 CHILD:

           a   Charles Daniel (Danny) b Aug.
                29, 1958

      2   Hamilton King b Apr. 22, 1943
[1] Daughter of Betty Phillips & Allen Lewis
Morgan, younger brother of Nancy McDavid Morgan,
wife of George M. White--grandparents of John Gwin
White.

B Elisha Ford IV b Feb. 3, 1915 m FIRST March 30, 1940 Mesu King b CHILD:

 1 Elisha Ford V, b Feb. 5, 1943

 m SECOND May 20, 1956 Juanita Moody Masters b Nov. 7, 1917 CHILDREN:

 2 Carolyn b Sept. 25, 1944 [1]

 3 John Charles b May 22, 1957 d in infancy.

 4 William Edwin b March 5, 1960

VIII Tom Randolph b June 12, 1887 d Dec. 19, 1942 m Helen Cinnamond b d NO ISSUE

IX Robert Stanley I b Oct. 6, 1889 Living Uniontown, Ala., m FIRST Dec, 30, 1909 Lucile Pratt b Dec. 8, 1889 d Nov. 4, 1918 CHILDREN:

A Robert Stanley II b Nov. 11, 1911 UNMARRIED

B William Bruce I b Feb. 2, 1914 m Sept. 7, 1940 Ellie Smyer b Oct. 6, 1920 Living Birmingham, Ala. CHILDREN:

 1 Ellie Lucile b Jan. 13, 1945

 2 William Bruce II b July 31, 1948

 3 Shuford Stanley b Oct. 19, 1949

 m SECOND June 17, 1924 Flora Howell b Nov. 13, 1900 NO ISSUE

[1] Daughter of Juanita Moody Masters by previous marriage.

Descendants of George Phillips White and (Mrs.) Nannie Ezelle Bates

X   Nancy Inez b Feb. 2, 1905 m Aug. 28, 1930
    John Newton Thomas I, D.D. [1] b March 28,
    1903 Living Richmond, Va. CHILDREN:

    A   Nancy White b Nov. 18, 1934 Roanoke,
        Va., m Oct. 18, 1957 Robert E. Hill
        b Feb. 24, 1930 NO ISSUE

    B   John Newton II b July 18, 1940 m June
        1, 1962 Nancy Tipton Wingfield b Nov.
        25, 1939 CHILD:

        1   John Newton III b April 4, 1963
            Charlotte, N. C.

XI Morriss Ezelle b Aug. 6, 1906 m Aug. 4, 1931
    Virginia Woody b July 31, 1909 CHILD:

    A   Harriett Louise b April 23, 1932 m Aug.
        25, 1953 Anthony Colacino b June 2,
        1931 CHILDREN:

        1   Linda Ann b Jan. 2, 1955

        2   William Anthony b June 28, 1958

        3   Anthony Paul b Jan. 12, 1962

XII Mary Louise b Feb. 4, 1910 m FIRST Oct. 1,
    1933 Jarnagin Chesley Rice II b Oct. 10,
    1907 d Aug. 5, 1939 (auto accident)CHILDREN:

    A   Mary Louise b May 26, 1935 m Aug. 2,
        1957 Billy Dabbs b Oct. 16, 1922 [2]
        CHILD:

        1   Paul Jarnagin b Feb. 20, 1963

    B   Jane Armistead b Sept. 20, 1937 UNMARRIED

    m SECOND May 10, 1942 Eugene Reese Dawson b
    Jan. 8, 1906 Living Mobile, Ala. CHILD:

    C   Jeanne Lewis b Jan. 26, 1945

[1] Trustee of Washington and Lee University.
[2] Head Phys.Ed. Dept., Bessemer High School.

Descendants of John Henry White and Ella Simms

I   John Henry (Harry) II b Nov. 15, 1872 d Oct. 4, 1920 m Dec. 27, 1894 Fannie Bradford, b June 26 1874 d Jan. 18, 1937 CHILD:

     A   Frances b Feb. 27, 1896 m June 3, 1917 Thomas Ralston Long b Jan. 18, 1892 d Oct. 27, 1936 CHILDREN:

         1   Thomas Ralston II b April 7, 1918 m Oct. 19, 1946 Kitty Grey Pharr b April 30, 1924 CHILDREN:

             a   Thomas Ralston III b Feb. 15, 1948

             b   Mary Dudley b May 3, 1950

             c   Harry Pharr b Dec. 28, 1953

             d   Frances White b Feb. 1, 1958

             e   Rose Scott b April 12, 1960

         2   Frances White b June 19, 1919 d Feb. 23, 1938

II   Weenona Davidson b March 30, 1874 d Jan. 17, 1933 m Dec. 29, 1897 Victor Henry Hanson b Jan. 16, 1876 d March 7, 1945 NO ISSUE

III   Viola Pearl b June 6, 1875 d Aug. 20, 1955 m June 27, 1900 Benjamin Goff Snyder b Aug. 14, 1873 d April 21, 1950 NO ISSUE

IV   Annie Simms b June 23, 1876 d Nov. 27, 1955 m June 8, 1897 Alvin Milton Spessard b Nov. 14, 1862 d Feb. 20, 1924 NO ISSUE

V   Isabel Houston b Oct. 25, 1881 d June 9,1949 m Oct. 12, 1904 Thomas Jefferson Heflin b Aug. 10, 1876 d May 15, 1928 CHILDREN:

     A   Henry White b Nov. 7, 1906 d Jan. 2,1907

     B   Isabel White b April 24, 1908 m June 18, 1932 Thomas Fuller Torrey b Aug. 25, 1905 NO ISSUE

C   Weenona b Aug. 14, 1916 m March 28,
     1936 Robert Lyell Hundley b July 14,
     1913   CHILDREN:

     1   Preston Garnett b Feb. 19, 1937 m
          April 11, 1959 Ian Campbell
          MacInnes b Sept. 25, 1935
          CHILDREN:

          a   Ian Campbell II b Dec. 30,
               1959

          b   Jill Hundley b March 12,
               1963 d March 14, 1963

     2   Robert Lyell II b Aug. 16, 1941 m
          June 14, 1963 Judith Elizabeth
          Carpenter b Dec. 5, 1942   CHILD:

          a   Weenona Hundley b Dec. 23,
               1963

     3   Isabel Heflin b Jan. 12, 1943

VI   Joe Walter b June 12, 1885 d Aug. 21, 1885

VII Eloise Simms b June 4, 1886 m April 24, 1907
     Charles Poellnitz Johnston II b March 15,
     1882 d Jan. 15, 1947   CHILD:

A   Henry Poellnitz b Jan. 26, 1908 m Dec.
     26, 1946 Margaret Louise Feagin b Nov.
     6, 1909   CHILDREN:

     1   Henry Poellnitz II b Oct. 26, 1948

     2   Margaret (Miss) Ann b Jan. 10,1951

Descendants of Thomas Jefferson White and Mary Katie Shearen.

I   Bertha b Sept. 25, 1876, living Atlanta, Ga.
m FIRST E. S. Bondurant, M.D., b July 28,
1874 d Sept. 5, 1906 NO ISSUE [1]

     m SECOND William Franklin Rothe b d Buried
Pa. NO ISSUE

II   Daisy Kathleen b May 15, 1878 d Oct. 4, 1956
m Nov. 16, 1897 Eugene L. Nonemacher b 1869
d May 1942 CHILDREN:

    A   Eugene Louis b Dec. 10, 1902 m Estelle
Morgan b NO ISSUE

    B   Thomas White b May 16, 1905 d March 11,
1962, lived in Atlanta, Ga., m Edythe
Eleanor Stevens b NO ISSUE

    C   Daughter, died in infancy

III Chris Shearen b 1881 d 1954 m 1916 Willie Bell
Johnston b 1894 d CHILDREN:

    A   Kathryn b 1918 m FIRST Ellis Lewis b 1913
d 1940 CHILD:

        1   Ellis b 1939 (adopted name Aycock)

        m SECOND Walter Roger Aycock b 1913
Living Goldsboro, N. C.

    B   Willie Bell (Billie) b 1919. Living
Goldsboro, N. C., m FIRST Huston Dotson
b 1919 NO ISSUE

    C   Chris Shearen II b 1920 m Irene Downing
b 1918

[1] It is believed that Thomas Morgan Bondurant,
father of Dr. E.S. Bondurant, was named for Thomas
Morgan, son of Mary Hopkins and Henry Morgan of
the Laurens District of S. C.

Descendants of Robert Allen White and Mary Adelaide Brown

I   Robert Allen II (M.D.) b Oct. 10, 1883 d Apr.
      15, 1924 m Jan. 12, 1912 Mary Gallacher b
      June 12, 1887 d Jan. 5, 1939 CHILD:

      A   Mary Jean b Oct. 15, 1912 m Nov. 9,1941
            John Goggans Balle b June 6, 1912 Liv-
            ing Dallas, Tex. CHILDREN:

            1   Jean Lang b Nov. 3, 1943

            2   Lois Goggans b Oct. 3, 1946

            3   George Allen b Oct. 21, 1949

II   William Thomas b Aug. 19, 1885 m Mar. 8,1912
      Lucile Boswell b Sept. 16, 1895 Living Shef-
      field, Ala. CHILDREN:

      A   Mary Frances b Mar. 3, 1913 m June 13,
            1936 Robert J. Thomas b Sept. 22, 1913
            CHILDREN:

            1   Mary Lou b Oct. 29, 1938 m Dec. 28,
                  1960 Herman Charles Peeper CHILD:

                  a   Herman James b Dec. 14, 1962

            2   Marjorie b Feb. 8, 1942

            3   Robert J. b Nov. 16, 1943

            4   Jane Elizabeth b April 6, 1953

      B   Lucile b June 7, 1916 m Nov. 21, 1942
            John Callaham b Oct. 16, 1905 CHILD:

            1   Mary Frances b Oct. 15, 1943 m Mar.
                  9, 1962 William H. Reeves CHILD:

                  a   Elizabeth Ann b Dec. 26, 1962

III   Elizabeth (Lizzie) b Oct. 21, 1887, Uniontown,
      Ala. m July 7, 1915 George Sidney Woods b
      March 1, 1877 d Dec. 23, 1949 CHILD:

      A   David Sydney b May 6, 1923 m Feb. 5,1943
            Barbara Morgan b Nov. 25, 1924 CHILDREN:

1   George Brooks b Jan. 23, 1944

2   Barbara Jean b April 1, 1946

3   Sidney b May 4,1953

IV   Milton Christian b Nov. 15, 1889 d Nov. 11, 1962 m June 15, 1915 Bessie Linn Bilbro b Aug. 26, 1891 CHILDREN:

A   Bessie Linn b Nov. 1, 1916 d Jan. 2, 1934

B   Milton Robert b Jan. 26, 1920 m Oct. 16, 1943 June Colbert b June 1, 1923 Lives New Orleans, La. CHILDREN:

1   Susan b Dec. 4, 1949

2   David Allen b May 18, 1955

V   Jean b Dec. 3, 1891 d Nov. 13, 1907

VI   Lawrence b Feb. 1, 1894 m July 2, 1931 Bessie Stainton b July 9, 1903 Live Jackson, Miss. CHILD:

A   Mary Elizabeth b June 11, 1932 m Aug. 29 1952 Billy Runnells b Mar. 5, 1935 CHILDREN:

1   Helen Rebecca b June 27, 1953

2   George Lawrence b Dec. 11, 1962

VII Clement Brown b Jan. 9, 1896 d June 28, 1954 m Dec. 29, 1924 Gladys Shaw b NO ISSUE

VIII James Walter b Aug. 25, 1899 m Nov. 7, 1923 Mary Elizabeth Douglass b Feb. 22, 1898 Live New Orleans, La. CHILDREN:

A   Mary Douglass b June 4, 1925 m Dec. 24, 1943 Lawrence Dorr b Nov. 4, 1922 Lives Meridian, Miss. CHILDREN:

1   Lawrence Augustine b Dec. 2, 1944

2   Carol Ann b Nov. 17, 1951

B   James Walter II b Oct. 9, 1929 m Jan. 19, 1952 Ann Adcock b Nov. 28, 1929 CHILDREN:

1   James Douglas b May 5, 1956

2   Thomas Gary b Jan. 28, 1959

Descendants of Joseph Johnston White and Virginia Randolph Sherman

I   Sherman b Sept. 23, 1886 d May 7, 1888

II   Edward Randolph b Dec. 26, 1887 m Nov. 10, 1909 Mary Adelaide Graves b July 31, 1888 Charles City Co., Va. CHILDREN:

    A   Edward Randolph II b Dec. 25, 1912 m May 16, 1935 Mary Ellen Barnes b Jan. 25, 1915 d March 25, 1962 CHILDREN:

        1   Edward Randolph III (Lt. U.S.Army, graduate Auburn Univ. 1962)b Sept. 5, 1939 m Jan. 30, 1960 Leonora Douglas Pride b June 29, 1941 CHILDREN:

            a   Susan Douglas b Oct. 17, 1960

            b   Edward Randolph IV b Feb. 15, 1962

        2   Marguerite Barnes b Sept. 13, 1941 m May 17, 1958 John Roger Thompson b April 2, 1933 CHILD:

            a   Phylis b March 8, 1960

        3   Augustus Barnes b Jan. 6, 1943 (Student Bellhaven College, Jackson, Miss.)

        4   Mary Susan b Sept. 18, 1951

    B   Frances Beverley b Feb. 14, 1920 m Mar. 28, 1940 William Ransom Johnson Dunn II b April 18, 1917 CHILDREN:

        1   Mary Beverley b June 8, 1941 (Sr. Randolph Macon Woman's College, Lynchburg, Va., 1963)

        2   William Ransom III b June 17, 1943 d Mar. 2, 1963 (Killed accidentally, student University of Ala.)

        3   Lucy Durr b May 25, 1948

Descendants of Joseph Johnston White and Grace Stewart Triplett

III   Virginia Portlock b May 18, 1890 d Sept. 28, 1915 m June 20, 1914 Richard Jacqueline Ambler b   d   CHILD:

     A   Virginia White b Sept. 28, 1915 m FIRST Baynard Benton b   CHILD:

         1   Betsy

         m SECOND Kenneth Glenn b

IV   Joseph Johnston II b May 10, 1893 d Oct. 13, 1957 Erie, Pa., m June 24, 1920 Lucy Turner Barbee b June 2, 1893   CHILDREN:

     A   Turner Shacklett b June 25, 1925 d June 25, 1925

     B   Joseph Johnston III b June 8, 1928 Erie, Pa.

     C   Betsy b Oct. 10, 1932 Erie, Pa., m Oct. 26, 1957 Thomas Donald Rigley b July 15, 1928

V   Norman Webb b Jan. 21, 1904 (Retired, U.S. Medical Corps), m Feb. 3, 1925 Geraldine Catherine Van Eyk b May 21, 1903, Living 1959 Westboro, Mass.   CHILDREN:

     A   Norman Triplett b Jan. 7, 1938 (Graduated from Harvard University June, 1959)

     B   Gerald deJonge b May 28, 1941 (Student Colgate University, 1959)

     C   Robert Granville b Mar. 12, 1947

Descendants of Alice Nancy White and Frank McConkle

I   Frank White [M.D.] b June 30, 1893 Living
Gadsden, Ala., m Aug. 6, 1919 Mamie Woodfin
b May 22, 1893 CHILDREN:

    A   Walter Woodfin [M.D.] b Sept. 16, 1922
    m Oct. 28, 1949 Margaret Ann McCrary b
    March 21, 1923 CHILDREN:

        1   Frank Scott b March 9, 1952

        2   Susan b Feb. 26, 1954

        3   George Walter b June 8, 1957

        4   Margaret Ann b April 26, 1959

    B   Elizabeth Noell [twin] b July 25, 1928
    m June 25, 1949 Lt. William McCoy Wads-
    worth b Jan. 25, 1926 d Dec. 3, 1950
    [killed in Korea] CHILD:

        1   Catherine Donna b June 8, 1950

    C   Catherine Marcella [twin] b July 25,1928
    m Aug. 15, 1953 Lt. Harry Warner Lombard
    b April 24, 1930 CHILDREN:

        1   Kathleen Marcella b July 1, 1954

        2   Harry Warner b April 2, 1957

II   Henry White b Aug. 1, 1899 Living Montgomery,
Ala. m Oct. 4, 1923 Merle Looney b May 9,
1902 CHILD:

    A   Anabel Farris b Oct. 1, 1926 d Feb. 16,
    1936

III   Walter White b Sept. 7, 1900 m Nov. 3, 1923
Ruth Smith b Feb. 11, 1902. Living Uniontown
CHILDREN:

    A   Alice White b Jan. 10, 1925 m June 13,
    1946 John Benjamin White b May 2, 1922
    CHILDREN:

        1   Walter Pryor b Feb. 4, 1948

2   John Thomas b July 19, 1951

3   Harrison McCorkle [Mac] b Mar. 7, 1954

4   Robert Wayne b March 22, 1955

5   Lee Osborne b Nov. 22, 1958

B   Ruth White b Dec. 29, 1930 m May 31, 1952 James William Goodloe b April 22, 1922 CHILDREN:

1   Peter McCorkle b Jan. 31, 1956

2   Ruth Pryor b Sept. 17, 1958

3   William Jamison b June 13, 1960

4   Walter White b May 25, 1962

Descendants of Mary Brown White and Ruben Edmonston

I   Martha Jane b Aug. 11, 1842 d Jan. 12, 1925
m   David Thomas Winston b April
28, 1840 d Oct. 27, 1906 [1]

II   George Wesley b Nov. 2, 1843 d April 24,
1917 m April 4, 1869 Mary Frances Young b
June 6, 1845 d Aug. 31, 1928 [2] CHILDREN:

    A   William Brown b May 8, 1870 d Nov. 10,
1946 m Dec. 26, 1895 Frances Jane
Oliver b Feb. 15, 1873 CHILDREN:

       1   Loubie Gray b Jan. 26, 1897 m Sept.
3, 1917 Carl Allen James b May 18,
1895   CHILD:

          a   Martha Louise b June 9, 1920

       2   Ethyle Frances b Dec. 23, 1898 m
June 23, 1923 William Harris
Pritchett b May 26, 1896 NO ISSUE

       3   Mary Virginia b Nov. 8, 1901 m Aug.
16, 1930 Roaley Raymond Smyth b
April 21, 1900   CHILD:

          a   Sandra Ann b Aug. 26, 1932 d
Aug. 27, 1932, one day old [3]

       4   Dorothy Dean b June 27, 1911 m
June 27, 1936 Dilma Lays Vaughn b
Sept. 28, 1911 d Sept. 11, 1962
[3]   CHILDREN:

[1] He was son of David Winston & Candace Jeter.
Candace Jeter was daughter of Robert Jeter and
Susanna Allen. Susanna Allen and Rachel Allen
were sisters; and Rachel was the mother of Mary
Brown White above.

[2] Both buried Liberty Cemetery, Weakley Co.Tenn.

[3] Buried Hopewell Cemetery, Gleason, Weakley
County, Tenn.

a   Jack Dale b Jan. 20, 1939

b   Joel Nelson b Mar. 17, 1942

c   Jane Ellen b Sept. 27, 1946 (twin)

d   Janice Ann b Sept. 27, 1946 (twin)

B   **Emma** Eudora b March 30, 1872 d June 9, 1953 m March 5, 1892 Robert Lee Wiggs b July 8, 1869 d April 9, 1960 CHILDREN:

1   Infant b   d   1895

2   Newton Cornelius b April 6, 1897 m May 22, 1924 Sadie Alberta Williams b Nov. 9, 1897   NO ISSUE

3   Geneva Clair b Oct. 20, 1901 m Dec. 26, 1933 Griff Ross Dodds b Sept. 22, 1898   CHILDREN:

    a   A girl, b   d in infancy 1936

    b   A boy, b   d in infancy 1937

    c   Child, died in infancy

    d   Child, died in infancy

4   Child, b   d in infancy

5   George Wesley b Mar. 20, 1904 m June 11, 1935 Orrin Deloma Brann b April 12, 1912   NO ISSUE

6   Daisy Bell b June 16, 1907 m Aug. 7, 1946 Wesley Francis Gardiner b Dec. 9, 1903   NO ISSUE

7   Hazel Young b June 24, 1909   UNMARR_ IED

[1]   Both buried Mt. Olive Cemetery, Nashville, Tennessee.

C   Thomas Wesley b Jan. 5, 1874 d Aug. 23, 1936 m Sept. 7, 1902 Lela Mai Jeter b Sept. 26, 1882 d Nov. 19, 1961 [1] CHILDREN:

    1   Edgar Ruben b July 24, 1903 UNMARRIED

    2   Carl Finch b Aug. 17, 1904 UNMARRIED

D   Martha Geneva (Jennie) b Mar. 10, 1876 d Dec. 15, 1942 m Dec. 26, 1900 Robert (Bob) Smith Green b Dec. 5, 1875 d June 6, 1954. Both buried Paragould, Ark. CHILDREN:

    1   Infant b and d Nov. 27, 1901

    2   Infant b and d Oct. 4, 1906

    3   Infant b and d Dec. 6, 1910

    4   Marcus Luther b July 6, 1915 m Mildred May Oakley b   NFI

E   Jenius Young b Mar. 10, 1876 (twin) d July 12, 1876 Buried family cemetery near Dresden, Weakley Co. Tenn.

F   Ruben Asbery b Sept. 25, 1878 d March 17, 1936 m Jan. 11, 1920 Mayme Agnes Wix b June 29, 1882 d Dec. 9, 1931 [2] CHILD:

    1   Ruben Wix b April 15, 1922 UNMARRIED

[1] She was daughter of George Samuel Jeter and Mary Tennessee Ward. George Samuel Jeter was son of William B. Jeter and Mary Boswell. William B. Jeter was son of Samuel Jeter and Ann Brasfield. Samuel Jeter was son of Robert Jeter and Susanna Allen---who was sister of Rachel Allen, wife of Joshua White.

[2] Both buried Liberty Cemetery, Dresden, Weakley County, Tennessee

G   Ivo Cleveland b June 17, 1883 (twin) m
    Dec. 21, 1904 Maude Hortense Clark b
    March 12, 1886   CHILDREN:

    1   Leroy b Dec. 21, 1905 m Oct. 8,
        1938 Lauretha May Travis b Oct. 11,
        1914   NO ISSUE

    2   Robert Aubrey b Apr. 3, 1908 m Aug.
        18, 1935 Mary Juanita Howard b Mar.
        1, 1915   CHILDREN:

        a   Gloria Lemon b Sept. 16, 1936
            m Sept. 3, 1955 Hal Jerome
            Taylor b July 18, 1935 CHILD-
            REN:

            i   Kennith Jerome b Aug. 9,
                 1956

            ii   Kimberly b Nov. 27, 1958

        b   Suzette b Sept. 11, 1946

H   Ione b June 17, 1883 (twin) d Aug. 6,
    1883

I   George Ella b Oct. 2, 1885 d Oct. 2,
    1885

J   Robert Ernest b June 25, 1888 d Feb. 12,
    1952 m Aug. 2, 1921 Onie Smyth b Feb.
    24, 1893   CHILD:

    1   George William b Mar. 22, 1922 d
        May 6, 1963 m May 26, 1957 Ruth
        Imogene Crawford b Oct. 25, 1930
        CHILDREN:

        a   Anthony William b July 17,
            1958

        b   Melanie b Sept. 25, 1960

III Mary E. R.   b Sept. 30, 1844 d Sept. 30,
     1844

IV   James Robert (Bob) b Sept. 24, 1846 d Oct.
11, 1900 m March 16, 1869 Sallie Pointer b
Aug. 2, 1846 d Dec. 10, 1917 Both buried in
Arkansas.   NO ISSUE

V   Rufus Elbert Granville b Aug. 19, 1848 d
1850

Descendants of Joshua Asbury White and Prudence Buchanan

I   Garland A.   b   d   New Orleans
    m   NFI   CHILDREN:

    A   Willie b   UNMARRIED   NFI

    B   Laura b   UNMARRIED   NFI

    C   Tennessee b   UNMARRIED   NFI

    D   Bell b   d   m   George
       Lucas b   d   CHILDREN:

       1   George II b   d   Lived
          in Illinois   NFI

       2   Erwin b   d   Lived
          in Mississippi   NFI

    E   George b   UNMARRIED   NFI

    F   Maggie b   d   m   a Mr.
       Smith b   d   CHILDREN:

       1   Annie Bell b   NFI

       2   Garland b

II   Elizabeth b   1835 d Oct. 8, 1881 m
    March 22, 1854 Elliott Dean Hornbeck b   1817
    d   CHILDREN: (had 8,   NFI)

III   Arthur b   1839 d   m   FIRST   a
     Miss Lynn b   d   CHILD:

    A   Egbert b   d   m
       Dave Campbell b   d   CHILDREN:

       1   Imogene b   NFI

       2   John Richard b   NFI

       3   Thomas Carry b   NFI

    m   SECOND_____ CHILD:

    B   Arthur II b   NFI

Descendants of Joshua Ashbury White and Prescilla Buchanan

IV   Sarah C.   b   1842 m   ____Fuller b
      CHILDREN: [1]

      A   Robert b   NFI

      B   Alice

      C   George

      D   Lizzy

V   Henry Logan b   1845 d   m
      Sarah Cornelia Wilson b   d   NFI

VI   Millard Filmore b   1850   NFI

VII   Josephine b March 24, 1855 d   m
      Alpheus Jones b   1845   CHILD:

      A   Ann Eliza b   (7 mos. in 1870 Cen-
           sus)

VIII Cullen Debrough b   d   m
      Bettie Reavis   b   d .   NFI

IX   Joshua Asbury II b March 24, 1855 d Sept.
      18, 1881

X   Julia Ann b 1857   d   m   John Jeter
      b   d   NFI

[1]   Sarah is shown as 8 yrs. old in 1850 Census.
The children are mentioned in WILL OF JOSHUA ASBURY
WHITE.

DUM SPIRO SPERO

𝔐𝔬𝔯𝔤𝔞𝔫

While I Breathe, I Hope

ALABAMA IN 1830

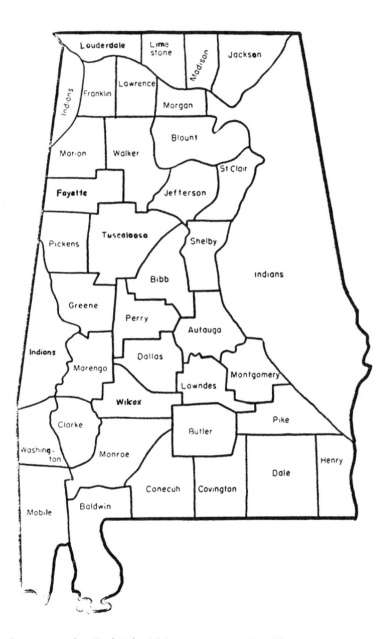

The Formative Period in Alabama 1815-1828, by Abernathy, page 177.

The Morgans

When and where the first of our Morgans reached America is still speculation and conjecture.

Perhaps the writing of this book may awaken a keen enough interest that others will join me in searching further for the parents of Henry Morgan, born Nov. 10, 1771 and died in Laurens District, South Carolina April 24, 1824.

Though there may be speculation as to whether Henry Morgan was born in old District 96 or whether he might have been born close to the Virginia-North Carolina line, there can be no speculation that the name Morgan is Welsh. We are assured by P. H. Reaney in his *Dictionary of British Surnames* that Morgan is Welsh and that it, in reality, is a very old Celtic name. Other ways of spelling the name, through the passing of time, have been *Morgans, Morganus, Morgrund, Morgane, Morcant, Morgum.* Charles W. Bardsley in his *Dictionary of British and Welsh Surnames* verifies Morgan is an old Welsh name, and so does C. L. Ewen in his *History of Surnames of The British Isles.*

But, that still leaves us wondering about the parents of our Henry Morgan, and when he, or they, moved to the Laurens District of South Carolina.

Some historians, by avocation, in our family think that the Morgans came from close to the Virginia-North Carolina line and then moved on to South Carolina; and that probably

Henry Morgan's father or grandfather was a brother of the famous Daniel Morgan of Revolutionary fame.....and this *could* be possible, though doubtful.

The first we hear of Daniel Morgan was in 1748 when he was a youth in Pennsylvania [1] and met his life-long friend Jeb Pellers, the woodsman. They had fought in the Indian wars together and as a young man the Morgan family did move to Virginia and the rousing, patriotic speeches of Patrick Henry aroused Daniel Morgan to such an extent that he formed a company known as *Morgan's Riflemen*. Of course, the rest of the story of Dan Morgan and his contribution to the Revolution is known,especially his terrific defeat of Tarleton and the battle of Cowpens. Morgan did spend much time, under command of General Greene in western North and South Carolina, but he retired near Winchester, Virginia.

Many of the families settling in old District 96 migrated from the eastern shores of Virginia to Brunswick, Lunenberg and Mecklenburg counties in Virginia. [2]

In our research we have found a John Morgan's will probated in Granville in 1786 and a Benjamin Morgan mentioned in the will of Winfield Wright in 1783. We also find Benjamin Morgan as a grantee of land in Granville on two occasions between 1779-90 and 1793-7, and we also find a Benjamin Morgan as a grantor of land in 1779-90.

Checking further into other North Carolina counties, we find James Morgan, son of William, to have had his will probated in

Perquimans Co.N.C. in 1741 and his lands were described as *"Morgan's Swamp."* His sons were Jacob and Charles, which does not seem to fit in our pattern of names in our Morgan line. In 1742 Jane Morgan's will was probated in Perquimans Co.and she names James as her son.

John Morgan of Pasquotank Co.,N. C. had his will probated in 1755 and names sons John and Joseph. He also had daughters and grand-children of his daughters were mentioned, but no grandchildren by his sons.

On Nov. 26, 1730, Robert Morgan's will was probated in Pasquotank and he names Bennett, Joseph, Robert and Moses as his sons and from the will must have been an extremely wealthy individual.

Of course, Perquimans and Pasquotank Counties adjoin each other and are on Alber-marle Sound.

Then we find Nathan Morgan's will pro-bated in 1750 in Onslow Co., N. C. Onslow Co. is on the Atlantic Ocean between New Bern and Wilmington.

Though, again, none of the above proves the parents of our Henry Morgan it does prove there were Morgans who were *Pioneers in Their Own Rights* in North Carolina. And, it could be that some of these Morgans moved to South Carolina, but we do not wish to imply any-thing other than a possible probability that they could be ancestors of our Henry Morgan.

The 1790 South Carolina Census shows in Old District 96 *Morgans* by the name of: Benjamin, Elizabeth, George, and Sarah (of course as heads of households). But none of this proved, nor does it prove the father of our Henry Morgan.

So we still find ourselves continuing to search for Henry Morgan's father.

We do find that *South Carolina In The Revolution* by Sara Sullivan Erwin shows a William Morgan as a Lieutenant in a Battalion of Artillery of Charles Town Militia and we find, from the *S. C. Historical and Genealogical Magazine,* a Jonathan Morgan on May 17, 1781 was sent aboard a prison ship. Finally, we find Benjamin, David, George and Spencer Morgan served in the Revolution.

This could be proof enough that the Benjamin Morgan on the Virginia-North Carolina line was not the same Benjamin who served in the Revolution of South Carolina and we still find ourselves hopelessly involved in the parents of our Henry Morgan, and whether they came direct to South Carolina or whether they migrated from the north.

But, let's get along with what we do know about Henry Morgan: he married Mary Hopkins, daughter of Solomon Hopkins and his wife Margaret (maiden name not known). Some think Solomon Hopkins might have come direct to South Carolina from Scotland, but we found a John Hopkins in Albermarle Co.,N. C. whose will was probated Nov. 8, 1721 and then the will of John Hopkins was proved in Chowan County in January Court of 1754 [3] and then in September Court of Orange Co., N. C. 1759 we find the will of James Hopkins of St.

Matthews Parish in which he names William and John Hopkins with William Phillips as executors.

Orange County, of course, was carved partially from Granville and Johnston Counties in 1752, and Granville was formed from Edgecombe in 1746. It was in this Virginia-North Carolina territory where the Cunninghams once lived and there were Morgans there, and Simms, and Underwoods, and there seemed to be a migration from around Jamestown, Williamsburg, Yorktown and the Albermarle County's easternmost section to the areas around Lunenberg and Mecklenberg counties of Virginia and old Granville and then southwestward (a wilderness route) west of the Fall Line. [4]

So, we could possibly speculate that Solomon Hopkins' forefathers came the same way to Old District 96. And, some of them came into Old 96 before the Revolution because we find applications for war pensions by David and Robert Hopkins.

The 1800 Census for Old District 96 shows the family of Solomon Hopkins included 3 boys under 10 years of age; 2 boys and 1 girl between 10 and 16; 2 boys between 16 and 26, and a male and female above 45. Also in the same district is a James Hopkins and his wife shown to be between 16 and 26, but we cannot connect this James with our Solomon.

At this point it might be interesting to note that our Solomon Hopkins was shown in the 1800 Census as living in the Laurens District, Enoree Regiment, Upper Battalion, XX Capt. Joseph Holmes' Co., the same as that of

John, William and James Dorroh. In connection with this I found the following statement (but not the source): "An interesting peculiarity of this Laurens enumeration is the use of military terminology to indicate geographical subdivisions. Old 96 had been so completely involved in Indian Wars, in the Whig-Tory atrocities, in Tarleton's butchery, and in the battles of King's Mountain and Cowpens that most of the heads of families in the 1800 Census were either veterans of the American Revolution or of an active Militia or both."

Solomon Hopkins died in 1815 and was survived by his widow Margaret, sometimes referred to as Peggy. He and Margaret had a total of eight children at the time of his death: Jeremiah, George, John, Solomon, Frank and Francis, who served as executor of his estate with his wife. The girls were: Nancy who married William Mahaffey, and Mary....the wife of Henry Morgan.

Henry Morgan lived in Laurens until his death April 24, 1824 and was buried in the Friendship Presbyterian Church not far from Gray Court. [6] The grave of Mary Hopkins Morgan has never been found nor the date of her death, but it is assumed she must have died before many and most of their eleven children moved westward into Alabama and Miss. issippi. Three of the children are known to have gone to Perry County, Alabama to join the Dorrohs and Cunninghams and thus became *Pioneers in Their Own Rights;* and six are known to have moved to Mississippi and thus became *Pioneers in Their Own Rights.*

Through the passing of the years connection between the Mississippi and Alabama families has been lost. Perhaps, it is not too much to hope that this chapter might possibly bring together these families again.

We find several of the Alabama Morgans moving onward to Texas and, today, some of them have even reached the Pacific shores of California.

Following the footnotes we will list the *Descendants of Henry Morgan and Mary Hopkins.*

F O O T N O T E S

[1] *Dan Morgan....Rifleman* by Ernest Tucker.

[2] Brunswick County was formed from Prince George, Isle of Wight, and Surry...in 1720. Then in 1746 Lunenberg was formed from Brunswick, and then Mecklenburg was formed from Lunenberg in 1764-5. As one can easily see, this makes documenting records quite difficult!

[3] Albemarle County was formed in 1663 and remained a county until 1751 when all of its districts were made separate counties. Chowan County, of which Edenton is the county seat, was formed Albemarle in 1672.

[4] The Fall Line actually ran from just west of Washington, D. C. to Richmond, to Raleigh, to Columbia, through Milledgeville, Ga., westward through Columbus, Ga., just north of Montgomery (Wetumpka) and on past Tuscaloosa.

[5] SOLOMON HOPKINS (No will in these papers
Box 33, Pkg. 7, Bk. D-1, pg. 198
Francis Hopkins, Executor

"A Warrent of Appraisal: By David Anderson,
Esq., Ordinary, to Tully Bolling (Justice),
Thomas Graydon, Thomas Matthews and Drury
Boyce---these are to authorize and empower
you or any three or four of you to repare to
all such parts and places within Laurens District as you shall be directed unto by Margaret Hopkins and Francis Hopkins, Executors--
late of Solomon Hopkins, Deceased wheresoever
any of the goods and chattels of the said deceased are or do remain with shall be shown
unto you by the said Executrix and Executor
and there view & appraise all & every said
goods & chattels being first sworn on the
holy evanglists of almighty God, to make a
true and perfect inventory and appraisement
thereof and to cause the same to be returned
under your hands or any three or four of you
to the said Margret Hopkins & Francis Hopkins
Executors on or before sixty days now next en-
suing dated this the 19th day of April, 1815,
and in the year of the American independence
the thirty ninth."

David Anderson, Ordy.

(Written on back in pencil: Jerry, John,
Frank, Solomon, George)

///////   //////   ////////

"The Petition of Francis Hopkins, Executor of
Solomon Hopkins, deceased order of sale granted agreeable to the within petition to be holden on the plantation of said decd.on a cred-

it twelve months from the sale thereof by me
this 23th day of December, 1819"

D. Anderson, Ordy.

"To David Anderson, ordinary of Laurens District whereas by Solomon Hopkins(deceased)hav-
ing date on the 19th day of July 1814 did by
said will give unto his wife Margret, a life
estate in the whole of his estate to his wife
and at her death to be sold in a credit and
the amount of the said sale to equally divided among the whole of his children---and as
the said will was proven in the court of ordinary on the 19th day of April, 1815, at the
same time was qualified that said Margret Hop_
kins and Francis Hopkins as Executors they
being named as such in the said last will and
testament, and there is no terms of credit
mentioned in said will therefore pray that
your honour would grant me an order of sale
agreeable to the said bill on a credit of
twelve months from the sale thereof-this 23rd
day of December, 1819.

Signed, Francis Hopkins,Ex.

/ / / / / / /   / / / / / /   / / / / / / / /

Appraise bill of Solomon Hopkins, deceased,
recorded adm. Book D, page 203-204 by me and
filed in my office on the 2nd day of May,
1815-D. Anderson, Ordy.

"You Thomas Matthews,Thomas Graydon and Drury
Boyce, do swear or affirm that you will make
a true and just apprsement of all and singular the goods and chattels ready money only
excepted of Solomon Hopkins, deceased, which
shall be produced by Peggy Hopkins and Fran-

cis Hopkins, Executors of the estate of the
said Solomon Hopkins, deceased, and that you
will return the same certified under your
hands unto the said Peggy Hopkins and Francis
Hopkins, Executors, within the time prescrib-
ed by law. Sworn and subscribed before me
this 24th day April, 1815"
(above three signed)

Tully Bolling, Justice

///////   //////   /////////

List of property appraised of SOLOMON HOPKINS
decd. this 24th April, 1815:

6 head of horses................$2.75
14 head of cattle.............. .73
34 head of hogs................ .53
etc., etc, etc, etc,
4 Negroes..........$1100 for all four
etc. etc, etc,   Totaled $2210.96 1/4
(Much household and farm goods)
                                   his
          Signed   Thomas Matthews X
                                   mark
                      Thomas Graydon
                      Drury Boyce

///////   //////   //////////

Sale Bill of the Estate of SOLOMON HOPKINS,
decd.------Recorded Adm. Book E, pages 60 -
61

---An Account of the sale 14th Jan., 1820--
Among some of those buying at sale were:

Jeremiah Hopkins
Mrs. Nancy Mahaffey

George Hopkins
Francis Hopkins
John Hopkins
Solomon Hopkins
Frank Hopkins
William Morgan

(Bulk of the estate was purchased by above fa
mily), but there were others.

///////   //////   ////////

[6]   HENRY MORGAN ESTATE--Box 53, Pkg. 1-1824
William Morgan, Adm.

A Citation on the Estate and Effects of HENRY
MORGAN, deceased, 1824:

"South Carolina, Laurens District: Whereas
Mary Morgan and William Morgan made suit to
me granted letters of administration on the
estate and effects of Henery Morgan,deceased.
--These are therefor to cite and admonish all
and singulor the kindred and creditors of the
said Henery Morgan before me in the court of
ordinary to be holden at Laurens Court House
on the first Monday in May next after the publication hereof to show cause if any they
have why the said administration should not
be granted as afouresaid--given under my hand
and seale this 13th day of April, 1824 and
in the yeare of the American independence the
forty eight."

                    David Anderson, Ordy.

On back of citation::::::::

    "The within citation was published at the

Quaker Meeting house, Raburn Creek on the third Sabbath in April, 1824---Hugh Dickson

The within citation was published at the Friendship Meeting house, by me this 2nd May,

Barnett Smith

Appraise Bill of the goods and chattels of Henery Morgan, Decd.
Recorded Adm. Book E, page 405-406

The above is a true inventory of the several goods and chattels with its various praisements of the estate of Henery Morgan, decd. which was shown to us by William Morgan, administrator of said estate and appraised this 24th May, 1824 by us

Mark Killingsworth
Jas. Dorroy
Jehu Pitts   Y (his mark)
Jas. Cunningham, Snr.
Abraham Bolt A (his mark)

//////// ////// /////////

The Sale Bill of HENRY MORGAN, Decd. recorded Adm. Book E, pages 427 and 428

Sale Bill October 22, 1824 of the Estate of Henry Morgan, Decd. Among those who bought goods and chattels were:

Polly Morgan (wife) - six negroes, and much household goods
Thomas Morgan (son)
James Morgan (son)
John Hopkins (brother-in-law)
Jeremiah Hopkins (brother-in-law)

William Mahaffey (husband of Nancy Hopkins,
sister of Mary Hopkins Morgan
James Dorroh II

Above family bought most of goods. Others buying were: Wiley Yeargin, son-in-law,
who married Nancy and Matthew Johnson who mar_
ried Dorcas Cunningham, daughter of William
Cunningham and Martha Dorroh.

Total of Sale $2,380.51 3/4

Descendants of Henry Morgan and Mary Hopkins

I   William b June 1799 d July 19, 1860 m FIRST
       ca 1818 in Laurens Dist. S.C. Margaret Cunn
       ingham b Sept. 28, 1798 d June 16, 1853
       CHILDREN: SEE SEPARATE LISTING.

       m SECOND Dec. 28, 1854 Nancy Cunningham b
       April 5, 1810 d June 16, 1885. (1)

II   Thomas b Laurens Dist.,S. C. d after Jan.
       1848 (No record of marriage)

III   John b June 18, 1811 d Oct. 30, 1844. (2)

IV   Allen J. b April 10, 1815 d Sept. 24, 1840
       NFI

V   Lawson b Laurens Dist.,S.C. d ca 1847.(3)

VI   James b Laurens Dist., S. C. d after Jan.
       1848. Lived Marshall Co., Miss. NFI

VII   Lewis M. b Laurens Dist.,S.C., d after Jan
       1848 Lived Marshall Co., Miss. NFI

VIII   Elizabeth b Laurens Dist., S.C., m Joseph
       Gaines. (4)

IX   Margaret b Laurens Dist., S.C. m John Gary
       Lived Tippah Co.,Miss. She died after Jan.
       1848. NFI

X   Sarah b Laurens Dist. S.C. m Felix Norris
       Lived Tippah Co., Miss. She died after Jan
       1848 NFI

XI   Nancy b Laurens Dist. m Wiley Yeargin. She
       died after Jan. 1848 NFI

FOOTNOTES

1] This marriage took place in Perry Co.,Ala. Margaret and Nancy were daughters of William Cunningham and Martha Dorroh. See Cunningham chapter for further information.

2] No record of marriage, and his brothers and sisters were listed as heirs of his Perry County, Ala. estate.

3] Presumably never married as his brothers and sisters were listed as heirs of his Perry County, Ala. estate which was settled Jan. 17, 1848. He was living in Marshall Co., Miss. at time of death.

4] They lived Marshall County, Miss. He was dead by July 1847. She died after Jan. 1848. NFI

Descendants of William Morgan and Margaret Cunningham

I   Henry b Aug. 27, 1819 Laurens Dist.,S.C., d
Jan. 19, 1899 Uniontown, Ala., m Sept. 7,
1857 Martha Caroline Mobley [1] b June 9,
1839 d Feb. 2, 1885 Uniontown, Ala. CHILDREN:
SEE SEPARATE LISTING.

II   John Frank b ca 1822 Laurens Dist.,S.C. d in
Tex, m FIRST Dec. 13, 1847 Louisa Jane Under-
wood b 1830 d May 21, 1852 [2] CHILDREN: SEE
SEPARATE LISTING

m SECOND Sept. 6, 1860 Lizzie Pitts b d in
Texas. CHILDREN: SEE SEPARATE LISTING.

III   Nancy McDavid b Aug. 2, 1823 Laurens Dist.S.C.
d Oct. 25, 1908 m Aug. 22, 1844 George M.
White b April 17, 1807 Granville Co.,N.C., d
Nov. 9, 1866 [3] CHILDREN: SEE SEPARATE
LISTING UNDER DESCENDANTS OF GEORGE M. WHITE
AND NANCY McDAVID MORGAN.

IV   William II b Nov. 2, 1825 Laurens Dist.,S.C.
d Oct. 20, 1845 UNMARRIED

V   James T. b Dec. 14, 1827 d Dec. 19, 1867 m
Feb. 12, 1856 Louisa Stewart b d

VI   Mary Jane b Mar. 13, 1830 d Nov. 28, 1908 m
May 15, 1851 Abraham Holland Underwood [4]
b April 22, 1822 d Mar. 21, 1895 CHILDREN:
SEE SEPARATE LISTING

VII   Thomas J. b Feb. 4, 1832 d Feb. 23, 1875
(buried Marion) m June 15, 1866 Nannie Alice
Bates b Jan. 23, 1847 d Oct. 29, 1934
CHILDREN: SEE SEPARATE LISTING

[1]   Daughter of Abner C. Mobley

[2]   Buried Fairview Presbyterian Cemetery in
western Perry Co., Ala.

[3]   Both buried Uniontown, Ala.

[4]   Son of Robert Underwood & Patience Holland.

VIII Samuel C. L. b July 6, 1835 Laurens Dist.,
S. C., d June 27, 1862 [1] UNMARRIED

IX Lewis Allen b Sept. 23, 1839 d March 24,1915
m Elizabeth Ann Phillips b Jan. 6, 1847 d
May 22, 1919 CHILDREN: SEE DESCENDANTS OF
LEWIS ALLEN MORGAN & ELIZABETH ANN PHILLIPS

CONFEDERATE MILITARY HISTORY
by General Joe Wheeler

"Captain Lewis A. Morgan, of Uniontown,a
veteran of the army of Northern Virginia, is a
native of Alabama, born near Marion, Ala. He enlisted April 25, 1861, in Company D, Fourth regiment Alabama infantry,Col. Egbert J.Jones command-
ing, accompanied this regiment to Virginia, and
fought at the battle of First Manassas July 21, in
the brigade commanded by General Bee. Bee and
Jones were both mortally wounded in that engage-
ment, and E. M. Law became colonel and later commander of the brigade until he was disabled and
succeeded by Gen. W. F. Perry.

"Captain Morgan served in the line at the
battles of Williamsburg, Seven Pines, the Seven
Days before Richmond, Harper's Ferry and Sharps-
burg, Fredericksburg, the Suffolk campaign, and
Gettysburg, and coming west with Longstreet's
corps fought at Chickamauga. General Perry then
took command of the brigade, and Morgan was appointed inspector-general on his staff, with the
rank of captain, in which capacity he served during the remainder of the war, including the Knoxville campaign, and the operations about Richmond
and Petersburg.

"He was surrendered with the army at
Appomattox, returned to Alabama, in 1865 made his
home in Selma for two years, and in 1867 engaged,
in business as a merchant at Uniontown, where he
resided until 1876. Since that date he has given
his attention with much success to cotton buying.
He is one of the leading men of his city, is president of the school board, and served as mayor in
1876=79 and 1897-1900."

[1] C.S.A., Fourth Alabama, died of wounds in
Civil War, in Danville, Virginia.

Descendants of Henry Morgan and Martha Caroline Mobley

I   Rebecca Mobley b Oct. 15, 1859, died young

II   Margarette L. (Mug) b Feb. 28, 1861 d
         ca 1924. UNMARRIED

III   Nancy b Dec. 5, 1862 d Dec. 18, 1937 m March
         5, 1891 Richard Henry Britton (Petersburg,
         Va.) b April 16, 1857 d Oct. 26, 1895. Both
         buried Uniontown, Ala. CHILDREN:

         A   William Henry I b Aug. 17, 1892 m July
                1919 Bettie Louise Tutt b Oct. 21, 1897
                d March 23, 1950 CHILDREN:

                1   William Henry II b July 13, 1920 m
                       July 11, 1946 Mabel Rose Levy b
                       March 18, 1919 Living Demopolis,
                       Ala. CHILD:

                       a   William Henry III b June 25,
                              1947

                2   Margaret Inda b Dec. 10, 1924 m
                       Oct. 6, 1945 Lawrence F. Pyle I b
                       May 14, 1923 CHILDREN:

                       a   Lawrence F. II b March 3,1947

                       b   Inda Louise b Oct. 14, 1951

                       c   George Vice b Sept. 1, 1954

                       d   Martha Virginia b April 12,
                              1956

                       e   James Barr b Aug. 15, 1959

         B   Richard Morgan b Aug. 17, 1894 d Aug.
                19, 1895

IV   Mary Elizabeth (Mamie) b Dec. 31, 1864 d
         Sept. 30, 1937

Descendants of John Frank Morgan and Louisa Jane Underwood

I   William James b Sept. 24, 1848 d Oct. 9, 1849

II   Henry Taylor b Oct. 20, 1849 d July 2, 1850

III   David S. b Dec. 17, 1850 d Sept. 27, 1906
      Buried Uniontown. UNMARRIED [1]

IV   Louisa Jane b May 11, 1852 d Feb. 2, 1853

Descendants of John Frank Morgan and Lizzie Pitts

V   Lewis Allen II b June 18, 1861 d Dec. 16,
      1920 m Jan. 3, 1888 Alberta Cope b Nov. 1,
      1859 d Oct. 28, 1943 CHILDREN:

     A   A girl, b Oct. 1, 1889 d Oct. 1, 1889

     B   Louise b Oct. 5, 1890 d May 27, 1891

     C   Carl Cope b July 2, 1892 m Nov. 12,
         1919 Evelyn Ellis b Aug. 19, 1892
         CHILDREN:

         1   Carl Cope II b Aug. 12, 1920 m
            Mar. 8, 1946 Carolyn Jane Umstad
            b Oct. 7, 1918 CHILDREN:

            a   Janie Ellis b June 17, 1947

            b   Carl Cope III b Nov. 28,
                1949

            c   Warnelle Eastmond b Dec. 14,
                1951

[1] Minute Book O, page 236,dated Jan.10,1873,
shows John Frank Morgan guardian for David S.
Morgan and Martha Morrison in division of land be-
tween them and Robert M. Underwood.This makes me
believe Louisa Jane Underwood was daughter of
James and Sarah Underwood. James b Mar. 10,1794 d
Feb. 28, 1842 and Sarah b Dec. 2, 1799 d Feb. 26,
1870. Sarah shown as buying the land in settlement.
Robert M. Underwood above mentioned must have been
nephew of the Robert M. Underwood b Oct. 13,1818 d
Sept. 26,1852 and he was brother of Louisa Jane
Underwood Morgan.

2   Lewis Allen III b May 23, 1922 m
Mar. 17, 1944 Jimmy Penelope Hardwick b June 22, 1922 CHILDREN:

    a   Lewis Allen IV b Nov. 6,1947

    b   James Hardwick b Feb. 11,1951

D   Ellalee b Oct. 5, 1894 m May 2, 1917
Everett Setzer b Sept. 23, 1883 Living
Uniontown, Ala. CHILD:

    1   Alberta b June 20, 1920 m Nov. 10,
1951 Robert Booth b NO   ISSUE

VI   Minnie Lee b June 3, 1863 d June 17, 1960 m
Dec. 24, 1862 John S. DuBose b   d Oct. 12,
1927 CHILDREN:

A   Katie Elizabeth b Sept. 19, 1883 d
Sept. 3, 1886.

B   Mabel M. b May 7, 1888 d Dec. 26, 1929
m Aug. 23, 1911 Parkie Maples b   d
1962 CHILD:

    1   Mary Lee b Sept. 20, 1912 m 1932
Garland Baker Goodson b NO ISSUE

C   Minnie b June 26, 1891 UNMARRIED

D   Tom Morgan b Sept. 3, 1893 m June 3,
1917 Gladys Forrester b Apr. 29, 1895
CHILDREN:

    1   Gladys b Jan. 1920 m May 1941
Ernest Wicker b d   1947 CHILD:

        a   Tommy b April 1943

    2   H. J. (Jay) b June 19, 1923
UNMARRIED

E   John Franklin b May 22, 1897 m Feb. 1,
1920 Jessie Ruth Giles b Feb. 6, 1898
CHILD:

    1   John Franklin II b Apr. 28, 1935
m June 4, 1957 Arnold Parsons b
March 11, 1934 CHILDREN:

a   Belinda b April 11, 1959

b   Bruce Kevin b May 7, 1960

VII   John Frank b 1865 m 1892 Kate Walton b 1876 CHILDREN:

A   Pitts b 1894

B   Ruth b 1896 d 1960 m CHILD:

1   Tom Mass b

C   Frank b 1898 d 1959 m CHILDREN:

1   Frank III b

2   Jack b

D   Marshall b 1903 d 1960

VIII   Joe b 1868 m 1901 Laura Denman b 1882 d 1962 CHILDREN:

A   Joe Arnold b 1902 d 1903

B   Nancy Nadine b 1904 d 1944 m

C   Gerald b 1908 d 1939 m

D   Denman b 1912 m Ruth Knox b CHILD:

1   Geraldine b Feb. 21, 1941 m Pepper b CHILD:

a   Kelly b Sept. 12, 1961

IX   Margaret Cole b April 2, 1871 d Dec. 28, 1925 m Jan. 7, 1897 Charles Sidney DuBose b Jan. 28, 1870 d March 18, 1947 CHILDREN:

A   Willard Morgan b Nov. 12, 1894 m Dec. 23, 1915 Nannie Belle Sparks b Nov. 4, 1896 CHILDREN:

1   Dorothy Fay b June 30, 1917 m FIRST July 25, 1937 M. L. Waldrop b Apr. 19, 1904 CHILD:

a   Martin Hugh b Feb. 19, 1945

m SECOND Oct. 29, 1953 J. R.
Harris, M.D., b Dec. 28, 1912

2   Raymond Carl b April 1, 1919 m
Dec. 6, 1947 Virginia Ashcraft b
May 16, 1925 d Jan. 23, 1962
CHILDREN:

    a   Diana Lynn b Oct. 15, 1949

    b   Raymond Douglas b Jan. 7,
        1952

3   Oleta Pearl b Feb. 10, 1921 m
FIRST William D. Comer b d May,
1942 CHILD:

    a   William D. II b April 6,
        1942

m SECOND July 27, 1944 William D.
Bogar b Oct. 21, 1919 CHILDREN:

    b   Patricia Ann b July 13, 1946

    c   Johnny b Jan. 19, 1948

4   Winnie Mae b Jan. 29, 1923 m Oct.
3, 1942 George A. Fields b Aug.
29, 1913 CHILDREN:

    a   Kay b Nov. 9, 1946

    b   Robert b Dec. 16, 1948

5   Willard Clayton b Dec. 21, 1925 d
Dec. 15, 1929

6   Truman Allen b Dec. 5, 1927 m Dec.
15, 1949 Gwendylon Franks b Sept.
10, 1926 CHILD:

    a   Wayne Allen b May 11, 1951

7   Mildred Inez b Oct. 19, 1929 m
April 30, 1950 Howard W. McIlroy,
M.D., b Nov. 22, 1927 CHILDREN:

    a   Sharon Lynn b Aug. 11, 1955

b   Gary Vance b June 18, 1960

8   Patsy Ophillia b Sept. 20, 1931 m Dec. 24, 1949 Roy Vance Wilson b CHILDREN:

    a   Cynthia Gail b March 1,1953

    b   Kim Denese b Sept. 9, 1955

9   Charlsie Bell b Aug. 31, 1933 m Sept. 21, 1952 James L. Willis b Dec. 24, 1933 CHILDREN:

    a   Carla Jan b Aug. 19, 1955

    b   James Mark b June 25, 1959

B   Katie Elizabeth b Sept. 28, 1897 m Apr. 20, 1926 John Earl Thompson b Jan. 21, 1895 CHILDREN:

1   Charles Brown b March 5, 1927 m Oct. 15, 1947 Billye Wes Jones b Sept. 14, 1931 CHILDREN:

    a   Sue Annette b Sept. 14, 1948

    b   Charles Brown II b Oct. 16, 1951

    c   Mary Alice b Feb. 20, 1956

    d   Ben Andrew b Sept. 3, 1959

    e   Pennye Dell b Oct. 9, 1961

2   Mansel Earl b Oct. 9, 1928 m May 1, 1958 Nell Smith b April 2, 1927 NO ISSUE

3   Gerald Neil b March 10, 1930 m March 24, 1950 June Hodges b Aug. 17, 1934 CHILD:

    a   Pamela Kay b Jan. 30, 1952

4   John Vern (twin) b Dec. 15, 1932 m July 28, 1958 Janet Weatherred b Sept. 30, 1935 CHILDREN:

a   Tracy Kemir b Oct. 21, 1959

b   Tammy Low b Sept. 20, 1960

5   Verna Janelle (twin) b Dec. 15, 1932 m Oct. 1, 1952 Harold Ray Pharr b Aug. 15, 1929 CHILDREN:

a   Jimmy Ray b Aug. 8, 1953

b   Johnny Keith b Oct. 11, 1954

c   Jerry Mack b March 10, 1956

d   Jacky Paul b May 21, 1958

e   Elizabeth Jo b Dec. 6, 1960

6   David Dwight b Aug. 21, 1937 d Oct. 28, 1940

C   Lee Pitts b March 1, 1900 m Dec. 20, 1928 Cleo Cleaveland b Aug. 27, 1908 CHILDREN:

1   Doris Wynelle b m March 22, 1950 Wayland Houchins b Sept. 27, 1925 CHILDREN:

a   Eddie W. b Aug. 25, 1952

b   Teena b Nov. 1, 1955

c   Chris b Feb. 13, 1960

2   Zelma Lee b Nov. 3, 1933 m Nov. 23, 1955 M. L. Williams b CHILD:

a   Mel b Aug. 5, 1960

3   G. L., b Aug. 3, 1941 UNMARRIED

D   Lewis Allen b June 14, 1902 m July 5, 1941 Mouryne Proctor b Nov. 14, 1914 CHILD:

1   Edreum b June 23, 1942 m James Jones b CHILD:

a   Kenneth Alton b Feb.24, 1962

2 Elbert Lynn b Nov. 14, 1943

3 Cretha b Dec. 16, 1953

E Jack Charles b April 9, 1906 m Dec. 17, 1931 Bobbie Oletha Cook b Oct. 5, 1910
CHILDREN:

 1 Jackie Yvonne b July 27, 1932 m Dec. 8, 1950 Audra Bernice Cary b April 13, 1929 CHILDREN:

  a Cynthia Jill b May 22, 1956

  b Brenda Elayne b Oct. 21, 1958

 2 Betty Dawn b Nov. 29, 1935 m Jan. 21, 1956 Tommy Loyd Hamilton b Sept. 21, 1935 CHILD:

  a Loyd Ray b May 18, 1961

 3 Terry Joe b March 3, 1944

F Frank Sidney b Dec. 17, 1909 m Aug. 27, 1939 Lela Wheatley b Nov. 7, 1912
CHILDREN:

 1 Deryee Wayne b Dec. 28, 1941

 2 James Sidney b Jan. 2, 1942

Descendants of Mary Jane Morgan and Abraham Holland Underwood

I   Margaret Ann b Sept. 8, 1852 d Jan. 14, 1892 Trinity, Texas, m Fred Hargrave Goff b April 13, 1846 d May 23, 1930 CHILDREN:

    A   Frederick McEwen b May 22, 1878 d May 3, 1947 m Mrs. Louise Shepard McCorkle b Jan. 8, 1872 d July 10, 1948 NO ISSUE

    B   Mary b Nov. 19, 1880 d Jan. 24, 1913 m July 31, 1910 C. L. Grubbs b d NO ISSUE

    C   Janie b April 22, 1885 m July 6, 1905 Robert Travis Hunnicutt b Dec. 18, 1882 d Jan. 12, 1945 CHILDREN: [All live Del Rio, Texas] [1]

        1   Margaret Alice b Feb. 23, 1907 m Sept. 2, 1932 Paul Henry Sultenfuss b Aug. 20, 1902 d April 28, 1958 CHILD:

            a   Susan

        2   John Gott b Sept. 26, 1908 m Sept. 18, 1937 Jewel Geraldine McDowell b NO ISSUE

    D   Lewis W. Morgan b Aug. 11, 1888 d Nov. 18, 1911 UNMARRIED

    E   Robert Ephriam b Aug. 3, 1882 d Aug. 31, 1883

II Ella Eugenia b April 15, 1854 d June 21, 1918 m Dec. 22, 1875 William Daniel McAuley b Mar. 13, 1849 in India, son of a Presbyterian Missionary, d Oct. 27, 1919 Both buried Uniontown. CHILDREN:

    A   Joseph Eugene b Oct. 30, 1876 d Sept. 2, 1942 m Dec. 12, 1906 Viola McClinton b Nov. 8, 1883 CHILDREN:

        1   Joseph Hester b Sept. 12, 1907 d Aug. 24, 1942 m 1935 Larena Pate b

2 Viola Eugenia b Feb. 2, 1910 m June 29, 1929 Robert Cochran Molette b Mar. 9, 1905 CHILDREN:

 a Eleanor Viola b April 9, 1932 m Dec. 30 1952 Charles Ramon Cobb b June 25, 1928 Living Selma, Ala., CHILDREN:

  i Eleanor Molette b Jan. 12, 1956

  ii Charles Ramon II b July 5, 1959

 b Robert Cochran II b Oct. 14, 1934 m July 7, 1962 Helen Garrison b March 29, 1941

 c Eugenia Page b Dec. 6, 1945

3 Louise b April 14, 1915 m Dec. 9, 1934 Walter Durand Poellnitz b Feb. 22, 1906 Living Uniontown CHILDREN:

 a Shirley Louise b Oct. 4, 1936 m Aug. 28, 1957 Frank Pride Scott b Oct. 1, 1933 CHILDREN:

  i Carrie Louise b June 24, 1958

  ii Jeanette McAuley b Dec. 9, 1959

  iii Marie Pride b Sept. 25, 1961

 b Walter Durand III b Oct. 13, 1938

 c William McAuley b Oct. 17, 1953

4 Jeanette b April 3, 1918 d June 1, 1955 m FIRST Feb. 11, 1937 Ben Clark b CHILD:

 a Ben b April 14, 1939, legally adopted, name changed to

Ben Severn.

m SECOND Aug. 17, 1945 Charles W. Severn b Sept. 11, 1916 CHILDREN:

b   Eveleen b Oct. 14, 1946

c   Charnette b May 13, 1939

5   Ruby William b June 27, 1912 d Dec. 11, 1946 m Sept. 5, 1937 Myrtle Fowler CHILD:

      a   Elizabeth Anne b May 13, 1938 m June 16, 1958 Horace Adair
      b   CHILD:

      i   Horace II b July 9, 1961

6   Solon Coleman b Dec. 12, 1920 m Apr. 24, 1954 Betty Jean Massey b June 1, 1933 CHILDREN:

      a   Thomas Coleman b Dec. 2,1955

      b   Robert Massey b Sept. 12, 1957

      c   Peggy Ann b Apr. 21, 1962

B   Mary Leona (Leila) b March 2, 1879 d Dec. 23, 1950 m Jan. 22, 1895 William Haywood Flinn b Aug. 22, 1855 d Dec. 17, 1922 CHILD:

1   William Haywood II b   d in infancy

C   William Hall b June 25, 1885 d Aug. 31, 1957 UNMARRIED

D   Jeanette Bayles (Nettie) b May 11, 1892 m Dec. 26, 1908 John Kirker b June 21, 1887 CHILD:

1   Jean b Feb. 18, 1927 m May 19,1948 John Lejeune Moter b June 28, 1925 CHILDREN:

      a   John Bayles b Aug. 21, 1949

      b   Guy Stanley b Mar. 6, 1951

      c   Gregory Allen b Jan. 21,1952

III William Thomas b Sept. 12, 1857 d May 1,
1943 m Dec. 16, 1879 Azoline King b Jan. 27,
1858 d April 3, 1929. Both buried Uniontown,
Ala. CHILDREN:

A Laura Pearl b Feb. 5, 1881 d May 31,
1960 m June 5, 1902 Prof. Kieffer
Glesner Hoover b Jan. 16, 1875 d June
12, 1953 Both buried Marion, Ala.
CHILDREN:

1 Elizabeth Azoline b May 4, 1903 m
June 18, 1929 William Henry Stewart
b Oct. 28, 1892 CHILDREN:

a Mary Elizabeth b April 8, 1931
m June 5,1953 Joseph David
Mooty b April 6, 1930 CHILD:

i Joseph David II b Oct. 13,
1959

b William Henry II b Jan. 26,
1934 m May 11,1957 LaFaye
Plummer b Aug. 6, 1936 CHILDREN

i William Hoover b March 26,
1958

ii James Michael b Feb. 8,
1960

c Robert Glesner b Sept. 14,1936
m Dec. 28, 1958 Annie Pauline
Logan b Jan. 20, 1939 CHILDREN:

i Charles Steven b Feb. 27,
1960 Twin

ii Richard Morgan b Feb. 27,
1960 Twin

2 Mary b Oct. 20, 1904 m Dec. 28, 1929
James Ormand (Jo) Speed b Nov. 26,
1901 CHILD:

a James Ormand II b Dec. 7, 1930
m Aug. 2, 1957 Flora Moore McDonald b Sept. 7, 1937 CHILDREN:

    i   Elizabeth LeBron b Sept. 29, 1959

    ii Mary McDonald b Oct. 21, 1961

3 Lillian b Dec. 6, 1906 m Aug. 10, 1929 Latimer Alan Epps b Aug. 4, 1901. Living Tulsa CHILDREN:

    a Latimer Alan II b June 11, 1935 m July 24, 1959 Deedrie Eden Ellis b Sept. 27, 1939 CHILD:

        i Zachary Alan b Oct. 12, 1961

    b Emily Pearl b Sept. 19, 1938 m June 1, 1959 James Joseph Manlandro II b April 18, 1936 CHILDREN:

        i Victoria Eden b March 3, 1960

        ii Monica b Nov. 7, 1961

4 Clara b April 19, 1910 m Oct. 10, 1945 Joseph Crowell Camp b Sept. 1, 1910 Living Linden, Ala. CHILDREN:

    a Frances b Feb. 24, 1948

    b Joseph Crowell II b Jan. 16, 1952

5 John Wesley b Feb. 24, 1916 m Dec. 14, 1939 William Clarence Jones (girl) b Oct. 25, 1912 CHILDREN:

    a Rose Failey b Dec. 20, 1943

    b John Wesley II b Sept. 4,1947

6 Katherine Glesner b Feb. 9, 1918 m Sept. 27, 1947 Renfro Banton Creager b Feb. 9, 1920 Living Memphis, Tenn. CHILDREN:

a   Katherine Alice b July 18, 1948

b   Renfro Banton II b April 23, 1950

c   Susan Terrell b July 3, 1957

7   Thomas Milton b Feb. 8, 1920 m Aug. 27, 1949 Mary Clark Sturdivant b Dec. 8, 1921 CHILDREN:

a   Jamie Clark b Oct. 20, 1950

b   Thomas Milton II b Oct. 3, 1953

B   Lillian Olene b Feb. 24, 1883 d Feb. 18, 1963 m Nov. 23, 1904 T. J. Cleveland b d NO ISSUE

C   Robert Fulton b May 19, 1884 d Nov. 9, 1958 m July 18, 1920 Leona Louise Koops b Sept. 24, 1898 Living Birmingham, Ala. CHILD:

1   Margaret b Aug. 11, 1921 d Sept. 21, 1954

D   Mary Kate b Nov. 17, 1885. Living Uniontown, Ala., m Feb. 24, 1910 George W. Underwood b Jan. 27, 1885 d Feb. 16, 1948 (son of Annie Nonnemacher and Joiner Underwood) CHILDREN:

1   Erin b Oct. 25, 1910 m July 9, 1935 Alfred C. Harrison b July 2, 1912 Living Opelika, Ala. CHILDREN:

a   Katherine Carlisle b July 25, 1940

b   George Underwood b Sept. 10, 1946

2   George W. II b Nov. 11, 1913 d Oct. 27, 1942, Hawaii. Buried there.

E   William Thomas II b Jan. 5, 1889 d Jan. 6, 1948 m Nov. 22, 1916 Edith DuBose b Sept. 3, 1891 Living Birmingham. NO ISSUE

F   John King b Jan. 17, 1890 d Feb. 15,
     1955 m Dec. 21, 1922 Mary Ray Blackburn
     b July 11, 1901. Living Birmingham,Ala.
     CHILD:

     1   John King II b Jan. 31, 1925 m Oct.
          27, 1951 Georgia Ann Fowler b Feb.
          26, 1929 CHILDREN:

          a   Cynthia Lynne b May 16, 1956

          b   John King III b June 29,1959

G   Herbert b Jan. 15, 1893 d July 28, 1893

H   Margaret Erine b Aug. 6, 1894 d Oct. 13,
     1894

I   Mattilee b Sept. 30, 1897 m Nov. 7, 1922
     John W. Dehnert b Nov. 25, 1890 d Oct.
     25, 1957 CHILDREN:

     1   Emoline b Dec. 2, 1924 m Mar. 30,
          1948 Myrven H. Cron b Nov. 5, 1923
          CHILDREN:

          a   Nancy Lee b March 1, 1949

          b   Elizabeth Dehnert b Oct. 6,
               1952

     2   John W. II b Sept. 20, 1930 m Feb.
          15, 1958 Annie Laurie Hewitt b Dec.
          5, 1930 CHILD:

          a   Laurie Grey b Aug. 13, 1959

IV   Robert Holland b Nov. 29, 1859 d March 17,
     1920 m May 24, 1881 Bettie B. West b May 24,
     1859 d Oct. 31, 1918 CHILDREN:

A   Walter West b July 26, 1882 d April 24,
     1957 m 1904 Alta Bruce b March 31,1886
     d Dec. 10, 1960 CHILDREN:

     1   Walter West II b Sept. 8, 1910 m
          Apr. 2, 1932 Elsie Adria Stokes b
          Oct. 19, 1913 Living Washington,
          D.C. CHILDREN:

a   Bradley Bruce b July 2, 1933
m Aug. 4, 1956 Dianne Wilks b
Feb. 7, 1938 CHILD:

    i   Sharon Aline b Feb. 15,
      1960

b   Gloria Anne b Dec. 5, 1944

2   Robert Bruce b Feb. 24, 1914 m Jan.
30, 1955 Carol Elizabeth Kay b Oct.
2, 1932 CHILDREN:

a   Elizabeth Ann b Nov. 14, 1955

b   Thomas Andrew b Feb. 24, 1959

B   Maggie Adele b Dec. 22, 1884 Lives Huntsville, Texas UNMARRIED.

C   Robert Abram b March 12, 1886 d Aug. 14,
1956 m Sept. 20, 1911 Mary West b
CHILDREN:

1   Robert Abram II b Nov. 14, 1912

2   John Tolliver b July 27, 1916 m
Sept. 17, 1937 Martha Jennings b
CHILD:

a   Mary Susan b Aug. 11, 1947

D   Nettie Lee b Aug. 22, 1888 d Nov. 15,
1952 m Aug. 20, 1913 Walter Alvis
Parish b CHILDREN:

1   Walter Alvis II b Aug. 13
CHILDREN:

a   Name and date not available

b   Name and date not available

2   Robert Underwood (Bobby) b Dec. 5,
1925

E   Evelyn b Sept. 27, 1890 m Dec. 26,1910
Caswell Forest b d July 1, 1925 CHILD:

1   Caswell II b m Lu Nell Patton b CHILD:

a   Pat

F   Mabel Oline b Jan. 25, 1895 d Oct. 21, 1946 m May 15, 1915 Jarrette D. Law b Oct. 27, 1892 CHILD:

1   Bettie Mildred b May 29, 1916 m De Los Cook b Dec. 9, 1909 NO ISSUE

G   John B. b Aug. 19, 1896 m Mary Duke b Aug. 19, 1902 d Feb. 12, 1953 CHILDREN:

1   John B. II b Feb. 14, 1932

2   Duke b Aug. 15, 1937

V   Jesse Eugene b Dec. 17, 1861 d **March 21, 1864**

VI   Lewis Abram b Nov. 28, 1864 d Aug. 19, 1868

VII   John Henry b Aug. 7, 1866 d June 17, 1924 Holland, Tex., m Maude Cox b d CHILDREN:

A   Mary Belle b m Sam Barton b

B   Isla b m Raymond Goddard b

VIII Mary Lee b March 20, 1869 d June 27, 1896 m Dec. 24, 1891 William Haywood Flinn b Aug. 22, 1855 d Dec. 17, 1922 CHILD:

A   Ruby Lee b May 13, 1893 m April 25, 1912 Charley Washington Wood b Nov. 6, 1885 d Dec. 6, 1939 CHILDREN:

1   Mary Lee b Oct. 4, 1913 m April 5, 1942 Charles Elliot Toole b April 30, 1915 CHILD:

a   Charles Elliot II b Sept. 23, 1946

2   Lois Elizabeth b Jan. 3, 1919 m Aug. 19, 1940 James Burnette Williams b Jan. 19, 1917 CHILD:

a   Isabelle Lee b Jan. 1, 1954

IX   Samuel Morgan b June 21, 1872 d Sept. 10,
1878

F O O T N O T E S

[1] Mrs. Robert T. (Janie Goff) Hunnicutt of Del
Rio, Texas writes:

"When Grandpa (Abraham Holland)Underwood left
home to go to war he went over to Selma, Ala., and
asked a colonel stationed there to send him a disabled soldier to stay with Grandma (Mary Jane Morgan Underwood) and the children, and he sent papa
(Fred H. Goff) as he had lost his arm at the Battle of Corinth, Miss. He was quite young and she
took him in and was like a mother to him. In fact,
I have heard him say that she was a most wonderful
woman. Papa's home was in the southern part of
Missouri and he went back after the war was over,
but he did not stay long.

"His mother and father were not living. Then
he went to St. Louis and took a course in bookkeep-
ing. Then finally settled in Alabama, near Uniontown. Later he and Mama were married. They lived
there for a while.

"Fred and Mary, my oldest brother and only
sister, were born near Uniontown, Ala. Then they
moved to Texas, settling in Holland, Texas. I was
born in Holland, also my younger brother Lewis.
When he was a baby they moved to Trinity, Tex. and
when he was about three years old our mother died,
leaving four young children. So Grandma (Mary Jane
Morgan) Underwood who was living in Alabama on
their plantation came to the funeral and never did
go back to Alabama to live.

"Then Grandpa (Abraham Holland) Underwood sold
the plantation and came to Trinity, Texas, and he
and Grandma (Mary Jane Morgan Underwood)lived with
us. She had the most wonderful disposition, never
was sick, only in later years when she fell and
broke her hip and got over that; then fell and broke
her leg and finally died as a result of a fall.

"She was visiting her sister, Aunt Nancy Morgan
White, in Uniontown, Ala., and a day or so after

Aunt Nancy died, Grandma tripped and fell and
injured her back. She was buried in Uniontown
Cametery on the McAuley lot by her daughter, Ella
McAuley. This has been a long story but will help
you to understand why Grandma and Grandpa Underwood were not buried together.

"Grandpa only lived a year or so after Mama
died, but he was buried in Trinity, Texas. That
was the reason you do not find anyone who remembered him."

Descendants of Thomas J. Morgan and Nannie Alice Bates

I Minnie Isabelle b Nov. 15, 1867 d Feb. 28, 1952 m Oct. 23, 1889 Walter Pancoast Levis b Nov. 12, 1866 d June 9, 1946 CHILD:

A Marshall Morgan b Aug. 30, 1893 Marion, Ala., m Jan. 15, 1919 Loretta Denise Sullivan b July 27, 1893,New York, N.Y. CHILDREN:

1 Donald Morgan b Nov. 1, 1919 San Francisco, m Aug. 30, 1941 Janice Bertha Lowell b May 17, 1921, Berkeley, Cal. Living in Belleview Wash. CHILDREN:

a Susan Carolyn b Feb. 9, 1943 (attends Univ. of Washington)

b Laurette Jane b Jan. 29,1947

2 Cornelia Morgan b July 13, 1924 Oakland, Cal., m Aug. 1, 1948 Berkeley, Cal. Yates Smoot Bleuel b Oct. 12, 1919 Oakland, Cal. Living Orinda, Cal. CHILDREN:

a Denise Marie b Feb. 8, 1950

b Molly Mae b June 21, 1951

II George William b Nov. 13, 1869 d Nov. 24, 1891 Buried Marion, Ala. UNMARRIED

III Lula b June 12, 1871 d Dec. 7, 1907 m James D. Smith b   d

IV Clara Ida b Dec. 29, 1873 d Oct. 4, 1961 m June 13, 1894 Arthur Dickinson Frost b Nov. 27, 1871 d May 31, 1946 CHILDREN:

A Marion Morgan b May 1, 1895 m Nov. 8, 1924 Burl Bryan b Aug. 22, 1897 Living Dallas, Tex.

B Vernice Louise b Mar. 17, 1898 d July 25, 1941 m July 15, 1929 Russell H. Henderson b   NO ISSUE

Descendants of Lewis Allen Morgan and Elizabeth Ann Phillips

I   Lewis Allen II b Oct. 21, 1876 d June 24, 1961 m FIRST April 17, 1900 Leonard Pitts b Sept. 9, 1877 d June 10, 1910 NO ISSUE

m SECOND 1914 Alice Marks b June 21, 1877 d Oct. 1, 1928 CHILD:

A   Allen Lewis b May 20, 1918 m Sarah Majors b Living Houston, Texas CHILDREN:

1   Hardie White b March 15, 1958

2   Alice Bisbee b April 6, 1959

II   Lottie b Dec. 15, 1878 d May 2, 1963 m Oct. 25, 1900 James Hardie Bradford b Feb. 8, 1876 Living Uniontown, Ala.* CHILDREN:

A   Elizabeth Ann b May 6, 1903 m June 5, 1930 William Adams Kimbrough b Jan. 11, 1900 Living Thomasville, Ala. CHILDREN:

1   Elizabeth Ann b Dec. 14, 1931

2   William Adams II b July 21, 1935 m Dec. 28, 1958 Kay Lindsey b May 7, 1938 Living Butler, Ala. CHILD:

a   Mary Elizabeth b June 9, 1960

3   Hardie Bradford b Jan. 4, 1938 m Jan. 2, 1961 Deanna Phillips b July 23, 1937 NO ISSUE

B   Robert Hardie b Dec. 12, 1904 m June 8, 1938 Thomasine Locke McCorkle b March 1, 1908 Living Uniontown, Ala. CHILDREN:

1   Louise Harrison b April 20, 1940

2   Charlotte Hardie b April 15, 1944

3   Gertrude Shepard b Jan. 7, 1948

C   Mary Isabelle b July 17, 1908 m June 4,
     1931 Percy Hatch b CHILD:

     1   Infant child, died

III Addie Poindexter b Jan. 14, 1883 d July 13,
     1951 m April 26, 1905 John Gwin White b April
     24, 1883 d May 10, 1956. Both buried Union-
     town, Ala. CHILDREN: [carried under *Descend-
     ants of George M. White and Nancy McDavid
     Morgan*

IV   Willie b May 22, 1886 d July 12, 1886

V   Bettie b July 19, 1888 d Jan. 29, 1889

*   James Hardie Bradford died Monday, Feb. 24,
     1964 and was buried Feb. 26, 1964. He was
     formerly a President of the PLANTERS AND
     MERCHANTS BANK of Uniontown, Ala.,for many
     years Mayor of Uniontown and also an Elder
     and Clerk of the Session of the Uniontown
     Presbyterian Church.

144

ALABAMA 1840

Adapted from Dorman's Party Politics in Alabama from 1850 Through 1860.

OVER FORK OVER

Cunningham

The Cunninghams

The name Cunningham is Scotch and the family name takes its name from the District of Cunningham in Ayrshire. The name occurs as early as the twelfth century.

The Gaelic name was: Mac Cuinneagain.[1]

The Scotch Clans, their plaids, their coat-of-arms and their crests have become a real fad in America and everyone of Scotch descent is proud of his ancestry, even though complete documentation beyond a progenitor is often difficult.

In search on the Cunningham family I found *The Scotish Tartans*, published by W. & A. K. Johnston Ltd. (of Edinburgh and London) quite interesting. Robert Bain's *Clans and Tartans of Scotland*, published by William Collins Sons & Co., London and Glasgow; *Tartans of The Clans and Families of Scotland*, by Sir Thomas Innes of Learney, published by Irving Ravin, New York City; and *Tartans* by Christian Hesketh, published by G.P. Putnam's Sons,New York are more than interesting reading for one interested in Scotish folk lore.

When in Edinburgh in August of 1962 brousing about her beautiful Library and other sources of information about various Scotch ancestors, it was my pleasure to meet Donald F. MacDonald, [2] a feature writer for *The Weekly Scotsman.* He is a native of Charlotte, N.C. and we had many things and people in common.

While visiting with Mr. MacDonald he was

kind enough to make available a very interesting article from *The Weekly Scotsman* of Thursday, Oct. 26, 1961. The article was on the Cunningham family, as you would expect, and its heading was *They Were Heroes of The Old,* and it was written by Allan Douglas, who knows more about the various Clans than most any other person. With their kind permission I reproduce it, as it tells more about our Cunninghams than I could ever tell otherwise:

"There's nothing in history to suggest that sailing is in the Cunningham Blood. Certainly land-locked Kilmarnock didn't offer the family many opportunities to show their paces on the sea.

"Yet the Cunninghams were to produce two Admirals of the Fleet, brilliant sailors who won their spurs in the grim heat of battle, and both of whom played a vital part in freeing the Mediterranean from German submarines and warships during the last war.

"The men, of course, were Admiral of the Fleet Viscount Cunningham of Hyndhope-----who was decorated by the French,Americans,Greeks, and Dutch as well as by his own country---and Admiral of the Fleet Sir John Cunningham who was C.-in-C. Levant in 1943, and C.-in C.Mediterranean and Allied Naval Commander Mediterranean from 1943-1946.

"The name *Cunningham* is territorial, and stems from an old parish called Cunningham,in North Ayrshire. First of the name is said to be Wernebald, who received a grant of Kilmaurs in Cunningham from the High Constable of Scotland, Hugo de Morville.

"Harvey de Cunningham fought at the Battle of Largs in 1263, and in the following year he got a charter of the lands of Kilmaurs from Alexander III.

"Sir William Cunningham married a daughter of Lord Dennieston, and with her received large possessions of land, especially Glencairn--from which his descendants took their title of Earl---in Dumfrieshire.

"Sir Alexander de Cunningham was created Lord Kilmaurs in 1445, and the Earl of Glencairn by King James III in 1488. Following his creation,he died fighting for the king at the battle of Sauchieburn.

"After the Recissory Act of 1488, the earldom was annulled, but was later restored to Cuthbert, as 3rd Earl of Glencairn. In 1526 Cuthbert joined the Earl of Lennox in an attempt to rescue King James V from the power of the Douglases. In the same year he was wounded at a battle near Linlithgow, where Lennox lost his life.

"The fourth Earl of Glencairn will be best remembered for his double dealings with the English. He joined the forces of the Earls of Angus and Lennox in 1524, when they captured Edinburgh and tried to take the young King from the Queen Mother. Two years later, he was appointed High Treasurer of Scotland, then sent on a matrimonial embassy to France where the treaty of marriage between Mary of Guise and James V was concluded.

"Glencairn was captured by the English at the rout of Solway Moss, but released on a ransom of 1000 lbs., and the promise to promote a marriage between Mary Queen of Scots and Edward VI.

"Glencairn at this time was one of Scotland's most powerful barons......so powerful, in fact, that he headed the intrigues and counterplots of the Anglo-Scottish party of the time.

"Not only that---When Henry contemplated an invasion of Scotland, Glencairn offered to lead his army from Carlisle to Glasgow..without opposition. But the Earl overstepped himself when he promised to deliver Mary Queen of Scots into Henry's hands. He led 500 spearsmen on Glasgow but his army was thrashed by the Regent and Glencairn fled to Dumbarton, abandoning Henry's cause.

"'If you can't beat them, join them,' seemed to be Glencairn's motto, for he accompanied the Regent's army that laid siege to Coldingham. The English dispersed them, so the following year Glencairn and his son renewed negotiations with Henry.

"Miraculously,he survived his treachery, and the Scots parliament virtually pardoned him and his followers for their treason.

"When John Knox began to make his violent presence known in Scotland, Alexander, the 5th Earl of Glencairn, sprang up to support the Reformer. He even took a letter from Knox to the Queen Regent, Mary of Guise, asking her to protect the Reformed preachers.

"When she read it,Mary handed it over to Bethune, Archbishop of Glasgow, adding contemptuously: 'Please you, my lord, read a pasquil.'

"Knox dined with Glencairn on several oc
casions, and the Earl was one of the Lords of
the Congregation who has subscribed to the
Covenant, drawn up for the support and de-
fence of Protestantism. Mary dealt harshly
with the Protestants, and when the Reformers
at Perth decided to arm for their own protection, Glencairn joined them with over 2000
men. He died shortly after the religion had
been established by Parliament in 1560.

"The ninth Earl of Glencairn was a firm
and courageous royalist. When General Monk
marched into Scotland at the head of Crom-
well's powerful army, the Earl remained faithful to Charles II.

"He fled north, and at Loch Earn, in
Perthshire, met Atholl and other Highland
chiefs who were loyal to the throne. Glencairn took command of the men and captured
Elgin. But the taste of victory turned bitter in his mouth when he learned that Charles
had appointed Middleton Commander in Chief of
the Army; accordingly, he handed over his men
and command at Dornoch in March, 1654.

"The men, too, were bitter at losing
their old general, but mere anger was soon
turned to hatred and resentment.

"Addressing Middleton, Glencairn said;
'My lord, general, you will see what a gallant
army these gentlemen and I have gathered together.....these men have come to serve His
Majesty, at the hazard of their lives and all
that is dear to them. I hope, therefore, that

you will give them   all the encouragement   to
do their duty that lies in your power.'

"In reply, Sir George Munro, Middleton's
tactless lieutenant general, shouted: ' The
men you speak of are nothing but a pack of
thieves and robbers. In a   short time I will
bring a   very different set of men into the
field.'

"Stung by his answer,the angry Glencairn
challenged Munro to a duel. Their pistol
shots flew wide of the mark and they fought
with swords. Though wounded in the hand, the
Earl cut Munro across the forehead, blinding
him with blood. His own servant restrained
him from running Munro through.

"Middleton ordered his arrest, and the
spirit of the whole army left with him.

"James, the fourteenth Earl, was chosen
one of the 16 Scottish representative peers
and was a patron and great friend of Robert
Burns. He sold the ancient family estate of
Kilmaurs to the Marchioness of Titchfield and
died at Falmouth, after a visit to Portugal,
in 1791. At his death Burns wrote the touching 'Lament for the Earl of Glencairn.'

"The title fell to his brother,John, who
took orders in the Church of England. He died
without issue and the title became dormant.

"The chiefship was eventually settled on
the Cunninghams of Corsehill, deriving from
Andrew Cunningham of Corsehill, second son of
the 3rd Earl of Glencairn.

"The present chief is Sir John Cunningham, of Corsehill, 12th Baronet."

Now that we have gotten a pretty interesting background of our Cunninghams in Scotland, we shall now proceed with our American line:

Worth S.Ray in *Colonial Granville County And Its People* (page 233)shows a map of Queen's Creek in York Co., Virginia with Skimmino Creek to its west,both emptying into the York River, just up stream from Yorktown. He shows a number of families living between Skimmino and Queen's Creeks and lists among them the Whites and the Cunninghams. He states that all of these families (the several he listed) settled in York County during the first half of the 17th century and "one generation after another toddled along. They intermarried and formed ties and alliances that have never been abandoned or dissolved."

And, it is easy to visualize the normal westward treck of many of these families. The first time we find what I definitely believe to be our ancestor is in Brunswick Co. Va. in 1745 when Thomas Cunningham purchased 685 acres near Cubb Creek, adjacent William Harwood and Andrew Cunningham [3]. We also find Andrew Cunningham in 1745 bought 768 acres for 22 pounds on Cubb Creek adjoining Thomas Cunningham. [4]

We were unable to find any more Cunningham deeds in Brunswick Co., but remember in that same year Lunenburg County was formed from Brunswick and the Cunningham property fell in the newly formed county.

We do find several Cunninghams as grantees in Lunenburg County between 1752 and 1772
[5].And, we find a number of grantors including our Thomas Cunningham [6].

Since so few people in the middle 18*th*
century had middle names, it is difficult to
keep everything *absolutely* straight. For ex-
ample, we mentioned that Thomas and Andrew Cunningham secured property on Cubb Creek in
Brunswick County, which in 1746 became Lunenburg. Between 1749 and 1778, we have found:
Thomas as grantor or grantee in deed books
twice; John four times; James 10 times; Matthew three times(once as Mathew); Robert three
times; William three times; and Jonathan once
Though there is no definite way to prove the
connection of these men, it seems likely that
Thomas and Andrew Cunningham were brothers.

William Perry Johnson, outstanding genealogist of Raleigh, wrote on July 11, 1961
that he likewise felt sure Thomas and Andrew
Cunningham were brothers.

The will of Thomas was dated Sept. 10,
1745 when he was living in Brunswick, and it
was proved April 7, 1752 in Lunenburg Co. In
this will he mentions his wife as Darkus,
which most likely was Dorcas. He names his
children as John, Thomas, and Mary; and his
executors as friends John Caldwell and William Cunningham. Apparently, he was old, or
at least sick, and quite feeble at this time
as it was signed *"his mark"*, while all other
deeds were signed by him personally. [7]

Andrew Cunningham's will was not proved
until 1761. His wife Jean was living at the
time and his eldest daughter, Mary, had married a Mr. George and had a daughter named
Margaret.He left two other daughters, single

Elizabeth and Jean. The executors of his estate were: James McMachen of Prince Edward Co. and John Cunningham of Prince Edward,and here again the will was signed by "his mark', witnessed by Mathew Cunningham, James Dougherty, and William Cunningham. [8]

The following year (1762) the will of James Cunningham was filed, leaving wife Jane and sons: John, William, and James.....and again, the will was signed by "his mark." [9]

Though I feel certain Thomas Cunningham is our ancestor I have mentioned briefly the three above wills to show how easy it is to confuse a researcher.

The will of Thomas mentions sons Thomas and John, witnessed by William and one of his executors was William. Andrew had no sons but appoints John as an executor and has his will witnessed by Mathew and William, and to further confuse researchers a John Cunningham died in 1764 [10]...But what John and whose John?

Earlier in this chapter we showed that Thomas Cunningham had purchased from Richard and William Kennon (see footnote 3) 685 acres of land in 1745 in Brunswick Co., Virginia. We found a very interesting bit of information in the Lunenburg County records for the year 1754 where John Cunningham sold to William Hardwick of the same county part of a tract of 342 acres for 62 pounds, being part of a larger grant from Richard and William Kennon, on the north side of the Staunton River, except 30 square feet where Thomas Cunningham was buried. (From the information I have been able to gather, the property

spoken of would be in Charlotte County today.
Thus we see that it was once in Brunswick,
then Lunenburg, and now in Charlotte.)

Worth S. Ray in his *Colonial Granville
County and Its People* (page 212) writes "a
large contingent of these Pinsons and Cunning
hams, of upper Granville County moved down
into Laurens Co., S. C., where numerous wills
deeds, etc...identify them on the records,
there. Old Aaron Pinson is mentioned in the
'Journey To The Land of Eden' by Col. William
Bird in 1733, who at that time lived on the
Roanoke, probably above Clarksville. There
was a Cunningham Store near the Virginia line
on Kyco Creek." [11]

We do find many Cunninghams around the
Virginia-North Carolina line bearing the same
name as those who later lived in old District
96; so they must have been the same ones or
their descendants.

Joseph A. Waddell, writing in *Annals Of
Augusta County, Virginia*, 1726-1871, tells us
of Cunninghams living in Augusta County about
the same time as Thomas and Andrew came to
old Brunswick. He tells us that Robert Cunningham,a native of Ireland, settled on a farm
called Rock Springs about 1735. He was one
of the first set of Justices of the Peace appointed in 1745 and afterwards served in the
House of Burgesses. He had no son but there
was a John Cunningham who lived in Staunton,
Va. on Lot 1, southwest corner of Augusta
Street and Spring Lane, and this John is believed to be a brother of the Robert Cunningham just mentioned. John's only son was
named Walter and he moved to Kentucky, thus
these two early cunninghams are removed from

our line.

Mr. Waddell tells of another Cunningham family settling on the "Forks Of The James" and John, of this family, appears first in Augusta County Aug. 18, 1752 when John Cunningham received a deed for 133 acres of land in Borden's Grant.

There was a James Cunningham in 1753 who conveyed to his son Jacob land on Tee's Creek a branch of the James River, which had been patented by James. He also conveyed land to his son Jacob in 1756 and in 1760.

We find a Hugh Cunningham conveyed in 1760 land lying on "Whistle Creek, Forks of The James River" and in 1764 he conveyed land to Jonathan Cunningham.

Remember back a few pages we spoke of a John Cunningham as dying in 1774? This John died before March 18, 1774 when his property was appraised. In the same year, though it was May 13, we find John Cunningham and his wife Mary conveyed land to their son Patrick "in consideration of their maintenance by him"

We then find in 1765 that a James Cunningham, wife Mary, left his estate mostly to son Moses. He also mentions son Hugh, grandson James (son of Jacob) and grandson John (son of Jacob) and others. Then we find the will of Jonathan Cunningham of "Carr's Creek" was recorded March 20, 1770 and he left his plantation to his "dutiful father", Hugh Cunningham.

Mr. Waddell credits Clarence Cunningham

of Charleston, S. C. with the fact that John Cunningham of "Kerr's Creek" [12] as having three daughters and four sons: Robert, Patrick, John and David. In 1769 Robert and Patrick removed to District 96, now Abbeville and were followed in 1770 by John and David.

Appleton's *American Biography* says: Robert Cunningham, loyalist born in Ireland about 1739; settled in District 96, S. C. in 1769 and soon became a judge. He opposed the cause of the colonies and was imprisoned in Charleston in 1775. After his release he joined the British forces and in 1780 was commissioned a Brigadier General. When the Revolution was over in 1782 he had left the country and petitioned to return, but his request was denied, his property confiscated and the remaining days of his life were spent in Nassau, where he died in 1813.

Brother Patrick Cunningham also entered the British army and became a colonel. Patrick did not create the enmity as did Robert, so after the Revolution he remained in South Carolina. He had a son named Robert who was a captain in the Mexican War and Robert's son John was a prominent lawyer, politician and journalist and it was John's daughter, Pamela, who organized and was the first Regent of the Ladies' Mt. Vernon Association....the organization which was responsible for making Mt. Vernon a memorial to our own George Washington.

We have no certainty as to whether the other brothers, John and David Cunningham, participated in the Revolution or not; but if they did, neither reached the rank as did Patrick and Robert. We do find that a John Cunningham did serve in the Revolution, according to Mrs. Jayne Conway Garlington Pruitt, of Washington, D. C., but unfortunately, we have not been able to ascertain whether this John was the brother of Robert and Patrick, or whether he was the John of our branch of the Cunningham family. There is no mention of a David Cunningham having served on the side of the colonies.

We do know that it was quite common in Old District 96, just as it was around Fayetteville, N. C., for father to be against son, and brother to be against brother during the struggle for our independence as those of the Scotch and Scotch-Irish were very strong in their views.

One of the best known of the Cunningham Torries was William Cunningham, otherwise known as "Bloody Bill". In Appleton's *American Biography* there is a sketch of William Cunningham. He was born in Dublin and came to America in 1774. He was appointed provost-marshal of the army (British) by General Gage. At one time he had charge of the military prisons in Philadelphia and New York. It is revealed that he literally starved to death 2,000 prisoners and hung 250 without trial. After the Revolution he returned to England where he became a very dissipated man and in 1791 was hanged for forgery.

It is believed that "Bloody Bill" Cunningham was a second cousin of Robert, Patrick, John and David. Whether the latter were distant relatives of our John Cunningham, the son of Thomas is not known, nor have I attempted to verify any connection.

Lunenburg County records show that John Cunningham disposed of 342 acres of land, being part of a large grant to Richard and William Kennon, on the north side of Staunton River, for 62 pounds. This was done in 1754, two years after the death of his father. Thomas Cunningham, brother of John, sold to Robert Andrew 143 acres on the north side of the Staunton River for 16 pounds and this land is described as part of a grant to Richard and William Kennon. This transaction was made in 1752, but after the death of his father Thomas.

In 1755 we find that James Cunningham, who we believe to have been a brother of Thomas and Andrew, sold in Lunenburg County 342 acres on the north side of the Staunton River, part of a grant to Richard and William Kennon, to William Hardwick for 62 pounds.

Here we should remember that Thomas and Andrew and James at one time bought land from the Kennon brothers and, therefore, must have migrated from a more eastern Virginia County to their new lands on the north of the Staunton River.

We also find in the Lunenburg County records where Mary Stevens sold to John Cunningham 200 acres on Nut Bush Creek in 1758. We believe this Mary to be the daughter of Thomas Cunningham, and that the John to whom she sold the property was her brother. This transaction was witnessed by James Kidd and we find just three years later, 1761, that James Kidd bought from John Cunningham 201 acres on Nut Bush Creek, probably the same land.

There were other transactions in Lunenburg County by John Cunningham as late as
1777, [13], but we have no means of identify-
ing which or what John might have been involved. And, we found no other transactions by
Thomas. Just when they might have left Virginia for old District 96 is purely speculative at this writing. We did find records
in South Carolina from 1785, and after,where
John and Thomas had purchased land and in the
section of Laurens where it is known our Cunninghams lived; namely, in the Gray Court
section and not far from the Friendship Presbyterian Church.

We find almost as many Cunninghams in
Laurens Co. as we did in the Virginia counties and no doubt some are related and some
are too far removed to claim any relationship.
It is pretty definite that those living along
Duncan Creek in the eastern portion of the
county were not closely related, if at all,
to our branch.

As we said, just when John Cunningham
and his family moved to District 96 is not
known to me, but we do know that John, the
son of Thomas, died in South Carolina. His
will was recorded in Will Book A-1, page 17
and was dated 1788. Though a complete copy
of the will was not available, what I read
does say in substance that John Cunningham,
was of the State of South Carolina, District
96, "now called Cambridge District, in Laurens County"' and he gives to his son Thomas
Cunningham, to his son James Cunningham, to
his daughter Ann Allison, to his daughter
Margaret and William (her husband) Hall and
to his daughter Dorcas and David(her husband)

Allison five shillings sterling, each. He gives to his sons John, *William,* and George one horse and saddle each; and then to his granddaughter Mary Allison he gives one mare, a dark bay, also a colt; and to his grandson, Samuel Allison, he leaves something, but this was unreadable.

John Cunningham further gives to his daughter Catherine Josephine five shillings sterling, and to his wife he gives his house and as much of the clear land as she desires to use during her lifetime. He provides that as his sons marry, she (his wife) may give them what property she shall think fit by the advice of the other executors. At his wife's death, her property is to be equally divided between his sons John, *William,* and George. He states that son Samuel Cunningham is to have the fourth part of the land that he (Sam uel) now possesses, and his part to be paid out where he now lives by the executor.

He then names his executors as being: his wife (no name mentioned), John Cunningham and Thomas Cunningham, but he does not ment- ion their relationship, but perhaps they were his sons.The will was witnessed by Dunlap and James Dorroh. We, of course, should bear in mind that the daughter of James Dorroh was Martha and she married William Cunningham, mentioned in the will. And, William Dorroh, son of James, was married to a Dunlap.....so this seems to conclude and prove that the father of our William Cunningham was this John and this John was the son of Thomas.

The name Dorcas, an unusual name, was of tremendous help in pegging our John Cunning- ham. His mother was Dorcas, he had a daughter named Dorcas, and his son William had a daughter named Dorcas, and Jane Cunningham Dorroh, his daughter, had a daughter named Dorcas.In none of the other Cunningham lines, have I found Dorcas, though there have been untold Johns, Thomases, Williams, Jameses, Roberts, etc.

The line which we have pursued, at this time, has been that of John's son William who was born Feb. 23, 1770 and married on February 11, 1795 in Laurens District to Martha Dorroh, daughter of James and Jane Brown Dorroh (see THE DORROHS). Though Martha's older brothers and sisters were born in County Antrim, Northern Ireland, she was born in District 96 near Gray Court on Sept.22, 1776.

William died Sept. 15, 1822, leaving his widow and a large family of children: John, Margaret, Jane, Catherien,Anna, Nancy, Dorcas William, and Martha. James Cunningham predeceased his father.

In William Cunningham's will [14] he leaves his son John a Negro boy, a mare, land cow, calf and the land he leaves John was already in his possession. He further provides for son William by leaving him a Negro boy, $225 when he arrives at age 21 (he was 8 yrs. old at his father's death) and he further states: "The rest of my estate, the executors to dispose of in the same manner as though I had not made a will or as the law appoints in case of intestate." He leaves his wife Martha (Dorroh)Cuñingham, as executrix with his son, John Cunningham, as executor. The will was signed Sept. 4, 1822 and witnessed by Henry Morgan, William Pitts, and S. Cunningham.

It was shortly after William Cunningham's death that John Dorroh and his wife Jane Cunningham moved to Perry County and settled in what is now Cunningham's Beat and he was followed by John Cunningham and his wife Sarah (Sally) Mahaffey. By 1835 Martha Dorroh Cunningham, with the rest of her children, came to Alabama.

From all appearances there was an unusual closeness between John Dorroh and his mother-in-law and aunt, Martha Dorroh Cunningham. We found in Deed Book D, page 124 of Perry Co. dated Nov. 13, 1837 that "John Dorroh, according to an agreement herein after contained to be performed by Martha Cunningham doth demise and lease to said Martha Cunningham, her executors, administrators and assigns, all tract or parcel of land whereupon the said Martha Cunningham now resides ......for the consideration of the clearing and building which she has or may do on said premises.....for the term of 5 years to commence on January 1 next, or as long as she may live after......and that she, the said Martha Cunningham, will take proper and nec essary care and cause to be done," Signed, John Dorroh. In presence of John Cunningham (her son) and Martha Cunningham, Jr.(who was her youngest daughter).

This land, given Martha Cunningham by John Dorroh, consisted of 160 acres and was about a mile south of the John Cunningham home on State Highway 5.

The John Dorrohs, the John Cunninghams, and the William Morgans all settled in what is now Cunningham Beat in Perry County; and since they all had large families, the early records of that part of Perry County are filled with Dorroh, Cunningham, and Morgan records.

John Cunningham's plantation was on Washington Creek, the home being in fork of the roads near where the Creek crosses Highway 5. The Morgans settled about five miles north of him just off Highway 5, on the road to Norman Station. The Dorrohs owned nearly 2,000 acres of land to the south and east of John Cunningham...much of this land being very rich creek bottom land and wooded. For several generations, the *Dorroh Woods* was a favorite hunting ground for the men and boys of the community.

The Morgans, Cunninghams, and Dorrohs... all intermarried in Laurens District before coming to Perry County....were all Presbyterians. John and Jane Dorroh gave a plot of land containing about four acres for a church and graveyard. This church was near the dwelling of John Cunningham, about four miles south of Marion.

This church was given by John Cunningham and John Dorroh. At first it was used by the Cumberland Presbyterian Church, who referred to it as *Providence Church,* and by the Presbyterian Church who referred to it as *Friendship Church*. This name was in memory and in honor of the Friendship Presbyterian Church, in South Carolina, whose land for the church had been given by James Dorroh and John Cunningham.

Here, in Alabama, in the old Friendship burying ground, are the remains of many Cunninghams, Dorrohs, and Morgans....all *Pioneers*

In Their Own Rights.

Regretably, the Friendship building no longer stands. Just a few feet to the west of the old site is now a Negro church. The family burying ground is in back of the church in a most deplorable condition. It is the hope of this author that a get-together, or reunion may be held, in the near future, with the hope that we can have the old cemetery cleaned and pay respects to our older generation......those who were truly *Pioneers In Their Own Rights.*

Following the footnotes we shall find the *Descendants of William Cunningham and Martha Dorroh.*

F O O T N O T E S

[1] Robert Bain's *Clans and Tartans of Scotland.*

[2] Donald F. MacDonald and his wife are presently producing recordings in story and song of various Scots clans. His wife is a native of Scotland. He may be reached in care of *The Weekly Scotsman,* 20 North Bridge, Edinburgh 1, Scotland. In this series of recordings Pipe Major John Archibald MacLelland head of the Army School of Piping at Edinburg Castle, is doing the pipe tunes and Alex Allan, a Scots TV personality, is doing the narration.

[3] Brunswick Co., Va. Deed Book 4, page 24, Deed dated 1745 Richard Kennon of Charles

City Co., and William Kennon Jr. of Henrico
Co. (Richmond) deeded to Thomas Cunningham
of Brunswick Co. 685 acres for 20 pounds
(Sterling) near Cubb Creek, adjacent William
Harwood and Andrew Cunningham. Both signed
the deed by name. Witnesses: James Munford,
Robert Kennon, Cadr. Jones, and it was proved
1746. It might be interesting to note that
Brunswick Co., Va. was formed in 1720 from
Prince George, Isle of Wight, and Surry Counties. Prince George County was formed in
1702/3 from Charles City Co. Surry County
was formed in 1652 from James City and Isle
of Wight was one of the original shires, or
counties, and was formed in 1634.

[4] Deed Book 4, page 34, Brunswick Co., Va.
Both parties signed their names and same
witnesses as in above transaction. This,
likewise, was proved in 1746.

[5] Cunningham grantees: 1749 James;1756
James; 1757 Mathew; 1758 John; 1761 James;
1761 Jonathan; 1761 James; 1762 Robert; 1762,
James; 1762 James; 1764 James; 1764 James;
1765 Robert; 1772 William.

[6] Cunningham grantors in Lunenburg County
between 1752 and 1778: Thomas in 1752; Thomas 1762; John 1754; James 1755; James 1756;
John 1762; Matthew 1764; Matthew 1764; Robert
1767; William 1772; William 1776; and John
1778.

[7] Lunenburg County, Will Book 1, page 59.

[8] Lunenburg County, Will Book 2, page 6. In
1761 Prince Edward County joined that of Lunenburg. Prince Edward was carved from Amelia
County 1753/4 and Amelia County was carved

from Brunswick and Prince George counties in 1734. Prince George was carved from Charles City 1702/3. Charlotte County was not formed until 1764/5 from Lunenburg.

[9] Lunenburg Co. Will Book 2, page 26. James Cunningham lived in Raleigh Parish, Lunenburg County. His will was dated Oct. 2, 1762 and probated Nov. 2, 1762. In this will his son John received 212 acres on Roberson River, part of 400 acres purchased from Capt. Joseph Williams; and son William received 213 acres.

[10] Lunenburg Co., Will Book 2, page 227. Inventory and appraisement of John Cunningham was dated May 30, 1764 per Court Order April 12, 1764. It was signed by Samuel Hopkins, Edmund Bugg and Anselm Bugg. Registered Aug. 9, 1764. (No other names given.)

[11] In the Granville Co., N. C. Will Book 5, page 143, dated April 5, 1801 and probated May 4, 1801, we find the Will of Aaron Pinson in which he mentions his wife, Delilah, evidently the widow Cunningham, when he married her as his second or third wife. The legatees mentioned are: William Cunningham, James Cunningham, Sally Cunningham and who shall have their mother's part of the estate: Thomas Pinson, Elizabeth Camel, Darcus Orston, Sarah Read, Amy Cuninghem, John Pinson, David Pinson, Isaac Pinson, Aaron Pinson, Zacharia Pinson and Mary Evens. The will was witnessed by John Graves, Ralph Graves, and John Stovall.

Delilah Pinson was before her marriage Stovall, for the will of John Stovall, 1-313, names son-in-law Aaron Pinson and the will

was dated July 29, 1781 and probed Nov. 1781
Granville Co. In this case, the name Pinson
was spelled Pincen....just when Delilah Stovall married Aaron Pinson is unknown but it
was certainly before 1765 when they were
grantors in Mecklenburg Co., Va. to Thomas
Pinson 100 acres of land. This full explanation is given because at one time there was
some speculation that the William Cunningham
mentioned in the will of Aaron might have
been our William Cunningham who married Martha Dorroh. This explanation disproves any
such assumption.

[12] The name Kerr's Creek and Carr's Creek
no doubt are one and the same creek. The
Kerr name is a well known family on the Virginia-North Carolina line for generations and
they pronounce the name as though it were
spelled Carr. A Kerr of North Carolina married into my *Johnston* family.

[13] Brief abstracts of the old Cunningham
deeds on record in Lunenburg Co., Va.: 3-519,
3-9, 5-352.

[14] Will of William Cunningham, Laurens Co.,
Book E, page 242---Box 15, Pkg. 4.

The 1790 Census of Laurens Co., S. C.
lists nine Cunninghams among which *Margaret
Cunningham* is listed, with 1 male under 16, 4
females and 2 slaves. It is believed that
she could be the wife of John Cunningham as
she is the only female listed as head of the
household in this Census.

Descendants of William Cunningham and Martha Dorroh

I   John b Sept. 11, 1796 d July 17, 1852 m March 4, 1819 Laurens Dist. Co.,S.C. Sarah (Sally) Mahaffey b Jan. 4, 1802 d CHILDREN: SEE SEPARATE LISTING

II   Margaret b Sept. 28, 1798 d June 16, 1853 m ca 1818 Laurens Dist. S.C. William Morgan b June 1799 d July 19, 1860 SEE LISTING UNDER WILLIAM MORGAN

III   Jane b Jan. 28, 1801 d Jan. 20, 1883 m John Dorroh b May 4, 1797 d Sept. 26, 1854 [1] CHILDREN: SEE SEPARATE LISTING

IV   Catherine b April 14, 1803 NFI

V   Anna b July 18, 1805 d m George W. Swindle b d NFI

VI   James b Nov. 7, 1807 d June 11, 1809

VII   Nancy b April 5, 1810 d June 16, 1855 m Dec. 28, 1854 William Morgan b June 1799 d July 1860 NO ISSUE. SEE LISTING UNDER WILLIAM MORGAN

VIII   Dorcas b Feb. 2, 1812 d m Matthew Johnson b d CHILD:

A   Rebecca b d m Burgis b d [2]

IX   William b Oct. 11, 1814 NFI

X   Martha b Nov. 2, 1818 d July 12, 1842 m Jan. 14, 1841 William A. Spears b Feb. 4, 1812 d May 26, 1856

[1]   Son of William Dorroh. Raised by his uncle, John Dorroh, of Tuscaloosa Co., Ala., and a nephew of Martha Dorroh Cunningham.

[2]   She lived with daughter, a Mrs. R. L. Smith in Albermarle, N. C.

Descendants of John Cunningham and Sarah (Sally) Mahaffey

I   Martin b Dec. 9, 1819 d ca 1844 m Rachel W.
     b May 5, 1814, in Clarendon Dist.,S.C., d Jan.
     23, 1891 CHILDREN:

     A   William Augustus b d ca 1862 [1] m Oct.
          31, 1854 Justina Ann Eskridge b d

     B   James E. b d [2] m March 28, 1861
          Mollie Q. McEachen b

II   William b Oct. 22, 1821 d Feb. 25, 1859 m
     May 18, 1850 Sarah Ann McKellar b Dec. 29,
     1829 d Nov. 17, 1908 CHILDREN:

     A   John Archibald b June 10, 1851 d May 1,
          1890 m April 19, 1877 Kate England b
          Oct. 25, 1857 d Sept. 3, 1936 CHILDREN:

          1   William Archibald b March 8, 1878
               d Nov. 10, 1930 m FIRST Aug. 17,
               1905 Polk Trimble b   d 1913
               CHILDREN:

               a   Frances b   1908 d 6 mos.

               b   b 1913, infant boy,
                    d same day   1913

               m SECOND April 12, 1916 Kate
               Alley b   NO ISSUE

          2   Kate b Feb. 3, 1880 m April 25,
               1907 Thomas F. Pollard b   d
               CHILDREN:

               a   Louise Phillips b Sept. 23,
                    1908 UNMARRIED

               b   Mary Elizabeth b Jan. 20,
                    1912 m April 27, 1934 Bernie
                    Daniel Hoffman b CHILDREN:

[1] Will dated Nov. 20, 1862 proved Nov. 12,
     1863

[2] He was away with the Confederate Army when
     his brother William Augustus died. Some be-
     lieve he did not return from the War.

i   Betty Louise b Sept. 14,
1936 m May 12, 1956
Thomas Edward Chapman II
CHILDREN:

(a)   Thomas Edward III b
Nov. 1, 1958

(b)   Tambolyn Elizabeth
b Aug. 20, 1960

ii   Michael Daniel b June 8,
1942

3   Robert E. b July 14, 1882 d June
29, 1905 UNMARRIED

4   Annie b Feb. 18, 1886 m Oct. 10,
1911 Nicholas Boddie Mason b Sept.
11, 1884 d Dec. 9, 1947 NO ISSUE

B   Amanda L. b Dec. 29, 1857 d Aug. 17,
1936 m FIRST W. M. Phillips b CHILD:

1   Louise b Feb. 8, 1880 d Nov. 13,
1892

m SECOND David Avery Dew b Oct. 12,
1851 d Dec. 9, 1899 CHILDREN:

2   Mary b Dec. 19, 1887 d May 2, 1946
m June 30, 1909 DeWitt King Mason
b Dec. 6, 1881 d Aug. 12, 1948
CHILDREN:

a   DeWitt King II b Nov. 30,
1911 m June 10, 1842 Evelyn
Brock b Mar. 25, 1917 NO ISSUE

b   John Dew b Sept. 21, 1915 m [1]
Harriet Jane Meyers CHILDREN:

i   John Dew II
ii   Mary Jane

3   John Cunningham b Nov. 23, 1889 d
Oct. 2, 1942 m Apr. 24, 1912 Nell
McNeill b Sept. 22, 1892 CHILD:

[1] m July 3, 1942 Falmouth, Mass.

a   Mary Frances b Mar. 12, 1925
m Aug. 28, 1946 Warner Lee
Bruner II b July 6, 1924
CHILDREN:

    i   John Lee
    ii   Warner Lee III
    iii   David Dew

4   Isabel b June 8, 1895 m Oct. 23,
1923 Alfred B. Shivers CHILD:

a   Mary Catherine b Feb. 26,1925
m June 9, 1941 Jesse Harrell
II b   CHILD:

    i   Jesse III (Rusty) b July
       7, 1943
C   William b Mar. 8, 1878 d Nov. 10, 1930
D   Rebecca, died as a child.   NFI
E   Edward, died as a child.   NFI

III   James D. b 1823 d m Margaret Ann__ CHILD:
A   George b d Aug. 11, 1856,age 13 mos.
3 days.
IV   John B. b June 27, 1825 d June 5, 1853 NFI
V   Sarah Manima b May 12, 1829 d Aug. 21, 1908
m Jan. 17, 1854 Eleazer J. Pierson b d July
30, 1861, Polk Co., Tex. CHILD:

A   Annabelle b Jan. 9, 1855 d Mar. 25,1911
m FIRST May 8, 1880 Timothy Thorpe Tallman b Mar. 10, 1850 d Sept. 26, 1883
CHILD   :

1   Timothy Thorpe II b 1882 d   1944

m SECOND Rev. David Abram Burns b Apr.
12, 1856 d Feb. 18, 1930 CHILD:

2   Ruth Craig b Nov. 4, 1892 m Dec.
20, 1923 Robert Ezekiel Campbell
b Nov. 4, 1893   CHILD:

a   Robert Ezekiel II b Dec. 19,
1928 m Aug. 30, 1952 Norma
Netherland b May 6, 1932
CHILD:

     i Robert McGregor b Aug.
       8, 1953

  3 Mary Louise b Feb. 19, 1897 m FIRST
   Miles Arnold Gresham b Nov. 7,1887
   d 1924 CHILD:

    a Annabelle Miles b Oct. 13,
      1922 m Nov. 29, 1947 Marion
      Holland Salmon b CHILDREN:

      i Spencer

      ii Louise

      iii Eleanor

    m SECOND Thomas Anderson Hanna b
    March 31, 1880 d Jan. 24, 1962
    CHILDREN:

    b Mary Orlean b Dec. 4, 1928 m
      Jan. 1950 John Donald Woodson
      (Lt. USAF).

    c Thomas Anderson II b Feb. 6,
      1931 m Nan Bond b July 16,
      1933

VI Rebecca b d m May 6, 1851 George W. Browder
  M.D., b d March 1862 CHILDREN: [1]

  A Tommy b April 6, 1852 d Oct. 2, 1856

  B George W. II   NFI

  C James D.

  D Frank L.

  E Minnie L. [2]

[1] Probate Minute Book, page 490 lists "the
  only minor heirs in Aug. '75."

[2] The 1880 census lists "Minnie Browder as age
  17'...this being the case, she was born after
  her father's death.

VII   Martha b   d   m Dec. 9, 1869 John Stevenson
       b   d CHILDREN:

       A   Lewers (girl) b   m   NFI

       B   Mamie b   m   Gibson, Lived in Texas

       C   Katherine b   m   Lived in Texas

VIII Nancy (Nannie) b Mar. 16, 1831 d July 27,
     1915 m Oct. 11, 1859 William W. Craig b
     d 1873 [1] CHILDREN:

       A   Robert A. b 1861 UNMARRIED NFI

       B   John S. b Feb. 13, 1866 d Jan. 25,
            1915 UNMARRIED NFI

       C   A. Thomas b April 18, 1867 d Oct. 6,
            1907 UNMARRIED

       D   J. Walter b Oct. 8, 1868 d May 22,
            1885 [2]

IX   Preston b after 1831 d before 1859 [3]

X   Cynthia Catherine (Kate) b June 2, 1835 d
       Jan. 12, 1915 m FIRST John A. Craig [4]
       b Sept. 22, 1831 d July 24, 1879 NO ISSUE

       m SECOND Dec. 14, 1886 William T. Boyd b
       Aug. 14, 1830 d April 10, 1898 NO ISSUE

XI   Mary A. b Oct. 15, 1837 d Nov. 13, 1902
       UNMARRIED

XII   Samuel P. b after 1838   UNMARRIED NFI

XIII Francis (Frank) M. b after 1838   NFI

XIV   Nathaniel G. b after 1838   UNMARRIED NFI

[1]   Son of Samuel Craig and Isabella Underwood.
[2]   Drowned at Sunday School picnic at Lake
       Lanier.
[3]   Not listed in father's will, so probably
       died as child.
[4]   Son of Samuel Craig and Isabella Underwood.

XV   Amanda L. b May 10, 1844 d Nov. 1, 1913 m
April 12, 1864 Thadeous Augustus Craig [1]
b Feb. 17, 1842 d Jan. 14, 1909 CHILDREN:

A   Thadeous Augustus II b 1865 m Dove
Cater b d CHILD:

    1   Raymond b

B   Katie Lewers b June 20, 1868 d May 6,
1870

C   Nannie Mae b   1871 m May 7, 1890
Augustus M. McBroom b   CHILDREN:

    1   Emily b d m James Earnest Dooly
CHILDREN:

        a   James Earnest II b m
CHILDREN:

            i   Joe [2]

            ii   Mary

            iii George

    2   Kate b m Tillman F. Wood, live
Birmingham, CHILDREN:

        a   Tillman F. II b m

        b   Mary Augusta b m Douglas
Goode b

        c   Mortimer b m

    3   Augusta b m Lacey Rawls b
live Gadsden, Ala. NO ISSUE

D   William (Will) b 1875 m Blanche___
CHILD:

    1   Bill   NFI

[1] Son of Samuel Craig and Isabella Underwood.
[2] Graduated from Marion Institute, June 1963.

E John Alex b 1877 m Mary_____
  NO ISSUE

F Samuel B. b 1879 m Eleanor_____
  CHILDREN: NFI

G Kathleen b m L. E. Claibourne b d
  Lived Sunflower, Miss. CHILDREN:

  1 Augusta NFI

  2 Edmond

  3   A son

Descendants of Jane Cunningham and John Dorroh

I Dorcas Cunningham b July 22, 1824 d Jan. 1,
1908 m Nov. 24, 1842 James Didlake b April
5, 1816 d Dec. 2, 1863 CHILDREN:

A Sarah Jane b July 1, 1844 d m Nov. 29,
1866 J. C. Nance b d CHILDREN:

1 Eugene b Feb. 27, 1875 NFI

2 Andrew D. b Nov. 6, 1876 NFI

B Samuel D. b May 4, 1846 NFI

C John D. b Feb. 17, 1848 d Oct. 16,1856

D Ella Lee b Jan. 29, 1850 d Aug. 1, 1919
m Nov. 28, 1872 Benjamin Franklin Roden
b Jan. 5, 1844 d Feb. 23, 1908 CHILDREN:

1 Viola Harrison b Feb. 23, 1875 d
Oct. 12, 1947 m Feb. 1898 George
Redin CHILD:

a Mahdah (Ella Lee) b Dec. 2,
1901 d March 18, 1953 m April
30, 1932 Leonard K. Kniffin II
b Oct. 23, 1904 NO ISSUE

2 Florence Lee (Flossie) b May 8,
1876 d Feb. 23, 1937 m Feb. 6,
1896 Charles Gracie Davis b Aug.
30, 1870 d Oct. 1, 1923 CHILDREN:

a Dorothy Roden b July 7, 1897
m Sept. 23, 1920 Henry Bram‑
lett Gray II b March 17, 1892
d May 18, 1953 CHILDREN:

i Dorothy Davis b April 19,
1926 m Nov. 26, 1948
Marshall Raymond Haynes
II b July 11, 1922
CHILDREN:

(a) Dorothy Gray b March
4, 1950

(b)   Elizabeth Martin b
March 2, 1953

(c)   Marsha Merritt b
July 27, 1954

ii   Henry Bramlett III b Jan.
29, 1929 m June 15, 1957
Mary Frances Adams b
CHILDREN:

(a)   Henry Bramlett IV b
Jan. 19, 1959

(b)   Dorothy Davis b Mar.
13, 1961

b   Eleanor Roden b Feb. 22, 1899
m Oct. 20, 1920 Howard Richards
Terry b Sept. 16, 1895 CHILDREN:

i   Howard Richards II, M.D.
b Aug. 10, 1923 m Mar. 9,
1952 Doreen Lusier b Apr.
19, 1925   CHILDREN:

(a)   Joanne C.   b Sept.
12, 1953

(b)   William Davis b Feb.
1, 1955

(c)   Patricia A. b Sept.3,
1957

(d)   Barbara L. b April
23, 1959

ii   Charles Roden b Aug. 15,
1928 m Sept. 2, 1950 Katherine Ann Anderson b June
23, 1928 CHILDREN:

(a)   Mary Eleanor b Nov.
28, 1951

(b)   Katherine Ann b Apr.
15, 1954

c   Charles Gracie II b March 11, 1908 m June 24, 1931 Ruth Hutchinson b Aug. 30, 1908 CHILDREN:

     i   Charles Gracie III b June 12, 1932 m Sept. 3, 1955 Mady Irene Von Dehn b Mar. 22, 1933 CHILDREN:

        (a)   Karin b March 12, 1937

        (b)   Deborah b March 17, 1938

    ii   Chester Hutchinson b Nov. 13, 1934 m June 22, 1957 Teresa Antoinette Weisbecker b July 19, 1935

    iii   Caroline b Oct. 11, 1944

    iv   Virginia b Nov. 27, 1946

3   Lillian b Nov. 15, 1878 m Oct. 26, 1904 Arthur John (Jack) Bowron b Jan. 19, 1875 d Dec. 16, 1951 CHILDREN:

    a   Arthur John (Jack) II b Jan. 1, 1907 d July 13, 1961 m June 25, 1936 Virginia Pero b July 20, 1907

    b   Lorol b March 21, 1913 m Apr. 18, 1939 Norris Rediker b Feb. 26, 1908 * CHILDREN:

     i   John Michael b Feb. 20, 1942

     ii   Diana Bowron b Sept. 8, 1944

4   Benjamin Franklin II b Oct. 5, 1883 d March 18, 1958 m Jan. 15, 1908 Elizabeth Bowman b Feb. 4, 1883 CHILDREN:

*   Norris Rediker died January 17, 1964

a   Benjamin Franklin III b Jan. 10, 1909 UNMARRIED

b   Calvin Bowman b Aug. 26, 1910 m July 6, 1936 Dorothy Wood b Oct. 11, 1915 CHILDREN:

i   Gayle Dorvin b Sept. 1, 1938 m April   1964 James Joseph Burden,M.D., b

ii   Carol Lee b May 15, 1942 m FIRST Dec. 15, 1959 Robert Brown   CHILD:

(a)   Benjamin Roden [1] b Sept. 30, 1960

m SECOND Dec. 5, 1961 Micajah Woods Lupton II b   CHILD:

(b)   Micajah Woods III b Sept. 8, 1962

iii   Calvin Bowman II b May 19, 1949 d May 23, 1951

c   Elizabeth b Jan. 16, 1912 m Oct. 1, 1935 Culpepper Exum II b March 23, 1908 d Dec. 24, 1950 CHILDREN:

i   Culpepper III b Feb. 8,

1938 m June 21, 1963 Barbara Ann Williams b

ii   Elizabeth Roden b Feb. 9 1948 UNMARRIED

5   Maibelle b May 8, 1885 d Dec. 3, 1961 [2] m April 19, 1911

[1] Adopted, and name legally changed to Benjamin Roden Lupton.

[2] Died Mattoon, Ill. Funeral services held there Dec. 5, 1961. Buried Elmwood Cemetery Birmingham, Ala., Dec. 23, 1961.

Isaac Croom Beatty II [1] b Dec.
20, 1878 d Nov. 11, 1956 CHILDREN:

a   Isaac Croom III b June 9,
1914 m FIRST July 18, 1936
Eleanor Fulford b July 18,
1916 CHILDREN:

    i   Isaac Croom IV b June 21,
           1937 Meriwether
           Tannahill b

    ii   Sandra Fulford b Dec. 22,
           1939 m Charles K. Cleaver

    iii   Susan Devereux b July 15,
           1943 d Aug. 27, 1960
           (Killed in auto accident)

    m SECOND Aug. 27, 1950 Helen
    North Miller b 1903

b   Child, died in infancy,
       Unnamed.

E   William Bradley b April 5, 1852 d Oct.
4, 1883 m Dec. 7, 1881 Bell Huff b
d (first cousins) CHILD:

1   Lurline

F   James Neely b Apr. 19, 1854 d Dec. 7,
1901 (age 47)

G   Willey b Mar. 12, 1856 d Nov. 4, 1873

H   Robert b Jan. 3, 1859

[1] Isaac Croom Beatty Jr. was born near Faunsdale, Ala. On Feb. 11, 1899 he married
Hughie Duffee born Feb. 26, 1879 died May,
1909. Of this marriage there were four children: Donald, Dorothy, Hughie and Malcolm.
The father of Isaac Croom Beatty Jr. was born
at Beatty's Bridge, N.C. Oct. 21, 1852. He
married on April 30, 1878 in Demopolis, Ala.
Marianna DuBrutz.

II   Martha Jane b June 10, 1829 d Sept. 5, 1899
m July 10, 1845 John Bates b Dec. 1, 1808 d
Aug. 2, 1868 CHILDREN:

A   W. D. b Aug. 22, 1847 d Oct. 22, 1847,
age two months

B   Sam b July 19, 1849 d Nov. 7, 1913 m
Nov. 22, 1870 Ida Bates b Nov.11,1850
d Oct. 24, 1932 [1] CHILDREN:

1   Annie b Sept. 20,1871 near Uniontown, Ala. Now living Globe,Ariz.,
m Dec. 24, 1891 in Bell Co., Tex.
Samuel Holland Underwood b Nov. 8,
1866 Perry Co.,Ala., d Feb. 15,
1947 [2] CHILDREN:

a   Ida b Sept. 23, 1893 Bruce-
ville, Tex., m Jan. 29, 1914
L. Lamar Moreland b Feb. 21,
1888 Living Globe, Arizona
CHILDREN:

i   Annie b Nov. 18, 1914
Ballinger, Tex., m June
28, 1932 Albert Sanders
II b Dec. 8, 1905
CHILDREN:

(a)   Albert Lamar b Mar.
31, 1933 m FIRST
Aug. 1954 Meryle
Baker b CHILDREN:

(i)   Carol Baker b
Oct. 22, 1951

(ii) Barbara Baker
b Sept. 1,1954

(iii)Pamela Kay b
Jan. 8, 1956

[1]   Daughter of George Bates who was brother of
John Bates.....thus, Sam Bates and Ida Bates
were first cousins.
[2]   Son of John Weyman Underwood and Fannie Nelms
and youngest brother of Isaac Nelms Underwood.

(iv) Kelly Jean b
Dec. 8, 1961

m SECOND Oct. 14,
1962 Laurel Rose
Johnson b

(b) Patricia Ann b Dec.
31, 1938 m April 21,
1958 Hugh N. Weech
CHILD:

(i) Tammie Lynn b
Aug. 12, 1962

(c) Melvin Lewis b May
12, 1943, Miami

ii   Weyman Lamar (Jack) b
Jan. 20, 1916 Maverick,
Tex. m June 28, 1947
Donna Lee Stewart b
CHILDREN:

(a) Cheryl Lee b Aug.
16, 1950 Phoenix

(b) Carol Lynn b Aug.
22, 1952

(c) Gerald Lamar (Jerry)
b Sept. 22, 1954

(d) Jackie Ann b May 14,
1956

iii   Martha (Mattie) b July 5,
1918 Globe, Ariz. m June
28, 1937 Mason H. Fitz-
gerald b   1912 CHILDREN:

(a) Marvin H. b Dec. 2,
1940 Globe, Ariz.

(b) Marsha Ann b Sept.
8, 1947 Phoenix

    b   Samuel Holland II (twin) b Dec. 29, 1897 Perry Co.,Ala. m Sept. 15, 1918 San Angelo, Tex. Ella Mae Lee b Apr. 5, 1901 CHILDREN:

        i   Mildred Lucile b Feb. 4, 1920 Maverick, Tex. m Feb. 9, 1940 Sanderson, Tex. Conway Ferrell Pickard b May 29, 1913 CHILD:

            (a)   Ann b Nov. 15, 1944 El Paso, Tex.

        ii   Samuel Ross b May 25, 1924 Maverick, Tex. m Aug. 14, 1954 Arcola, Miss., Martha May Shaw b Sept. 15, 1927 CHILDREN:

            (a)   John Ross b June 20, 1956 Greenwood,Miss.

            (b)   Lee Holland b June 10, 1958

            (c)   Martha Ann b Sept. 21, 1959

    c   Annie (Lady) (twin) b Dec.29, 1897 Perry Co., Ala., d June 1904 Perry Co., Ala. [1]

2   John b   1876   UNMARRIED

3   Samuel b   1879   NFI

4   Joe (or Joel) b   NFI

5   Ida (Queen) b   m_____Burchett

[1] Died from fall from swing.

C Annie E. b Aug. 29, 1851 d Sept. 8, 1870 m June 22, 1870 Jesse W. Wells b NO ISSUE

D John b d in Texas, UNMARRIED

E Martha Jane (Mattie) b Dec. 29, 1855 d March 5, 1906 m Dec. 12, 1878 Robert A. Craig b June 22, 1840 d Dec. 29, 1899 CHILDREN:

 1 William (Will) b d young, m NO ISSUE.

 2 Robbie (girl) b Feb. 8, 1882 d Nov. 7, 1928 m June 7, 1905 Samuel W. Barkley b Mar. 7, 1880 d May 14, 1933 CHILDREN:

  a Joe Bates NFI

  b Martha NFI

F Julia b Nov. 24, 1857 d Nov. 3, 1953 m Dec. 24, 1890 George C. Bell b Dec. 25, 1858 d April 10, 1906 NO ISSUE

G Joel M. b Aug. 20, 1859 d Nov. 15, 1900 UNMARRIED

H Lettie L. b Nov. 17, 1860 d May 23, 1927 m Jan. 10, 1889 Harwell C. Smith b July 28, 1860 d Oct. 9, 1938 NO ISSUE

III Malinda Lenora b d m Sept. 4, 1846 Donaldson Huff b d CHILDREN:

A   Nancy Jane (Nannie) b April 5, 1848
     d June 27, 1938 m March 19, 1872 Jesse
     White Wells [1] b April 16, 1839 d Jan.
     5, 1897 CHILDREN:

     1   Katie Craig b Jan. 23, 1873 d July
          30, 1884

     2   Mary Drula b Mar. 21, 1875 d Dec.
          31, 1876

     3   Theodore Leonard b Dec. 13, 1876
          d Jan. 23, 1934 m   NFI CHILD:

          a   Frederick Wells b   NFI

     4   John William (Jack) b Mar. 28,
          1878 d Nov. 13, 1916 UNMARRIED

     5   Jessie White   b Aug. 3, 1880 d
          May 27, 1959 UNMARRIED [2]

     6   Neal Christine b Aug. 30, 1883 d
          Jan. 13, 1914 m William Oscar
          Stroud   CHILD:

          a   Billy   m   CHILDREN:

               i   (boy) NFI

               ii   (boy) NFI

     7   Janie b   d   m FIRST   Fonville
          CHILD:

          a   Margaret m Lt. Col. Coats,
               Med. Corps. NFI

          m SECOND Emery Miller CHILDREN:

          b   Jane   NFI

          c̄   Emery II   NFI

     8   Walter b Nov. 9, 1889   NFI

[1] Sometimes shown as "Wills"

[2] Teacher in Birmingham for many years.

B   Cornelia Donaldson b Mar. 25, 1850 d April 8, 1932 m Jan. 21, 1873 William T. Dobyns b Jan. 8, 1848 d Sept. 28, 1908 CHILDREN:

1   Willie D. (girl) b Jan. 5, 1874 d in infancy.

2   Emma Olga b June 27, 1876, d in infancy.

3   Fannie Elizabeth b Feb. 4, 1878 d Jan. 25, 1945 m Feb. 20, 1901 Frank Sanger England b Aug. 12, 1853 d June 16, 1916 CHILDREN:

    a   Frances Cornelia b Feb. 19, 1902 d Feb. 6, 1940 m 1935 Harold Butts Collins b CHILDREN:

       i   Cornel England b Aug. 29, 1939 UNMARRIED

       ii   Cornelia Eden* b Aug. 29, 1939 m July 1959 Carl R. Stiffler   CHILDREN:

          (a)   Darwin Joel b May 6, 1960

          (b)   Candalyn Frances b Sept. 27, 1961

    b   Helen Brown b Mar. 27, 1905 d Mar. 8, 1963 m FIRST John Lee James   NO ISSUE

       m SECOND E. Joseph Galibardy NO ISSUE

    c   Mannie Dew b Oct. 29, 1907 m June 12, 1929 Otha Wright Nichols b Dec. 18, 1894 CHILD:

       i   Otha Wright II b Feb. 15, 1939 m FIRST Jan. 19, 1957 Ellen Grey Tucker CHILD:

*   Twins

(a)   Tena Marie b Aug. 6,
1960

m SECOND Emily Taylor b
Dec. 15, 1961

4   Lucy b Apr. 26, 1880, d in infancy

5   William Donaldson b Oct. 20, 1881
d m * FIRST Willie Lee Underwood b
June 9, 1880 d July 10, 1903
NO ISSUE

M SECOND April 24, 1904 Susie Roan
CHILDREN:

a   Bettie b m   Weiner

b   Christine   NFI

c   Mamie   NFI

d   Thomas b   d   m Anne   NFI

6   Annie Lee b Feb. 20, 1888 d Sept.
1, 1898

7   Lenora Jane b Oct. 4, 1890 m June
14, 1914 Fred Gowan England b Apr.
18, 1885 CHILDREN: [1]

a   Fred Gowan II b Sept. 29,1915
[2] m Sept. 19, 1937 Nancy
Catheren Ritter b Jan. 21,
1920 CHILDREN:

i   Nancy Louise b Dec. 23,
1938 m July 1, 1958
Robert Leslie Hancock b
Sept. 27, 1938 CHILDREN:

(a) Robert Leslie II b
Sept. 13, 1959

[1] All born in Perry County, Ala.

[2] Long time POW in Germany, AF Major

*   Marriage date was Nov. 26, 1902

      (b)   Shawn Lee b Aug. 13,
          1960

      (c)   Rita Lynn b May 23,
          1963
          [1]

b   Samuel Donaldson b Nov. 26,
     1917 d Sept. 13, 1944 m Sept.
     10, 1938 Eugenia Eloise
     Mellown b Apr. 23, 1920
     CHILDREN:

     i   Samuel Donaldson II b May
           26, 1941

     ii   Julia Eloise (Judy) b
           Nov. 5, 1942 m July 18,
           1961 Robert Lee Massey b
           Nov. 18, 1941 CHILD:

           (a)   Susan Michelle b Apr.
               22, 1962
             *

c   Arthur Eugene b Feb. 29, 1920
     d Mar. 1, 1942 [2]

d   Stanley Earle b Sept. 29,1921
     m Sept. 24, 1947 Virginia
     Allen Oxford b Feb. 4, 1925
     NO ISSUE

e   Jane Elizabeth b Aug. 10,1924
     m Jan. 24, 1948 Rodney George
     Freeman II b Apr. 15, 1918
     CHILDREN:

     i   Hilma Jane b Oct. 7,1950

     ii   Donna Jean b Sept. 17,
           1955

     iii   Janet Ann b May 23, 1962

[1] Died in sinking of USS Warrington.

[2] Died in sinking of USS Edsell.

 *   Stephanie Susan b July 24, 1963.

   f Robert Gordon (Bill) b May 27, 1927 m Oct. 12, 1952 Emily **Raye** Bamberg b July 23, 1933
CHILDREN:

     i Emily Diane b Oct. 13, 1955

     ii Cynthia Dawn b May 22, 1959

     iii Robert Eugene (Bob) b Apr. 27, 1961

   g Neil Huff b Dec. 2, 1928 m Feb. 6, 1953 Lillian Ione White b July 31, 1933
CHILDREN:

     i Neil Bradley b Sept. 5, 1955

     ii David Bryant b Apr. 27, 1960

     iii Suzanne b Aug. 9, 1963

C William b   d as a child

D John Green b Aug. 23, 1854 m Jan. 23, 1881 Ada Belle Hayles b Jan. 26, 1862
CHILDREN:
1 Maud b 1881 d 1900
2 John b and d 1883
3 Belle b 1885
4 Pearl b Aug. 30, 1887 d 1887
5 Edgar Lafayettte b Aub. 30, 1887
6 Lessie b July 4, 1889
7 Charlie Wesley b Feb. 24, 1891
8 Roy William b June 28, 1893
9 Skeeter b Dec. 25, 1896
10 Raymond b Jan.1, 1902 d Jan.29,1909
11 Mark E. b Dec. 3, 1907 m 1933
  Ada L. CHILD:

   a Mark Huff (Dr. Wichita Falls Tex.)

E Malinda Lenora b m Jan. 10, 1886 Benjamin Franklin Cook b 1850
CHILDREN:

1   Benjamin Franklin II

2   Nannie (Dixie) m C, W. Rogers
CHILDREN:

    a

    b

3   Annie Bell   m   Jesse Sconyers

4   John b d

F   Donna M. b Nov. 25, 1857 d May 5, 1884
m Nov. 11, 1874 Benjamin Franklin Cook
b   1850 CHILDREN:

1   Lenora (Lenny) b 1875 d about age
16

2   Mary Clayton b   1877   NFI

3   Eula V. (twin) b July 18, 1879 d
Mar. 27, 1883 (from burns)

4   Drula (twin) b July 18, 1879 d

5   R. Dorroh

6   Donna (Beaut) b   m   ____Morrison

    CHILDREN:

    a   Donna

    b   Billy

    c

G   Drula b UNMARRIED

H   Anna Belle b m FIRST Dec. 7, 1881
Bradley Didlake b CHILD:

1   Lurline b d, as a young girl

m   SECOND Joe Pellerin   NO ISSUE

IV   Margaret Caroline b   m March 14, 1847 Bird
H. Gilliam b   d ca 1862   CHILDREN:

A   John D. b Sept. 19, 1852 d Oct. 24,
1853

B   Lenora H. b Feb. 11, 1856 d Nov. 8,
1856

C   Cora

D   Josephine

E   Samuel

F   Robert

G   Caroline

V   Samuel J. b   d July 12, 1858 m Dec.
14, 1854 Perry Co., Ala. Frances I. Howze b
ca 1835 d   CHILDREN:

A   Julia H. b ca 1855 d ca 1875 m May 5,
1875 J. W. Long b Jan. 1, 1853 d Oct.
1897   CHILD:

    1   Julian b   1876 d   1888

B   Mary E. b ca 1859 d   m June
12, 1877 Benjamin N. Bobbs b
Lived Selma, Ala.   CHILDREN:

    1   Mary Thomas b   1884 d   1954
        m J.Goodwin Scott b

    2   Benjamin b   d   UNMARRIED
        [1]

    3   Julia b   d   1944
        m James Claudian Octavius Moroso b
        Sept. 21, 1885 Charleston, S. C. d
        Oct. 29, 1929   CHILDREN:

        a   John A. III b March 23, 1910
            Charleston, S. C. m Sept. 8,
            1934 Anna Catherine Dale b

[1]   Served in Canadian Army in World War I.

a   CHILDREN:

    i   Nancy Gail b March 8,
       1938 (Nurse)

    ii John A. b July 20, 1939
       (Sgt., U.S.A.)

b   James Claudian Octavius II b
    Charleston, S. C., m
    Dorothy Douglass b
    CHILDREN: (3 sons   NFI)
    Live in Old Greenwich, Conn.

c   Henry J. b Nov. 23, 1914 d
    May 15, 1941 [1] m
    Dolores Becker b   CHILD

    i   Steven

d   Mary Alice b Dec. 1923 Colum-
    bia, S. C., m Jan.   1942
    Ralph Baeuerle b
    CHILDREN:

    i   Ralph II b   Jan. 1943

    ii Robert b Sept.   1945

VI   J. M. b Dec. 19, 1834 d Sept. 7, 1847

VII William R. b Jan. 8, 1837 d Aug. 3, 1846

[1] Killed in boat collision.

ALABAMA IN 1850 and 1860

* Benton County's Name changed to Calhoun. Jan. 29th, 1858.
* Hancock County's Name changed to Winston, January 22, 1858.

The Love of My Country Leads Me On

The Phillipses

It was in the spring of 1947 that I made my first visit to Hillsboro, Orange Co. N. C.My father had passed away on January 15, 1947 and my mother and my wife, Louise, and I were taking a little spring trip through Hillsoborǫ where I knew my Johnston relatives had lived, and then it was on to Williamsburg and to Lynchburg for a visit with my cousins, Isabel and Tom Torrey.

My final destination was Washington and Lee University where I was to attend an Alumni Association Meeting.

Roads then were not as good as today and neither was my knowledge of my kinfolks, but I did know the Johnstons were good Presby-terians and I wanted to visit the Hillsboro Presbyterian Church and just browse about the Cemetery with the hope I would find something about my Johnston kin.

In the church building was information. But, in the cemetery I found nothing. I was a wee bit disappointed until I, quite by ac-cident, ran across a family plot with the name Phillips. This struck me as interesting and I immediately began to check each marker carefully.

I found a D. D. Phillips and this name struck me as identical to Cousin Dan Phillips who I had known from early childhood. I felt sure that those buried in this cemetery must, and had to be, related to our Perry County, Alabama Phillipses. And, Mother remembered,

having heard her mother say we had some Phillips kin who lived in Hillsboro, and thus my
interest and curiosity about the Phillips
came to life.

Unfortunately, I have not been able
to trace this family as far back as I would
like, but I have tried to see just what would
come to light.

At first I had been told that D.D.
Phillips and Solomon S. Phillips, and Elizabeth (Ann) Nancy Phillips, brothers and sister, and their parents had come from Wake Co.
N. C., the adjoining county to Orange; and
it is possible that they might have lived
for a while in Wake, but certainly, as historians go, they were not from Wake, but from
Northampton County which is bound on the east
by Hertford and on the west by Halifax. Northampton was one of the older North Carolina
counties being formed from Bertie in 1741.

We found that Jesse Phillips married
Mary A. Smith in Northampton in Sept. 1808,
that in 1814 he enlisted in the War of 1812
for a period of six months and he died in
late 1822. [1] Jesse Phillips' will was
written Oct. 6, 1822 and probated in North-
hampton Co. in December 1822, which would cer.
tainly indicate he was living in Northampton
Co. at the time of his death. [2] His will is
filed in Will Book 3, page 272 and mentions
Polly and "my children". He names his wife
as executrix and Willie Langford as executor.

There are only two earlier Phillips
wills in Northampton and they are in the

Jesse b. 1764 - 1774.
m. 1808
d. 1822.

corporal in
McDonald's NC
militia
Discharged
a sergeant

North Carolina Archives, File 71.018.

The will of Mark Phillips shows as legatees Martha Bottom, and the two daughters of his brother Thomas, Morning and Martha. This was signed Feb. 18, 1778 and probated March 1778. Apparently, brother Thomas wrote his will very shortly after brother Marks' death, for it was dated March 1778 and he lived only a short time for his will is proved September 1778.

We find on the 1789 tax list of Northampton (to be found in the N. C. Archives, Raleigh, File LP 46.1) John Phillips, Mark Phillips, William Phillips,and Lucy Phillips. The 1790 Census of Northampton Co., shows only one Phillips, that being a Mark Phillips and Deed Book 10, page 83 shows that by 1794 he had moved to Bladen Co., which is south and east of Fayetteville.

The 1800 Census of Northampton shows a *Drury* Phillips as living in this county, but Deed Book 10, page 150 speaks of Drewry Phillips as first buying land 1790 and speaks of him as living in Northampton. Of course, he could have moved to the county shortly after completion of the census.

Drury (or *Drewry*, as you please) is shown as buying more land in Northampton in 1810 and this was witnessed by Solomon and Jesse Smith (Deed Book 15, page 19). In 1812 he deeded land to a son Nathaniel, and a Benjamin Phillips was a witness. In 1817 Drewry Phillips sold land with his wife, Lucretia with his son, Jesse, as a witness.

The last we find of Drewry Phillips in Northampton was in a Deed of Trust, 1827(Deed Book 23, page 227). Drewry left no will in Northampton, but Samuel Stancell, Jr. did leave a will dated and probated in Northampton in 1817 in which he names among others his sister, Lucretia Phillips, which verified that Drewry's wife was Lucretia Stancell, daughter of Samuel Stancell, Sr.

Tracing *Drewery* or *Drury* Phillips ancestors proved to be quite a task. To begin with, Creasey or Lucretia Stancell was apparently his second wife. There is a Northampton Co. marriage bond, 1812, for Drury Phillips and Creasey Stancell which means this marriage took place four years after Jesse Phillips, his son, was married to Mary A. Smith. Unfortunately, we have not been able to find to whom he was married the first time and thus who was the mother of Jesse.

The 1800 Census of Northampton shows Jesse to be between the age of 26 and 45; thus he was born between 1755-74 and his wife name not given, was born in the same period. It also lists one male between 16 and 26, who was Jesse, and one male under 10.

The 1810 Census lists only two Phillips' men as heads of households: Drury as being over 45, which would have made his birth before 1765. And, in his household, are also listed one female 26-45; one female 10-16 and one male 10-16. The other male listed was Jesse and he was listed between 16 and 26;his wife in the same age bracket; and one male under 10.

By 1820 the Jesse Phillips family had grown to 4 females under 10; one male between

10-16; and one female under 10. Our records only show three children: Solomon Smith ; Elizabeth (Nancy) Ann; and Daniel Day, so no doubt the others either died in their youth or for some reason separated from their family as we have no other information on them.

Northampton was formed from Bertie in 1741. In scanning the Bertie Cross Index to Deeds, we find the following grantees: 1724, Thomas Phillips, Jr.; 1735, Richard Phillips; 1737, Thomas Phillips; and grantors: 1738, Richard and 1741, John Phillips.

Grimes, page 288, shows the will of Thomas Phillips of Northampton Co., N. C. dated and probated 1751. His wife was Patty and sons: Thomas, Mark, and William and daughters: Patty Simpson, and Mary Phillips.

William Perry Johnson, writing me on June 19, 1962, says: "I do not see how Jesse and Drury can escape being descended from one of the three sons of Thomas, who left the 1751 will! But, the line of descent is not yet clear."

After Jesse Phillips died, his wife and children moved to Wake Co., but when it is not known; and it is not known just when her son D. D. Phillips and his family moved to Hillsboro, but Mary Ann Smith Phillips' life in Orange Co. was not for long as she died there Jan. 16, 1852, two years after filing papers for land bounty for Jesse's services in the War of 1812.

The oldest of the Jesse and Mary Ann Smith Phillips children was Solomon S. Phillips. He moved to Perry Co., Alabama. He married Elizabeth Smith in Wake Co., N. C.

It is not known whether he came back for his bride or married her before coming to Alabama because we do know that Elizabeth (Nancy) Ann Phillips, his younger sister,married James J. Simms in Perry Co., Alabama on Oct. 11, 1839. It would be safe to assume, for sure, that Grandma Simms must have been visiting someone in the family, or closely connected with it, for her to marry in Alabama when her mother and other members of the family were in North Carolina. We shall cover more about Nancy Phillips Simms under the chapter on *The Simmses*.

It might be interesting to note that Elizabeth Smith was a twin and her twin sister married Henderson M. Cope and they too moved to Alabama. There were all together 9 children in the family: Hilliard J. Smith... never married, died in Perry Co., Ala. 1882; we have mentioned Sarah and Elizabeth; James moved to Tennessee; William Asbury died as a young man in North Carolina; Griza Ann died unmarried in North Carolina; Nancy Grant died in North Carolina married to B. W. Matthews; and Mary Louisa married Thomas M. Cope, and moved to Alabama.

The father of these nine children was William F. Smith (his wife being Rachel Olive daughter of Jesse Olive) and he was the son of Sihon Smith, a Methodist preacher who contributed in our American Independence.

We find that Solomon Smith Phillips died intestate and Hilliard Judge Smith, brother of Elizabeth Smith Phillips, the wife of the deceased, was appointed administrator of the estate and was bonded for $12,000 with Wilson Ethridge and L. N. Walthall as sureties. The appraisers of the estate were John N. Walthall, Thomas Walthall, George M. White Thomas Bondurant, and L. G. Drake.

For those not too familiar with the family connections: George M. White was the father of John Henry White who married El-giva (better known as Ella)Simms, a niece of Solomon S. Phillips and Thomas Bondurant was the father of Emma Bondurant who married Solomon Frank Phillips---Solomon Smith Phillips' son.

One little matter which has been somewhat of a puzzle to me is that in April 14, 1845 we find a Hilliard J. Phillips bought some land in Sumter Co., Alabama and it was recorded in Greene. This has made me wonder how this Hilliard J. Phillips might have been connected with our Phillips family!

What we have on our Phillips family follows:

F O O T N O T E S

[1]   Information from J. Fred Dorman, a pro fessional genealogist of Washington, D. C. , in a letter written Nov. 23, 1956. This was written to Mrs. T. F. (Isabel Heflin) Torrey of Lynchburg, Va., Mr. Dorman stat-es that Mary A. Phillips, the widow of Jesse, applied for the bounty land given by the government for services in the War of 1812, and stated she was married to Jesse Phillips in September 1808, in Northampton. Her applicat-

ion was made on Dec. 7, 1850 in Wake Co.,N.C. and she was then 62, which agrees with her tombstone in Hillsboro. She did not state how long she had lived in Wake, or when she left Northampton.

[2] This information, with the condensation of his will, was furnished me by William Perry Johnson, professional genealogist of Raleigh, North Carolina.

Author's Note:

The following information which follows on the PHILLIPS' family was furnished by members of the family, but does not concurr with the 1850 Census of Perry County, Ala. which was copied from the ALABAMA GENEALOGICAL REGISTER, Vol. 3, No. 3, page 126 and is reproduced here:

NAME	AGE	SEX	BORN
Smith, Hillard J.	33	M	N.C.
Phillips, Elizabeth	31	F	N.C.
" William	7	M	Ala.
" Mary L.	5	F	"
" Betsy Ann	3	F	"
" Solomon F.	2	M	"
" James M.	6/12	M	"

Descendants of Jesse Phillips and Mary A. Smith

I   Solomon S. b April 1814 d Feb. 16, 1850 m
       Jan. 13, 1843 Elizabeth Smith b May 1, 1818
       d Feb. 25, 1900 [1] CHILDREN: SEE SEPARATE
       LISTING

II   Elizabeth (Nancy) Ann b April 27, 1817 d May
       3, 1888 m Oct. 11, 1839 James J. Simms b 1815
       d before 1871 CHILDREN: SEE LISTING UNDER
       SIMMS

III   Daniel Day b April 19, 1819 d Nov. 7, 1870
       m May 31, 1843 Tamesia M. Cooley b Feb. 11,
       1827 d Oct. 26, 1899 [2] CHILDREN:

       A   Alonza b Jan. 30, 1845 d April 29, 1884

       B   Mary Eliza b Mar. 31, 1851 d Nov. 5,
              1876 (Twin)

       C   Henry Butler b Mar. 31, 1851 d June 14,
              1862 (Twin)

       D   Laurence Fisher b Dec. 27, 1856 d Aug.
              27, 1867

       E   Lucy Ann b Dec. 23, 1858 d Feb. 13,1910
              m May 9, 1878 Hillsboro, N. C. Rev.
              Hiram Pearson Cole b * d   CHILDREN:

              1   Elizabeth Malantha (Elma) b April
                     4, 1880 d March 14, 1948 m 1904
                     Charles Ashby Pamplin I b June 12,
                     1869 d Sept. 30, 1951 CHILDREN:

                     a   Charles Ashby II b March 25,
                            1907 m Oct. 10, 1936 Mary
                            Harris Hubbard b CHILDREN:

                            i   (boy)   NFI

                            ii   (boy)   NFI

[1] He is buried in DeYampert family lot in west
Perry Co.,Ala,having died of typhoid fever. She is
buried in Phillips lot, Uniontown, Ala.
[2] Both buried Hillsboro,N.C.Presbyterian Cem.
*   Year born Sept. 1840

b   Hiram Cole b July 31, 1908 m
Sept. 30, 1939 Ruth Burnett b
CHILDREN:

    i   (boy)   NFI

    ii   (girl)   NFI

c   Lewis Anderson b Sept. 2,1911
d Sept.   1917

d   Jack Cole b Sept. 23, 1913 m
Dec. 23, 1941 Mollie Baker
Glass b   CHILDREN:

    i   (girl)   NFI

    ii   (girl)   NFI

e   Elma Cole b Sept. 14, 1915

2   Lucy Mayfield b June 7, 1882 m Oct.
19, 1909 Goldsboro, N. C. Thomas
Jefferson Gattis II b   1879 d
Nov. 10, 1938   CHILDREN:

a   Patsy b June 25, 1909 (legally
adopted) m June 5, 1944
Clarence Mitchell Lamb b
CHILDREN: NFI

b   Thomas Jefferson III b Dec. 5,
1910 d Feb. 10, 1913

c   Austin Phillips b Dec. 3, 1917
m Dec. 18, 1945 Mary Alice
Stone b   1918   CHILDREN:

    i   Austin Phillips II b

    ii   Mary Alice b Sept. 13,
    1951

F   Emma Cooley b July 3, 1860 d Oct. 31,
1942 m_____Boyd   NFI

G   Fanny Tamesia b July 31, 1863 d July 1,
1938 m_____Springs   NFI

Descendants of Solomon S. Phillips and Elizabeth Smith

I   William Thomas b Nov. 1843 d Sept. 1917

II   Elizabeth Ann b Jan. 6, 1847 d April 22,
     1919 m Lewis Allen Morgan b Sept. 23, 1839
     d March 24, 1915 CHILDREN: SEE LISTING
     under MORGAN DESCENDANTS.

III James Markham b Nov.   1848 d July 1913

IV   Solomon Frank b July 2, 1849 d Sept. 27,
     1928 m Dec. 6, 1871 Emma Bondurant b March
     13, 1851 d Jan. 26, 1932 Buried Uniontown,
     Ala. CHILDREN:

     A   Mamie Lelia b Nov. 24, 1872 d Oct. 1,
          1892 UNMARRIED

     B   Thomas S. b Feb. 16, 1874 d March 19,
          1923   UNMARRIED

     C   Louis M. b Aug. 14, 1875 d Dec. 8,
          1956 m Oct. 7, 1897 Maggie Nola Roberts
          b Sept. 7, 1880 d July 2, 1957 CHILDREN:

          1   Arthur Frank b Nov. 15, 1898 m 1916
               Myrtle Palmer b Sept. 25,1896 CHILD

               a   Kathryn Rhea b Nov. 16, 1917
                    m April 5, 1936 J. M. McEl-
                    waine b Sept. 7, 1900
                    CHILDREN:

                    i   Kay b Aug. 22, 1941 m
                         Nov. 18, 1958 Murry
                         Alewine b Apr. 15, 1938
                         CHILD:

                         (a) Allen b Feb. 14,
                              1960

                    ii   Jimmie b May 18, 1947

          2   Lola Mae b July 12, 1900 m Dec. 7,
               1917 Moran Kirk Bell b Feb. 3,
               1897   CHILDREN:

               a   Audrey Lee b Jan. 15, 1924 m
                    Aug. 19, 1939 Mitchell Bryant
                    b July 15, 1922 CHILDREN:

    i   Phil b May 14, 1942

    ii   Odell b Nov. 30, 1947

    iii Sandra b Nov. 29, 1952

3   Henry Lee b Feb. 24, 1902 m Aug. 12, 1925 Kate Popejoy b Oct. 31, 1902 CHILDREN:

    a   Dale b Nov. 8, 1928 d Jan. 29, 1962 m March 18, 1949 Billie Stribling b June 19, 1932 CHILDREN:

        i   Denny Carl b Jan. 4, 1950

        ii   Lynn b Oct. 15, 1953

    b   Frank b Sept. 13, 1934 m April 4, 1953 Leona Smith b May 9, 1934 CHILDREN:

        i   Larry b May 18, 1956

        ii   Danny b July 18, 1954

        iii Darla b Sept. 24, 1958

    c   Kenneth b Feb. 15, 1933 m Oct. 2, 1954 Vincennette de Ponceau b Feb. 16, 1932 CHILDREN:

        i   Steve b Aug. 28, 1955

        ii   Sherry b May 12, 1957

        iii Jason b March 2, 1959

        iv Bryan b Aug. 7, 1960

4   Agnes Mildred b April 28, 1904 m April 29, 1922 Lloyd Lane b Oct. 21, 1902 CHILD:

    a   Mildred b Mar. 3, 1924 m April 7, 1942 Edward Haley b Mar. 2, 1919 CHILDREN:

    i   Denny b Jan. 27, 1947

    ii   Darlann b Feb. 14, 1950

5   Martha Emma b Feb. 19, 1907 m Mar. 13, 1926 Cash Hettler b March 22, 1904 CHILD:

    a   Terry b May 29, 1945

6   Maggie Louise b Sept. 28, 1909 m July 5, 1940 Leon Wall b May 10, 1902 CHILDREN:

    a   Rubye Louise b Mar. 12, 1942 m June 17, 1960 Jimmie Triplett b Mar. 14, 1941 CHILD:

          i   Mark Wayne b Sept. 14, 1961

    b   Dee Royce b May 14, 1945

7   Rubye Anita b Sept. 27, 1918 m Dec. 24, 1949 Charles Rust b March 4, 1918

D   Bettie Alvice b April 7, 1877 m Oct. 29, 1902 Forrest H. Lavender b Aug. 21, 1879 d 1959 CHILD:

1   Forrest H. II b Jan. 3, 1905 m Dec. 12, 1929 Dora Leach b March 14, 1909 CHILDREN: [1]

    a   Sydney Leach b Sept. 8, 1932 m Aug. 4, 1956 Carol McNeal b Feb. 22, 1932

    b   Mary Lee b Nov. 24, 1937 m June 19, 1960 White Gibson III b March 26, 1934

E   Daniel Day b May 19, 1878 d Sept. 19, 1956 m Nov. 27, 1901 Golda Howell b Aug. 26, 1883 CHILDREN:

1   Eleanor Elizabeth b Jan.3, 1903 m

[1] Forrest H. Lavender II d Dec. 1, 1963

Nov. 27, 1935 Claiborne Clifton Myers I b Feb. 5, 1892 d Oct. 24, 1960 CHILDREN:

a   Claiborne Clifton II b July 24, 1937 m Feb. 8, 1957 Mary Elizabeth Collins b CHILDREN:

     i   Claiborne Clifton III b March 16, 1959

     ii   Darrell Wayne b May 30, 1961

b   Frank Arthur b Feb. 26, 1946 Lives Barlow Bend, Ala.

2   Golda Helen b June 18, 1904 m May 5, 1927 James Philip Waters b Mar. 25, 1906 CHILDREN:

a   James Philip II b Dec. 27, 1927 m June 17, 1950 Claire Anne Walker b Aug. 16, 1930 CHILDREN:

     i   Karen b Dec. 19, 1950

     ii   James Philip III b Jan. 9, 1958

     iii   Charles Keith b Oct. 3, 1960

     iv   Kelly Walker b Aug. 31, 1961

b   Daniel Howard b June 1, 1934 m June 17, 1956 Virginia Elizabeth Canant b June 8, 1957 CHILDREN:

     i   Martha Elizabeth b Jan. 17, 1959

     ii   Melanie Virginia b Sept. 14, 1961

3 James Markham I b Aug. 6, 1906
m Feb. 26, 1927 Pauline Story b
Dec. 1, 1910 CHILDREN:

 a Elizabeth Story b Sept. 26,
  1928 m FIRST Henry Hudson b
     CHILDREN:

  i James Vaughn b Aug. 20,
   1947

  ii Laura Beth b June 23,
   1954

  m SECOND William E. Cobb b
     CHILD:

  iii William Judson b Aug.
   29, 1961

 b James Markham II b Feb. 12,
  1952

4 Lucile Alice b Feb. 15, 1908 m Oct.
4, 1930 Charles Wilson Foster b
Oct. 6, 1903 CHILDREN:

 a Silvia Lucile b May 1, 1932 m
  July 17, 1951 Charles Hugh
  Vaughn II b June 17, 1931
  CHILDREN:

  i Michael Philip b Dec.
   26, 1956

  ii David Keith b Aug. 29,
   1958

  iii Brian Douglas b June 18,
   1961

  iv Jeffery Foster b May 22,
   1962

 b Golda Elizabeth b May 21,1934
  m Jan. 29, 1955 Billie Wayne
  Spain b June 17, 1933
  CHILDREN:

      i   Susan Elizabeth b Nov. 14, 1956

      ii   Billy Wayne II b Nov. 19, 1959

      iii   Alan Nolan b July 29, 1961

c   Helen Wilson b Mar. 29, 1936 m Dec. 8, 1956 Robert Fay Brooks b Aug. 1, 1932 CHILD:

      i   Bari Renee b Dec. 16, 1960

d   Charles Wilson II b June 27, 1941 UNMARRIED NAS,Pensacola, Fla.

e   Frederick Phillips b May 28, 1945 UNMARRIED

5   Daniel Day II b Nov. 10, 1910 **d** July 1, 1911

6   Solomon Frank b July 24, 1922 m Jan. 2, 1948 Mary Ann Coney b Dec. 3, 1926 CHILDREN:

     a   Amy Lynn b July 3, 1950

     b   Daniel Day III b Mar. 4, 1954

F   Frank S. b Sept. 10, 1880 d Dec. 31,1880

G   Emma Frances b Nov. 16, 1881 d Mar. 15, 1961 m Sept. 25, 1918 Junie C. Edwards b March 12, 1881 CHILD:

     1   Joseph William b Aug. 20, 1919 UNMARRIED Living Winston-Salem,N.C.

H   Ella Sims b Sept. 13, 1883 m April 20, 1904 William Carl Howell b Jan. 29, 1879 d June 2, 1940 CHILDREN:

     1   Frank Benton b March 29, 1905 m

May 30, 1929 Emma Lucille Boone b *d 3 Nov 1998*
April 20, 1907 CHILD:

a   Betty Ann b March 29, 1934 m
    Aug. 19, 1961 Robert Milton
    Gay b Oct.   1935

2   Carl Phillips b Nov. 24, 1907 m *d. 6 Nov 1989*
    Jan. 10, 1933 Margaret Alma Hisey
    b Oct. 5, 1912 CHILD:

a   Margaret Janice b Aug. 7, 1935
    m Feb. 12, 1954 Victor Gustaff
    Schneider II b Oct. 19, 1926
    CHILDREN:

        i   Sheryl Margaret b June
             26, 1956

        ii   Victor Scott b May 8,
             1958

        iii Stephen Carl b July 27,
             1961   *d. Nov 1998*

3· Alvice b March 5, 1913 m July 14,
    1937 Harold Frederick Parler b Dec.
    15, 1904 d Sept. 13, 1954 CHILD:

a   William Harold b Feb. 14,1953 *d.28 Nov 1998*

4   Mary Frances b Mar. 26, 1916 m Oct.
d. June 2009   17, 1936 Mark Edwin Lemley b Aug.
    29, 1909 CHILDREN:

a   Rhoda Jane b July 17, 1938 m
    Sept. 29, 1962 Charles Bolton
    Hall b July 18, 1933

b   Mary Carol b April 25, 1943 m
    March 29, 1961 Henry Hamilton
    Gary II b April 14, 1940
    CHILDREN:

        i   John Paul b Dec. 25, 1961

        ii   Mark Hamilton b Dec. 25,
             1962

  c Edwin Phillips b Sept. 15, 1947

I Lucy b July 16, 1885 m Oct. 15, 1908
Joseph Theodore Pack b Oct. 22, 1879
d Jan. 6, 1957 CHILDREN:

 1 Mary Louise b Aug. 10, 1909 m Jan.
19, 1940 Noble Wilson King b Jan.
14, 1892 NO ISSUE

 2 Joseph Theodore II b March 22, 1911
m Jan. 1, 1945 Marian M. Armes b
May 4, 1909 NO ISSUE

 3 John Franklin I b April 24, 1917 m
Nov. 23, 1941 Elizabeth Buck b Dec.
16, 1915 CHILDREN:

  a John Franklin II b April 5, 1948

  b Joseph Carlton b Feb. 8, 1952

  c James Stallworth b Oct. 12, 1957

J Annie b Sept. 7, 1887 m Jan. 21, 1917
Selby Hardenberg b CHILD:

 1 Mary Gordon b Oct. 29, 1917 m Nov.
19, 1940 V. F. Crabtree II b
CHILDREN:

  a V. F. III b Jan. 19, 1942

  b Mary Ann b Aug. 11, 1943

  c Selby Phillips b July 4, 1947

K Nettie b Aug. 2, 1890 d July 25, 1892

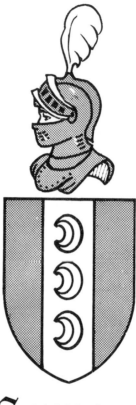

Symes

The Simmses

This is an English family name. The meaning or significance of the name is not known. Though I found during the research on this family from the middle sixteenth century that there were numerous spellings of the name, the pronounciation seems never to have changed.

We found the following spellings of the name: Simms, Sims, Semmes,Semes,Simes,Simmes, Symms,Symmes, Sim, Sym, Syme, Simm, Syms and Symes. All of these spellings appear in the 1790 Census of the United States, our first official census.

It is interesting to note that the 1790 Census shows 215 people under heads of families by one of the various spellings of the name, and that the average size of the family was 5.9. There was another total of 1,043 persons by the same names who apparently were not heads of families. [1]

We have found the various spellings very constant in our family line since the middle of the eighteenth century when George Symes' son picked up the name *Sims* and since then it has been interchanged from *Sims* to *Simms*. And this has made my research all the more confusing.

In the family cemetery in Uniontown we find the marker on Grandma Simms' grave showing her name with two Ms and that of her son Cadmus, while three of her other sons have their grave marked with the single M. Thus, it is Annie Phillips Simms and Cadmus Worth Simms and W. C. Sims, C. D. Sims and J. D. Sims. In the same cemetery, in another lot, we find Eleanor Simms, daughter of J. K. and T. E. Simms, while the marker of her father shows him as John K. Sims. My grandmother's marker shows her as Elgiva Simms, and my mother says she was Eloise Simms White.

But, let's not waste too much time on the spelling. You may take your choice.. ...but for consistency, we shall henceforth use the double M or spell the name *Simms*, except when referring to the older generations, where we shall use the spelling as we find and found, in our study and research.

The first of our line was John Symes, of Barwick, England, who married Jane, daughter of Robert Hill, of Yard, and his wife, Alice Clark. His will was proved June 15, 1581 in County Somerset.

His son was William Symes, born ca 1540 and died 1597. He was of Chard and was born at Poundsford in Pitminster, County Somerset. He was a very profitable merchant and held manors of Barwick, Boure, and Stoford in County Somerset, and Franklin in County Dorset. His wife was named Elizabeth and her maiden name was believed to be Hill. His will was proved July 27, 1597. He stood in good favor with the king and received his coat of arms (reproduced foreward) in 1592.

Among the children of William Symes were William and John Symes, who likewise were given coat of arms and in *The General Armory* by Sir Bernard Burke, C. B., LL. D., Ulster King of Arms atates they were from Chard and Poundsford, County Somerset...the former from Chard and the latter from Poundsford. And, this corresponds with the information we have gathered elsewhere that John was of Poundsford and was born March 4, 1572 and matriculated at Exeter College, Oxford on February 23, 1587/8 [2] and received his A. B. degree July 9, 1591. He also was a student at Lincoln's Inn in 1589. He was appointed high sheriff and died Oct. 21, 1661 at the age of 86 and his will was proved Dec. 19, 1661.

Thomas was a son of John Symes and was known as Thomas Symes of Winterbourne, County Gloucester, late of Poundsford.....meaning he had originally come from Poundsford, County Somerset. He married Amy, daughter of Edward Bridges of Keynsham. They were married about 1640 and his will was proved Aug. 22, 1639.

Thomas Symm had among his children a son named George who moved to Antigua, British West Indies about 1672. He was a very suck cessful merchant and a member of the council. In 1681 he was granted 260 acres of land on the island and in 1688 became speaker of the council. He married Dorothy, daughter of Thomas Everard. I have no record of his death.

George's son, George Symes, moved to the colony of Virginia when he was about 16 years old and settled in the Isle of Wight County. His wife was Elizabeth Sherwood. Among their children were Adam and John Symes.

Since both of these enter into the interest of our family, let us treat them separately:

John, the younger brother, lived in Hanover and New Kent Counties in Virginia and here we find a change in the spelling from the old *Symes* to *Sims*. John married about 1705 Mary Rice, the daughter of Thomas Rice. This couple had a large family, including probably six or seven sons........one of whom was John Sims who married Sarah Bullock about 1734. She was the daughter of Richard Bullock. John and Sarah Bullock Sims moved on to Granville County, North Carolina.

Mrs. Zebulon Judd, Auburn, Alabama, is a descendant of this line and has done considerable research on the *Symes-Sims-Simms* family. Some of her work has been available to me and most helpful in this research. I have not attempted to follow her line, but to take this branch only in its relationship as it ties into the *Whites*.

John Sims died in Granville County in 1769 and left ten children, among them was Elisha Sims. He married Farah Howard. Of this marriage there were known to have been eleven children: John; Herbert; Zachariah, who settled in Georgia; Elisha, who moved to Tennessee; *Guilford Dudley* who married *Jacksey White* and moved to Tennessee; Irena ; Thiria; Mahala; Susan, who married David Royster, Jr.; Saunders; and Leonard Henley.

Of these eleven children, *Guilford Dudley Sims* interests us most in that he married *Jacksey White*. He was born in 1789 and died in 1854 and was a physician. She was born about 1800 and died about 1875. Both are bur_ied in Liberty Cemetery, near Dresden, Weakley Co., Tennessee. *Jacksey White* was the third and youngest child of *Phillip White* and Ann Mann,who were married Feb. 7, 1797.*Phillip White* was the son of *George White* and *Susannah Read,* and this complete line is covered in an earlier chapter under *The Whites.*

Adam Sims, the older brother of John who we have just covered, was born ca 1689 and died in July 1733. He married ca 1708 Mary Isham and she died ca 1747. *Adam* lived for a while in Prince George County and later in Brunswick. Since *Adam* died in Brunswick County before Lunenburg County had been carved from it and before Mecklenburg was carved from Lunenburg, it would be almost impossible to know just where in the old Brunswick County Adam Sims lived, but....in any event....it was not far from the North Carolina line.

We find that the will of *Adam* Simms mentions his wife and nine children: Adam, Isham, John, William, David, Mary, Charles,James and *George.*

George Simms was born in Brunswick County Virginia ca 1709 and died in September 1763. He married Martha Walton ca 1728 and she died in 1772. *George* left a will and named eleven children: George; Adam; Millington; Hannah; Nathaniel, who married Ann Harwell and moved to Warren Co.,N.C.; *Burwell Boswell,* whose wife we have not ascertained, did move to Wake Co., N. C. sometime around 1764 to 1766, and it is known that among his children was *William.*

We then see that *William Simms*, son of *Burwell*, married Martha Cook, daughter of Arthur Cook.

The 1790 Census of Wake Co., N. C. lists six families by the name of Simms (or Sims): Adam; Isham, Sr.; Isham, Jr.; Mark; Murry; and William. In this household, that of *William*, there were three free white males of 16 years old and upwards; 3 males under 16; 7 free females; and 8 slaves.

Wake Co. Estate Papers has a file on *William Simms*. These papers are in the Archives in Raleigh and they show *William* died "about 15 April 1820" intestate. He left a widow, Martha, who "died last February". There was no date on the paper, but William Perry Johnson, in a letter to me on Sept. 12, 1961 states the date 1829 was on the back of the paper, so I presume that sometime between June 11, 1826 and the year 1829, possibly February 1828, to be the date of her death.

In the settlement of *William Simms'* estate we find he had the following heirs: wife Martha Cook Simms and the following children: Burwell; Joel; Rhoda; Winifred; wife of Nathaniel Thompson; Martha, wife of Edward Rigsbee; Berry; Mary, the deceased wife of Isham Garrett; John; and Penney, wife of Joseph Lloyd.

In 1821 the Negro slaves of *William Simms* were divided among: Martha, his widow; and children; Burwell; Redding; Rhoda; John, who was living in Helena Parrish, Louisiana in 1822; Winnifred; Martha; Polly Garrott; Penny Lloyd, wife of Joseph W. Lloyd; *Joel;* and Berry. We find Burwell was administrator of the estate.

We found in Record Book 21, page 88 of
Wake County a will of Martha Symms (note the
spelling). She mentions her children as:
Burry D. (who is without doubt the same as
Berry D. mentioned in the papers of William
Simms,); Martha C. Rigsbee; Burwell Symms
Joel Symms; Mary Garrot; Penelope Loyed (note
difference from former spelling of Lloyd);
Rody Symms; Winniford (spelled Winnifried in
former records) Thompson; and the executor
was her son-in-law, Edward Rigsbee. The will
was signed June 11, 1826.

Wake County marriage bonds show that
Joel Simms married in 1804 Patsy Hunter. [3]

We have found much difficulty in getting a thorough and complete record of *Joel,*
but we do find him on the 1805 Tax List of
Wake Co., St. Matthews Dist., with no land,
1 free or white poll and 1 black poll. *Joel*
must have moved from Wake Co., for the next
time we find him in the St. Matthews Dist.
of Wake Co. was 1816 through 1823. He was
not shown as owning land except in 1823
when he was shown with 90 acres. *Joel* then
does not show in Wake Co. until 1834 when he
appears in House's Creek Dist., again with no
land. We did not find him in Wake Co. until
1837 and '38 when he was again in St. Matthews Dist., and again with no land. We found
him back in House's Creek Dist.in 1839-40-41,
and here our research stopped on his where-
abouts.

William Perry Johnson suggests that *Joel
Simms* apparently left Wake Co. within a few

years after his marriage and did not return to Wake County until sometime in 1815 or '16, and that he must have again left Wake and did not return until sometime in 1833 or '34.

Mr. Johnson further states that he has learned that Martha (Patsy) Hunter Simms died rather young. In the Wake Co. Estate papers in the Archives at Raleigh, are guardian papers showing that in 1832 Jesse Powell was appointed guardian to the children of *Joel Simms*, and names the children as: Redding; *James J.*; Sarah W.; Joel D. and John H. (believed to have been John Hunter).

We then found a will of a *Joel Sims* (note spelling) in which the legatee was named as Sally W. Lewis, my daughter. The will was signed Aug. 9, 1858 and probated in February term of court 1859. Whether this can be, indisputably, the same *Joel Simms* who had Redding, *James J.*; Joel D., John H. and Sarah W. is only speculative, but most likely. The question is still asked just why were his other children omitted if the *Joels* are one and the same? The answer can be that his sons moved from Wake Co. into other states and in some way forfeited their inheritance, for whatever it might have been.

Just when *James J. Simms* came to Perry County is not known, but he was definitely a young man when he did come.....for as best as we can ascertain.....he was born in 1815; and according to Perry County Marriage Book, we find that he married in 1839 when he was 24 years old.

Just why and how *James J. Simms* happened

to come to Perry County, Alabama is not clear to us, unless it was that he followed certain of his kinsmen into Alabama....as was a common thing in the early nineteenth century.

We have mentioned earlier about the various ways of spelling the name and that there had been a consistent interchange in the spelling of *Sims* and *Simms*. And, William Perry Johnson has pointed out that in the eighteenth century a middle name was not common and with the spelling of the name both *Simms* and *Sims*, it is most confusing in trying to document people and their descendants.

It is most likely that many of the early members of the *Sims* family in Perry County, Alabama were related to our *James J. Simms*. For instance, in Perry County Orphans Court Records, we find a William Sims in 1836 appointed a guardian Green B. Sims, son of Green Sims, deceased. We find William Sims was appointed, in 1834, administrator for estate of Miles W. Sims, deceased. We also found a Henry Sims transferring property to James Crawford, Dec. 7, 1838, and we find a Johnathan Sims purchasing land in Uniontown on Sept. 24, 1838.

Green Sims sold 80 acres to Henry Sims on Feb. 13, 1830 and Henry Sims on Dec. 11, 1832 sold this same 80 acres to Burrell G. Sims and William W. Sims. On Oct. 23, 1834 Burrell G. Sims sold 79.79 acres to William W. Sims. No doubt this Burrell G. Sims and Burwell G. Sims, mentioned in Perry County court records of March 1841, was one and the same......and since we found a *Burwell Simms* to have been the son of *George Simms* born ca

1709 and Burwell had a son named William who married Martha Cook. Though undocumented, we have no doubt that *James J. Simms* came to Perry County, Alabama following his cousins, though the spelling of their names might have been different. As we have said earlier , these varied spellings make it very confusing for researchers. The 1850 Perry County Census shows *Sims*, James; the 1860 Census shows *Simms* J. J.; and in the 1870 Dallas County Census (Bellview Beat), we find *Sims*, James J.!

As shown a few paragraphs earlier *James J. Simms* and Nancy A. Phillips, formerly of Wake Co., N. C., were married in Perry County. Their descendants are shown in the tabulation which follows.

The *Simms* family has been interesting and fascinating to many. Earlier we have mentioned the interest shown by Mrs. Judd of Auburn. Henry Upson Sims, deceased of Birmingham, has made a very interesting study of the family and has published a book on his family which can be found in our Birmingham Library, and it was very helpful in my work. He, like Mrs. Jane Morris, of Little Rock , Arkansas, is a descendant of *Adam Symes*. Mrs. Morris, in 1938, published a book, *Adam Symes And His Descendants*. I have been unable to locate a copy of this book.

The name *Simms* and *Sims* is now, to the best of my knowledge, extinct in Perry County. Nancy A. Phillips Simms is buried in Uniontown, Perry County, Alabama. James J. Simms is buried in a family cemetery out from Port Gibson, Claiborne County, Mississippi, with his son Ludolphus A. Simms. We located other members of the Sims family in Jefferson County, Mississippi whom we believe to be of the same descent   as   our Virginia-North Carolina family.

This family research has   been most fas-cinating   in   that the   older generation   has been much easier to trace than the later gen-erations. Unfortunately, we have   not   found the   interest in   the   present generation   of this family that we have in   others and, as a result, are lacking all too much.....but with what we have......may we invite you to take a look at *Descendants of James   J. Simms*   and *Ann Phillips* following   the   FOOTNOTES.

F O O T N O T E S

[1] Information furnished   by *William Perry Johnson*, professional genealogist of Raleigh, N. C. He points   out   that the schedules   of the 1790 Census for   the   states of Delaware, Georgia, New Jersey, and Tennessee are   miss-ing. The   1790   Census for   Virginia,   which included Kentucky, was also lost, but Virgin-ia's 1790 Census was replaced by   a   compila-tion of tax records taken from the 1780s.

[2]   The English were using the *Julian* Calen-dar rather than the *Gregorian* Calendar.There-fore, 1587/8 would mean the former year under the Julian Calendar and the latter year under the Gregorian. The year under the Julian Cal-endar changed   in   the middle of March rather than January 1. Thus, any date in January and February, and   the first couple   of   weeks in March, would show as   one year earlier on the Julian Calendar than on   the Gregorian Calen-dar as we use today.

[3] Patsy Hunter, otherwise Martha Hunter, was the daughter of Jacob Hunter and Sarah Rogers who according to Wake County Marriage Bond Records were married Nov. 25, 1783. In the N. C. Archives, under Wake County Estates Feb. Term of Court, 1807 on back of one of the documents reads: "On the Petition of Joel Simms and Patsy his Wife & others Who are Infant children orphans of Jacob Hunter decd. being exhibited to this Court, It is Ordered that Isaac Hunter Senr. the Grandfather of the said Infants be and he is appointed their Guardian pending the proceedings on the said Petition to guard their rights and Interests in the same." Wake Co. Marriage Bonds show that on Dec. 18,1822 Sarah Rogers Hunter, the widow of Jacob Hunter, married James Nance. Thus, we see that Martha (Patsy Hunter) was the daughter of Jacob Hunter and Sarah Rogers and the granddaughter of Isaac Hunter whose wife is unknown to us.

Descendants of James J. Simms and Ann Phillips

I   Ludolphus A. b   1841 d   [1] m
June 5, 1875 Mrs. Alice Wheeler Patton [2]
b   d   CHILDREN:

    A   James   NFI

    B   Anne   NFI

    C   Louie   NFI

    D   Henry   NFI

    E   Allie May   NFI

    F   Myrtle   NFI

II   Camillus Duke b March 30, 1844 d July 22,
1844 *

III J. D.   b Feb. 12, 1849 d Aug. 29, 1870 *

IV Ella A. b Dec. 10, 1850 d April 2, 1937* m
Nov. 16, 1871 [3] John Henry White b May 17,
1849 d Mar. 3, 1901 CHILDREN: SEE SEPARATE
LISTING under DESCENDANTS OF JOHN HENRY WHITE
and ELLA SIMMS

V   W. C. ** b Mar. 25, 1853 d *   1896**
UNMARRIED

VI C. L., b   (Shown as girl, age 5, 1860
Census, died before 1870 Census.)***

VII J. Y., b   (Shown as girl, age 5 1860
Census, died before 1870 Census)***

VIII Kate Hunter b   1858 d   [4]
m   George Washington Wheeler b
d   [5] CHILDREN:

    A _____a boy, died at birth

*   Buried in Uniontown Cemetery

**   His name is spelled *Sims* on the tombstone &
has the date 1895 as when he died. But, if
you will refer to WILLS, COURT RECORDS and
OLD LETTERS you will find a letter dated
July 6, 1896, Holland, Tex.

*** Buried in family plot,Bellview Bt.,Dallas Co.

B Charlotte Ann b   **m**   Dewey
Newman b   d   CHILDREN:

1 Kate Eller b   d   1908,
3 years old

2 Emma Elizabeth b   **m** FIRST
Walter J. Rothchild b   d
NO ISSUE

   m SECOND   Lee Le Blanc b
CHILDREN:

   a L. A.   NFI

   b Michael

   c Charlotte

C Charles Dochtoman b Nov.   1883 d Aug.
1946 m Sept.   1912 Lucille Berry b
March 1, 1896 d   CHILDREN:

1 Lois Marjorie b Jan. 20, 1914 m
FIRST Feb. 16, 1935 Richard Earl
Tackett b July 24, 1907 d Aug. 27,
1958   CHILDREN:

   a Elizabeth Dee Ann b Sept. 5,
1938 m June 2, 1961 John
Edward Forsythe b   CHILD:

      i Elizabeth Ann b Jan. 1,
1963

   b Marjorie Gayden b Mar. 18,1944
m Mar. 8, 1963 James DeWayne
Bone II b   NO ISSUE

   m SECOND July 22, 1960 Gilbert
Cleatus Maynard b Feb. 25, 1917
NO ISSUE

2 George Dochtoman b July 6, 1916 m
Dec. 7, 1941 Ruby Inez Milstead b
Aug. 1911 d June   1963 CHILDREN:

   a George Hardy b Oct.   1942

   b Ruby Lucille b Aug.   1944

      c   Dick Milstead b

D   Ella Pearl b   m FIRST   W.J.
     Poche b   d   CHILDREN:

    1   Lucille b   m   F. W.
       Smith b   CHILDREN:

       a   Robert b   m
          Betty Weller b

       b   Frentiss Ann b

    2   Charlotte b   m   L.E.
       Martin II b   CHILDREN:

       a   Charlotte Ann b

       b   Nancy b

    m   SECOND   W.C. Gill b

E   Emma Belle b Jan. 27, 1888 m April 15,
    1905 Ralph Joseph Poche b
    d July 9, 1955   CHILDREN:

    1   Ralph James b   m
          CHILD:

       a   Marvin James b   m
          Mrs. Peggy Forgy b
          NO ISSUE

    2   b   m
       Edward Abdalla b   CHILDREN:

       a   Carolyn Ann b

       b   Edward II

    3   George Herbert b   m
       Cecile Rousseaux b   CHILD:

       a   George Herbert II

F   A boy, died as an infant

IX   John K.   b Dec. 31, 1859 d Sept. 21, 1916 m
    July 20, 1891 T. (Tillie) Eleanor Dykes b
    d   [6]   CHILDREN:

A   Eleanor b May 29, 1893 d Oct. 12, 1901

B   James K. b Aug. 9, 1895 d Dec. 17,
      1933 [7]   UNMARRIED

F O O T N O T E S

[1] Dr. Peter A. Brannon, Director State of Ala.,
Dept. of Archives & History, states: "L. A. Simms
on original roll for Co. D, 4th Alabama Infantry
Regt., and dated from 25 April 1861 to Jan. 1865,
shows the following: 'Lew A. Sims (spelled Simms)
private, age 20; enlisted 26 April 1861 at Perry
County, Ala. for one year. He was present at the
Battle of First Manassas; Gains Farm; Suffolk;
Gettysburg; Hazel River; Chickamauga; Dandridge;
Spottsylvania; Wilderness; Hanover Junction; Cold
Harbor; Draytown; Mechanicsville Pike and Howlet
House. The record further shows he was born in Ala.
was single; a clerk and resident of the county.' "

[2] Widow of J. B. Patton who died Oct. 2, 1873.
J. B. Patton and Alice Wheeler had a daughter,
Bourrough, who married Jake Colson. Of this marr-
iage there were two sons: Milton Patton Colson and
Charles Foster Colson. It is my understanding
Henry Simms now lives with "Pat" Colson in Columbia
Marion Co., Miss.

[3] John Henry White and Ella Simms of Perry Co.,
were married at a plantation known as "The Sibley
Place" Nov. 16, 1871 by Rev. John S. Arbuthnot.

[4] Shown as age 2 in 1860 Census and as 12 in
1870 Census.

[5] George Washington Wheeler is brother of Mrs.
Alice Wheeler Patton who married L. A. Simms (see
I, page 1)

[6] Moved to Texas. All contacts lost.

[7] Though exact date of birth is not known, the
death certificate shows death as Dec.17, 1933, 38
years, 4 months, 8 days. Cause of death.....result
of coronary occlusion.

The Dorrohs

James Dorroh left the eastern shores
of County Antrim, with his wife Jane Brown,
and four children, for Charleston, South Carolina 200 years before I landed in Belfast on
a BOAC Vanguard.

James was coming across the Atlantic
to become a *Pioneer in His Own Right.*

I was visiting Northern Ireland with
the hopes of learning something about my ancestors.

Many changes had taken place in the
lapse of these 200 years. James and Jane had
come on a sailboat, taking weeks to make the
crossing. On my return I was flying a D-6B..
...returning in less than 11 hours from Glasgow to New York.

The first spot I visited was the House
of Records where a Miss Embleton made available much material.

My first obstacle was finding anything
about the Dorrohs. I looked and I looked.
Finally, in desperation, Miss Embleton heard
my story......you see, all family tradition
had said the Dorrohs not only came from North
ern Ireland, Ulster, but they came from County Antrim and here I was in the House of
Records in Belfast, head of the government
for County Antrim, and for all Ulster.

It did not take long for me to realize
people have a way of changing the spelling of

their names.

Only seconds passed, with the help of Miss Embleton, when I found James *Doragh* of Tully in Ballyclug Parish in a census taken in 1669 and a John *Doragh* of Connor Town, Connor Parish also in County Antrim. From the map of County Antrim, in the House of Records, these two towns are a matter of only a few miles apart....north and west of Belfast and nearly due west of Larne, then the second largest port of eastern Ulster.

Some have ventured that the Dorrohs sailed to Charleston from Belfast. However, without documentation, I have serious doubts. In the eighteenth century Larne was a thriving port itself. It was the closest port to Tully and to Connor Town....and to have sailed from Belfast would have meant traveling almost twice as far as had they left from Larne. While in County Antrim I did have the pleasure of visiting the seaports of Larne and Belfast.

Now that we found a James and a John Dorroh and we have come up with the belief that our James Dorroh most probably had sailed from Larne, we might even venture to say that our progenitor could have easily been either the grandson of James Dorroh of Tully, or the great grandson of John, of Connor Town. These two names (James and John) are so common in descendants of James Dorroh, the immigrant. And, while making these ventures, it could be that the progenitor's father was William Dorroh, because in the Scotch and Scotch-Irish custom of those days, the oldest son was always named for the paternal grandfather.

The most reliable information we have been able to find indicates James Dorroh was born May 25, 1738 and died June 24, 1820, age 82. His wife Jane Brown was also born in County Antrim the same year and died Oct. 22, 1836 at the ripe age of 98.

One of the real challenges in securing information on the Dorroh family has been the variable spelling of the name. Just as in the case of our James Dorroh, we find James *Daragh* as securing 200 acres of land in Craven County on a creek of Broad River and Brown Forks. This was certified by him on Nov. 2, 1762, and was surveyed by John Gaston on Jan. 27, 1763. We further find in Memorial Tax Return Book 6, page 107, that Eli Kershaw made a tax return for 200 acres of land in Charleston (then capitol of the colony) on Dec. 14, 1763 which belonged to James *Darragh* which had been surveyed by John Gaston on Jan 27, 1763....making the two one and the same), and we find in the Colonial Deeds that this same land was sold in 1764 to Eli Kershaw.

This information might lead us to wonder if our progenitor actually was living in America in 1762, 63 and 64; for we find in the South Carolina Archives that James *Daragh* "lately arrived from Ireland with his family" and was allowed 350 acres of land. This land was situated on Duncan Creek and was certified for him on Nov. 8, 1772. This land was on the branch water of the Enoree River in then Berkeley County, South Carolina. It was surveyed by Patrick Cunningham (of whom we shall read more about under the chapter on *The Cunninghams*) Sept. 30, 1774.

This property was described as bound on one side by vacant land and the other by Roger Brown, believed to have been the brother of Jane Brown [1]....wife of James Dorroh. This information is found in Memorial Book 13 page 504 and the plat is marked Irish, which means that James *Daragh* came with his wife and children direct from Ireland as immigrants through the Port of Charleston. This record shows that James *Daragh* was over age 16, and so was his wife; and he had four children between the age of 2 and 16.

Memorial tax returns made in Charleston by James *Daragh* was made June 9, 1775 for his 350 acres of land and more specifically identifies its exact location by stating it was on Duncan Creek of the Enoree River where Brown Fork empties into Duncan Creek in Berkeley Co., S. C.

We were talking about the various spellings of the family name and here we seem to have digressed slightly to prove the location of the Dorroh property and to document the time he and his family did come to America to make their permanent home, so let's go back to the various spellings of the name!

Albert J. Huber, Bakersfield, California, has done considerable research on the Dorroh family and came up with the 1800 Census to find a John Dorroh, William and a James, but all three of the brothers were listed as *Dorough*. Mr. Huber made a real study of the different spellings and has come up with 21 different ways: Mac Oara or Mac Oarac which means *Son of Dubhdarach*, or in our own every day language means *Black man of the Oak*.....or, I freely interpret this to mean, that the Dorrohs were brunettes or darker than many of the fair-haired people of Northern Ireland and they were strong and sturdy as the oak.

He adds that "I found others such as : Dorroh, Daragh, Darragh, Darrogh, Darra, Darrock, Dara, Darrah, Darrow, Darrough , Darral, Darroh, Dorra, Dorrah, Dorrough , Dorough, Doroh, Durrah, Mac Dara,Mac Adarra, and Mac Dara."

(And, please let me add that the 1790 Census of South Carolina, District 96, Pendleton Co., shows one James *Durrow*, still another way of spelling the name Dorroh. This census shows him head of the household with one son under 16 and one daughter under 16. This would account for Martha who was then 14 and James II who was 11. No other Dorrohs were listed as heads of households in South Carolina and where the other children were living is not known.)

Many of the various spellings of the name may be contributed to errors in recording deeds or wills in courts, and others may come by the actual inability (lack of education) of certain county officials to spell or that they spelled a name as they thought it sounded and, thus, wound up with a type of phonetic spellings.

Let's take some court records in Laurens Co., S. C. where we find in Book L, page 159 where James *Dorrah* and his wife Sarah *Dorrah* signed a deed April 10, 1824. Book G, page 655 shows James *Durroh*, signed a deed

May 24, 1787 to Matthew Brown for 35 acres of land on Duncan Creek "which was an original grant to me on Dec. 9th, 1774, but this James shows his spelling the first time in America as *Daragh*.

We could go on and on with other illustrations, but this should be sufficient to show the difficulty in documenting accounts, but since the present descendants of the original James have adopted the spelling of Dorroh, we shall henceforth use this spelling.

Fortunately, the spelling does not give one away in the pronunciation of the name. But, I found difference in pronunciation as well as the spelling. Some pronounced Dorroh as though its first o was a long o; some as though it was Dur; and some as though the first o was a short o; and I argue not which pronunciation is correct.

But, let's get back to our immigrants, James and Jane Brown Dorroh:

Information in the South Carolina Archives from Memorial Book 13 shows them to have had four children between the ages of 2 and 16 when they came to America in 1772, in this order:

I   Margaret b ca 1765 County Antrim [2]

II   Nancy b ca 1766 County Antrim d 1840 Madison Co., Alabama m 1792 William McDavid   NFI   [3]

III   William b ca 1767 County Antrim d ca 1807 Laurens Co.S.C. m ca 1792 a Miss Dunlap b ca 1770 d ca 1807 Laurens Co.

S. C. [4] CHILDREN: See listing under DESCENDANTS OF WILLIAM DORROH AND MISS DUNLAP.

IV John b March 16, 1769 County Antrim d Nov. 23, 1851 Tuscaloosa Co., Ala. m Rebecca Jones b Aug. 27, 1770 d Aug.4 1852 Tuscaloosa Co., Ala. [5]CHILDREN: See separate listing under DESCENDANTS OF JOHN DORROH AND REBECCA JONES.

V Martha b Sept. 22, 1776 Laurens Co.S.C d Oct. 28, 1855 Perry Co., Ala. m Feb. 11, 1795 William Cunningham b Feb. 23, 1770 d Sept. 15, 1822 Laurens Co.,S.C. CHILDREN: See separate listing under DESCENDANTS OF WILLIAM CUNNINGHAM AND MARTHA DORROH under chapter on: *The Cunninghams.*

VI James b ca 1779 d Feb. 25, 1842, age 63 [6] m Sarah Ross b Dec. 22, 1783 d July 20, 1856. Both lived and died in Laurens Co. and he was executor of his father's estate. CHILDREN: See separate listing under: Descendants of JAMES DORROH II AND SARAH ROSS.

When James Dorroh reached Charleston with his wife and four children (family tradition relates) he secured a Negro slave who he named Antrim for his old home county. The two, by horseback, proceeded across the state to Old District 96, which was truly the back woods section of South Carolina. After clearing the new ground he went back to Charleston for his wife and four children. This section was not settled by whites until the 1760s and rather slowly until near the beginning of 1770 when the immigration picked up.

Charleston was the capitol of the Colony and all deeds and records were supposed to be kept there, of course, because of the long and hazardous distance many of the early transactions never reached the capitol and, thus, have never been recorded. Charleston remained the capitol of South Carolina until 1790 when Columbia was selected because of its more central location.

The Carolinas (North and South) got their name in 1629 when Charles I of England gave a large patent to Sir. Robert Heath which he specified should be called Province of Carolana from the word *Carolus*, Latin name for Charles. A new patent was granted by Charles II to the Earl of Clarendon and others when its spelling was changed to Carolina. In 1729 the Carolinas were divided into North and South.

In 1768 an Act of the South Carolina Assembly divided the colony into seven judicial districts, District 96 being one of them.

In 1783 an ordinance was passed to divide District 96 and other districts into counties of a convenient size, none more than 40 miles square. Under the ordinance the counties of Edgefield, Abbeville, and Newberry appear to be the first laid out. The Act of the General Assembly of March 12, 1785 divided the remainder of Old 96' into Laurens Spartanburg, and Union Counties. The counties in South Carolina remained as counties until 1799 when their names were changed back to Districts, i.e. Laurens District. Again, during Reconstruction days, after the Civil War, the Districts reverted back to counties.

With all the boundary switching and changing in the early days of South Carolina, it is easy to see how difficult it is to locate documented information. Let's take for instance: It was not until 1913 that it was required to register a marriage license or a birth. Back in those old days the boundaries were changing so rapidly that in one year you would find papers, or documents, about a certain person in one county, and then you would go back to check on other transactions and find nothing. What happened is that a year or two after the first transaction was recorded, the person was in another county, though he had not even moved the front porch rocker in that time.

On the whole, court records are drab, but some do bring out interesting light...... for instance: April term of Court, 1814 James Dorroh, Sr. was drawn as a juror. His excuse for not attending was that he was upwards of 74 years old and "dull of hearing." He was excused!

Another interesting venture in the Dorroh research is that there is a grave in the Union Baptist Church Cemetery between Reedy River and Rabon Creek on S. C. Highway 54, south of Friendship Presbyterian Church, saying "Capt. James Dorroh, died Sept. 17, 1857, age 57 years.......(b 1807)

"As a husband, master and neighbour,
In every relation exemplary,

"Each lonely scene shall thee restore
For Thee the tear be daily shed,
Belov'd till life could no more,
And mourn'd till pity's self be
dead"

Beside his grave was that of his wife:

"Mrs. Martha (Hamilton) Dorroh, wife
of Capt. James Dorroh.....died July 18, 1873,
age 74"(b 1799) and the inscription reads:

"Remember mortal as you pass by,
As you are now, once was I,
As I am now, so you must be
Prepare for death and follow me."

And, of course the same old saying
comes up "not until I know where you went!"

This one gave trouble as we could not
locate the parents nor have we ever under-
stood anything even since glancing over the
contents in Box 129, package 5 (Laurens Co.)
where we find the settlement of the Capt.
James Dorroh estate in which Martha Dorroh
was the executrix. His will starts "I, James
Holliday, otherwise called James Dorroh....."
and he leaves his property to his wife. The
will was witnessed by W. D. Simpson, Alexander McCarley and Thomas M. Young. The appraisal of his estate shows he had 19 slaves and
his total estate was valued at $23,371.45.

All of this would indicate there were
no children, but we even ventured to review
the will of Martha Hamilton Dorroh! Her will
was dated Aug. 28, 1858 and was proved July
21, 1873. This is recorded in Laurens Co.

Book B, pages 279-80 and letters on page 597. It is shown that Mary Downey and her husband, Samuel Downey, are the closest of kin residing in the State of South Carolina. It is also brought out that Martha had a brother residing in the State of New York, named Alexander Hamilton, which verified her maiden name, and she has also a sister living in Ireland "beyond the seas". Her nephews James Downey and John Hamilton were appointed trustees.

We find the estate of Capt. James Dorroh settled and that of his wife, but we have never been able to tie-in why James Holliday should have changed his name to James Dorroh!

Another mystery, never completely resolved, is the name of the Dunlap girl who married William, oldest son of our progenitor. Footnote 4, which follows, will be interesting.

We know that William had a son named James and he married Belinda Hyle Wright. We have this complete line, but we were puzzled with a Perry Co., Alabama marriage license, showing James *Dorrough* married Catherine Gary Oct. 22, 1833. This was puzzling as "our James" first child was born ca 1827. Search and search we did until we found the 1850 Census of Alabama which shows living in Perry Co., Alabama a James *Dorrah*, age 47, who was born in Virginia and his wife, Catherine, born in South Carolina....they had six children. To confuse the matter even worse, one of the children bore the name John, another Martha, and another James.....all so common in our Dorroh family.

Catherine Gary's father was William and his will signed July 7, 1836 was recorded July 1, 1839 and among his provisions he states, "It is my will and desire that slaves and all cash to my daughter, Catherine, should be secured for her benefit and used during her natural life and to her children after her death. Everything of hers is to be vested in William Hartley (not her husband James *Dorrah*) in trust to be managed and controlled by the said Hartley. At her death everything remaining and the slaves are to be conveyed by title (the slaves) to her children." Thus, after hours and days of research, we find there to be no family connection between James Dorroh and James *Dorrough*, later spelled *Dorrah*.

And, I mention the above to indicate the patience and pains we have extended in trying to be as accurate as possible in all information and statements in our book.

James and Jane Brown Dorroh lived out their lives in South Carolina. On the grave of James is written "Sacred to the memory of James Dorroh, Sr., who departed this life, 24th of June 1820, aged 82 years, Blessed are the dead that die in the Lord." He is buried in the Dorroh Cemetery located in a patch of woods called "Dorroh Fields" near Friendship Presbyterian Church.

Beside his grave is that of his wife. The inscription reads, "Here lies the body of Mrs. Jane Dorroh who died Oct. 22, 1836, having lived to the extraordinary age of 98 years. All flesh is grass and all the goodlings thereof is at the flower of the field. Isaiah XL 6th verse." In this same plot is the grave of Jane Dorroh, daughter of Sarah Ross and James Dorroh, Jr. (d July 22, 1810) and one "to the memory of William Holliday, deceased, who departed this life Oct. 18, 1826, age 70."

The next stone is so badly broken that only the word Holliday can be seen. Nine other graves are in this cemetery with only old field stones as markers.. It be believed that all are members of the Dorroh family. Older members of the family in South Carolina recall being told that William Dorroh, son of the immigrants, and his wife are buried in this cemetery and this is more than likely as William and his wife died 13 years before his father.

In the very early days of District 96 churches were scarce, but the old Scotch and Scotch-Irish were deep in their religion and would meet in various homes on the Sabbath and then, finally, in Meeting Houses. Near Gray Court neighbors built a Presbyterian Church, known as Friendship Church, which is located between Rabun Creek and Reedy River, and the church was built on land given by James Dorroh and John Cunningham, according to Mrs. C. D. Wilson in her pamphlet on EARLY HISTORY OF FRIENDSHIP PRESBYTERIAN CHURCH. The church was organized about 1819 and was the fifth church in the county. When the church was first built it was used by the Methodist and Baptist as well as the Presbyterians, and in the passing of time, only the Presbyterians remained.

The present church building is its third one. Records show several family names mentioned prominently in these books such as the Dorrohs, Simpsons, Boyds, Blakelys, Lewers, and Cunningham as taking active part.

It is interesting to note that when the Dorrohs and Cunninghams migrated to Alabama they, too, established a Presbyterian Church. It was located about five miles south of Marion at the intersection of present day State Highway 5 to Mobile and the 183 Farm-to-Market Road to Uniontown....and, as expected, the church was named Friendship Church. In this church, like the South Carolina Church, members of "our" family played prominent parts, serving as Deacons and Ruling Elders;even to the donating of the ground for the erection of the church.

Just as James and Jane Brown Dorroh came to Charleston nearly 200 years ago and moved to the undeveloped western section of South Carolina and became *Pioneers in Their Own Rights*, we find Nancy Dorroh and William McDavid came early to Madison County, Alabama and thus became *Pioneers in Their Own Rights*. Then, John and Rebecca Jones Dorroh moved to western Kentucky about the turn of the nineteenth century and then to Alabama almost two years before it became a state on December 14 1819, and thus John and Rebecca truly became *Pioneers in Their Own Rights*.

William Dorroh and his wife, son of the immigrant, died in South Carolina in 1807. We find their sons John, William and James living in Perry County before this state was ten years old;and thus, these three brothers became *Pioneers in Their Own Rights*.

Martha Dorroh Cunningham, the youngest daughter of the immigrants and their first child born in South Carolina, came to Perry County shortly after her husband's death and settled near her nephew John Dorroh who had married her daughter Jane Cunningham, and thus Martha and her unmarried children truly became *Pioneers in Their Own Rights*.

The only children of the immigrants , our progenitors, to remain in South Carolina were Margaret, William and James, Jr.

To make the moves into the wilds and pioneer, there is no wonder that we can truly believe the original name of Dorroh had an English meaning: *Black man of the Oak*...with oak being symbolic of strength and sturdiness.

F O O T N O T E S

[1] In the Laurens Library is a book on the Roger Brown Family of Ireland. It states a sister of Roger Brown married in Ireland to a man by the name of *Darrough* and he came over to America later and settled on Duncan Creek by his wife's brother, Roger Brown, Sr. Perhaps this clarified the confusion that has existed that James Dorroh's wife was Jane; or Jean Rankin. Mrs. Sarah Dorroh Wilkes, in a paper on the Ross family, lists David Ross and his wife, Jean Rankin, to have come to America from County Antrim and to have had 5 children. Their second

child was Mary Ross and married first a
Mr. McCullough and married second John B.
Simpson who bought much of the property
left the children of William Dorroh.

[2]   George F. Dorroh, the son of David Ross
Dorroh and Susan B. Lewers and the grandson of James Dorroh II, who inherited
the lands of his father, the immigrant,
wrote a letter to Henry Phillips White,
of Marion, Perry Co., Alabama on May 21,
1920, stated Margaret was a daughter of
the immigrants, but did not give her age
nor her marital status. All other children are accounted for.

[3]   No attempt has been made in working out
the line of Nancy Dorroh and William Mc-
David as Mrs.Rosa McDavid Munger is pre-
paring to include this in a book she
later hopes to -publish. However, under
WILLS,COURT RECORDS AND OLD LETTERS will
be found what we have about this line
which is in the Tutwiler Room (Southern
History)of the Birmingham Public Library.

[4]   The 1800 Census of South Carolina, Dist-
trict 96 shows William Dorroh to be head
of a household and to have two sons under 10 years of age who would, of course,
have been John and James F., which means
Samuel and William were born after 1800
as is shown. This same Census also
shows William Dorroh to have had 2 girls
under 10 years of age living in his household and one girl between 10 and 16.
The name of the latter is not known nor
is it known for sure she was a daughter.

In the Administration of the estate of William Dorroh (Nov. 29, 1808) by James Dorroh, the father, it is stated that there were 6 children (the proceeding of the estate is in File 19-10 Laurens Co., S. C.). If the girl listed in the 1800 Census as between 10 and 16, was a daughter, then she, or one of those under 10 in the 1800 Census, died before their parents; and the other must have died before the settlement of the estate as we have only been able to locate five who shared in the division. Perhaps this book will bring to light the children of William Dorroh who are unaccounted for and clear up the name of his wife.

[5] John Dorroh lived in South Carolina for a while after his marriage and then moved to Kentucky in the western section before 1809. From Kentucky he moved to Tuscaloosa Co., Alabama by 1818 and had been living in the Alabama Territory more than a year before Alabama became a state in December 1819.

[6] The will of James Dorroh was written April 23, 1810 and was proved Oct.2,1820. He named his son James as executor and says, "he is to have all since for many years he cared for me in my old age." Other children were not listed by name as he states he has already provided for them. Witnesses to the will were John Taylor, George Grace, and William Downs. The appraisers of his property were William Arnold, John Wiseman and Henry Burrows.

Descendants of James Dorroh and Jane Brown

I   Margaret b ca 1765 County Antrim

II   Nancy b   1766 County Antrim d   1840 Madison Co.,Ala. m   1792 William McDavid b   d

III   William b   ca 1767 County Antrim d   ca 1807 Laurens Co., S. C. m ca 1792 Miss Dunlap b ca 1770 d   ca 1807 CHILDREN: SEE SEPARATE LISTING under DESCENDANTS OF WILLIAM DORROH AND MISS DUNLAP

IV   John* b March 16, 1769 County Antrim d Nov. 23, 1851 Tuscaloosa Co. Ala. m   Rebecca Jones b Aug. 27, 1770 d Aug. 4, 1852 CHILDREN: SEE SEPARATE LISTING under DESCENDANTS OF JOHN DORROH AND REBECCA JONES

V   Martha b Sept. 22, 1776 Laurens Co. S.C. d Oct. 28, 1855 Perry Co. Ala. m Feb. 11, 1795 William Cunningham b Feb. 23, 1770 d Sept. 15, 1822 Laurens Co. S. C. CHILDREN: SEE SEPARATE LISTING under DESCENDANTS OF WILLIAM CUNNINGHAM AND MARTHA DORROH

VI   James II b   ca 1779 d Feb. 25, 1842 age 63, buried Laurens Co. S.C. Friendship Church, m   Sarah Ross b Dec. 22, 1783 d July 30, 1856 Both lived and died in Laurens Co. S.C. CHILDREN: SEE SEPARATE LISTING under DESCENDANTS OF JAMES DORROH II and SARAH ROSS

*   Deed of Gift of John and Rebecca Dorroh can be **found** in Tuscaloosa Co. Court House.

Descendants of William Dorroh and Miss Dunlap

I   Ann b May 16, 1794 d July 27, 1885 m Jan.
26, 1815 John Owings b Sept. 12, 1783 d Aug.
12, 1872 Lived and died in South Carolina
CHILDREN: SEE SEPARATE LISTING under
DESCENDANTS OF ANN DORROH AND JOHN OWINGS

II   John b May 4, 1797 Laurens Co.,S.C., d Sept.
26, 1854 Perry Co.Ala., m ca 1818 in S. C.
Jane Cunningham b Jan. 28, 1801 Laurens Co.
S. C., d Jan. 20, 1883 Perry Co.,Ala.
CHILDREN: SEE SEPARATE LISTING under
DESCENDANTS OF JANE CUNNINGHAM AND JOHN
DORROH

III   James F. * b   1799 d May 9, 1864 m
Belinda Hyle Wright b   ca 1808 d Nov. 13,
1873, age 65, CHILDREN: SEE SEPARATE LIST-
ING under DESCENDANTS OF JAMES F. DORROH and
BELINDA HYLE WRIGHT

IV   Samuel b   ca 1801 d Dec. 23, 1874 m [1]
CHILD: SEE SEPARATE LISTING UNDER DESCEND-
ANTS OF SAMUEL DORROH

V   William b   ca 1804 d   1870 m FIRST
Jane Gordon Baird (sometime spelled Beard)
b ca Sept. 17, 1808 in Ga., d Jan. 29,1857,
age 48 yrs, 4 mos. 12 days CHILDREN: SEE
SEPARATE LISTING under DESCENDANTS OF
WILLIAM DORROH AND JANE GORDON BAIRD

     m SECOND Oct. 22, 1857 Mrs. Eliza Ann Evans
Fagan b   d   CHILDREN:
SEE SEPARATE LISTING UNDER DESCENDANTS OF
WILLIAM DORROH AND ELIZA ANN EVANS FAGAN

[1] Date and name of wife unknown. She died
early for he sold his lands inherited from
his father on Sept. 17, 1823 and there was
no renunciation of dower by his wife. (South
Carolina marriage records as a whole in the
early days are very incomplete.)

*   Settlement of Estate of James F. and Belinda
Dorroh may be found in Greene Co., Ala.

Descendants of Ann (1) Dorroh and John Owings

I   William Butler b Oct. 13, 1815 d Jan. 28,
    1871 m March 14, 1839 Greenville, S. C.
    Cisely Ann Jenkins b   d 1889 [2]
    CHILDREN:

   A   Adolphus John   NFI, other than
       he lived Huntsville, Ala.

   B   Juliet Caroline b   NFI

   C   David William b   d in early man-
       hood

   D   Sarah Matilda, died young

   E   Samuel Dorroh, died in early manhood

   F   Butler Spillman b   d in infancy

   G   James Rapley, b   d in infancy

II Richard Rapley b June 13, 1818 d Nov. 20,
    1858 Anderson Co., S. C. m Dec. 22, 1842
    Laurens Co. S. C. Elizabeth Reeves b
    d Jan. 22, 1907 Atlanta, Ga. CHILDREN:

   A   James Archibald Lafayette b   [3]

   B   Susan Wesley b   NFI

   C   John Dorroh   b   NFI other than he
       lived in Atlanta, Ga.

   D   Amelia Caroline b   NFI

III James Berry b Sept. 8, 1820 d Oct. 16, 1884
    m FIRST Oct. 9, 1845 Laurens Co., S. C.
    Nancy Caroline Boyce b   d Mar. 8,
    1860 [4]   CHILDREN:

[1] Quite frequently called Nancy

[2] Moved from Laurens Co.,S.C. to Miss. & lived
     in Columbus & Louisville. Both buried Cedar
     Hill Cemetery, Columbus, Miss.
[3] Killed in Civil War
[4] Both buried Byhalia, Marshall Co.Miss.

A   Emily Creswell b   d young

B   John Dorroh b   NFI other than he
lived Byhalia, Miss.

C   William Anderson b   NFI

D   Caroline Boyce b   NFI

m SECOND Jan. 16, 1866 Shelby Co., Tenn.
Martha Elizabeth Small b   d March
26, 1928 Miller, Miss. Buried Byhalia,
Marshall Co., Miss.   CHILDREN:

E   Cora Lee b   NFI

F   James Rapley b   NFI other than
he lived DeSoto Co., Miss.

G   Lulu Jane b   NFI

IV   John Dorroh b March 23, 1823 d Jan. 31, 1847
Killed at Buena Vista., Private Co.D, 2nd
Miss. Infantry

V   Catherine b June 1, 1825 d   m Jan. 4,
1844 Laurens Co., S. C. Simeon Putnam b   NFI

VI   Sarah b Oct. 5, 1827 d   m Dec. 14,
1848 Laurens Co., S. C. Leonard Griffith NFI
other than understand they moved to Texas.

VII Jonathan Hellams b June 29, 1830 d May 15,
1915 m FIRST Jan. 29, 1857 Nancy Mary Stoddard b   d July 13, 1864. Both
buried New Harmony Cemetery, Owings, S. C.
CHILDREN:

A   John Calvin   NFI

B   Sarah Catherine   NFI

m SECOND Dec. 12, 1865 Sarah Elizabeth
Ranson b   d Feb. 14, 1920 Buried
New Harmony Cemetery, Owings, S. C. CHILDREN:

C   William Rapley b   NFI other than
moved to Quitman, Ga.

D   Robert Cresswell b   NFI other
     than lived in Laurens, S. C.

E   Mary Nancy   b   NFI

F   Caroline Lee,   died at birth

VIII Archibald Cresswell b Dec. 23, 1832 d Dec.
     28, 1922 m Feb. 4, 1858 Nancy Williams
     Brooks b   d Oct. 22, 1916 Both
     buried Dial's Cemetery near Gray Court,S.C.
     [1]   CHILDREN:

A   Sarah Emily b   NFI

B   James Franklin b   NFI other
     than lived Greenville, S.C.

C   Jane Monima   NFI

D   John Dorroh b   NFI other than
     lived Laurens, S. C.

E   Bartlett Brooks, b   d in infancy

F   Anna Maria b   NFI

G   Susan Allen   NFI

H   Archibald Cresswell II b   NFI
     other than lived Gray Court, S. C.

I   Charles Butler b   NFI other than
     lived Owings, S. C.

J   Claude Lamar   b   NFI other than
     lived Laurens, S. C.

IX   Samuel Dorroh b Aug. 15, 1836 d Nov. 12,
     1869 m Dec. 6, 1855 Nancy Dial b
     d June 11, 1911 Both buried Dial's Cemetery
     near Gray Court.   CHILDREN:

A   Ella Ann b   NFI

B   John Franklin b   NFI other than
     lived Laurens, S. C.

[1] He served as 2nd Lieut. Co.E, S.C.InfantryCSA

C   Richard Rapley b   NFI other
than lived Owings, S. C.

D   Mary Susan b   NFI

E   Catherine Elizabeth   b   NFI

F   Samuel William   b   NFI
other than lived Owings, S. C.

Appreciation goes to Prof. D. M. Owings, Dept. of
History, University of Oklahoma, Norman, Oklahoma
for the above information.

Descendants of James F. Dorroh and Belinda Hyle Wright

I   Julia Ann b ca 1827 d before 1864 m Nov. 19,
     1842 Greene Co., Ala. James A. Tallman b ca
     1820 S. C. d   CHILDREN:

     A   Lizzie Oliver b   d   [1]
          m before 1864 Benjamin Franklin Roden
          b Jan. 5, 1884 d Feb. 23, 1908 [2] NO
          ISSUE

     B   Timothy Thorpe b Mar. 10, 1840 d Sept.
          26, 1883 m May 8, 1880 Annabelle Pier-
          son b Jan. 9, 1855 d Mar. 25, 1911 [3]
          CHILD:

          1   Timothy Thorpe II b   1882 d 1944

     C   Harriet (Hattie) [4] b   d   m
          a Mr. Smith b   d   NFI

II   Susan Anderson b   ca 1832 d before 1864
     m William Robert Sample b   d
     (Lived in Gadsden)   CHILDREN:

     A   Willie   b   d   m
          Marcus Lucellus Foster b   NFI

     B   Lutiola Levert b   d age 14

     C   NFI

[1] Understand she lived only six months after
     her marriage.

[2] He married a second time to Ella Lee Didlake,
     a granddaughter of John Dorroh & Jane Cunn-
     ingham. John & James Dorroh were brothers.
     Refer to DESCENDANTS OF JANE CUNNINGHAM &
     JOHN DORROH.

[3] Annabelle Pierson was daughter of Sarah Man-
     ima Cunningham and Eleazer J. PAerson. See
     DESCENDANTS OF JOHN CUNNINGHAM & SARAH
     MAHAFFEY.

[4] Living in Etowah Co.,Ala. in 1875, mentioned
     in the settlement of her üncle Samuel Dorroh
     of Perry Co.   John Dorroh, husband of Jane
     Cunningham, was brother of Samuel as was
     James F.above mentioned.

III John Hyle [1] b   1839 Erie, Ala. d
Dec. 6, 1888 New Orleans, La. m FIRST   Molly
Melton b   d   CHILDREN:

A   Marie Eloise b Oct. 30, 1859 Forkland,
Ala. d June 5, 1931 Shreveport, La., m
Nov. 2, 1894 Alexander Covington Monette
b Dec. 31, 1843 Adams Co.,Miss. d Feb.
2, 1899 Tallulah, La. CHILDREN:

1   Julian Dunbar b Sept. 14, 1894
Madison Parish, La. m Apr. 20,1927
Georgine W. Frentz b Dec. 15, 1900
CHILDREN:

a   Jean Elizabeth b Aug. 10,1928
m Feb. 16, 1953 Lawrence D.
Stout b June 29, 1926 CHILDREN:

i   Linda Jean b Dec. 26,
1953

ii   David Lawrence b May 30,
1956

iii Kathaleen Louise b July
29, 1960

iv   Wesley Eugene b June 6,
1962

b   Betty Eloise b July 21, 1933
m Aug. 9, 1958 Dr. John D.
White b Nov. 17, 1935

c   Nell Dunbar b Dec. 4, 1937 m
Nov. 21, 1956 Ray N. Hemphill
b Aug. 28, 1937 CHILDREN:

i   Christopher b June 22,
1960

ii   Wendy (girl) b Mar. 24,
1963

[1] Third Lieut. Co. B, 7th Ala. Cav. joined
at Eutaw, Alabama.

2   Anita Dorroh b Aug. 12, 1898 Madison Parish, La. m Sept. 8, 1924 Ellis F. Brakefield b Mar. 10,1892 CHILD:

    a   Marjorie Ann b July 16, 1929 m Sept. 14, 1957 Julian F. Martin b Jan. 12, 1927 CHILDREN:

       i   Monica Jeanette b Mar.26, 1958

       ii   Tobi Roxanne b Feb. 29, 1960

                        *

3   Arthur Gayle b Aug. 12, 1898/ Madison Parish, La. m Feb. 24, 1924 Laura Perreand b Sept. 10, 1902 d Sept. 2, 1961   CHILDREN:
* d Nov.13,1963,Shreveport, La.
a   Louis Gayle b July 13, 1925 m Nov. 29, 1957 Patricia Ann Penny b   CHILD:

       i   David Page b Sept. 4, 1959

    b   David Ogbourne (twin) b Aug. 1, 1929 m Nov. 11, 1953 Betty Jean Browne b   CHILDREN:

       i   Glen Arthur (twin) b July 18, 1955

       ii   Benjamin Roe (twin) b July 18,1955

       iii   Laura Elizabeth b June 4, 1958

       iv   Betty Browne b Nov. 20, 1961

    c   John Dorroh (twin) b Aug. 1, 1929 m June 4, 1955 Sara Eudora Lemmons b Aug. 27,1934 CHILDREN:

       i   Michael Andre b Sept. 28,

1959

    ii   Martha Ann b Sept. 18,
          1963

B   Julia Elizabeth b   ca 1863 m
    McGehee b   CHILDREN:

    1   Balfour b

    2   Clinton b   d   1914
         m   CHILD:

         a   NFI

    3   Julie E. b   1889 m June 14,
         1911 E. C. Mohtgomery b July 13,
         1891   CHILDREN:

         a   Alex b   NFI

         b   Olivia

         c   Mona

         d   Retta

C   Molly Epps b Feb. 22, 1865 Forkland, Ala
    d Jan. 2, 1949 m Dec. 18, 1888 John
    Henry Thurmond b April 25, 1861 Jeffer-
    son, Marengo Co., Ala., d Nov. 22, 1924
    Both died Dallas, Tex. CHILDREN:

    1   Robert H. b April 28, 1890 d April
         28, 1890

    2   Clifton D. b Aug. 25, 1891 d Aug.
         25, 1891

    3   Marie b Jan. 20, 1893 Hollandale,
         Miss. m Aug. 30, 1912 Francis M.
         Rembert b Mar. 20, 1893 Living
         Big Spring   Tex. CHILDREN:

         a   Frances Thurmond b Aug. 17,
              1913 d June 17, 1915

         b   Ruth b May 4, 1915 m Aug. 8,
              1936 Andrew G Edmonson I b
              Aug.10, 1910 d Mar. 8,1963

b   CHILDREN:

    i   Andrew G. II b Jan. 24, 1938 (teacher SMU,Dallas)

    ii   Bernadene (Bebe) b May, 25, 1939 m Jan. 20, 1962 Ardis McCasland II b

4   Robert Hyle b May 30, 1895 Murphy, Miss. m Etta Caspary b CHILDREN:

    a   Robert Hyle II b

    b   James Edward b

5   Clifton Dorroh b July 8, 1904 Longview, Tex. m Aug. 2, 1929 Lorene Amyette b   CHILD:

    a   James Edward b

III m SECOND Jan. 7, 1867 Orline Baldwin Melton b Nov. 30, 1850 Hollow Square, Greene Co.,Ala d April 10, 1934 Durant, Miss. CHILDREN:

D   Alice b Mar. 1, 1868 d July 18, 1873

E   Nan (twin) b Nov. 6, 1869 d Nov. 13, 1869

F   Linda (twin) b Nov. 6, 1869 d Nov. 13, 1869

G   James Hyle b Feb. 3, 1873 d June 12, 1874

H   Iva May b June 22, 1875 d Aug. 30, 1878

I   William Gayle b April 29, 1878 Madison Co. Miss. d Aug. 10, 1945 m Nov. 29, 1905 Mary Lee b April 22, 1880 d Mar. 17, 1953. Both died Jackson, Miss. CHILDREN:

    1   Katie Lee b Nov. 12, 1906 Jackson, Miss. m June 26, 1930 Winton Houston b Jan. 19, 1902 CHILDREN:

a   Thomas Gayle b April 7, 1932 Pacific Grove, Cal. m Sept. 17, 1954 Nell Rose Reese b July 21, 1933 CHILD:

     1   William Talmadge b Dec. 14, 1962 Greenwood,Miss.

b   Katie Lee b Sept. 4, 1940 Jackson, Miss. m June 30,1962 Howard Terry Worrell II b Sept. 3, 1935

2   John Hunter b Dec. 20, 1910 Jackson, Miss. m Nov. 28, 1935 Marie Lillian Verchota b Sept. 6, 1904 CHILDREN:

    a   John Hunter II b Feb. 2, 1937 UNMARRIED

    b   William Gayle II b Mar. 12, 1938 Jackson, Miss. UNMARRIED

J   Ida Virginia b Sept. 22, 1880 Madison Co. Miss. Living Canton, Miss. m March 9, 1902 George Robert Bennett b May 14, 1874 Camden, Miss. d Sept. 8, 1952 CHILDREN:

1   Robert Hyle b March 22, 1904 m July 1, 1930 Gladys Lowery b NO ISSUE   Lives Springfield, Ill.

2   Walter Gayle (Buddy)(twin) b June 9, 1910 m Dec. 2, 1933 Elizabeth (Tib) Blalock b April 23, 1916 CHILD:

    a   Raye Wayne b Jan. 20, 1935 m Oct. 24, 1953 Craig Morris b April 2, 1933 CHILDREN:

      i   Walter Craig b Oct. 12, 1956

      ii   Randall (Randy) Ray b April 10, 1959

3   Albert George (twin) b June 9,
      1910 m July 5, 1935 Caroline Weir
      b Nov. 29, 1911 CHILDREN:

      a   Albert George II b Aug. 8,
           1937 (teacher, Miss. State Un.
           Starkville, Miss.) m May 28,
           1960 Sarah Lyle b June 30,
           1938

      b   Alma b Nov. 28, 1940 UNMARRIED

      c   Robert Horace b Apr. 10, 1946

K   Omega b June 5, 1883 Issaquena, Miss. d
    March 13, 1956 m June 6, 1906 Clifton D.
    Mann b May 9, 1880 d Dec. 26, 1939 Both
    buried Mannsdale, Miss. CHILDREN:

    1   Lois Baldwin b June 8, 1908 m FIRST
         June 21, 1931 John Law II b Jan. 4,
         1905   CHILD:

         a   Sara Jane b Nov. 12, 1935 m
              Aug. 5, 1961 Robert Anthony
              Marchese b   CHILD:

              i   Michael Watson b Sept.
                   14, 1962

         m SECOND   Walter Charles DeHority
         b Nov. 10, 1895 d Feb. 24, 1958
         Laurel, Miss.   CHILD:

         b   Debora (Debbie) Mann b Nov. 8,
              1952

    2   Ruth b Nov. 9, 1910 m Jan. 19,1936
         Henry Elner Watson b Jan. 1, 1908
         CHILD:

         a   Henry Clifton b Jan. 9, 1945

    3   Julius Daniel (Dee) b Oct. 18, 1914
         m Nov. 2, 1940 Anita Vigil b Oct.
         8, 1919   CHILDREN:

         a   Ann Dee b Aug. 2, 1941 Mag-
              nolia, Miss. m April 5, 1962

J. K. Stringer II b Aug. 10,
1940   CHILD:

i   J. K. III b Dec. 6, 1962
Quantico, Va.

b   Ellen Ruth b March 27, 1944
Magnolia, Miss.   UNMARRIED

c   Robbie Fay b Sept. 6, 1953
Magnolia, Miss.

IV   Samuel [1]b   ca 1840 Erie, Ala. d Sept. 25,
1861

V   Ida Virginia b ca 1841 d   m Feb. 28,
1868 James Polk Rogers b Dec. 5, 1841 d
after 1901   CHILDREN: SEE SEPARATE LIST-
ING under DESCENDANTS OF SAMUEL DORROH

VI   Inez Clifton b   ca 1842 Erie, Ala. d   1885 m
Thomas Jefferson Mayfield b   d
Both buried Monroe, La.   CHILDREN:

A   Andrew Middleton b   d   NFI

B   James Dorroh b July 12, 1875 d Oct 31,
1930 m Aug. 4, 1897 Susie Katherine
Epperson b Nov. 8, 1880 d Nov. 4, 1935
CHILDREN:

1   Morris Taylor b Aug. 22, 1899 m
Dec. 27, 1926 Oneal Thomas b Dec.
17, 1903   CHILDREN:

a   William Vaughn b May 12, 1927
m Dec. 8, 1960 Louise Nichols
b June 25, 1932   CHILD

i   William Scott b Dec. 6,
1962

[1]   CSA, Co. I, Fifth Ala. Inf. Died of typhoid
in Civil War.

b   Morris Cecil b Aug. 22, 1930
m May 12, 1953 Margaret
Christenberry b May 14, 1932
CHILDREN:

    i   John Richard (Ricky) b
        Dec. 6, 1955

    ii   Robin Elise b Dec. 29,
        1958

c   Doris Oneal b Mar. 2, 1933 m
Dec. 25, 1955 Robert Lee
Langham b Nov. 14, 1932
CHILDREN:

    i   Donna Lynn b Dec. 6,
        1960

    ii   Brenda Lee b June 12,
        1962

2   Aimee b Dec. 6, 1902 m Dec. 1, 1926
John Houston McCrory b Dec. 16,1894
CHILD:

    a   James Houston b Dec. 27, 1927
        m Dec. 24, 1949 Loretta Burt
        b July 3, 1930 CHILDREN:

        i   Loretta Kay b Oct. 5,
            1952

        ii   Pamela b Sept. 28, 1956

3   Alma b Nov. 20, 1905 m Jan. 4,
1928 James Dallas Rayfield b Oct.
14, 1904   CHILD:

    a   Mary Lucile b Nov. 22, 1928 m
        Sept. 23, 1944 Valcus George
        Smith b Dec. 31, 1925
        CHILDREN:

        i   Debra b Aug. 2, 1947

        ii   Jimmy b Nov. 26, 1951

b   Jamey b April 3, 1930 m Sept. 11, 1954 Helen Boyd b June 14, 1935   CHILDREN:

     i   Ruth Alma b Mar. 17, 1956

     ii   Rickey b Jan. 11, 1958

c   Peggy R. b Aug. 20, 1938 m Dec. 19, 1958 George Simpson b Aug. 24, 1936   CHILDREN:

     i   Darrel b May 24, 1960

     ii   Melissa b Mar. 15, 1962

4   Lucy Dell b Jan. 27, 1908 m Nov. 28, 1931 Richard Marvin Thomas b May 18, 1907   CHILDREN:

a   Richard Marvin II b Jan. 12, 1935 m Oct. 4, 1962 Edith Richards b July 3, 1936 CHILDREN:

     i   Michael Richards b July 14, 1954

     ii   Lucy Leigh b Apr. 17, 1956

     iii   Bruce Delane b Dec. 10, 1958

     iv   Rose Myra b Dec. 11,1960

b   Allen Boyd b June 4, 1937 m Jan. 17, 1957 Joe Stewart Thomas b   CHILDREN:

     i   Allen Scott b Dec. 12, 1958

     ii   Bryan Boyd b Dec. 24, 1960

     iii   Candice Allene b June 28, 1961

5   James Dorroh II b Aug. 6, 1911 m Jan. 28, 1933 Elizabeth Britton b Oct. 14, 1915   CHILDREN:

a   Mary Catherine b Nov. 1, 1934

b   Jimmy Dorroh b April 15, 1939 d Dec. 22, 1945

6   William M. b May 28, 1915 m Nov. 24, 1938 Lucy Carr b Nov. 22, 1918 CHILDREN:

a   Carolyn Inez b Oct. 30, 1939

b   Barbara Ann b Jan. 17, 1946

C   William Thomas b April 24, 1880 Living Birmingham, Ala. m Nov.   Eunice Helton b Aug. 28, 1887 d June 12, 1957 CHILDREN:

1   Margaret Helton b Sept. 23, 1908 m FIRST   Frank Chambers b NO ISSUE

m SECOND   George Welch b CHILDREN:

a   Patricia Ann b Jan. 7, 1937 m Richard (Dick) C. Hitt b CHILDREN:

    i   Deborah Lynn b March 30, 1957

    ii   Donna (twin) b Dec. 8, 1960

    iii   Deanne (twin) b Dec. 8, 1960

b   Bettye Jane b July 28, 1938 m William Carl Goodwin b CHILDREN:

    i   Katherine Lee b June 30, 1958

ii   William Carl II b Oct.
      14, 1959

iii   Gregory Thomas b March
      1, 1963

c   Barbara Jean b July 28, 1938
    m   Douglas Charles
    Davies b   CHILD:

    i   Douglas Charles II b Feb.
          14, 1962

m   THIRD   Dan W. Horton II
b   NO ISSUE.

2   Annie Clifton b May 29, 1914 m June
    28, 1933 William Courtenay Renneker
    b Sept. 14, 1910   CHILDREN:

    a   William Courtenay II b Dec.
        30, 1936 m June 3, 1961
        Dorothy Kendrick b Sept. 12,
        1937   CHILD:

        i   Margaret Ann b Sept. 24,
              1962

    b   Ann Mayfield b June 8, 1940 m
        Sept. 2, 1961 Lucian Ferris
        Bloodworth b Nov. 7, 1940
        CHILD:

        i   Lucian Ferris II b June
              21, 1963

3   William Thomas II b Oct. 29, 1923
    m   Mary Clyde Deaver b
    CHILDREN:

    a   Mary Clyde b July 10, 1949

    b   Margaret Ann b Apr. 2, 1953

    c   William Thomas III b March 1,
        1954

    d   Marsha b April 14, 1956

D   _____ b   d in infancy

VII   India b   d age 18   UNMARRIED

VIII Elmira b   d in infancy

IX   James F. II b   d in infancy

X   William Gayle [1] b Oct. 2, 1844 Erie, Ala.
d Feb. 16, 1929 m Jan. 31, 1866 Greensboro,
Ala. Eliza Jane Robinson [2] b ca 1841 d Jan 12
1926   CHILDREN:

    A   Clara Leslie b Sept. 18, 1868 Madison
        Co. Miss. d July 16, 1958 m   Thomas
        Landrum Darden b   d
        Lived Fayette, Miss.   CHILDREN:

        1   Robert Leon b Apr. 16, 1899

        2   Clara Dorroh b Dec. 19, 1903 d
            Feb. 1960   NFI

        3   John Gayle b Sept. 29, 1906 m
            Frances Marie Bombeck b

        4   Annie Fleming b Apr. 1, 1910 m
            John Thomas Dalton b   CHILD:

        a   John Thomas II b

    B   William Gayle II, M.D., b Aug.   1870 d
        Feb. 6, 1931 m   1898 Estelle Stewart
            1875 d Mar. 1, 1929 Buried
        adison, Miss.   CHILDREN:

        1   Will Edwin b Mar. 15, 1900 m Nov.29,
            1935 LaVerne Hollingsworth b
        CHILDREN:

        a   Will Edwin II b June 28, 1937
            m Jan. 13, 1962 Zelma McPher-
            son
        b   James Robert b Jan. 24, 1940
            UNMARRIED

[1] Left Univ. of Ala. to join CSA. When he was 81,
the University gave him a degree. His will may
be found in Canton, Miss.& his son James
Franklin's will also.
[2] Great great granddaughter of William Robinson,
a Colonial Governor.
* We are indebted to Mrs. Marie Upton for help here.

2   Eleanor b June 5, 1905 m   Jacob Alexander Lonas b   CHILDREN:

      a   Jacob Alexander II   NFI

      b   Edwin Gayle   NFI

      c   Ellen

      d   Marilyn

               1874 *
C   James Franklin b ca/ UNMARRIED   NFI

D   John Hazard b Apr. 29, 1878 Madison, Miss. d May 1, 1961 m FIRST 1905 Louise Laurence Dawson b April 18, 1880 Yazoo City, Miss. d May 8, 1925 CHILDREN:

    1   Mary Louise b May 13, 1907 Oxford, Miss. m Nov. 12, 1930 Byron Patterson (Pat) Harrison b Sept. 24,1908 Living Gulfport, Miss.[1] CHILDREN:

      a   Patricia Louise b June 10, 1933 m Jimmy Roy Webb b Aug. 30, 1928 CHILDREN:

          i   Louise Adell b June 24, 1954

          ii   James Patton   20, 1955

          iii John Harrison b   7, 1960

      b   Mary Ann b July 24, 1936 m FIRST   Bruce Allen b CHILDREN:

          i   Mary Catherine b Dec. 25, 1955

          ii   Patricia Gale b Aug. 19, 1957

[1] Son of former Senator Pat Harrison of Miss.
*   James was a poet. He died Oct. 11, 1943.

b   m SECOND Samuel Franklin
Everett Warren b Jan. 20, 1935
CHILD:

     iii   Samuel Franklin b April
11, 1963

c   Louise b July 3, 1944

2   John (Jack) Hazard II b Oct. 6,
1910 Oxford, Miss. d Sept. 4, 1963
m FIRST   1932 Martha
Crymes b   CHILDREN:

a   Mary Nele b Aug. 10, 1933 m
James O'Neal b
CHILDREN:

     i   James Allen b May 10,
1956

     ii   Nelessa Lee b Sept. 13,
1959

b   Jacqueline Cordelia b June 4,
1936 m   Louis
Hernandez b
CHILDREN:

     i   Robert Clayton b   NFI

     ii   Theresa

     iii   Joseph Coleman b April,
1963

c   Suzanne Catherine b
m   Robert Coleman
Cash b   CHILDREN:

     i   Laurie Elizabeth b March
18, 1960

     ii   Tammy Lynn b May 8, 1963

m SECOND   1951 Marion
Wheeler b   d Apr. 12,
1957 Claremont, Calif. NO ISSUE

2   m THIRD Dec. 25, 1960 Vivian Ellen
     Holstrom Milbauer b Nov. 6, 1923
     NO ISSUE

D   m SECOND Mrs. Mattie Cavett Thompson[1]
     b Dec. 11, 1882

[1] Her children are: Allen Cavett Thompson (may-
or of Jackson, Miss. since 1948) and John Cavett
Thompson.

Descendants of Samuel Dorroh (wife unknown)

I   Annis Caroline b 1823 d 1902 (grave marker
Marion Cemetery) m   George C. Rogers
b ca 1814 in N. C.,   d   [1] CHILDREN:

    A   James Polk b Dec. 5, 1841 Tenn. d
          m Feb. 28, 1868 Ida Virginia Dorroh b
          ca 1841 d   [2]   CHILDREN:

        1   Samuel W. b 1870 Perry Co. Census
             shows 1 year old. Does not appear
             in 1880 Greene Co. Census. Died
             in between.

[1] The 1880 Perry Co. Census shows Annis Caroline Dorroh's mother & father were born in S. C.
and the mother & father of George C. Rogers were
born in N. C. The Rogers' lived in Tenn. a while,
then moved to Perry Co. where Samuel Dorroh had
recently moved to join his brother John. George C.
Rogers was editor of The Marion Commonwealth for a
number of years. The 1870 Perry Co. Census shows
he was living in Cunningham Beat about a mile
north of Washington Creek. His property ran about
a half mile on both sides of present Highway 5.
When he became editor of the paper they apparently
moved to town, or very near the town; for in 1899,
April 20 to be exact, the George C. Rogerses trans=
ferred their home site to their son John C. Rogers
unmarried; and at that time they were living in
Brazos Co. Tex.

[2] Ida Virginia Dorroh was the fifth child of
James F. Dorroh & Belinda Hyle Wright. James F.
Dorroh was a brother of Samuel Dorroh; thus James
Polk Rogers was a grandson of Samuel. Perry Co.
1870 Census shows this couple was living with Samuel Dorroh and Mr. Rogers was shown as a lawyer.
The Greene Co. 1880 Census shows him as a grocer
in Forkland and that his mother was born in S. C.
and his father was born in N. C., and he was born
in Tenn. The Register of the University of Ala.
(Officers & Students) 1831-1901 shows him living
when the book was published in 1901 and him to be
a planter, and that he entered the University in
1859 from Marion, and that he was a private in
Co. G, Fourth Alabama, CSA.

2   Annis Kathleen (Kate) b Dec. 5,
1880 Forkland, Greene Co.,Ala.
Living Monroe, La. m Nov. 22,
1899 George Augustus Klie b March
12, 1870 Demopolis, Ala. d June
1948   CHILDREN:

a   Annis b Jan. 28, 1906
UNMARRIED Girl Scout District
Adviser.

b   Lu McClinton b Nov. 12, 1909
m Jan. 25, 1935 Howard Yeild-
ing b Jan. 25, 1899 d Jan.
21, 1964   CHILDREN:

    i   Lu Klie b Dec. 7, 1935
Birmingham, m Nov. 2,
1957 James Asbury Downey
III b Aug. 23, 1930
CHILDREN:

       [a]   James Patton b Oct.
4, 1960 Huntsville,
Ala.

       [b]   Howard Yeilding b
July 8, 1963 Hunts-
ville, Ala.

    ii   Howard Bee b March 7,
1945 Student Vanderbilt

c   Roger Preston b July 15, 1912
Pine Bluff, Ark. m July 15,
1938 Nathalie Counce b March
11, 1917 Grady, Ark. Living
Grady, Ark.   CHILDREN:

    i   Catherine Sue b Sept. 1,
1939 Grady, Ark. m Aug.
12, 1959 Nesbit Morgan
Ryall II b   1937
CHILDREN:

       [a]   Sandra Sue b May 27,
1961 Yorktown, Ark.

       [b]   Nesbit Morgan III b
Dec. 20, 1962

d   Clifton Dorroh b Jan. 9, 1920
Pine Bluff, Ark. m Feb. 13,
1952 Evelyn Anita West b Nov.
16, 1931 Clanton, Ala. Living
in Birmingham. CHILDREN:

i   Elizabeth Anita b Nov.
17, 1952 Clanton, Ala.

ii   Larry West b Jan. 16,
1955, Clanton, Ala.

iii   William David b Dec. 27,
1960 Birmingham

3   Inez E. b   d   [1]

B   Amanda D. b ca 1844 d   m Nov. 1,
1864 John A. True b ca 1831 d   [2]
CHILDREN:

[1]   The 1880 Greene Co. Census shows no mention
of Samuel W. who was listed in the 1876
Census. The 1880 Census shows Annis C. who
no doubt is Annis Kathleen (Kate) Rogers, as
2 years old and it shows Inez E. as four mo.
old. Miss Annis Klie, 502 Roselawn, Monroe,
La. on Oct. 30, 1963 wrote, "The sister, Inez
E., died at the age of 18 or 19." She further advised "there were a good many more
children before my mother, none of them whom
lived long." She further advises James Polk
Rogers, her grandfather, was wounded in the
Battle of Mannassas in 1863.

[2]   Perry Co. Tax records show the True land on
Washington Creek, south of Marion, about five
miles. It was listed as J. A. True in 1905-6,
while the 1907 list had a line drawn through
J. A. and Amanda was written in. For 1908 and
9, the listing showed Mrs. A. D. True. This
could indicate Mr. True died in 1907.

```
1      Samuel b ca 1870 d          NFI [1]

2      Ella Lou b           d             m
       Charles C. McLendon b           d

C      Cora b ca 1850 d         [2] m    Luman G.
       Crawford b          d             NFI

D      Samuel b ca 1853 d            m   Bettie
            _____ b ca 1858 d           NFI

E      George b ca 1855 d       NFI   [3]

F      John C.  b ca 1861 d          [4]

G      Willie (girl) b ca 1863       NFI
```

[1] Sam True was quite a baseball player. Have no
record as to his having married nor when he died.
It is most likely that he died before Oct. 10,
1909 because on that date Amanda D. True, her
daughter Ella Lou and her husband Charles C. Mc-
Lendon, sold to L. A. Morgan Jr. and F. Meyer 200
acres on Washington Creek. Amanda D. True and the
McLendons gave notarized statements from Tarrant
Co. Tex. indicating they were living away from
Marion. L. A. Morgan is listed under DESCENDANTS
OF JOHN FRANK MORGAN.

[2] Older living citizens of Marion remember her
as living with her brother John C. Rogers in the
old George C. Rogers home and to have married
"late in life". She graduated from Judson College
in 1876.

[3] Perry Co. 1880 Census shows him as 25 and a
student.

[4] Perry Co. Book 99, page 241, Apr. 20, 1899
shows Annis Caroline Dorroh and her husband George
C. Rogers, both Brazos Co.,Tex. to deed to their
son, John C. Rogers of Perry Co., a tract of land
1/2 mile from Marion containing 10 acres. Book 113
page 67, Jan. 7, 1901 shows John C. Rogers, an unmarried man (would be 40 years old) transfers the
same 10 acres of land described to James B. Jones
of Dallas Co. This is the last land transaction of
John C. Rogers we can find in Perry Co.; so we
could assume he moved from Marion or that he might
have remained there unmarried & without property.

Descendants of William Dorroh and Jane Gordon Baird (Beard)

I   William [1] b ca 1828/30 d ca 1853 Jackson,
     Miss. m ca 1848 Rhoda Blake (or Flake) b
     CHILDREN:

     A   William Wells b ca 1849 Miss. d 1883
          Milam Co. Tex. m Rebecca Elizabeth Brooks
          b 1849 Tex. d 1889 Tex. CHILDREN:

          1   Ida Elizabeth b Oct. 22, 1870 Milam
               Co. Tex. d Nov. 13, 1956 Clay, Tex.
               UNMARRIED

          2   James b   1873 d young [2]

          3   Rhoda b Sept. 18, 1875 Milam Co.,
               Tex. d Sept. 10, 1955 m Dec. 23,
               1905 James A. Bass b   NO ISSUE

          4   Henry H. b July 20, 1877 Milam Co.
               Tex. d   1937 McClennon, Tex.
               m   1899 JAsie Smith b
               NO ISSUE

          5   Nettie b Feb. 5, 1880 Milam Co.,Tex.
               m Aug. 19, 1903 A. T. Ray b Mar. 2,
               1882 d Nov. 27, 1943 Kaufman, Tex.
               CHILDREN:

               a   Elizabeth Ann b Oct. 20, 1904
                    Bexar, Tex. m June 8, 1927 J.C.
                    Cunningham b   CHILDREN:

                    i   Robert Gibson b Oct. 22,
                        1931 m   1952
                        Sarah Caldwell b
                        CHILDREN:

                        (a)   Dianne
                        (b)   Sally

                    ii   Jo Ann b Aug. 8, 1934 Clay
                        Tex. m   1957 Ray
                        Thomas b   CHILD:

[1] Tradition says this son was William.....we
have been unable to find authentic records on him.
However, he was listed as head of Household in
1830 Census.
[2] Found in 1880 Census, Milam Co., Texas.

        (a)   Mark b   1961

b   Avriett T. b June 6,1906 d Nov.
27, 1951 Arizona m July 18,1937
Marguerite McMurry b
CHILDREN:

    i   Alfred T. b Apr. 14, 1941
           m   1963 Nan
           Collins b

    ii   Nancy Beth b Dec. 26, 1938
           m Dec.   1961 Alton
           White b

c   John H. b Oct. 2, 1908

d   James Bass b Dec. 29, 1910 m
1937   CHILDREN:

    i   Rita Ann b Oct. 15, 1939 m
           Ray Castle b

    ii   Georgia Beth b Sept. 24,
           1942
    iii   J. C. b Mar. 12, 1947

e   Florence b Apr. 4, 1913 m June
8, 1933 A. D. Donnell b
CHILDREN:

    i   George Lee b Apr. 18, 1934
    ii   Peggy Ray b Apr. 15,1937

f   Nettie Dorroh b Nov. 8, 1915
Coleman, Tex. m Aug.   1938 E.
I. Hall, M.D., b
CHILDREN:

    i   Janette b Dec. 14, 1942
    ii   Ray Edward b June 4, 1945
g   Frances b Aug. 30, 1918 Coleman
Tex. m Apr. 29, 1937 Wayne O.
Watts b   CHILDREN:
    i   Waynette b June 8,1938 m
           1960 Tom Welch b   CHILD:
           (a) Milinda
    ii   Bill Orville b Aug.19,1940
           m   Mary Ann
    iii   Linda b May 8, 1945

iv   Sharon b Nov. 7, 1952

h   Charles W. b Dec. 29, 1923 m Sept. 24, 1952 Mary Lynne Fox b   CHILDREN:

      i   Rush b Apr. 12, 1954

      ii   Ricky b Aug. 30, 1956

      iii   David b Nov. 7, 1958

6   Jesse Robert b Sept. 29, 1881 Cameron, Milam Co., Tex. d Aug. 1941 m   1903 Ruth Elizabeth Porter b Dec. 22, 1885 d Jan. 24, 1954   CHILDREN:

  a   Joe Lee b Sept. 22, 1904 m June 3, 1931 Jaime Raquel Benson b Sept. 12, 1908 CHILDREN:

      i   James Robert b Apr. 21, 1937 m Aug. 1959 Elizabeth Jones Brett b July 22, 1935   CHILD:

          (a)   Rebecca Ruth b Apr. 7, 1960

      ii   Edgar Joe b Aug. 14, 1938 m Dec. 1957 Barbara Ann Spinks b July 6, 1940 CHILDREN:

          (a)   Beverly Jean b July 9, 1958

          (b)   Joe Barber b Oct. 11, 1959

      iii   Basil Raymond b Oct. 25, 1944 d May 26, 1947

  b   Ruth Elizabeth b Nov. 13, 1908 m Apr. 29, 1934 Louis Milton Bennett b Nov.15, 1905 CHILDREN:

      i   George Samuel (Sam) b June 21, 1941

      ii   James Dorroh (Jim) b Dec. 20, 1946

B   Henry Jethro b Dec. 1, 1850 Jackson, Miss. d Jan. 17, 1929 Hays Co. Tex. m Nov. 17, 1874 Frances (Fannie) Abigail Shaw Mathis b Oct. 17, 1850 Mo., d Aug. 28, 1926 Austin, Tex.   CHILDREN:

1   John Washburn b March 8, 1876 Rockdale, Tex. d Sept. 11, 1928 m Nov. 11, 1898 Annie Zepora Olive b Jan. 19, 1881 Taylor, Tex.   CHILD:

    a   Henry William b April 19, 1900 Fitzhugh, Tex. m FIRST Lila Simms b   CHILDREN:

       i   Jerald b

       ii   Harold b

       iii   Jack

       m SECOND   Melba Ratcliff b   CHILD:

       iv   Douglas b

    b   Floyd Clifford b July 23, 1902 Fitzhugh, Tex., d   as infant.

    c   John Olive b Sept. 5, 1904 Fitzhugh, Tex. m Sept. 4, 1928 Nellie Roland b June 25, 1904   CHILD:

       i   John Olive II b Dec. 30, 1946

    d   Fannie Elizabeth b Nov. 12, 1907 Cameron, Tex., m Nov. 15, 1927 Thomas Bracey II b   CHILD:

    i   Thomas III b Oct. 28, 1930

e   Mable Emily b Nov. 16, 1909 Cameron, Tex. m Apr. 6, 1953 Lowell H. Pearson b June 18, 1904   NO ISSUE

f   Floye Bee b Jan. 3, 1912, Fitzhugh, Tex. m Mar. 19, 1933 L. K. McKnight b Jan. 4, 1900   CHILDREN:

    i   James Irving b Nov. 9, 1943

    ii   Pamela Ann b Nov. 25, 1945

g   Lola May b June 1, 1914 Beaukiss, Texas m June 15, 1933 Fred Solomon b Aug. 16, 1909 CHILDREN:

    i   Katherinne Ann b Feb. 23, 1935

    ii   Eugene Fred b Aug. 29, 1937

    iii   Floyd Dean b Mar. 5, 1940

h   Edward Charles b Nov. 21, 1918 Houston, Tex., m FIRST Dec. 21, 1940 Verna Ozenne b CHILD:

    i   Janeen Ann b Sept. 21, 1941

m   SECOND Aug. 4, 1951 Kathryne Glasscock b CHILD:

    ii   Kimberly b Dec. 4, 1957

2   Wells William b Feb. 13, 1879 Fitzhugh, Tex. d Jan. 5, 1925 m Nov. 1902 Ophelia Townsend b CHILDREN:

a   Edgar b Sept.   1904

b   Dolly Mae b Feb. 17, 1912

c   Rose b

d   Robert

e   Wells William II b

3   Addie Eugenia b Sept. 13, 1881 m
FIRST   James Gunn b
CHILD:

    a   Thomas Franklin b July 26,
         1899 Fitzhugh, Tex. m Sept. 6,
         1919 Vivian Alice Davis b
         Nehawka, Neb.   CHILDREN:

        i   Vivian Ellouise b Aug. 1,
             1920, Fullerton, Calif.
             m July 19, 1940 Robert
             Cutler b July 13, 1917

        ii   Thomas Franklin II b
             Sept. 24, 1923 m July 7,
             1946 Rosemary Alber b
             Dec. 30, 1924

        iii   William Davis b May 26,
             1929 d Dec. 1, 1957 m Apr
             28, 1950 Faye Kellstrom
             b Apr. 15, 1933

        iv   Robert James b May 7,
             1931 m Sept. 21, 1952
             Marilyn Fredrick b Aug.
             21, 1932

    m SECOND Jan. 9, 1912 Charles
    Wilson Sullivan b   d   1962
    CHILD:

    b   Eugenia Illeen b Dec. 9, 1919
         m   S. L. McBride b

4   James Robert b July 26, 1884 d
      June 8, 1926   UNMARRIED

5   Mattie Roberta b Feb. 27. 1887 m
     Aug. 4, 1909 Edward Franklin Pres-
     nall b   d June 17,
     1954   NO ISSUE

6   Jefferson Davis b March 17, 1889
     Fitzhugh, Tex. m June 5, 1920 Eva
     Nell (Jean) Stout b Sept. 17, 1903
     CHILDREN:

     a   Jefferson Davis II b Mar. 14,
          1921 m Mar. 17, 1942 Mary
          Freel b Oct. 20, 1920
          CHILDREN:

          i   Jean Marie b Aug. 22,
               1943, Miami, Fla.

          ii   Jefferson Davis III b
               Dec. 8, 1944 Riverside,
               Calif.

          iii Catherine Mary b Nov. 15,
               Nyssa, Oregon

          iv   Anita Fay b Mar. 19,
               1953, Nyssa, Oregon

          v   Phyllis Craig b April 12,
               1955, Nyssa, Oregon

          vi   Susan Marie b Oct. 20,
               1959, Ontario, Oregon

     b   Raymond Phillip b Feb. 4, 1923
          m   Joetta Adams b
          CHILD:

          i   Adams b

     c   Jacqueline Fay b July 9, 1925
          m   1945 Gerald
          R. Clevenger b Feb. 24,
          CHILD: NFI

     d   Roberta Joyce b Mar. 26, 1937
          m   Robert F. Keller
          b   CHILDREN: NFI

II   Sarah Jane b Aug. 5, 1832 Ala. d Aug. 15,
      1897 m Dec. 24, 1848 Spencer May Atkinson b
      May 2, 1818 Ala., d Oct. 19, 1888 CHILDREN:
      SEE SEPARATE LISTING UNDER DESCENDANTS OF
      SARAH JANE DORROH AND SPENCER MAY ATKINSON

III   Frances [1] b   m   Jones
      b   CHILDREN:

      A   L. L. b   NFI
      B   Sallie b   NFI

IV   John A. b ca 1835 Ala. d Sept. 30, 1882
      UNMARRIED

V   Samuel B. [2] b ca 1841

VI   James Madison [3] b Dec. 3, 1844 Noxubee,
      Miss. d July 31, 1910 Big Sandy, Tex. m Aug.
      17, 1874 Sallie Pillow Durham b Mar. 23,
      1848 CHILDREN:

      A   Cameron Durham b Nov. 4, 1875 Tex. d
           Dec. 1, 1904 m July 20, 1896 Katie Baird
           b Nov. 20, 1879 d June 13, 1904CHILDREN:

           1   Cameron Durham II b Mar. 29, 1900
                Big Sandy Tex. d Dec. 23, 1931 m
                Nov. 1, 1924 Emma Lou (Louise)Banks
                b Aug. 7, 1907 CHILDREN:
                a   Corinne b Oct. 25, 1925
                b   Cameron Durham III b Sept. 5,
                     1927 m Oct. 3, 1959 Patricia
                     Ann Bennet b Oct. 28,1938
                     CHILD:
                     i   Cynthia Ann b May 9,1961
                          Truth or Consequences,N.Mex.

[1] In Newton, Miss. in 1875. Listed as heirs of
William Dorroh in Samuel Dorroh's estate settlement.
Believe her name was Frances, but unverified.
[2] In 1850 Noxubee Co.Miss.Census, age 9. Not in
heirs of Samuel Dorroh in 1875 as an heir of Samuel-
's brother William Dorroh.Must have d before Oct. 2,
1875. In Kemper Co.Miss. Marr.Records, Ben Dorroh m
Emiline Brooks on Oct. 28, 1874.

[3] A member of the Legislature of Upshur Co. Tex.
in 1897.

2   NFI

B   Pearl b Aug. 26, 1877 d Oct. 26, 1889
aged 12 yrs., 2 months.

C   James Madison II b Mar. 7, 1879 m April
17, 1900 Minnie Lowery b July 1, 1882
CHILDREN:

    1   Evelyn b Feb. 28, 1901 d Jan. 1,
1960 m FIRST May 27, 1924 W. B.
Knox b

        m SECOND July 19, 1939 V. H. Sholl
b   d Oct. 21, 1954

    2   Lois b June 26, 1903 m Dec. 26,
1923 Hilary B. Hebert b Feb. 15,
1896   CHILD:

        a   Jane b Feb. 21, 1928 m Dec. 1,
1945 E. A. Dunn b Dec. 21,
1927   CHILDREN:

            i   Jan Evelyn b Oct. 21,1945

            ii   Hilary Jennifer b Nov. 3,
1948

D   Corinne b Feb. 28, 1885 d Mar. 8, 1931
m Dec. 3, 1902 Jesse Barker b   CHILD:

    1   Infant,   b Jan. 17, 1904 d Jan.
19, 1904

VII   Zachary Taylor b May 30, 1847 Noxubee Co.,
Miss. d Sept. 26, 1919 m Feb. 11, 1873 Laura
F. McDonald b Oct. 31, 1846 d Jan. 10, 1912
CHILDREN:

A   Nellie G. b Dec. 5, 1874 d Nov. 14, 1893

B   Iva Lamar b April 11, 1876 d Sept. 31,
1931 m Apr. 7, 1909 Bessie Mae Greer b
1878   CHILDREN:

    1   Lamar Greer b May 25, 1911

    2   Elizabeth Justa b Oct. 30, 1913 d
June 8, 1942

3   Martha b Feb. 18, 1917 m Victor
        Parker b

C   Lillie E. b Feb. 19,   m W. W. Shannon
        b   d May 8, 1960

D   Lallie Whitsett b Mar. 23, 1887
        UNMARRIED

E   Ethel H. b March 20, 1890 m J. N.
        Lipscomb b July 3, 1886 CHILD:
        1   Jane b Feb.14,   m J. B. Agnew b
VIII (child) b   NFI   [1]

[1] Goodspeed in BIOGRAPHICAL AND HISTORICAL
MEMOIRS OF MISS. states there were eight children.
We have been unable to find the name of the eighth
child. Goodspeed mentions three: Sarah Jane,
James M., and Z. T......as being alive in 1891.

Descendants of William Dorroh and Mrs. Eliza Ann Evans Fagan

IX   Chastain Brackett (Tenie) b July 13, 1861 Noxubee Co.,Miss. d Aug. 8, 1914 m Nov. 28, 1882 Willie Jane Edwards b Jan. 13, 1863 Kemper Co.,Miss. d June 15, 1941 Buried Macon, Miss. CHILDREN:

    A   Herbert Eugene b Feb. 28, 1885 Noxubee Co.,Miss. d Feb. 2, 1962 m Sept. 22, 1910 Nell Clement b   CHILDREN:

        1   George Clement b Dec. 3, 1913 UNMARRIED

        2   Infant daughter b and d July 17, 1920

    B   Clinton Edwards b April 3, 1887 Shuqualak, Noxubee Co.,Miss. d Feb. 24, 1957 Jackson, Miss. m Dec. 8, 1928 Betty Durfree b May 30, 1884 NO ISSUE

    C   Jehn Evans b Dec. 20, 1889 Shuqualak, Noxubee Co.,Miss. Living Hot Springs, Ark. m Sept. 9, 1909 Jeannette Harkins b   CHILDREN:

        1   Walter Evans b Dec. 31, 1919 West Point, Miss. m April 26, 1952 Adrienne Prince b Jan. 11, 1923 Living Olla, La. CHILDREN:

            a   Walter Evans II b Feb. 11, 1953, Ferriday, La.

            b   William Edward b Jan. 26,1954 Ferriday, La.

            c   Adrienne Stephanie b Feb. 21, 1959 Vicksburg, Miss.

    D   Annie Maude b July 11, 1895 d Aug. 14, 1897 Macon, Miss.

    E   Elisha Edwards b Jan. 11, 1899 Macon, Miss. Living Dothan, Ala. m June 21, 1921 Alice Calmes b Apr. 14, 1898

E   CHILDREN:

1   Alice Calmes b Dec. 25, 1922 m Dec. 28, 1947 Macon Miss. Walter Frank Wood b March 9, 1917 Helena, Ark. CHILDREN:

     a   Walter Edwards b July 22,1954 Cleveland, Miss.

     b   Clinton Frank b Aug. 23, 1955 Cleveland, Miss.

     c   David Dorroh b June 5, 1958 Cleveland, Miss.

2   Jane Eloise b Feb. 13, 1929 m May 28, 1955 Dothan, Ala. Jack Tyson Brawley b April 11, 1925 CHILDREN:

     a   Jack Tyson II b May 24, 1957 Dothan, Ala.

     b   Edwards Dorroh b June 26, 1960, Bothan, Ala.

3   Brooks Reed b May 26, 1931 UNMARRIED

F   Mary b March 25, 1900 d March 25, 1900

X   Mary Ellen b Sept. 4, 1863 Mashulaville, Miss. d July 20, 1952 Jackson, Miss. m April 1, 1886 Shelton Minor Thomas b Dec. 6, 1860 d April 14, 1947   CHILDREN:

A   Shelton Minor II b Jan. 15, 1892 Macon, Miss. d April 3, 1959 Ellisville, Miss. m Nov. 28, 1917 Valera Sigrest b July 9, 1894   CHILDREN:

1   Elton Sigrest, M.D., (twin) b Sept. 29, 1921 Jacksonville, Miss. Living Columbus, Miss. m Aug. 19, 1944 Gene Webb b Dec. 16, 1923 CHILDREN:

     a   Elton Sigrest II b Dec. 1, 1949, Japan

      b   Keith Eugene b Nov. 10, 1953
           Vicksburg, Miss.

      c   Robert Craig b Oct. 5, 1957
           Vicksburg, Miss.

  2   Shelton Minor III (twin) b Sept.
       29, 1921 m Oct. 28, 1951 Laura
       Williams b Feb. 13, 1927 CHILDREN:

      a   Shelton Minor IV b Feb. 28,
           1955

      b   Laura Ellen b Oct. 2, 1957

B Annie Belle b Nov. 28, 1894 Macon, Miss.
  m June 7, 1916 William Albert Lyle b
  CHILDREN:

  1   Mary Evelyn b Jan. 30, 1919 Lauder-
       dale, Miss. m Oct. 10, 1947
       William Harold Davis b
       Living Tulsa, Okla.   NO ISSUE

  2   Katherine Thomas b Oct. 25, 1921
       Lauderdale, Miss. m Dec. 18, 1944
       Sid Adams b   CHILDREN:

      a   William (Bill) Sidney b Feb.
           20, 1948 West Palm Beach,Fla.

      b   Alan Clark b Aug. 11, 1952
           West Palm Beach, Fla.

      c   Karen Ann b Oct. 21, 1957
           Del Ray Beach, Fla.

C Ruby b April 5, 1896 Macon, Miss. m May
  13, 1918 William Verdo Westbrook b Mar.
  19, 1889 Living Jackson, Miss.
  CHILDREN:

  1   William Verdo II b Dec. 2, 1929
       Jackson, Miss. m Nov. 10, 1950
       Anderson, S. C. Barbara Ann Thomson
       b July 18, 1929 CHILDREN:

      a   William Verdo III (Chip) b
           Oct. 2, 1951

b   Mark Thomas (twin) b Jan. 18, 1957 Jackson, Miss.

c   Holley Ann (twin) b Jan. 18, 1957 Jackson, Miss.

XI Orlando Mays b Aug. 26, 1866 Gholson, Miss. d Aug. 28, 1938 Jackson, Miss. m April 3, 1894 Linnie Slaughter b April 26, 1877 Bastrop, La. d Sept. 6, 1959 Memphis, Tenn. CHILDREN:

A   James Zachary (Zack) b June 21, 1895 Mashulaville, Miss.   d   m Lois George b   Living Tupelo, Miss.   CHILDREN:

    1   Neal b   NFI

    2   Clifford

    3   Helen

    4   Katherine

B   Lillian Pearl b Feb. 20, 1897 Mashulaville, Miss., m March 2, 1929 Marcus R. Coleman b   NO ISSUE

C   Nellie May b Jan. 22, 1900 m March 11, 1919 James L. Jones b   NO ISSUE

D   William Hugh b Jan. 18, 1902 m Jan. 16, 1926 Mary Rogers b   CHILDREN:

    1   Lillian Lee b Oct. 30, 1927 m Oct. 17, 1957 Jesse James Green b Sept. 21, 1914   CHILDREN:

      a   Jesse James II b Jan. 19, 1960

      b   Dolly Gene b Sept. 22, 1962

    2   William Hugh II b Oct. 25, 1929 UNMARRIED

E   John Allen b May 17, 1905 m Aug. 7,1923 DuVergn Russell b Sept. 3, 1906 CHILDREN:

      1   Audrey Vivian b Nov. 8, 1924 m
             Jan. 27, 1945 Audrey Earl Hendrix
             b   CHILD:

           a   Audrey Earl II b Dec. 19,
                1946 Memphis, Tenn.

      2   James Allen b Oct. 25, 1927
             UNMARRIED

   F   Annie Bea b Feb. 12, 1910 m
       J. A. Stuckey b   Living
       Pine Bluff, Ark.   NO ISSUE

XII Eliza Ann b Aug. 18, 1868 Gholson, Miss. d
Nov. 16, 1941 Macon, Miss. m Jan. 19, 1886
John Plummer Hunter b Sept. 9, 1848 CHILDREN:

   A   William Mays b April 9, 1887 Noxubee Co.
       Miss. d July 21, 1907 Aliceville, Ala.
       UNMARRIED

   B   Ella Nora b Jan. 9, 1891 Macon, Miss. m
       July 6, 1915 George Mark Richardson b
       July 18, 1876   CHILDREN:

      1   Margaret b March 1, 1917 m Mar.
             23, 1952 Stanley Lawrence Perkins
             b Nov. 16, 1916   CHILD:

           a   Stanley Lawrence II b Sept. 3,
                1956

      2   George Mark II b July 18, 1921 m
             July 17, 1943 Sarah Louise Mitchell
             b Dec. 14, 1920

   C   Mary Kate b Dec. 11, 1893 m Aug. 16,
       1917 Wilson Ross Little b   NO ISSUE

   D   Ernest Dorroh b Jan. 22, 1896 d Dec. 6,
       1941 Macon, Miss. m June 24, 1920 Essie
       Mae Daniel b   CHILDREN:

      1   Ernest Dorroh II b April 25, 1923
             m June 26, 1946 Martha Elizabeth
             McVey b   CHILDREN:

a   Martha Elizabeth b Dec. 11,
     1948

b   James McVey b Aug. 1, 1951

2   Ann Daniel b Dec. 13, 1940
     UNMARRIED

E   Clara Louise b March 7, 1901 m April 10,
     1923 Tom White Crigler b Sept. 15, 1896
     CHILD:

1   Katherine b Nov. 12, 1924 m April
     25, 1950 Ernest Lee Hendrix b June
     3, 1924   CHILDREN:

     a   Katherine Harvey b April 20,
          1951

     b   Ernest Thomson b Sept. 15,
          1953

Descendants of Sarah Jane Dorroh and Spencer May Atkinson

I   William Henderson b Sept. 8, 1849 Choctaw, Ala., d Oct. 12, 1873

II   Henry Jefferson b Nov. 8, 1851 Choctaw, Ala., d Jan. 8, 1872

III   John May b Jan. 5, 1854 d Oct. 9, 1909 m Apr. 15, 1875 Nettie Handley b Feb. 26, 1855 d June 14, 1936   CHILDREN:

A   Edith b March 6, 1876 d Sept. 22, 1882

B   Handley b Sept. 22, 1877 d Dec. 31, 1877

C   Ella Mai b Nov. 5, 1879 m Apr. 22, 1902 John Trimble Palmer b Oct. 15, 1878 d May 25, 1948 CHILD:

    1   John Handley b June 27, 1906 Lincoln, Ark., m Feb. 25, 1932 Virginia Elizabeth Hopkins b Apr. 16, 1910 CHILDREN:

       a   Virginia b Sept. 5, 1938 m June 16, 1962 William Swan Yerger b June 11, 1932

       b   Jan b July 24, 1943 m Sept. 15, 1962 Lawrence Harley Stone b Oct. 24, 1943

D   Essie Gray b Jan. 17, 1881, Lincoln, Ark. d Sept. 22, 1882

E   Clair b Aug. 3, 1883, Lincoln, Ark., d Aug. 18, 1890

F   Spencer b Sept. 26, 1885 d May 4, 1889

G   John b Feb. 17, 1888 d Mar. 24, 1889

H   Grady b Feb. 20, 1890 d Sept. 28, 1890

I   Abbie b Sept. 10, 1891 d Sept. 19, 1937

J   Nettye Lois b April 15, 1894 m Dec. 12, 1912 Clyde Ester Fish b Aug. 8, 1892

CHILD:

1 Clyde Kimmel I b Oct. 18, 1914 m June 27, 1937 Loretta Clary b Aug. 14, 1914 CHILDREN:

 a Clyde Kimmel II b Oct. 17, 1938 m Aug. 26, 1961 Linda Haygood b July 20, 1924 CHILD:

  i Kimmela b Jan. 16, 1962

 b Curtis Ray b Mar. 19, 1949

K Charles Chris b Oct. 6, 1897 m Nov. 14, 1918 Irva Sanward Rupe b Mar. 8, 1899 d Aug. 22, 1944 CHILDREN:

1 Charles May b Sept. 6, 1919 m Oct. 4, 1942 Virginia Louise Oakley b April 15, 1925 CHILDREN:

 a Irva Annette b July 27, 1944

 b Charles Michael b May 4, 1947

2 Cecil Ray b Nov. 13, 1922 m * Martha Elizabeth Vick b Jan. 5, 1925 CHILDREN:

 a Robert Ray b July 29, 1946

 b Cathy Sue b Apr. 26, 1952

 c Martha Jill b May 3, 1953

 d Candace Jane b July 4, 1956

3 Donald Maurice b Dec. 19, 1925 m Sept. 15, 1942 Mary Catherine McGregor b Aug. 12, 1927 CHILDREN:

 a Larry Don b June 11, 1945

 b John David b Dec. 1, 1948

 c Mary Dee b Oct. 21, 1955

IV Robert Gray b Nov. 6, 1855 Choctaw, Ala., d Nov. 14, 1877
* m Nov. 5, 1944

V   Fannie Dorroh b Sept. 25, 1858 Choctaw,Ala.
     d Mar. 12, 1932 m Nov. 27, 1878 Marion Scott
     Winters b Aug. 16, 1852 d Sept. 12, 1931
     CHILDREN:

   A   Marion May b Dec. 6, 1880 d June 9,
        1887

   B   Fay Atkinson b Oct. 3, 1882 d

   C   Clifton Mose b Oct. 26, 1884 d Sept. 6,
        1947 m Jan. 24, 1906 Cathrine Ryall b
        Oct. 10, 1885 CHILD:

        1   Frances b Jan. 2, 1907 m June 9,
             1924 Clyde Oliver McFadden I b
             Nov. 2, 1904 d Mar. 1, 1961
             CHILDREN:

             a   Frances Ann b Jan. 14, 1925
                  m June 14,* Garland Eugene
                  Monk b Oct. 9, 1924 CHILDREN:
                  i   Michael Eugene b Dec. 29
                       1960

                  ii   Daniel Ellis b Sept. 7,
                       1962

             b   Clyde Oliver II b May 22,1934
                  m June 30, 1956 Patrica Eliz-
                  abeth Pate b Dec. 10, 1932
                  CHILD:

                  i   Steven Clyde b Apr. 21,
                       1960

        2   Virginia b Mar. 9, 1908 m Oct. 28,
             1944 William J. Alexander b Nov.
             26, 1906

        3   Cathrine Ryall b Jan. 4, 1921 m Fe
             2, 1946 Elbert Kermit Harbaugh b
             July 9, 1914 CHILDREN:

             a   William Winters b Mar. 25,
                  1948 d Mar. 25, 1948

             b   Jeffrey Allen b July 2, 1950

   * 1949   c   James Kermit b May 15, 1953

d   Jane Ellen b Nov. 12, 1957

D   John Dorroh b Oct. 7, 1886 m May 22, 1916 Ruth Williams b Mar. 22, 1892 d July 20, 1930 CHILD:

1   James Dorroh b Oct. 28, 1918 m Sept. 3, 1943 Barbara Johnson b Aug. 14, 1924 CHILD:

    a   Sharon b Jan. 4, 1947

E   Bessie Caroline b Mar. 10, 1889 m Sept. 6, 1911 Wallace Percie McGeorge I b June 24, 1880 d Dec. 23, 1943 CHILDREN:

1   Mary Frances b Aug. 29, 1913 m June 30, 1938 Henry Richard Henes b June 22, 1910 d Oct. 7, 1958 CHILDREN:

    a   Elizabeth Cauthon b Apr. 26, 1940 m Feb. 6, 1956 Sam Motes b July 12, 1938 CHILDREN:

         i   Richard R. b Oct. 2,1956

         ii   Elizabeth b Feb. 2, 1958

         iii   John Thomas b May 17, 1960

         iv   Myra Lucinda b July 28, 1962

    b   Fay Helen b Aug. 19, 1949

2   Wallace Percie II b Nov. 13, 1915 m Sept. 20, 1939 Nancy Margaret Boswell b Jan. 26, 1915 CHILDREN:

    a   William Scott b Nov. 21, 1943

    b   Nancy Margaret b Mar. 1, 1946

    c   Wallace Percie III b Jan. 7, 1948

3   Harvey Winters b Nov. 26, 1923 m Nov. 15, 1945 Patricia Ann Triplett b Sept. 25, 1927 CHILDREN:

        a   Patricia Ann b Sept. 27, 1947

        b   Marilyn Hearne b Dec. 20,1952

        c   Jane Carolyn b Aug. 27, 1954

     4   Carolyn Scott b Mar. 19, 1932 m *
         Joe Treadwell Henslee b March 5,
         1932 CHILDREN:

        a   Louise Cheryl b Nov. 9, 1958

        b   Julia Lynn b Sept. 20, 1960

        c   Susan Gail b Oct. 9, 1961

        d   Donna Kay b June 24, 1963

F   Ethel b Jan. 20, 1891

G   Willie Scott (Scottie) b Jan. 10, 1893

H   Etta b Nov. 5, 1896 d Feb. 21, 1944 m
     Dec. 9, 1919 Lester Holman Carnahan b
     June 23, 1895 d Sept. 26, 1926

VI Elizabeth York b Oct. 1, 1860 d Dec. 6, 1951
    m Jan. 17, 1883 Marion Alexander Hudson b
    Oct. 27, 1855 d March 23, 1932 CHILD:

A   Virginia b Sept. 13, 1885 m April 6,
     1910 James Robert Ryland I b Aug. 3,
     1880 CHILDREN:

     1   Marion Virginia b Dec. 19, 1910 m
         Mar. 2, 1933 William Earl Love I b
         Nov. 11, 1907 CHILDREN:

        a   Marion Virginia b Sept. 21,
            1935 m June 17, 1955 Daniel
            Dunaway b   CHILDREN:

            i   David Alexander b Oct.
                 27, 1958

            ii   George b Sept. 28, 1960

        b   William Earl II b July 31,
            1942 m Aug. 10, 1963 Janet
            Gray b   1942

* Jan.28,1957

2   Nancy Bess b July 5, 1916 m Sept. 14, 1940 Charles Francis Williamson b Jan. 4, 1912 CHILDREN:

    a   Charles Francis II b Oct. 3, 1941

    b   Esther Ann b Apr. 25, 1946

    c   Martha Ryland b July 27, 1948

3   James Robert II b July 12, 1919 m Nov. 28, 1942 Mary Elizabeth Johnson b Feb. 22, 1923 CHILDREN:

    a   Mary Elizabeth b Apr. 26, 1944

    b   James Robert III b Sept. 7, 1946

    c   John David b Sept. 28, 1948

    d   Nancy Virginia b Jan. 5,1962

4   Martha Virginia b May 16, 1924 m Oct. 16, 1948 James Adam Jarvis I b   CHILDREN:

    a   James Adam II b Feb. 7, 1950

    b   Robert Ryland b Apr. 12, 1953

    c   Benjamin Campbell b June 1, June 1, 1956

B   James Atkinson b Jan. 26, 1886 m Apr.17, 1912 Mary Fitzhugh Banks b Oct. 31, 1888 d   Oct. 16, 1954 CHILDREN:

1   Mary Virginia b Jan. 12, 1913 m Mar. 28, 1939 Donald D. Wood I b July 9, 1912 d Aug. 3, 1955 CHILDREN:

    a   Donald D. II b Jan. 30, 1941

    b   Mary Banks b Apr. 3, 1942 m Aug. 27,1963 Charles Patrick McCarty b Dec. 22, 1942

    c   Kathryn Virginia b Sept.24, 1946

2 Jamie Fitzhugh b Jan. 13, 1914 m June 8, 1940 Charles Allen Conditt b Oct. 23, 1913 CHILDREN:

 a Jamie b Sept. 10, 1942

 b Charles b June 1, 1947

 c Banks b Dec. 4, 1951

3 Crawford b Lincoln, Ark. m Aline Cargill b CHILDREN:

 a Rosemary b El Paso, Tex., m William Fiske I b CHILD:

  i William II b

 b William b m

 c Lois

C Charles Fred b July 7, 1893 m May 27, 1921 Emma Thedford White b Jan. 12, 1898 CHILDREN:

1 Emma Jean b Oct. 21, 1922 m Nov. 21, 1942 Altus B. Goodgame b Dec. 23, 1919 CHILDREN:

 a Richard Hudson b May 25, 1944 m Feb. 18, 1963 Peggy Jeanne Holt b Sept. 19, 1944

 b Carol Ann b May 28, 1948

2 Joseph Marion b Jan. 28, 1925 m Oct. 21, 1950 Patricia Ann Williams b March 30, 1931 CHILDREN:

 a Elizabeth Ann b June 6, 1953

 b Norma Lynn b Sept. 5, 1955

3 Charles Fred II b Aug. 8, 1929 m Aug. 22, 1952 Eunice Joy Nichols b May 7, 1930 CHILDREN:

 a Donna Kate b June 29, 1956

b   Cheryl Hollis b Nov. 12, 1958

c   Joy Adrienne b March 5, 1961

D   Sarah Jane b Sept. 17, 1899 m June 6, 1922 James Ralph Dunning I b Jan. 29, 1898 CHILD:

1   James Ralph II b Sept.   1923

VII   Rufus Clayton b Jan. 13, 1863 d April 9, 1879

VIII Charles Price b Oct. 27, 1865 d Oct. 23, 1960 m April 17, 1897 Lollie (Lawrence) Calloway b Oct. 28, 1876 d Dec. 20, 1956

A   Mary b Dec. 9, 1901 m Jan. 18, 1922 Saul Isaac Towery b Sept. 14, 1899 Oct. 7, 1947 CHILDREN:

1   John Edward b July 12, 1925 d July 14, 1941

2   Charles b Feb. 5, 1928 d Feb. 14, 1931

B   Frances b Sept. 6, 1910 m Nov. 13, 1935 Calip Washington Smith b April 25, 1905

B   CHILDREN:

    1   James Rufus b June 23, 1942

    2   Mary Jean b Nov. 4, 1946

IX   Sarah Temperance (Jeffie) b Sept. 27, 1868 d April 26, 1956 m April 19, 1893 William Harris Fox b March 4, 1859 d Dec. 27, 1934 CHILD:

A   William Spencer b June 29, 1894 m Dec. 16, 1917 Elizabeth Clayton Daniel b Feb. 21, 1897 CHILDREN:

    1   William Harris I b May 1, 1920 m Sept. 5, 1942 Vera Sue Puckett b Nov. 9, 1921 CHILDREN:

        a   William Harris II b June 3, 1947

        b   Joseph Spencer b Apr. 30,1951

        c   Susan Elizabeth b July 22, 1953

    2   John Edward I b Feb. 1, 1924 m Dec. 9, 1947 Mary Helen Tillman b Aug. 4, 1925 CHILDREN:

        a   John Edward II b Jan. 5, 1949

        b   Fred Tillman b Dec. 9, 1950

        c   Mary Melissa b Nov. 30,1953

    3   Elizabeth b May 29, 1925 m July 12, 1947 Adam Benjamin Robinson I b Oct. 10, 1924 CHILDREN:

        a   Adam Benjamin II b Oct. 11, 1949

        b   Spencer Fox b Dec. 22, 1951

        c   Margaret Elizabeth b Oct. 21, 1954

X   Mary b Sept. 21, 1871 d Oct. 1, 1871

XI   Mattie Alsey b April 8, 1873 d June 4, 1960
m Oct. 25, 1899 James Osborne Hutcheson b
Mar. 18, 1870 d Feb. 18, 1947 CHILDREN:

    A   James Edwin b Sept. 29, 1903 m June 10,
1929 Bessie Ethel   b June 11,
1906 CHILD:

        1   Marion Virginia b Dec. 18, 1930 m
April 3, 1955 A. W. Wickware b
1930 CHILDREN:

            a   Carol Anne b Dec. 6, 1955

            b   Susan Lynn b May 29, 1960

    B   Maye Virginia b Nov. 29, 1905 m Sept.
15, 1927 George Sizer Yerger II b May
29, 1903 CHILDREN:

        1   Martha Hutcheson b Jan. 16, 1933
m Aug. 4, 1957 Carol Ferdinand
Andre b April 16, 1929 CHILD:

            a   Sigrid Elizabeth b Mar. 19,
1962

        2   Elizabeth b July 31, 1939 m Aug.
24, 1957 DAniel James Wray b May
2, 1935

        3   George Sizer III b Dec. 17, 1946

    C   Fred Atkinson I b May 6, 1908 m June 11,
1942 Carmen Works b Apr. 18, 1910
CHILDREN:

        1   Fred Atkinson II b May 26, 1944

        2   Barbara b Nov. 14, 1946

    D   James Osborne II b Jan. 12, 1911 m Feb.
10, 1934 Lesteree George b Sept. 2,1912
CHILD:

        1   Alyce Carole b Jan. 7, 1936 m Nov.
28, 1959 Ronald Duane Whitten b
July 13, 1933

We are grateful to Miss Ethel Winters and Mrs.
Mary Towery for help on this line.

Descendants of John Dorroh and Rebecca Jones

I   Sarah m FIRST March 10, 1810 Livingston Co.
     Ky. [1] Asa Mitchell b   NFI

     m SECOND Dave Mitchell [2]   NFI

II   Mary (Polly) m March 20, 1809 Livingston Co.
     Ky. Thomas Bennett   [3] CHILD:

     A   John P. b 1829 Pickens Co. Ala. d Sept.
          18, 1853 m ca 1849 Dorcas Ann Fox [4] b
          Dec. 17, 1833 d Sept. 4, 1893 CHILDREN:
          SEE SEPARATE LISTING *

III Jane (Jennie) m July 28, 1812 Livingston Co.
     Ky. James (Jim) Mitchell   NFI
     m   SECOND Arch McDowell *   NFI
IV   James b ca 1795 d ca 1849 [5] m Dec. 7, 1815
     Caldwell Co., Ky. [6] Elizabeth Sullivant b
     1797 d ca 1857 Both buried Dorroh Plantation
     Cemetery, Pickens Co., Ala. CHILDREN:

[1] Livingston Co. is northeast of Paducah, Ky.
     and is on the Illinois-Kentucky border, with
     Smithland its county seat.
[2] It is our understanding that Dave Mitchell
     was an uncle of Asa Mitchell.
[3] An old Dorroh record gives "Tommy Bennett was
     father of John, Asa, Tom L. and Brown Bennett
     It is believed that "Tommy Bennett" is the
     same Thomas Bennett who married Mary (Polly)
     Dorroh in Livingston Co. Ky. on Mar.20,1809.
[4] Dorcas Ann Fox was the daughter of Mary Ann
     Caroline Hughes (Finnell) by her second marr-
     iage to Jacob Fox; so Dorcas and Leroy M.
     Finnell II were half-brother and sister as he
     married Elizabeth Dorroh b Jan. 21, 1831
[5] He is shown in the 1840 Census of Pickens Co.
     Ala., but is not shown in the 1850 Census,
     though his wife & children are; thus making
     us assume he died during the latter part of
     the 1840s.
[6] Caldwell Co. Ky. is east of Paducah with
     Princeton as its county seat. See VII

*   m date Aug. 14, 1829 Tuscaloosa, Co.,Ala.

*   We are indebted to Mr. Z. F. Shelton for
     material furnished on these two lines.

A   Jane (Jincey) b ca 1816 d   m   Asa
    Bennett [1]

B   Martha b ca 1818   m John Henry. Lived
    Double Springs, Miss.--west of Stark-
    ville.   CHILDREN:

    1   Mary b m Dr. Dotson   NFI

    2   Jane (Jennie) b   m Andrew Gartin
        [2]   NFI

C   Joel b Nov. 1, 1820 Ala., d May 11,1891
    m Jan. 2, 1845 Emily Abigail Gregg b Dec
    21, 1828 d May 16, 1914. Both buried
    Dorroh Plantation Cemetery, Pickens Co.
    Ala. [3] CHILDREN: SEE SEPARATE LIST_
    ING under: DESCENDANTS OF JOEL DORROH ‾
    AND EMILY ABIGAIL GREGG (His Estate Sett-
    lement can be found in Pickens Co. Ala.

D   Matilda b ca 1822 m FIRST Bird Henry b
    CHILD:

    1   Bird II   NFI

    m SECOND Tom Parkinson (or Parkerson)
    b   CHILD:

    2   Tom II   NFI

E   Rebecca b ca 1824 m William A. Parker b
    ca 1810 d Nov. 28, 1911 CHILDREN:

    1   Sarah Ann   died young [4]

    2   Nancy Emily, died young

    3   James Henry died young

    4   John died young

[1] In 1896 Asa was living in Hopkins Co.Tex. He
had several children...among them, John b ca 1850
and Jess. After Asa's first wife died, he married
a woman who was part Indian.
[2] Have been told, though unverified, there were
two children.
[3] This cemetery is near Kennedy, Ala.Pickens Co
[4] Three of these children died, according to
family tradition, on the same day from diarrhea.
These four buried in Dorroh Plantation Cemetery.

5   Martha Melvina m Mr. Livingston NFI

6   Matilda m Harvey Sanders   NFI

7   Bird m Linnie Nabors   NFI

8   Stephen Decatur b Jan. 5, 1856 m
     FIRST Pickens Co.,Ala. Margaret
     Mitchell b   1856 d   1881 CHILD:

     a   Zelda Ann b Sept. 6, 1880
          Pickens Co.,Ala. m Dec. 19,
          1895 Joel Curtis Ashcraft b
          Mar 25, 1877 CHILDREN:

          i   Letha Estelle b Oct. 6,
               1896 m July 13, 1924
               Lewis Hoffman Houston b
               Feb. 6, 1890 CHILDREN:

               [a] William Robert b
                    July 28, 1927 m Apr.
                    12, 1958 Clara
                    Christine Evans b
                    Aug. 21, 1925
                    CHILDREN:

                    (i) William Robert
                         II b Dec. 29,
                         1959,Tuscaloosa

                    (ii) John Temple b
                         Sept 28,1963
                         Tuscaloosa

               [b] Samuel Ashcraft b
                    Sept. 18, 1932 m Aug
                    8, 1962 Merry Helen
                    Hatch Napier b Dec.
                    25, 1931 CHILDREN:

                    (i) Whitfield b Dec
                         23, 1950

                    (ii) Gale b Sept. 8,
                         1952

                    (iii)Jennifer Napier
                         b Aug. 23, 1957

ii   George Grady b Dec. 22,
      1899 m Faye Gibbons b
      CHILD:

      (a)   Bettye Fay b July 2,
            1924 m Dec. 30, 1943
            William Jeffress
            Senter,M.D. b Oct.
            16, 1917 CHILDREN:

            (i)   Virginia Faye
                  b Apr. 7, 1947
            (ii) Sara Elizabeth
                  b July 10,1950
            (iii) Anne Ashcraft
                  (twin) b July
                  13, 1953
            (iv) William Jeff-
                  ressII b July
                  13, 1953(twin)
iii   Walter Lee b Aug. 3,1901
      m June 2, 1938 Eva Miller
      b Aug. 10, 1907 CHILDREN:

      (a)   Judith Ann b June 24,
            1939
      (b)   Jack Grady b Jan. 11,
            1944

iv   Jack Smith b Mar. 24,1903
      m Sept. 4, 1936 Lillian
      Louise Jinks CHILDREN:

      (a)   Linda Marie b Aug.
            20, 1946
      (b)   Jack Lanier b Dec.
            28, 1947

8   m SECOND Clersie Adaline Thornton
      CHILDREN: [1]

      b   Martha Melvina (Melvie) b Jan.
           19, 1887 m Nov. 16, 1909 And-
           rew Jackson Mills CHILDREN:
           i   Abston
           ii   Aletha
           iii   Thornton
           iv   Olivia
           v   Emma Nell

[1] Data given by Icie Parker Free & Steve Parker.

c   George Belton b Jan. 4, 1888
    m Della Gordon.CHILDREN:

    i   Eva Lois

    ii   Otis

    iii   Inez b   m   Melton b
          CHILDREN:

          (a)   Edgar b   m FIRST
                m SECOND   CHILD:

          (b)   Gordon b

d   Dessie Beulah b Feb. 6, 1889
    m William Meredith McCool b
    CHILDREN:

    i   Castle

    ii   Colen

    iii   Olen

    iv   Leon

    v   Alonzo

    vi   Arline

    vii   Howard

    viii Parker

e   Icie Willie b Apr. 22, 1890
    Pickens Co.,Ala. m May 24,
    1909 Robert Earl Free b Dec.
    25, 1888 d July 19, 1963
    NO ISSUE.

f   William Alonzo b 1892 m Emma
    Free b   CHILDREN:
    i   Herman b m___Broughton
    ii   Beatrice b m Crawford
    iii   Opal b   m   Hannah
    iv   Ruby b   m Ralph Windle

g   Rebecca Eliza b   1894 m Mont-
    ezuma Williams b CHILDREN:

      i   Charles

      ii   Eugenia

      iii Mary Agnes

      iv   Robert Earl

h   Mary Orzula b Oct.   1896 m
    Willie Elmore b   CHILDREN:

      i   Avie Lou

      ii   Morris

      iii Lorene

      iv   Bernice

i   Dolly Ardell b   1898 m
    John Latham b   CHILDREN:

      i   Bertrice

      ii   Marie

      iii Pearce

      iv   Causey

      v   Bettie

      vi   Reba

      vii   Katie

      viii Jacqueline

      ix   Michael

j   John Bascom b   1900 m
    Velma Gordon b   CHILDREN:

      i   Louis

      ii   John

k   Joel Stephen b Mar. 30, 1902 Holman, Ala., m FIRST Lucy Hannan b   CHILDREN:

    i   Ava Nell b Nov. 30, 1922 Gordo, Ala., m Ernest M. Yeatman b

    ii   James Hugh b Mar. 20, 1926 m Sept. 3, 1950 Jeannine Britt b Nov. 4, 1929

    iii   Helen Ruth b Mar. 15, 1929 m Aubrey C. Smelley

    m   SECOND Minnie Cubell Cork b

9   Mary b   m   Louie McCracken

10   Jennie b   m Billy Nabors b
CHILDREN:

    a   Zeb b   m   Lillian Ashcraft

    b   Daisy   m   Blakeney

    c   Fannie b   m   Blakeney

    d   Walker b

    e   Zackie

11   Rebecca b   m   John Hannah

12   Mellie b   m   William Porter

13   Willie b   m   Major Moore

IV   F   John, M.D., b ca 1826 Pickens Co. [1] Ala., m Louise Wallace b   CHILDREN:

1   Annie Bell b ca 1859 m Dec. 7, 1882 Cornelius Ware Robinson b

2   Lelia b   m   CHILD:

[1] Practiced medicine at Pittsboro, Calhoun Co. Miss. Wounded in Civil War. Served Co. F, Fourth Miss. Moved to Pointblank, Tex.

      a   Annie Belle b   m   C.B.
           Melton b

   3   Charles Dickens

   4   Ellen

   (3 other children, NFI)

IV G   William b ca 1828 [1]   d
                                [1]
   H   Stephen b Jan. 19, 1830 d May 17, 1863
        m Mar. 2, 1853 Sarah Fox b Mar. 19,1837
        d Mar. 15, 1919 Buried Slate Springs,
        Calhoun Co.Miss. CHILDREN: SEE SEPAR-
        ATE LISTING under DESCENDANTS OF
        STEPHEN DORROH AND SARAH FOX

   I   Elizabeth b Jan. 21, 1831 d Aug. 4, 1861
        m Dec. 20, 1848 Leroy Montgomery Finnell
        II b Mar. 24, 1827 d Sept. 3, 1867 [2]
        CHILDREN: [3] SEE SEPARATE LISTING
        under DESCENDANTS OF ELIZABETH DORROH
        AND LEROY MONTGOMERY FINNELL

V   William b Jan. 30, 1797 Laurens Co. S.C., d
     Aug. 18, 1834 Caldwell Co. Ky., m March 12,
     1818 Caldwell Co. Ky. Mary (Polly) Stone b
     June 26, 1799 d May 1, 1876 Buried New Bethel
     Cemetery, near Kuttawa, Ky. [4] CHILDREN:
     SEE SEPARATE LISTING under DESCENDANTS OF
     WILLIAM DORROH AND MARY STONE

VI Rebecca b   m   Dudley Pruett NFI

[1] Wounded in Civil War by minie ball which
    according to family, caused carbuncle which
    became infected and caused his death.

[2] After death of Elizabeth Dorroh, Leroy Finn-
    ell married Lucinda Cook in 1862 and had 3
    children: Margaret Caroline, Jesse Montgomery
    & John Calvin. Margaret Caroline Finnell
    married Rev. Joel Dorroh. Refer to DESCEND-
    ANTS OF STEPHEN DORROH and SARAH FOX
[3] All born in Pickens Co., Ala.

[4] Came to Ala. Oldest child b Ala. Territory.
    Other children were born in Caldwell Co.,Ky.

VII   Elizabeth b   [1] m William Sullivant

VIII   John b   m Aug. 30, 1822 Tuscaloosa Co.,
       Ala. Elizabeth Willingham   [2]

IX   Martha b   ca 1805 d after 1864, m FIRST
       Feb. 23, 1826 John Roberson Pumphrey b   1804
       Ga., d Oct. 8, 1857 Union Co., Ark. CHILDREN:
       SEE SEPARATE LISTING UNDER DESCENDANTS OF MAR-
       THA DORROH AND JOHN ROBERSON PUMPHREY.

       m SECOND Nov. 20, 1964 George W. Cook b ca 1800

X   Clarissa b Nov. 11, 1806 Caldwell Co., Ky., d
       Mar. 20, 1847 Tuscaloosa Co., Ala., m Jan. 18,
       1826 Dave Cole b May 3, 1806 Laurens, S.C., d
       July 30, 1856 CHILDREN: SEE SEPARATE LISTING
       under DESCENDANTS OF CLARISSA DORROH AND DAVE
       COLE

XI   Margaret b Nov. 25, 1808 d May 5, 1867 m Feb.
       19, 1829 Tuscaloosa Co., Ala. Leven Pumphrey b
       Aug. 28, 1807 Ga., d Mar. 29, 1890 Buried Big
       Hurricane Cem.,Tuscaloosa Co., Ala. CHILDREN:

       A   Rebecca b Mar. 20, 1830 d May 12, 1920 m
            Jan. 14, 1847 Owen Collins b
            d July 28, 1902, aged 78 CHILDREN:

            1   Permelia Susan (Toodie) b
                 m   Sam Black b   CHILDREN:

                 a   Carver

                 b   Dave

                 c   William

                 d   Alice

                 e   Leven

                 f   Delma b   m Jesse Scales

[1] William Sullivant & Elizabeth Sullivant were
children of Stephen Sullivant b 1768 d 1857 Union
Co., Kentucky. See IV preceding.

[2] John accidentally shot & killed himself.

2　　Margaret b

3　　James b

B　Margaret b Feb. 14, 1832 d　　m July 25
　　1850 James P. G. Kyle b　　　　NFI

C　James Marion b Mar. 28, 1834 d Apr. 26,
　　1862 Richmond Hospital, Va., Served
　　Co. G, 26th Ala., Reg. CSA.

D　Susan b Feb. 8, 1836 d　　　m Feb. 11,
　　1854 Rufus Kyle b

E　Cornelia b Apr. 17, 1838 d　　m Isaac
　　Cox b　　　　　　CHILDREN:

　　1　　Ida

　　2　　William

　　3　　Jesse

　　4　　Oscar

　　5　　Grover

F　Permelia Ann b June 26, 1840 d Nov. 15,
　　1924 m Feb. 7, 1860 David B. Curry b
　　Aug. 9, 1833 d Aug. 20, 1875 CHILDREN:

　　1　　Margaret Annie b Feb. 10, 1862 d
　　　　Jan. 1, 1926 m Thomas H. Wildsmith
　　　　b Aug. 28, 1856 d April 24, 1899
　　　　CHILDREN:

　　　　a　　Amy Eliska b March 9, 1882 d
　　　　　　April 23, 1956 m
　　　　　　B. D. Selman b

　　　　b　　Ada Belle b Aug. 11, 1884 d
　　　　　　Feb. 24, 1960 m　　　Alfred
　　　　　　H. Olive b April 10, 1879 d
　　　　　　June 12, 1953

　　　　c　　Fannie May b Dec. 20, 1886 d
　　　　　　May 21, 1887

d   Hugh b April 4, 1888 d May 18, 1962 m June 15, 1920 Margaret Ercill Brown b

e   Ethel Clyde b   m William Thomas Dowdle b
CHILDREN:

      i   William Thomas II b Apr. 18, 1925 CHILD:

            (a)   William Thomas III b Aug. 7, 1954

      ii   Joseph Clyde b July 3, 1927 CHILDREN:

            (a)   Barbara Jan

            (b)   Jeanne Olive

      iii   Laurel Curry b   m Clarence Burton Cosby b
CHILDREN:

            (a)   Margaret b Apr. 22, 1917 m William Marshall Redick b
CHILDREN:

                  (i)   William Marshall II b June 27, 1939

                  (ii) Joseph Cosby b Aug. 15, 1951

            (b)   Clarence Burton II b Sept. 23, 1919 m Mae Welch b   CHILD:

                  (i)   Laurel Mae

f   Thomas Edward b Nov. 26, 1897 UNMARRIED

g   Henry Hunter (girl) b Oct. 25, 1899 m   William K. Vardeman b   CHILDREN:

        i   William K. II b Oct. 15,
               1927 m   NFI
               CHILDREN:

               (a)   Sheila

               (b)   Debra

        ii   Hunter W. b Oct. 15,1927
               b   CHILDREN:
               (a)   Hunter W. II

               (b)   Pamela

2   Jessie Lorena b May 26, 1864 d Nov.
     16, 1912 m   N. M. Adams b
     Sept. 4, 1857 d Aug. 14, 1912 NO
     ISSUE

G   Mary Jane b July 9, 1842 d   m
   Hiram C. Peterson b   NFI

H   Jesse b Jan. 12, 1845 d June 27, 1862
   [1]

I   John Lewis b Feb. 19, 1847 d   m   1875
   Mary Deaton b   NFI

J   William Morgan b March 18, 1849 d
   m ca 1876 M. E. Wilcox b   NFI

K   Luther Levin b Jan. 12, 1852 d   m
   Frances Vines b   CHILDREN:

    1   Morgan V.   b Aug. 24, 1873 d Mar.
      9, 1906 m Nov.   1896 Mary Jane
      House b Apr. 3, 1874 d   1931
      CHILDREN:

      a   John Robert b Mar. 20, 1898
         m   1920 Betty Autrey
         b   CHILDREN:

        i   Morgan Webster b Mar. 14
           1921

In Battle of **Richmond.** Family Bible says,
"Wounded in the breast"....served Co. G,11th
Reg. Inf. Alabama

          ii   Leon W. b Aug. 15, 1922

          iii Forest E. b May 24, 1924

          iv   Janie Mae b Mar. 7, 1926

          v   Lewis A. b   1929
               d   1961 [1]

          vi   Pauline b   1932

     b   Gordon P. b Aug. 1, 1905 d
           July 21, 1943 [2]

2   Lydia b Oct. 28, 1875 d Jan. 25,
     1936 m Oct. 19, 1898 Usrey Law-
     rence b   NFI

3   Alma b   m   Barney Persons
     b   NFI

4   Cullie b   m   Hubert Bacon

5   Samuel b Mar. 4, 1883 d Nov. 19,
     1960 m   Hester Smalley b

L   Martha Josephine b Mar. 6, 1854 d
    m   Jacob Anders b   NFI
    CHILDREN:

1   Percy

2   Levin

3   Susan Brown

4   Sam b   lives in Northport, Ala.

[1] Served in concentration camp in Korea.

[2] Died from wounds of World War II

Descendants of John P. Bennett and Dorcas Ann Fox

I   Martha Angeline b July 5, 1850 Pickens Co.Ala
    d Feb. 26, 1922 m FIRST ca 1866 James J.
    Cook b   d 1874-5 CHILDREN: [1]

A   Mary Frances b Nov. 16, 1867 d Aug. 11,
    1871

B   John William b Mar. 4, 1870 d Oct. 27,
    1873

C   Annie b Dec. 21, 1871 d Apr. 4, 1910 m
    ca 1890 William Pinkney Richardson b ca
    1870 d Jan. 26, 1949 CHILDREN:

1   Pearl b Feb. 27, 1892 m Oct. 6,
        1909 Tollie H. Branyon b July 14,
        1887 Live Kennedy, Ala. CHILDREN:

a   Royce Roy b Dec. 30, 1911 m
        Oct. 13, 1935 Docia Loueng
        Howard b Dec. 1, 1919CHILDREN:

i   Martha Ellon b Mar. 10,
        1940 m Mar. 3, 1962
        Marion Wayne Robinson

ii   Glenda Gail b Nov. 15,
        1945

b   Lucile b Nov. 20, 1913 m Sam
        Whetstone b   NO ISSUE

2   Clarissa Evelyn (Evie) b Feb. 1,
        1894 m Feb. 15, 1920 Lewis T.
        Winters b Jan. 18, 1893 CHILDREN:

a   Annie Lois b Apr. 24, 1922 m
        June 24, 1942 Thurman H. Hood
        CHILDREN:

i   Russell b

ii   Dorothy Ann

iii   Ellen Marchelle

[1] All children born in Pickens Co.Alabama.

b   Lewis Dupree b Mar. 26, 1925
m Mar. 12, 1943 Mable Johnson
CHILD:

    i   Sarah Carroll b

c   Frederick Burnell b Nov. 17,
1928 m Mar. 6, 1954 Gladys
Jeannette Kyser b CHILD:

    i   Ronald Frederick b 1955

d   Oleta Pearl b Oct. 6, 1933 m
Sept. 1, 1949 Monroe Virgil
Allen b   CHILDREN:

    i   Melba Dianne b Dec. 30,
1951

    ii   Retha Kay b   1956

3   Ottie Lee b Apr. 5, 1897 m Feb. 5,
1920 Ellis Newman Doss b Nov. 3,
1890 CHILDREN:

a   Evelyn Varada b Jan. 13,1921
m Aug. 18, 1937 Thomas Wesley
Poore b Aug. 24, 1911 CHILDREN

    i   Grady Marshall b June 13,
1938

    ii   Joseph Ellis b Sept. 20,
1939 m July 14, 1962
Janie Delight Rose b July
11, 1946

    iii   David Loy b Mar. 17,1942

    iv   Helen Elaine b Aug. 23,
1944 d July 11, 1946

    v   Billy Wayne b July 22,
1947

    vi   Thomas Eugene b Nov. 9,
1952

    vii   Robert Clyde b Nov.9,1954

b   Perry Oscar b Dec. 20, 1922
m Nov. 11, 1942 Evelyn Shirley b Sept. 9, 1925 CHILDREN:

    i   Brenda Jean b June 7,1945
m June 9, 1962 Frank
Mizell b Nov. 22, 1937

    ii   Marsha Lynn b June 19,
1951

    iii   Vickie Jo b Mar. 10,1956

c   Sybil Elaine b Dec. 20, 1924
m Aug. 4, 1943 Randolph M.
McDowell b June 6, 1922
CHILDREN:

    i   Audrey Mae b Sept. 2,1945

    ii   Linda Louise b June 19,
1947

    iii   Michael Bruce b June 28,
1949

d   Billie Nuna b Jan. 11, 1928 m
Feb. 1, 1947 Ralph Harold
Gossett b Mar. 30, 1928
CHILDREN:

    i   Patricia Eileen b Mar. 12,
1949

    ii   Dale Jean b Jan. 19,1953

e   Clara Addis b Sept. 5, 1930 m
Feb. 10, 1951 William Madison
Cabaniss b Aug. 28, 1924
CHILDREN:

    i   Ralph Theodore b April 10
1952

    ii   Betty Loraine b Sept. 17,
1953
    iii   Karen Elaine b May 24,
1955

        iv   Timothy Blair b Oct. 6, 1961 d Dec. 20, 1961

D   Jerusha b 1874 d Feb. 3, 1935 UNMARRIED

m SECOND   1880 William T. Adcox b July 25, 1842 d Apr. 21, 1932, almost 90, CHILDREN:

E   Eugene b 1881 d   age 3

F   Honnie Lee b April 11, 1882 d Aug. 1937 m Annie   b   d 1939 CHILDREN:

    1   Nora Lee b   m   Lawrence Purser b CHILDREN:

        a   Claude Lee b   m

        b   Nellie Joanne b

    2   Sidney Ethel b   m   First Oct. 28, 1924 Jesse Parker b   d CHILDREN:

        a   Honnie O'Neal b   m   Elizabeth Abbott b   CHILDREN:

            i   Honnie Kaye b

            ii   Cheryl

            iii Jesse Eugene

            iv   Kari Sue Ell.

        b   Anna Sue b   m   Hal Stephenson b   CHILDREN:

            i   Karen Lynn b

            ii   Paul Scott

        c   Marion Pearl b   m   Jerry Wilson b   CHILDREN:

            i   Jerry Richard b

            ii   Jesse Victor b

        m   SECOND   Malone b

3   Elizabeth Angeline b   d   1938 m
     Ira Whiteworth b   CHILDREN:

     a   Don Mark b   m

     b   Ira Glenn b ca 1937

4   Minnie Mary Jane b   m   Ackers

G   Thomas b Oct. 17, 1884 d Mar.   1923 m
CHILDREN:

1   Jewel b   d   age 5

2   Estell b   d   age 3

3   G. T. b   d   age 3 1/2 (Killed by
horse.)

4   Roland Austin b

5   Grady Leonard

H   Kittie Estelle b Sept. 9, 1889, Lives
Byers, Tex., m Sept. 23, 1906 Rube Roy
Hulse b   d   Mar. 1, 1963 CHILDREN:

1   Mattie Estelle b Oct. 17, 1907 m

2   Marcus Allan b Aug. 28, 1910

3   Rev. William Roy b Nov. 14, 1913 m
FIRST   d   1958 CHILDREN: 3
NFI

     m SECOND Jan. 1963 Mrs. Mary Gregg
Williams b

4   Dolly May b July 20, 1915 d Oct. 5,
1918

5   Bailey Bennie b Apr. 19, 1918 m   d
1955

6   Maggie May b Oct. 22, 1920 m
Manness   b   CHILDREN: 9   NFI

7   C.Z.Arlene b Feb. 10, 1922 m Thos.
C. Moxley b   Dec. 28, 1906
CHILDREN: 5   NFI

8 Rev. Harvey Wayne b Oct. 15,1925
  m CHILDREN: 4 NFI

I Tula b May 27, 1895 d Feb. 27, 1912 m
 Charley Smith b   NO ISSUE

II William Thomas (Will) b Pickens Co.,Ala.
 Sept. 22, 1852 d July 27, 1934 m June 19,
 1879 Telula Evelyn Linebarger b June 19,
 1860 d Nov. 21, 1926 CHILDREN:

 A John Worth b Nov. 3, 1880 m Nov. 14,
  1909 Lillie Phelan b Nov. 10, 1893
  CHILD:

  1 Allen Worth b July 23, 1912 Fisher
   Co.Tex., m June 18, 1932 Lula
   Emily Kallen b May 26, 1914
   CHILDREN:

   a Robert Allen b Oct. 24, 1933

   b John William b Oct. 26, 1936
    m Dec. 16, 1961 Carol Hope b

   c Constance Emily b Feb. 28,
    1947

 B James Jackson (Jimmie) b Oct. 12, 1882
  d Dec. 1918 m ca 1913 Eula Neves b
  Apr. 2, 1893 d Dec. 3, 1918 CHILDREN:

  1 Herbert George (twin) b Aug. 30,
   1914 m Jan. 15, 1947 Ophelia Estell
   Kincaid b June 22, 1926 CHILDREN:

   a Sherrye Ranell (twin) b Dec.
    29, 1953

   b Terrye Lagail (twin) b Dec. 29,
    1953

  2 Hubert William (twin) b Aug. 30,
   1914 m FIRST ca 1940 Mamie Smith
   b 1921 CHILDREN:

   a Jimmy Joel b ca 1940

   b Judy b Dec. 29, 1943

2   m SECOND Ora Melton Carlton b

3   Mattie Louise b Feb. 12, 1916 m
Dec. 16, 1932 Richard Clyde Eaton
b Dec. 12, 1911 CHILDREN:

    a   Janice b Jan. 1, 1935 m Aug.
        14, 1953 Donald Fred Park b
        Feb. 24, 1926 CHILDREN:

        i   Jane Donice b May 13,
            1955

        ii   Deanna Jean b Jan. 13,
            1958

    b   Evelyn Louise b Oct. 17, 1936
        m Mar. 10, 1954 Melton Eugene
        Murff b Aug. 25, 1934 CHILDREN

        i   Melta Lou b Nov 11,1956

        ii   Melinda Sue b July 9,
            1958

    c   Royce Lynn b Mar. 26, 1938 m
        Barbara

    d   Marsha Gayle b Oct. 22, 1949

Susie Pearl b Sept. 27, 1886 m Oct. 6,
1907 Hugh Thomas Neves b Dec. 26, 1885
d Mar. 18,1960   CHILDREN:

1   Claud Morris b Sept. 8, 1908 m Dec.
12,1926 Ola Lee Eaton b CHILDREN:

    a   Robert Worth b Mar. 13, 1928
        m ca 1949 Dean Palmer CHILDREN

        i   **Linda Dale**

        ii   Tricia Juan

    b   Lowell Gene b Oct. 14, 1932 m
        July 12, 1953 Mary Lou Nichols
        b Jan. 1, 1937 CHILDREN:

        i   Marti Gene b Nov. 12,
            1954

        ii   Debra Lee b Sept. 30, 1957

        iii   Terry Elaine b July 3, 1959

        iv   Cynthia Ann b May 24, 1961

2   Pearl Pauline b Oct. 7, 1912 m Apr. 12, 1943 Robert Worth Norwood b Sept. 27, 1904   NO ISSUE

3   Hugh Thomas II b May 10, 1916 m Sept. 30, 1940 Inez McClure Brumfield b Oct. 19, 1917 CHILD:

        a   Betty Ann bJune 3, 1945

D Willie Mae b Dec. 31, 1888 m Dec. 23, 1906 Guy Dewitt Johnson b Jan. 21,1887 CHILDREN:

1   William Leander b Dec. 17, 1908 m Dec. 20, 1930 Ethel Vera Carey b Jan. 26, 1912 CHILDREN:

        a   Vera Lee b Feb. 13, 1932 m July 22, 1961 William Martin Feil b

        b   Jean LaRue b Apr. 13, 1934 m Sept. 20, 1952 Covert Allen Beaver b Sept. 5, 1931

        c   Larry Claud b Aug. 24, 1936

2   Mildred b Nov. 23, 1910 m June 26, 1932 Raymond Knox b Oct. 22, 1904 CHILDREN:

        a   Edwin Ray b June 5, 1933

        b   Rex Wayne b Feb. 19, 1935

        c   Linda Mae b Apr. 17, 1941

3   John Robert b Sept. 21, 1916 d Dec 16, 1916

4   Edith LaRue b Dec. 23, 1920 m Apr.
    23, 1939 Littleton Pierson Henry b
    July 20, 1915 CHILDREN:

    a   Sherry Ann b Feb. 16, 1944 m
        April 2, 1962 James Roy Crisp

    b   Kathie Lea b Oct. 15, 1949

    c   Teri Sue b Jan. 4, 1955

5   James Weldon b Sept. 4, 1927 m Dec.
    25, 1944 Meta Faye Ashley b Jan. 5,
    1928 CHILDREN:

    a   Michael Weldon b Oct. 15,1948

    b   Ashley Dwayne b June 3, 1950

    c   Stephen Fayne b Oct. 25,1956

E   Timmons Herd b April 19, 1892 d   1948/9
    m Dec. 1915 Zola Nail b   CHILDREN:

1   Thomas Laverne b

2   Oscar Mae

3   Claudine

4   Peggy

F   Elbert Oran b Apr. 20, 1896 m Nov. 15,
    1914 Jessie Mae Parker b Sept. 15, 1896
    CHILDREN:

1   Naomi Evelyn b May 8, 1916 d April
    12, 1927

2   Elba Jean b Dec. 21, 1929 m May 13,
    1945 G. W. Wilkerson b May 21,1927
    CHILDREN:
    a   Sharon Elaine b Jan.23, 1948
    b   Gary Oran b Oct. 9, 1951

G   Oscar Burris b Sept. 13, 1898 d Mar. 14,
    1917
H   Tom L. b Oct. 13, 1901 d Nov. 6, 1954 m
    Audie Mae Owens b   CHILD:
    1   Helen Faye b

Descendants of Joel Dorroh and Emily Abigail Gregg

I   Jane Elizabeth b Oct. 22, 1845 d Nov. 24, 1846

II Martha Melvina (Mellie) b May 22, 1847 d Jan. 11, 1931 Clarendon, Tex., m June 7, 1868 John Alexander Shelton b Oct. 13, 1844 Lincoln Co. N. C. [1] CHILDREN:

    A   Clough b Jan. 22, 1870 d Dec. 15, 1943, Tex., m FIRST Nov. 16, 1897 Ethel Bass b July 1878, Corinth, Miss., d Sept. 6, 1903, Tex., CHILDREN:

        1   Virginia b Aug. 5, 1898 d Nov. 15, 1954 m June 4, 1924 Charles Chilton Harlan b Oct. 13, 1898,Moberly, Mo. CHILD:

            a   Charles Chilton II b Dec. 21, 1925

        2   Clough II b July 24, 1901 m Nomah Hughes b Aug. 29, 1903, Okla. CHILD:

            a   Clough III b Oct. 16, 1932, Dallas, Tex., m FIRST

            m SECOND May 14, 1955 Mary Sue Works b (Live in Calif.) CHILDREN:

                i   Clough IV

                ii   Vicki

        m SECOND Ottsie Bird b 1884 d 1947 NO ISSUE

    B   Adelle (Adella) b Nov. 11, 1871 d March 6, 1872

[1] Mellie and John kept a hotel in Kennedy, Ala. and sold out in 1895-6, moved to Rosebud,Tex., about 1905 moved again to Clarendon, in the Pan-handle. Their children were b in Pickens County, Alabama.

C   Ottis b Dec. 8, 1874 d Dec. 23, 1943 m
April 6, 1927 Addie Marie Holmes b
NO ISSUE

D   Joel (Joe) Tunstal b Aug. 15, 1875 d
June 2, 1959 m July 2, 1899 Estelle
Claire Jamieson b d May 29, 1954
CHILDREN:

  1   Joel Jamieson b Aug. 5, 1901, Tex.,
      d 1903

  2   Claudius Tunstall b May 26, 1903,
      Tex., m Mar. 2, 1929 Anne Turner b
      CHILDREN:

      a   Michael (girl) b Feb. 22, 1943
          Amarillo, Tex.

      b   Charles Turner b Oct. 7, 1946,
          Tulia, Tex.

  3   Laurence (Claire) b March 26, 1905,
      Clifton, Tex., m June 10, 1928 Ray-
      mond D. Holt b d 1946

  4   Malcolm Kenneth b May 13, 1910 d
      May 23, 1910, Bellevue, Tex.

  5   Helen Loraine b June 28, 1911, Bell-
      evue, Tex. m July 2, 1938 Lofton S.
      Little b CHILDREN:

      a   Janis Lynne (twin) b May 10,
          1940

      b   Lofton Shelton (twin) b May 10,
          1940

  6   Abbye Elaine b June 20, 1919 m May
      6, 1942 Edwin B. Ledbetter CHILDREN:

      a   Janis Elaine b Dec. 10, 1944

      b   Joel Austin b Aug. 27, 1947

      c   James Edwin b Apr. 2, 1949

      d   Jill Anne b June 7, 1953

e   Joan Claire b Oct. 23, 1954

E   Mary Abigail (Abbie) b Aug. 17, 1877 d Aug. 5, 1954 m June 20, 1897 Edward Miles Ozier b Sept. 27, 1869 d Nov. 21, 1942   CHILDREN:

1   Manley Shelton b June 4, 1899 d July 30, 1961 m FIRST April 20, 1921 Odelle Blair b Aug. 5, 1899 CHILD:

   a   Edward Blair b July 11, 1922 m June 26, 1942 Mary Frances Manning b June 26, 1924 CHILDREN:

      i   William Byron b Apr. 8, 1947
      ii Mary Odelle b Jan. 14, 1949
      iii Alyson Blair b Mar. 7, 1956

   m SECOND Dec. 19, 1938 Bess Jackson b Nov. 21, 1902 NO ISSUE

2   Pauline b Apr. 29, 1902 m June 6, 1926 Marion Dixon Stephens b CHILD:

   a   Carolyn Jane b June 5, 1931 m Jan. 16, 1960 Lawrence Berkmanns Schwarzbach II CHILDREN:

      i   Laurie Anne b Oct. 14, 1960

      ii Carol Marie b July 6, 1962

      iii Christine Renee b Sept. 6, 1963

3   Edward Byron b July 25, 1904 d Aug. 26, 1950 m Apr. 25, 1943 Willie Maude Pratt b Oct. 15,1918 NO ISSUE

F   Edgar (Paul) b Oct. 5, 1879 m Nov. 5, 1913 Edith Gorrisen b July 13, 1888 CHILD:
1   Pauline b Oct. 18, 1914 m Knox Dunlap b May 8, 1903   CHILD:

        a   Mary Pauline b Nov. 26, 1937 m
             Apr. 22, 1961 Richard J. Ecuy-
             er b Jan. 24, 1936

   2   Edith   b July 23, 1921 m
        Aug. 3, 1948 Thomas James McCand-
        less b Aug. 12, 1918   CHILD:

        a   Deborah Sue b June 3, 1952

G   Lonnie b   1881, d   in infancy

III John Marion b Mar. 29, 1849 Pickens Co.,Ala.
d Jan. 10, 1922 m Nov. 4, 1869 Wincy (Leona)
Rosabelle Shelton b Sept. 17, 1854 d Mar. 21,
1935   CHILDREN: [1]
A   Infant b   d
B   Samuel R. Kirk b Sept. 3, 1873 d July 11
     1956 m Oct. 18, 1904 Rosa H. Davis b Aug
     28, 1879 d Jan. 1959 CHILDREN:

   1   Joe Cooper b   d in childhood
   2   Samuel b Dec. 18, 1907 UNMARRIED
   3   John Quinn b Aug. 27, 1912 m July
        7, 1943 Janie Sue Pratt b CHILDREN:

        a   Barbara Sue b Mar. 30, 1947
        b   John Wayne b June 18, 1953

   4   Sarah b Aug. 5, 1914 m Wheeler
        McCrary b   NO ISSUE

C   Leonidas (Steven) b July 1, 1875 d Dec.
     9, 1958 m Sept. 13, 1899 Matilda Ash-
     craft b Aug. 9, 1878 d Mar. 7, 1938
     CHILDREN:
   1   Henry Lee b July 26, 1900 Pickens
        Co.,Ala. m July 1929 Adelyn Man-
        derson b July 30, 1909   CHILD:
        a   Minnie Florence b Mar. 15,1933
             m Jan. 10, 1959 Kenyon B.
             Fretwell b
   2   Emma Ralls b May 14, 1902 d Apr. 28,
        1946
D   Joe Frank b June 21, 1877 d Aug. 1954
     Edinburg, Tex. UNMARRIED
E   James Bascom b Aug. 1, 1880 m Aug. 29,
     1905 Louisa Mullican b Dec. 1, 1878
     CHILDREN:
[1] All born in Pickens Co., Shelton Beat.

1   Barney b Aug. 20, 1906 d June 4,
        1933 Drowned

2   Olivia b Sept. 28, 1908 m Oct. 23,
        1942 Ralph R. Carter b CHILD:

        a   Son, b and d Aug. 13, 1943

3   Joe Frank b Oct. 4, 1910 [1]
4   James Avery b Mar. 1, 1913 m Sept.
        26, 1942 Katie Rebecca Lewis b Oct.
        10, 1919 CHILD:

        a   Harriet Beverly b Aug..13,1943

5   Eulese b June 30, 1917 m June 28,
        1941 James Ralph Walker b Jan. 17,
        1920 CHILDREN:

        a   Wayne b Apr. 23, 1949

        b   Mary b Jan. 24, 1952

6   Fred b Aug. 14, 1922 m June 18,
        1960 Frances Hunt b CHILDREN:

        a   Deborah Ann b Mar.23, 1961
        b   Fredna Kay b Jan. 5, 1963

F   June O. b Dec. 30, 1882 m May 18, 1913
      Lucile Jackson b   NO ISSUE

G   Kittie Ola b Mar. 28, 1885 d Oct. 10,
      1946 m July 5, 1905 William Samuel
      Mullican b Feb. 22, 1882 d July 1954
      CHILDREN:

      1   Ann (Clora) b May 21, 1907 m April
              15, 1937 James Manley Garner b Oct.
              14, 1909 CHILDREN:

              a   Jimmie Ann b June 15, 1943
                    Miami
              b   Sarah Catherine b Jan. 15,
                    1945, Aliceville, Ala.
              c   Manley Bascom b July 9, 1948
                    Tuscaloosa, Ala.
              d   Virginia Ola b Aug. 16, 1950,
                    Tuscaloosa, Ala.

[1] m Dec.31,1959 Mary Neomia Burgess Ruffin

2   Eula Ola b Sept. 23, 1909 m L.
     Brooks Gregg b CHILDREN:

     a   Redus b Feb. 25,

     b   Kenny Word b Aug. 12, 1938

     c   Jerry

3   Jessie Lou b June 14, 1912 m Paul
     Booker b July 8, 1911 CHILDREN:

     a   Peggy Ann b Aug. 18, 1937 m
          Charles Clifton Jones b
          CHILDREN:

          i   Sheila Ann b Oct. 7, 1957

          ii   Charles Mikel b Jan. 19,
               1960

     b   Charles Gordon b July 16, 1942

     c   Mary Joyce b May 10, 1945

4   William (Harwood) b Sept. 16, 1914
     m Dec. 23, 1939 Laverne Adell Colvin
     b Sept. 1, 1919 CHILDREN:

     a   Bonnie Sue b May 29, 1941

     b   William Dallas b May 8, 1944

Parrie (Lacy) b July 17, 1887 m Oct. 25,
1911 Joseph (Joe) Fitzgerald Langdon b
July 6, 1887 CHILDREN:

1   John William b June 9, 1913

2   James Rufus b Apr. 22, 1917

3   Elizabeth (Lucile) b July 22, 1920

4   Zora (Opal) b Sept. 18, 1926 m
     Leroy F. Hughes

Zora b Dec. 22, 1890 m May 19, 1937
Vernon Etheredge b   NO ISSUE

J   Tracy b Feb. 22, 1895 d Dec. 26, 1901

IV   James William (Dee) b Apr. 12, 1851 d May 9, 1921 m 1878 Missouri McCullough b 1854 d Mar. 19, 1899 CHILDREN:

    A   Esse b 1879 d 1883

    B   Lellon b Apr. 14, 1880 d Feb. 6, 1909 m Nov. 13, 1904 Rufe Mathis b CHILDREN:

        1   Vera Mae b Oct. 1905 m John Weathers b CHILDREN:

            a   James Gary b Dec. 9, 1939
            b   Nancy Carol b Jan. 10, 1942

        2   Clarence K. b Nov. 7, 1907 d March 16, 1944 World War II

    C   Louie Bell b Jan. 22, 1883 m Apr. 20, 1930 Mavis Suddeth b Oct. 26, 1895 CHILD

        1   Mary Suddeth b Sept. 6, 1932 m Mar. 18, 1952 Leon Childress b July 15, 1930 CHILDREN: [1]

            a   Sandra Ann b Mar. 15, 1953
            b   Doris Lynn b Mar. 14, 1954
            c   Lamar Keith b Oct. 17, 1955
            d   Lagena Gail b Mar. 28, 1963

    D   Eldie Toxie b Jan. 13, 1884 d Jan. 29, 1956 m June 2, 1910 Mary Virginia Fowler b Aug. 20, 1892 CHILDREN:

        1   Marjorie M. b Apr. 23, 1911 m Oct. 17, 1950 George O. Sorrell NO ISSUE
        2   Gladys R. b Apr. 8, 1913 m 1930 Harold M. Cannady b Jan. 1, 1914 CHILD:
            a   Charles S. b Oct. 23, 1931 m July 13, 1961 Vera Jeanette Sayles CHILD:
               i   Danny Joseph b Dec.26, 1962
        3   William James b Oct. 17, 1916 m June 4, 1942 Louise B. Fort b Jan. 4, 1922 CHILDREN:

[1] All children born in Clanton, Ala.

a   Linda Louise b Aug. 29, 1943
m Oct. 12, 1963 William Joseph
McDonald

b   William James II b Aug.27,1946

c   Thomas Louis b July 9, 1948

4   Eldie Fred b Jan. 1, 1918 m Jan.13,
1941 Gloria L. Landry b Sept. 16,
1922 CHILDREN:

a   Ronald David b Nov. 16, 1941

b   Billie Lynne b Feb. 10, 1943
m Feb. 23, 1960 Samuel L.
Stubbs b CHILDREN:

    i   Gloria b Sept.26, 1960
    ii   Samuel Earle b Jan.9,
        1962

c   Richard Moreland b Sept. 11,
1949

5   Kitty Ennis b Dec. 17, 1919 m Sept.
13, 1941 Woodrow Wilson Thomas b
April 3, 1913 CHILD:

a   Woodrow Wilson II b July 27,
1946

6   Dan David b Dec.24, 1921 d Aug. 9,
1933

7   Frank Roland b Jan. 1, 1923 m Nov.
27, 1947 Martha Hughes b Feb. 15,
1921 CHILD:
a   Frank Roland II b Apr.24,1950

8   Mary Etta b July 15, 1925 m Nov.27,
1944 Jimmie P. Piliouras b May 23,
1926 CHILD:
a   Gloria Jean b Feb. 20, 1948

9   Mattie E. b Oct. 11, 1926 m Jan. 11
1944 Jack Leroy Bewley b Mar. 15,
1926 CHILDREN:

a   Jack Leroy II b Sept.18, 1946

b   Lawrence Eldie b July 21,1948

10   Sybil B. b Mar. 4, 1928 m Dec. 13, 1947 Walter Harold Moreland b Nov. 16, 1923 CHILD:

a   Walter Harold II b Mar.29,1951

11   Parrie Lou b May 27, 1929 m Billy Ray Hartzog b Jan. 16, 1928 CHILDREN:

a   Cathy Leigh b Nov. 11, 1951

b   Brent Ray b Nov. 9, 1954

12   Clyde Leighton b June 13, 1931 m Nov. 23, 1950 Emma Jean Wear b Jan. 7, 1931 CHILDREN:

a   Clyde Leighton II b May 19, 1951
b   Walter David b Jan. 15, 1954
c   Joseph Marshall b Aug. 25, 1955
d   Danny Keith b Sept. 12, 1960

13   Delano Ross b Mar. 8, 1933 m Mar. 31, 1956 Juanita J. Johnson b Dec. 15, 1937 CHILDREN:

a   Robin Denise b Jan. 15, 1957
b   Risa Dawn b Jan. 9, 1959

E   Mary b Apr. 23, 1886 d June 24, 1957 m Leland Conner b Nov. 24, 1882 d Apr. 23, 1919 CHILDREN:
1   Infant b & d Sept. 25, 1911
2   James Leroy b June 16, 1912 d Mar. 13, 1925
3   James LeFoy b May 22, 1915 d Mar. 29, 1939
4   Henson b & d Jan. 16, 1916
5   William Dorroh b Aug. 8, 1917 d Apr 20, 1947 (World War II)

6   Jessie b Apr. 7, 1919 m FIRST
Albert Bailey b

m SECOND George Wheat b CHILDREN:

    a   Calvin b Jan. 25, 1957

    b   Kelvin b Jan. 10, 1958

    c   Marcelyn Mary b Nov. 26, 1962

F   William Joseph (Willie Joe) b 1888 d
Jan 3,1927

G   Sarah Abbie b Jan. 5,

H   Worth Kennedy b   1893

I   Benjamin Hale b Oct. 25, 1896 m May 28,
1932 Grace Smith b

V   Mary Frances b Aug. 18, 1853 d Jan. 20, 1934
m Feb. 25, 1880 David Jordan Lacy, Capt. CSA
b July 11, 1836 d Nov. 12, 1903 CHILDREN:

A   David Murray b Mar. 8, 1881 m FIRST Dec.
1902 Effie Mae Reed   NO ISSUE

m SECOND Nov. 25, 1909 Bertha Youngblood
b Feb. 28, 1885 d May 26, 1953 CHILDREN:

    1   George David b Feb. 25, 1913 d May
5, 1958 m Nov. 28, 1935 Cora
Foster Sims b May 24, 1914 CHILDREN:

        a   George David II b Dec. 3, 1940
m July 14, 1962 Elizabeth Cook

        b   Richard Murray b Oct. 2, 1944

    2   Mary Estelle b July 4, 1914 m Sept.
14, 1933 Atwell Hughson McNees b
Dec. 5, 1910 CHILDREN:

        a   Atwell David b Dec. 10, 1934
m Apr. 19, 1963 Johnnie M.
Mullins b Nov. 21, 1941

        b   James Lacy b Apr. 27, 1942

3   Murray Reed b Aug. 6, 1917 m June
     28, 1942 Ann Ruth Scott b Nov. 2,
     1920 CHILDREN:

     a   Elizabeth b Oct. 12, 1949

     b   Scott Douglas b Apr. 30, 1951

4   Bertha Virginia b Feb. 2, 1921 m
     March 22, 1941 Joseph Philip
     D'Angelo b Aug. 1921 CHILD:

     a   Murray Eugene b June 3, 1946

5   Paul Edwin b Jan. 11, 1923 m Jan.
     15, 1946 Betty Jean Stansbury b
     Nov. 18, 1923, Mitchell, Ind. NO
     ISSUE

6   Carolyn Elizabeth b Aug. 15, 1925
     m Nov. 28, 1946 John Nelson Blas-
     ingame b Jan. 8, 1926 CHILDREN:

     a   Nancy Carol b May 22, 1948

     b   Barbara Kay b Mar. 9, 1952

     c   Lillian Elizabeth b June 17,
          1959 Selma, Ala.

B   Joe Frank, D.D., b Aug. 8, 1882 d Mar.
     12, 1958 m Oct. 12, 1909 Grace Hollings-
     worth b Sept. 20, 1889 CHILDREN:

1   Grace Stinson b Oct. 20, 1912 m
     Dec. 23, 1933 John Donelson John-
     ston b March 27, 1902 d Sept. 1,
     1962   NO ISSUE

2   Frances Isabelle b May 9, 1916
UNMARRIED

3   Joe Frank II b July 14, 1918 m
April 10, 1952 Jane Rogers b
CHILD:

     a   Joe Frank III b Sept. 15,
      1962

C   Will Brown b Jan. 8, 1886 d July 1949
m Oct. 12, 1910 Linnie Bell Cash b Feb.
22, 1894 d Feb.   1947   CHILD:

1   Will Brown II b Nov. 29, 1923 m
Sept. 15, 1948 Patsy Ruth Carter
b Dec. 9, 1928   CHILDREN:

     a   Patricia Lynn b June 3, 1953

     b   Will Brown III b April 13,
      1960

D   Parrie b Feb. 27, 1887   Lives Memphis,
Tenn.

E   Gay b Jan. 20, 1890 m Jan. 15, 1919
Julia Cox b Oct. 10, 1887 CHILDREN:

1   Gay II b Feb. 26, 1920 m Mar. 15,
1945 Ila Jo Boren b Aug. 23, 1925
CHILDREN:

     a   Melinda Kay b June 12, 1946

     b   Gay III   b July 5, 1948

     c   Ila Elaine b Aug. 4, 1950

2   Julia b Oct. 2, 1921 m June 4,
1954 J. L. Loftin b Aug. 19, 1913

F   Emma Ralls b July 2, 1892   UNMARRIED Living Memphis, Tenn.

VI   Cemantha Amanda b Jan. 18, 1856 d June 30, 1897   UNMARRIED

VII Stephen Bell b May 3, 1858 d June 10, 1937 m Jan. 17, 1893 Sallie Belle Linebarger b Oct. 16, 1866 d Jan. 27, 1941   CHILD:

A   Mary Abigail (Abbie) b Aug. 8, 1895 m July 3, 1920 John Dillard Williams b June 2, 1892   CHILDREN:

1   Bryan Dorroh b Mar. 20, 1922 m Mar. 31, 1941 Jessie Louise Sahm b July 2, 1922   NO ISSUE

2   Mary Elizabeth b May 11, 1931 m April 12, 1958 Judson Jones Copeland b Dec. 4, 1929   CHILDREN:

a   Carole Elizabeth b Dec. 6, 1961

b   Lisa Ann b Aug. 7, 1963

VIII Joel Young (Joe) b Apr. 3, 1860 d [1] m Nov. 7, 1883 Mary Emily (Kate) Hammond b Mar. 25, 1864 d May 25, 1957, age 93   CHILDREN:

A   Parrie Augusta b Nov. 12, 1885 m Jesse Lee Cook b Oct. 10, 1884 d Apr. 1951 CHILD:
             [2]
1   Eugene (Col.ANG) b Mar. 26, 1911 m Sept. 4, 1938 Floyd Cosby b May 16, 1913   CHILD:

[1] Lived and died old Dorroh place, Pickens Co. Ala.; all children born there.
[2] Awarded Bronze Star Medal 8 Aug.1944 for heroic achievement on the Island of Guam.

       a   Eugene Cosby b Jan. 19, 1942

2   Earlene b May 8, 1915 m William G. Bagnall b Mar. 7, 1911 CHILD:

       a   Bonita Ann b Feb. 24, 1948 Washington, D. C.

B   Tom Slaughter b Oct. 20, 1887 m Dec. 26, 1915 Bera Emily Richardson b Nov. 21, 1893   CHILDREN:

1   Tom Slaughter II b Dec. 2, 1916 d (World War II) m 1942 Onzelle Duckworth b   NO ISSUE

2   Emily b Oct. 13, 1919 m FIRST Dec. 23, 1939 William Larence Whitson CHILD:

       a   William Larence (Larry) II b Jan. 13, 1941 m Jan. 12, 1961 Barbara Ann Ivy b   CHILD:

             i   Pamela Ann b July 30, 1962

       m SECOND Feb. 3, 1951 Gerald J. West b   CHILD:

       b   Ava Sue b June 23, 1953

C   Frank Marvin b Mar. 7, 1892 m Sept. 14, 1919 m Ruby Conner b Sept. 22, 1898 CHILDREN:

1   Marvin Lacy b July 5, 1920 m Nov. 28, 1946 Jewel Richards CHILDREN:

       a   Katherine Elizabeth b May 10, 1952

       b   William Marvin b Dec. 26,1953

       c   Rebecca Ann b Jan. 26, 1955

       d   James Frank b Apr. 19, 1960

2　Mary Elizabeth b Apr. 8, 1922 m June 6, 1940 George B. Farrer b CHILDREN:

    a　Robert Franklin b Aug.24,1950

    b　Beth b Oct. 3, 1953

3　Nellie Jo b Jan. 21, 1932 m Nov.24, 1950 Harvey Lee Davis CHILDREN:

    a　Harvey Stephen b Jan. 21, 1951

    b　Marsha Jo b Sept. 29, 1955

    c　Karen Elizabeth b Feb.9, 1957

    d　Janice Carol b Dec. 27, 1958

D　Charlie Young b Aug. 8, 1895 m Mary Walker b Sept. 29, 1900 CHILDREN:

1　Rachel b June 24, 1924 m Ed Jones CHILDREN:

    a　Mike b Aug. 26, 1954

    b　Bekie b Apr. 16, 1957

2　Annalene b Aug. 7, 1926 m FIRST__ Clayton b　　NO ISSUE

    m SECOND George Saunders CHILDREN:

    a　Georg Ann b Sept. 24, 1953

    b　Charles Edwin b Jan. 18,1957

3　Edward Lawrence b Feb. 22, 1930 m Dec. 22, 1956 Jean Jennings b May 7, 1937

E　Kirk L. b May 12, 1902 m Jennie Stokes b Aug. 30, 1906 CHILD:

1　Joe Earl b Nov. 14, 1932 m Norma Crittenden

IX   Emily Paralee (Parrie) b Dec. 18, 1861 d July
        13, 1957 (almost 96) m Nov. 30, 1898 Armond O
        Propst b May 22, 1860 d April 12, 1946 CHILD:

A   Paul Nelson [1] b Feb. 9, 1905 m FIRST
        Glenna Roper

        m   SECOND Margaret Self Trippi

X   Ella Louisa b May 3, 1864 d July 5, 1946 m
        Dec. 16, 1880 William Robert (Bob) Babb b
        Oct. 27, 1856 d Mar. 8, 1935 CHILDREN: [2]

A   Annie Bell b Dec. 6, 1882 d Dec. 4, 1942
        m Dec. 16, 1900 John Lee (Dock) Plowman
        b   d Nov. 13, 1963 CHILDREN:

        1   Oscar b Nov. 9, 1901 d Aug. 12,1961
                m FIRST Oct. 2, 1920 Dixie Luther b
                Aug. 15, 1900 CHILDREN:

                a   Herman b Feb. 17, 1928 m May 8
                        1945 Bonnie   b May 7, 1918
                        CHILD:

                        i   Larry b Feb. 14, 1946

                b   Beatrice b Apr. 19, 1936 m
                        Sept. 16, 1955 Johnny Williams
                        b June 24, 1932 CHILDREN:

                        i   Vickie b Apr. 12, 1959

                        ii   Wendy b Apr. 1, 1961

                m SECOND Mollie_____

        2   Frank b Oct. 27, 1903 m June 27,
                1925 Dora Brandon b   CHILDREN:

                a   Ray b   m   Betty Graham b
                        CHILDREN:
                        i   Steve
                        ii   Darrell
                b   Carolyn b   m Howard Kitchens
                        b   CHILDREN:
                        i   Lisa
                        ii   Tommy
[1]   A Methodist minister in North Ala.Conference.
[2]   All born in Pickens Co. except eldest, Annie.

c   Barbara b m Claude Gray b
    CHILDREN:

    i   Mark

    ii   Pamela

d   Dennis b UNMARRIED

3   Ola Mae b Apr. 22, 1906 m Lee
    White b   CHILDREN:

a   Mary Lois b Dec. 6, 1926 m
    Tommy George b CHILDREN:

    i   Veronica b Apr. 26, 1948

    ii   Thomas Lee b Sept. 7,
        1949

    iii Robert Andrew (Bobby) b
        July 17, 1951

b   Billy

c   James b Sept. 18, 1934 m
    Jeanette Halbrook b June 28,
    1935 CHILDREN:

    i   Robert Lee b Dec. 12,
        1954

    ii   James Edward b Jan, 24,
        1956

    iii Harold Wayne b May 22,
        1957

    iv   Barbara Jo b Dec. 30,
        1958

    v   Delores Ann b July 8,
        1961

    vi   John David b Aug. 24,
        1962

4   Fred b Jan. 21, 1913 m Dec. 25,
    1934 Eloise (Edna) Shelton b Jan.
    25, 1916 CHILDREN:

a   James Adrian b Nov. 4, 1938
m Nov. 5, 1961 Betty Reeves

b   Hayes b July 10, 1944

5   James Osville b May 28, 1918 m Nov.
9, 1942 Mary Vaudine Plyler b July
18, 1923 CHILD:

a   James Lee b Dec. 10, 1954

B   Tullie O. b May 30, 1885 m July 12,
1919 Ozie Johnson b   Live Palmetto,
Pickens Co., Ala. CHILDREN:

1   Olon b July 1, 1920 d Dec. 13,
1958 m Aug. 30, 1940 Kittie Mae
Kyles b Jan. 25, 1925 CHILDREN:

a   Billie Jean b Dec. 7, 1941 m
Jan. 26, 1959 Michael Lan-
caster b   CHILD:

i   Kathy Jean b Mar. 1,1960

b   William Charles b Jan. 6,1945

c   Joe Donald b Aug. 5, 1949

2   Dorothy Jean b June 13, 1922 m Dec.
18, 1937 William Davis Foley b Jan.
18, 1917 CHILDREN:

a   Bobbie Sue b Aug. 20, 1938 m
Sept. 11, 1953 Paul Gene Pugh
b Sept. 1936 CHILDREN:

i   Vickie Paulette b Mar.
13, 1955

ii   Shela Kay b June 26,1957

b   Davis Eugene b Sept. 13, 1940
m Dec. 23, 1959 Ruby Nell
McDill b Mar. 8, 1942 CHILD:

i   Mary Dean b Apr. 12, 1963

c   Robert Earl b Jan. 6, 1945

d   Roger Dale b Mar. 10, 1950

e   Danny Ray b Jan. 22, 1955

f   Michael Olon b Jan. 20, 1960

C   Arrie b Sept. 24, 1887 m Eli Edwards
CHILDREN:

1   Phillip Preston Babb b Sept. 11,
1908 m Aug. 9, 1931 Sarah Lois
Duckworth b July 18, 1914 CHILDREN:

    a   Donald Denney b Feb. 12, 1937
    m June 4, 1958 Ruth Elizabeth
    Thaxton b July 6, 1937
    CHILDREN:

        i   Paul Donald b Feb. 13,
        1960

        ii   Mark Dennis b Dec. 6,
        1961

    b   Bobby Joe b Jan. 29, 1940 m
    Aub. 25, 1962 Peggy Ruth
    Meaders b Aug. 21, 1942

2   George b July 17, 1918

3   Vera b Aug. 25, 1920

4   Ruby Gray b Oct. 7, 1922 m Dec. 9,
1940 Kenneth Floyd Schneider b
CHILDREN:

    a   Kenneth Michael b Oct. 20,
    1956

    b   Wayne Frederick b Sept. 26,
    1958

    c   Sheila Lynne b Jan. 21, 1960

    d   Robert b Nov. 9, 1961

D   Joel Austin (Joe) b July 13, 1889 d Dec.
11, 1932 m FIRST Jan. 14, 1914 Nellie
Dulcie Grace b Dec. 30, 1894 d July 12,
1919   CHILDREN:

1   Ella Katherine b Nov. 8, 1914 m
    July 22, 1934 John Bluford Price
    b Nov. 27, 1914 CHILDREN:

    a   John Austin I b June 13, 1935
        m Feb. 3, 1956 Billie Jean
        Baldridge b Feb. 1, 1937
        CHILDREN:

        i   Vickie Sue b Jan. 28,
             1957

        ii   John Austin II b Feb. 8,
             1959

        iii Virginia Katherine b Mar.
             6, 1963

    b   Charles Russell b Feb. 13,
        1937 m May 28, 1960 Alene
        Favella b Sept. 30, 1938
        CHILD:

        i   Russell Allen b Mar. 11,
             1962

    c   James Bluford b Sept. 17, 1940
        m Mar. 30, 1963 Martha Jean
        Bodine b Feb. 15, 1942

    d   Joel Hayes b July 29, 1944

2   Nellie Elizabeth b Oct. 5, 1918 m
    Sept. 22, 1935 James Boyd Price b
    Sept. 19, 1916   CHILDREN:

    a   Nellie Jo b July 1, 1936 m
        June 22, 1958 John Jacob Cole
        b Oct.4, 1935 CHILDREN:

        i   John Jacob II b Oct. 23,
             1959 d Oct. 24, 1959

        ii   Kenneth Randle b Dec. 12,
             1961

    b   Dorothy Faye b Sept. 3, 1943

D   m SECOND Sept. 30, 1923 Lissie Lee
    Allen b Nov. 28, 1899 CHILDREN:

3 Nomilee b Feb. 22, 1925 m Dec. 19, 1941 Andrew Flynn b Sept. 24, 1923 CHILDREN:

 a Romana Ann b Mar. 20, 1947 m April 27, 1963 James Austin b Mar. 19, 1943

 b Patricia Lee b Dec. 5, 1949

 c Donald Joe b Aug. 21, 1951

4 Modean b Apr. 20, 1927 d July 13, 1928

5 Nettie Mae b Apr. 10, 1930 d Dec. 16, 1937

6 Joel Stanley b May 12, 1932 m Billie CHILDREN:

 a Gregg b May 16, 1955

 b Mina b Apr. 16, 1956

 c Tammy b June 21, 1958

 d Mark b Mar. 9, 1960

E Nellie (twin) b May 17, 1892 d ca 1892

F Mellie (twin) b May 17, 1892 m Dec. 12, 1913 Julius Wilson b Feb. 1, 1888 Live Palmetto, Pickens Co., Ala. CHILDREN:

1 Robert b Dec. 24, 1914 m Aug. 16, 1942 Annie Dell Hanks b CHILDREN:

 a Martha Ann b Apr. 9, 1943 d Aug. 26, 1949

 b Jimmy b Dec. 27, 1947

2 Glover b Dec. 25, 1917 m July 3, 1943 Lou Ella Homan b CHILDREN:

 a Doris Nell b Dec. 10, 1944

 b Juanita b Aug. 7, 1947

c   Ricky Eugene b Mar. 7, 1952

3   Homer b Jan. 20, 1921 m FIRST
Helen Kidd b   CHILD:

a   Gary b Apr. 27, 1945

m SECOND Mar. 20, 1952 Katie
Madison b   CHILDREN:

b   Paula Kay b Jan.6, 1950

c   Nadine b May 21, 1952

4   Elton b Apr. 1, 1923 m Apr. 26,
1942 Evelyn Moore b   CHILDREN:

a   Bobby Elton b Sept. 13, 1944
m Jan. 29, 1962 Sharon Little

b   Kandice b June 2, 1948

c   Kathy b May 13, 1950

d   Phylis b Dec. 19, 1952

5   Estelle b Apr. 3, 1926 m Jan. 8,
1944 Webster Butts b CHILDREN:

a   Jerry Douglas b Nov. 28,1947

b   Alford Lynn b Aug. 2, 1954

c   Frances Rena b Oct. 24, 1957

6   Linnie V. b Nov. 20, 1927 d Dec.
27, 1927

7   William Ernest I b May 24, 1929 m
Feb. 19, 1955 Virginia Arnold b
Jan. 15, 1935   CHILDREN:

a   William Ernest II b June 19,
1956

b   Trena Ann b   1960

8   Velma b Dec. 19, 1930 m June 24,
1950 Amos Aldridge b   CHILD:

a   Reba Dianne b Sept. 24, 1957

9   Ralph L. b Oct. 13, 1932 m
Nelly Angulo b Apr. 20,
1935 CHILDREN:

    a   Kennoth Allen b June 2, 1955

    b   Shirley b Nov. 17, 1956

    c   Sheila b Nov. 27, 1959

10   Emily b May 3, 1937 d May 3, 1937

G   Minnie b Apr. 20, 1894 m Dec. 30, 1916
Rube Sherrill b   CHILDREN:

    1   Douglas b   m   Curtis White b

    2   Nathan b m Beverly Smith b

    3   Clarence b m Marie Snipes b

H   Murray Doss b Apr. 6, 1897 m Feb. 26,
1920 Luna Holliman b Feb. 11, 1899 Live
Hot Springs, Ark.   CHILDREN:

    1   Lois Vivian b Apr. 14, 1921

    2   Betty b Oct. 20, 1928 m Clarence E.
Henson b Mar. 8, 1925 CHILD:

    a   Rita Ann b Jan. 27, 1947

I   Kenley Jackson b Oct. 27, 1901 m Aug.
13, 1927 Edna Inez Lord b May 27, 1911
CHILDREN:

    1   Kenley Earl b Nov. 3, 1928 d Nov.
14, 1928

    2   James Edgar b Aug. 12, 1930 m July
30, 1949 Lorraine Wilhams b May 21,
1931 CHILDREN:

    a   Patsy Jane b Nov. 20, 1951

    b   Phyllis b June 13, 1953

    c   Cathy Ann b

    d   Belinda Fay b

3 Mary Ella b Dec. 1, 1932 m Apr. 1948 Charles Gary Manley b Mar. 14, 1929 CHILDREN:

 a Michail Gary b Apr. 4, 1950

 b David Patrick b Feb. 5, 1952

 c Steven Edward b

 d Ruth Ellen b

4 Lily Evelyn b Oct. 20, 1934 m Oct. 17, 1953 Jessie Strickland b Dec. 28, 1925 CHILDREN:

 a Linda Maureen b May 21, 1955

 b Bonnie Sue b Mar. 22, 1957

 c Judy Evelyn b Nov. 29, 1958

 d Rebecca Ruth b Sept. 5, 1960

5 John Floyd b Jan. 8, 1937 m 1960 Connie Wedge b Feb. 4, 1940

6 Barbara Jean b July 9, 1940 m 1958 William Gilbert Perkins b May 12, 1931 CHILDREN:

 a William Gilbert II b Apr. 1959
 b Thomas Craig b 1961

7 Edna Annie b May 21, 1944 m July 7, 1961 Bruce Allen Peer b Aug. 19, 1934 CHILD:

 a Dennis Oneal Babb b Feb.4,1947

J William Ernest (Willie) b Nov. 19, 1903 m Mar. 21, 1926 Roberta Porter b Nov. 8, 1910 CHILDREN:

1 Ernest Levern b Feb. 26, 1927 m June 15, 1946 Maudine Ayers b July 8, 1929 CHILDREN:

 a Gwendolyn Ann b Oct. 19, 1948

b Gregory b July 9, 1958

2 Herbert Dennis b Oct. 15, 1929
m Oct. 8, 1952 Barbara Fulmer b
Oct. 21, 1921 CHILDREN:

 a Debra Jean b Apr. 11, 1954

 b Kathy b July 4, 1956

 c Jeffery b Feb. 10, 1959

3 Willie Nell b May 11, 1934 d Feb.
8, 1952

4 Martha Sue b Apr. 20, 1937,Fayette
Ala., m Aug. 22, 1953 James Allen
Shepherd b Aug. 24, 1933 CHILDREN:

 a Pamela Leigh b Feb. 22, 1955

 b Patricia Allen b Dec. 10,
1956

5 Billie Joyce b Aug. 3, 1942 Mill-
port, Ala. m June 6, 1959 Olis T.
J. Carey b Mar. 1, 1937 CHILDREN:

 a Atona b Oct. 24, 1960

 b Terri Jean b Dec. 11, 1961

6 Bobby Clarence b and d Nov. 22,
1948

K Grady b March 15, 1898 d May 15, 1898

XI Andrew Thompson b May 27, 1866 d July 22,
1868
[1]

XII Lewis Francis (Frank) b April 29, 1870 d May
19, 1954 m Oct. 22, 1899 Lola Sudduth b Apr.
20, 1877 d Sept. 4, 1958 CHILDREN:

[1] Frank Dorroh taught for thirty five years in
Pickens, Lamar and Fayette counties in Ala.
His will is recorded in the Lamar Co. and
Pickens Co. Court Houses.

A   Mary Lucile [1] b Feb. 15, 1901 m Dec.
    26, 1942 Steven Clay Burton b Aug.16,
    1902
B   Gay Irven b Apr. 7, 1903 d July 13,
    1963 m Dec. 23, 1933 Almeda Christian
    b Sept. 21, 1907 CHILDREN:

    1   James Willard b Mar. 28, 1935 m
        June 8, 1963 Amanda Irene Beckert

    2   Ralph b Apr. 30, 1936 m Aug. 24,
        1958 Shandry Calhoun b April 11,
        1936

    3   Bobby b Jan. 13, 1939 d Dec. 3,
        1949

C   Robert Burdette b Dec. 2, 1907 d Nov.
    7, 1962 m Dec. 29, 1939 Charlean Crow-
    ley b Nov. 2   NO ISSUE

D   B. J., b April 6, 1909 m May 13, 1939
    Nueal Conner b May 14,   CHILD:

    1   Lola Jean b Nov. 16, 1940

E   Charles Hill b May 24, 1916 m Apr. 7,
    1947 Elizabeth Snow b April 14,
    CHILDREN:

    1   Patricia Gail b Aug. 25, 1950

    2   Ann Marie b May 21, 1953

F   Lola Frances b May 22, 1923 m June 7,
    1950 August W. Kuhn b Aug. 30,
    CHILDREN:

    1   Kenneth August b Jan. 3, 1954

    2   Keith Frank b April 10, 1959

[1] Lucile is family historian for Dorroh, Sulli-
    vant, Gregg, Sudduth, Shepherd, Bell, Middle-
    ton and Nall families. Lives in Birmingham,
    Alabama.

Reverend Joel Dorroh

The history of this family would not be complete with nothing more than mere statistics on this remarkable man, Joel Dorroh. When his grandfather Jacob Fox moved to Mississippi in the fall of 1866 with most of his children and their families, there was a severe shortage of men as Jacob Fox had only one son, John M. Fox; the other seven children were girls and the youngest, Angeline, was not married. His daughter Dorcas and her husband Jack Hollingsworth remained in Pickens Co. Ala. His daughter Martha's husband William T. Gregg had died in 1860 and his daughter Sarah's husband Stephen Dorroh father of Joel, had died in Tennessee in the Civil War.

Joel Dorroh was only eight years old when they moved but took the place of a man and drove a yoke of oxen in the wagon train all the way from Alabama to their new home in what is now the northern part of Webster Co. Miss. He had a first cousin also named Joel (Joel Y. Dorroh, son of Joel and Emily Gregg Dorroh) who lived back in Ala., both of them called "Joe" and both of them were first cousins to my mother Dora Gregg Shelton. When the families visited and mention was made of Joe Dorroh, someone would invariably say, "which Joe are you talking about, 'Mississippi Joe' or 'Alabama Joe'?"! An account of the feats and accomplishments of Rev. Joel Dorroh would be too long to include here, but the most amazing one was that two days after the community had helped him celebrate his 91st birthday, he was discovered climbing a 40-foot high gum sapling which he topped with the dexterity of a 30-year-old! His accomplishments - too numerous for this record but he was a Baptist Minister for about 55 years and four of his sons became ministers. His funeral was attended by 27 preachers and over a thousand people - a fitting testimonial to the passing of a great man.

Article contributed by Z. F. Shelton

Descendants of Stephen Dorroh and Sarah Fox

I   Jarusha b Feb. 24, 1854 d Aug. 17, 1863
UNMARRIED

II   James Jacob b June 29, 1856 d Jan. 15, 1876
UNMARRIED

III   Joel (Rev.) [1] b Nov. 1, 1858 d Mar. 27,
1951 (age 92) m FIRST Dec. 11, 1883 Margaret
(Mag) Caroline Finnell [1] b Feb. 17, 1863 d
Feb. 26, 1925   CHILDREN:

    A   Jerusha (Pearl) b Nov. 22, 1884 m Nov.
4, 1908 John (Newt) Bennett b
NO ISSUE

    B   John Bunyan b Jan. 30, 1886 d Nov. 14,
1958 m   Cecil Rankin b
                CHILD:

        1   Kathleen b   ca 1933

    C   Leroy Finnell b Apr. 25, 1888 m Dec.
26, 1911 Manie West b June 11, 1886
CHILDREN:
                                      m
        1   Maggie Louise b Jan. 15, 1913 T.J.
Vance b Aug. 11, 1934   CHILD:

            a   Bobby b   d as infant

        2   Harold Finnell b Dec. 18, 1913 m
Nov. 14, 1949 Geralden Tompson b
Sept. 4, 1932   CHILDREN:

            a   Debra b Apr. 3, 1952

            b   LuNell b Nov. 24, 1953

            c   Malissa b Apr. 6, 1959 d

[1] Rev. Joel Dorroh & his wife "Mag" Finnell
were cousins---"Mag's" father, Leroy M. Finnell
Jr. was a son of Mary A. C. Hughes by her first
marriage to Finnell, & Joel Dorroh's mother Sarah
Fox was a daughter of this same Mary A. C. Hughes
(Finnell by her second marriage to Jacob Fox.

3   Ella Pauline b Nov. 28, 1915 m
Sept. 30, 1934 Odia McPhail
b   CHILDREN:

    a   Iris b   m Wally
        Simpson b

    b   Harold Wells b

    c   James Rone b

D   Joel (Ira) b Feb. 24, 1890 d July 21,
1918 m   Janie West b
NO ISSUE

E   Susie b April 25, 1892 d July 19, 1939
m   1913 Claude Denton b Mar.
2, 1891   CHILDREN:

1   Joel Russell b July 29, 1914 m Aug.
5, 1933 Nancy Skelton b
CHILDREN:

    a   Margaret Carolyn b Sept. 5,
        1934 m July 14, 1956 John
        Alan Phillips b
        CHILDREN:

        i   John Alan II b May 3,
            1957

        ii   Russell Lord b Apr. 21,
            1959

        iii   Mary Catherine b Feb. 9,
            1962

    b   Joe Grady b Mar. 7, 1939 m
        Dec. 16, 1959 Barbara Ann
        Ogglesley b   CHILD_
        REN:

        i   Deborah Kay b Sept. 8,
            1960

        ii   James Russell b Jan. 27,
            1962

2 Samuel Bunyan b Mar. 13, 1916 m
Apr. 30, 1937 Bertie Lollar b
CHILDREN:

 a Patricia Jean b Aug. 10, 1938
  m June 28, 1956 William Wray
  Allen b   CHILDREN:

  i Tammeron Lynn b Nov. 20,
   1957

  ii William Terry b May 20,
   1962

 b Bobby Jerome b Oct. 31, 1940
  m May 8, 1958 Mamie Lavern
  Pullen b   CHILDREN:

  i Rennee b April 21, 1959

  ii Samuel Jeffery b Apr. 15,
   1962

 c Prudie Fay b July 18, 1945

3 Claude Haven b Nov. 5, 1921 d Nov.
2, 1943

4 Mary Finnell b Oct. 3, 1932 m Oct.
1950 Douglas V. Mallory b
CHILDREN:

 a Claudia Kate b July 8, 1951

 b Mary Douglas b Oct. 6, 1952

 c Peter Jackson b Sept. 21,1962

F Jesse Stephen b Jan. 2, 1894 m Apr. 14,
1918 Ruth Macon b July 3, 1897 CHILDREN:

 1 James Stanley b May 1, 1920 m Dec.
  22, 1941 Dolores Langston b June 4,
  1923 CHILDREN:

  a Eric Stanley b Apr. 2, 1943

  b James Elton b Dec. 18, 1946

        c   Joel Langston b Feb. 21, 1957

2   Annie Lucille b Oct. 9, 1922 m Mar. 25, 1946 James H. Langston b NFI

3   Mildred Pearl b July 18, 1924 m April 11, 1942 Curtis Pounds b CHILD:

        a   Donald Curtis b Oct. 25, 1953

4   Robert Grady b March 13, 1932 m July 19, 1952 Nellie Fay Wooten b   CHILDREN:

        a   James Grady b Aug. 26, 1953

        b   Linda Ruth b July 10, 1955

        c   Thomas Allen b Sept. 10, 1957

G   Jimmie Bell b May 11, 1896 d March 3, 1957 m Nov. 10, 1917 Georgia Lee Carroll b Feb. 26, 1897 CHILDREN:

1   Ralph Edgar b June 25, 1920 Belle-fontaine, Miss. m Nov. 21, 1948 Grace (Gay) Darling Schell b May 24, 1922 CHILDREN:

        a   Mark Lee b May 10, 1951 Fort Madison, Iowa

        b   Shelby Kay b Oct. 30, 1955, Hollywood, Fla.

2   James b April 4, 1925 m Aug. 12, 1951 Jeanette House b CHILD:

        a   Sharla b   d (age 4 yrs.)

H   Grady b Jan. 23, 1898 d Oct. 29, 1929 UNMARRIED

I   Mary Lackey b Jan. 26, 1900 d Sept. 14, 1900

J   Nelson Trueman b Feb. 21, 1902 m
       CHILD:

       1   Lillie Jean b

III m SECOND   Lillie Gregg b Jan. 9,
      1880 d Dec. 19, 1958

IV Montgomery Bell b Sept. 2, 1860 d Jan.   1915
    m   Hattie Strong b March 23, 1865
    d March 5, 1937   NO ISSUE

V   John William Stephen b March 17, 1862 Pick-
    ens Co., Ala. d March 26, 1953 m April 22,
    1908 Mattie L. Thompson b Feb.22, 1877 d Aug.
    CHILDREN: 24, 1943

A   Sarah Irene b Feb. 1, 1909 d Feb. 2,
       1909

B   Stephen T. b Jan. 17, 1910 d Nov. 10,
       1951

C   William Judson b Sept. 10, 1912 m Nov.
       9, 1956 Edna Jackson Campbell b May 5,
       1911

D   Joseph Bell b July 24, 1914 d Oct. 18,
       1916

E   Curtis H. b Aug. 31, 1916 m Nov. 27,
       1942 Emma Jean Thorne b Aug. 14, 1923
       CHILD:

       1   Curtis Wayne b Jan. 18, 1946
          Grenada, Miss.

354

Descendants of Elizabeth Dorroh and Leroy Montgomery Finnell *

I   Mary Elizabeth b Sept. 29, 1849 d 1852

II   Frances Jane b June 23, 1851 d   1918
     m   Henry Cook b   CHILDREN:

     A   Sallie b   m   Whitaker

     B   Ethel b

III Martha Ann b July 27, 1853 d   1861

IV   Emoline (Em) b Jan. 27, 1855 d Sept. 8,1888
     m FIRST Oct. 16, 1872 James Henry (Jim)Shaw
     b Sept. 16, 1849 d Sept. 20, 1874 CHILDREN:

     A   Lois Edna b Aug. 12, 1873 d Dec. 1960
          m Dec. 24, 1891 James William West b
          Sept. 21, 1870 CHILDREN:

          1   Clara Emma b Aug. 18, 1895 m April
               2, 1912 Elbert Elmore Lunceford b
               CHILDREN:

               a   William Herbert, M.D., b June
                    26, 1913 m June 12, 1941 Mary
                    Clay b   CHILDREN:

                    i   Judith Clarilee b Jan.
                         12, 1943

                    ii   William Herbert II b May
                         18, 1945

                    iii David Eugene b Sept. 16,
                         1948

                    iv   Elizabeth Joy b June 16,
                         1952

               b   Leroy Elmore b Feb. 13, 1915
                    m Nov. 9, 1938 Christine
                    Flemming b   CHILDREN:

                    i   Lois Marie b July 29,
                         1939

* We are indebted to Mr. Z.F.Shelton for help on
this line.

ii   Leroy Wayne b Nov. 14,
      1946

c   Jasper Hycock b Jan. 18, 1917
     m Nov. 2, 1940 Mavis Allday
     b   CHILDREN:

i   Roma Ann b Aug. 24, 1941

ii   Timothy b Aug. 10, 1946

d   James Ovis b April 7, 1919 m
     Aug. 14, 1939 Grace Brooks b
     CHILDREN:

i   Patricia Ann b Apr. 1,
     1942

ii   Jimmie Lynn b Dec. 4,
     1943

e   Edna Opal b May 4, 1921 (school
     teacher) m Oct. 17, 1941
     Gilbert Allday b   CHILDREN:

i   Gilbert Wayne b June 4,
     1943

ii   Jerry Nelson b Nov. 4,
     1946

f   Martha West b Aug. 28, 1923

g   Marvin Lee b May 4, 1925

h   James Shaw b Aug. 12, 1927

i   Travis Eugene b Jan. 8, 1930

j   Henry Durell b July 1, 1932 m
     Sept. 2, 1952 Eva Nell Whit-
     Worth b

k   Joe Elbert b Jan. 20, 1937

l   Infant b and d   1939

2 Henry Jerome b Mar. 18, 1901 m Aug. 13, 1927 Wrispy Ida Spencer b Nov. 17, 1900 CHILDREN:

 a Infant son b and d May 2,

 b Willie Jobe b Sept. 24, 1935

 c Henry Green b Nov. 19, 1939

3 William Everett I b Mar. 24, 1906 m Apr. 29, 1924 Dollie Putman b CHILDREN:

 a William Everett II b June 17, 1925 m Sept. 14, 1947 Alma Magress b CHILD:

  i Michael b July 4, 1950

 b Imogene b Sept. 19, 1929 m July 26, 1948 Bennie Lee Norwood b CHILDREN:

  i Bennie Harold b Aug. 26, 1950

  ii Sherry Darnell b Nov. 10, 1952

 c James Frank b Mar. 4, 1946

4 Connie Dorcas b Dec. 1, 1908 m July 13, 1924 Irby Patterson b CHILDREN:

 a Winford b Aug. 23, 1926 m Jan. 25, 1945 Johnny Bervis Sutton b CHILDREN:

  i James Irby b Mar. 5,1947

  ii Linda Kav b Sept. 21, 1948

  iii Boyd Wavne b July 29, 1951

 b Willie Katherine b July 20, 1928 m May 11, 1946 Royce

Langston b   CHILD:

  i   Nancy Sherryll b May 25, 1952

 c   Sarah Frances b Jan. 27, 1932
   m   Buddy House b

 d   Anna Lois b July 13, 1934 m
   Jimmy Porch b

 5   Infant girl b and d June 30, 1911

IV   m SECOND Jan. 15, 1878 Joseph E. Pryor b
CHILDREN:

B   Mary Virginia b May 3, 1879 d June 18,
   1897   UNMARRIED

C   Fannie Eustatia (Stacia) b Feb. 24,1881
   m April 14, 1901 Thomas Sidney Fox b
   CHILDREN:

 1   Emma Camilla b April 20, 1903 m
   July 18, 1925 Sidney B. Thomas
   CHILDREN:

  a   Sidney Jeanne b Aug. 12, 1931
    m April 7, 1951 Mark Fairman
    b   CHILDREN:

    i   Mike

    ii   Robert
  b   Sidney B. II b Jan. 25,1935[1]
 2   Edna Opal b Aug. 6, 1906 m FIRST
   Feb. 10, 1929 Thomas Felton Camp I
   b   CHILD:

  a   Thomas Felton II, M.D., b
    Sept. 20, 1930

   m SECOND Oct. 14, 1939 Joe Page b
   CHILDREN:

  b   Carey Pryor b Jan. 7, 1943

  c   John Hulon b Jan. 9, 1945
[1]   m June 1952 Mary Zell Jones

3   Lillian Estelle b Aug. 7, 1908 m
     July 3, 1930 William C. Payne I b
     CHILD:

     a   William C. II b

D   Connie b April 19, 1884 d Mar. 11, 1943
     m Mar. 22, 1907 Claiborne Crain b
     CHILDREN:

     1   Joseph Ballard b April 1, 1908 m
          1938 Bonnie_____ b

     2   Virginia b Sept. 1, 1909 m   1934
          Jack Turner b   NO ISSUE

     3   Jerry Christler b Sept. 27, 1911 m
          March   1936 Betty Hicks b
          CHILDREN:

          a   Claiborne Hicks b

          b   Jerry b

V   Gracy Matilda b Dec. 18, 1857 d   1860.

VI   James Leroy b Sept. 1, 1860 d   1865.

Descendants of William Dorroh and Mary Stone

I Jonathon Wesley b Jan. 22, 1819 [1] d July 1,
   1896 m FIRST Feb. 22, 1841 Catherine Glenn
   b   ca 1823 d   before 1870 CHILDREN: SEE
   SEPARATE LISTING under DESCENDANTS OF JONA-
   THON WESLEY AND CATHERINE GLENN

   m SECOND Helen Langston b April 8, 1842 d
   Nov. 6, 1911 CHILDREN: SEE SEPARATE LISTING
   under DESCENDANTS OF JONATHON WESLEY AND
   HELEN LANGSTON

II Rebecca b April 27, 1820 d June 11, 1896 m
   Oct. 10, 1838 William C. Martin b
   CHILDREN:

   A   Thomas b

   B   Henry b

III James J. b   1823 d   1904
    m FIRST   Mary T. Glenn b Jan. 26,
    1835 d May 13, 1866 [2]   CHILDREN:

    A   William A.   b   1858 d   1934
        UNMARRIED

    B   James Franklin b   1860 d May 17,
        1946 m Nov. 21, 1893 Linnie Crayne b
                1869 d   1949
        CHILDREN:

        1   William Robert b Nov. 10, 1894 m
            April 5, 1925 Frances Adams b June
            26, 1894   CHILD:

            a   James Robert b Feb. 11, 1926
                m Sept. 24, 1958 Jackie Eliz-
                abeth Howard b May 24, 1939
                CHILDREN:

[1] Jonathon Wesley was born in Alabama; all
    other children born in Caldwell Co.,Ky.

[2] Both buried in New Bethel Cemetery, near
    Kuttawa, Kentucky.

        i   Patty Elisa b July 26, 1959, Crayne, Ky.

       ii   Pamela Anne b May 23, 1963, Crayne, Ky.

2   Eugene b Sept. 5, 1896 d Aug. 22, 1956 m May ₁8, 1918 Iva Bigham b
CHILDREN:

    a   Dorothy Glenn b Jan. 24, 1924 Crittenden Co.,Ky., m Nov. 3, 1946 Curtis Hill b
CHILDREN:

        i   Gary Eugene b Dec. 30, 1947

       ii   James Richard b Sept. 19, 1952

      iii   Bonnie Kay b Dec. 10, 1959

    b   Norma Jean b Aug. 23, 1927 d Dec. 1, 1941

3   James Tinsley b Sept. 25, 1901 d Dec. 14, 1958   UNMARRIED

4   Mary Emma b June 19, 1906 m April 29, 1929 Allie Myers b

C   Rebecca b   1862 d   1901
m   Press Martin b
CHILDREN:

1   Ollie b

2   Frank

3   Mary

4   Jimmie

5   Willie

6   Ras

D   Maggie b   1864 d   1938
    m   Joe Perryman b

III m SECOND Oct. 28, 1868 Esther J. Cole b
            d   CHILDREN:

E   Bell b Dec. 16, 1873 d May 29, 1959 m
    William Clement b   CHILD

    1   Florence b Jan. 22, 1911 m May 8,
        1929 Raymond Johes b   CHILD

      a   Billy Wayne b Dec. 22, 1931

F   Dickie b   d   young

IV Elizabeth b   ca 1825 m Nov. 26, 1842 M. S.
    Freeman b   CHILDREN:

A   Jim b   m   Mollie
    Bice b

B   Sarah b   m   Joseph
    Deboe b   CHILDREN: [1]

    1   Philip b   NFI

    2   Thomas

    3   Robert

    4   Henry

    5   Charles

    6   Bell

    7   Nellie

    8   Carrie b   m Thomas
        Ordway b

V Sarah b Sept. 18, 1826 d June 29, 1842

VI William Washington b Feb. 21, 1827 d Feb. 18,
1904 m FIRST Rachel Frost b May 19, 1832 d
June 7, 1855   NO ISSUE

[1] All deceased except Carrie

VI   m SECOND   Mary Avery Easly b
Sept. 23, 1831 d Feb. 9, 1892 CHILDREN:
SEE SEPARATE LISTING under DESCENDANTS OF
WILLIAM WASHINGTON DORROH AND MARY AVERY
EASLY.
    m   THIRD   Miss Craig b   NO ISSUE [1]

VII Caleb Clark b Aug. 16, 1828 Caldwell Co.Ky.
d   1910 m Dec. 9, 1845 Nancy
Dyson b   d April 7, 1909
CHILDREN: SEE SEPARATE LISTING under
DESCENDANTS OF CALEB CLARK DORROH AND
NANCY DYSON   [2]

VIII Mary b March 21, 1830 d Aug. 20, 1834
UNMARRIED

IX   Martha A.   b ca 1832 m   _____   Bice
b   CHILDREN:

    A   Fleet

    B   Gideon

    C   Mollie b   m   James
       Freeman b

    D   Lee

X   Francis (Frank) M. b ca 1833/34 d April 6
or 7, 1862 (Civil War)

XI   Malinda b   ca 1834 m   _____   Lynn
b   CHILDREN:

    A   William b

    B   Nancy b   m   _____ Bowers
       b

[1]   Buried Princeton, Kentucky.

[2]   Some descendants include the name Clay in
the name of Caleb Clark Dorroh

Descendants of John Wesley Dorroh and Catherine Glenn

I   Nancy E. (Nannie) b ca 1842 m   Mr. Stone

II James Thomas b Feb. 17, 1942 d Jan. 16, 1917
    m   Nannie White b Oct. 14, 1847 d
    July 7, 1932   CHILDREN:

A   Sarah b March 6, 1868

B   Viola b ca   1870 d March 18, 1953
    m   Harvey G. McElroy b
    CHILDREN:

    1   Archie

    2   Allie

    3   Nannie

C   Mary Katherine b Feb. 12, 1875 d Feb.
    28, 1956 m   Joe Guess b
    CHILDREN:

    1   Edward

    2   William

    3   J. D.

    4   Eugene

    5   Sudie

    6   Lucy

    7   Dora

D   Homer b Dec. 24, 1876 d   1877

E   George Henry b June 28, 1878 d Oct. 17,
    1961 m   Lelia George b May
    22, 1890 d Dec. 2, 1916   CHILD:

    1   Juanita b

F   Thomas Collins b Jan. 22, 1883 d Sept.
    16, 1950 m Caroline (Cad) Brasher*b Nov.
    4, 1880   CHILDREN:

1   Leslie b Feb. 2, 1905 m July 16, 1923 Rebecca Cash b   NO ISSUE

2   James Thomas b July 8, 1910 m Dec. 24, 1927 Hester White b CHILDREN:

     a   James Lester b July 8, 1933 m Oct. 15, 1961 Patricia Gray b Nov. 4,____

     b   Caroline Ann b May 30, 1954

G   Lucy Cornelius b Apr. 10, 1885 d Dec. 20, 1920 m   Claude George b CHILDREN:

1   Cecil

2   Ruth b   m Ralph Churchill

3   Hershall

4   Anna b   m Roy Rosengreen

5   William'

6   J. I.

H   Infant b Aug. 17, 1887 d Aug. 30, 1887

I   Infant b   1888 d   1888

III   Sarah Malissa b Jan. 1, 1845 d   15, 1903 m   Garrett George b

     CHILREN:[1]
IV   Sue b   ca 1847 m   Will Grace b CHILDREN:

A   Pearl b   m   George Keaton

B   Ruby b   m   Lester Hodge

V   Virginia Ellen b   1849 d   1926 m   Col Hammack b   CHILD:

A   Col II

VI   Elizabeth A. (Eliza) b Sept. 20, 1850 d Jan. 31, 1918 m   S.C. McGill b   CHILDREN:

A Nannie b Sept. 26, 1874 d July 17, 1899
A. R. Hammack b   CHILD:
 1 Seldon b
B Archie b   m   Tom
Hammack b CHILD:
 1 Earl b   m Willie Virginia

VII William Henry b Oct. 12, 1854 d Dec. 27,1903
m   Minnie Riddle b Feb. 1,
1881 d May 15, 1956 CHILD:

A William Glenn b Nov. 5, 1900 m Oct. 28,
1937   Charline Nunn b Oct.26,1899
NO ISSUE

VIII Florence b July 13, 1858 d Aug. 23, 1873

IX George F. b ca 1859

* Thanks go to Mrs. Cad Brasher Dorroh for help
on material in this line.

[1] CHILDREN ARE:

1 Albert

2 Patrick

3 Cora b m Will Davis

4 John b   UNMARRIED

Descendants of John Wesley Dorroh and Helen Langston

I   Lillian b Jan. 21, 1862 m July 4, 1887
Phillip Matlock b   CHILD:

A   John

II   Robert H. b Aug. 22, 1864 d Oct. 29, 1906 m
March 22, 1892 Allie Young b March 22, 1878
d Aug. 17, 1922   CHILDREN:

A   Janie F. b   1898 d
1959

B   Robert Francis b Oct. 30, 1901 m
Tiny Hall b

III May b Oct. 15, 1867 m   Kirk
Brasher b

IV Frederick C.   b March 1, 1873 d Feb. 13,
1943 m   1897 Enola White b Jan.
22, 1878 d Aug. 5, 1958   CHILDREN:

A   Bryan Clifton b Sept. 20, 1898 m
Naomi Cash b Oct. 9, 1899 d March 23,
1956   CHILDREN:

1   Bryan Clifton II b April 9, 1921
d Jan. 16, 1922

2   Rachel Ruth b June 22, 1923 m
William S. White b July
21, 1918   CHILD:

a   Rodney b May 10, 1947

3   Barbara Nell b Sept. 11, 1925 m
Joseph S. Barnes b Nov.
8, 1923 d Sept. 22, 1962   CHILD:

a   Penny Jo b Aug. 31, 1953

4   Carl Elwood b July 4, 1928 m
Sidney Wood Satterfield
b Nov. 2, 1933   CHILDREN:

a   Randy b Dec. 17, 1953

b   Sandra Lynne b Sept. 23,1957

5   Frances Elizabeth b July 23, 1930
m   Richard Brandon
Lester b June 16, 1930 CHILDREN:

    a   Charles Bradley b Oct. 20,
          1956

    b   Richard Bryan b Dec. 10,1958

    c   Andrew Perry b Sept. 13, 1962

6   Billy Joe b Jan. 14, 1936 m
Melba Joyce Holt b March 8, 1939
CHILD:

    a   Jochael Ruth b Dec. 28, 1961

B   John Richard b Feb. 24, 1901 m Oct. 19,
1921 Dorris Garner b Sept. 15, 1902
Lyon Co., Ky.   CHILDREN:

1   Gloria b Dec. 30, 1923 m
T. E. Joiner b March 13, 1910

2   Margo Jean b July 21, 1930 m Dec.
20, 1948 John L. Dixon b March 7,
1930

3   Charles Richard b Feb. 9, 1936 m
Sept. 23, 1960 Rebecca Joy Tabor
b Oct. 21, 1937

       Elizabeth
C   Helen b April 30, 1903 d Sept. 18, 1923
m Aug.   1923 Frank Arnold b

D   Frederick W. b May 31, 1916 m Oct. 10,
1932 Louise LeFan b Dec. 14, 1914
CHILDREN:

1   Wilford Wayne b Sept. 22, 1933
Lyon Co.Ky., m Oct. 3, 1956
Patricia Ann Bennett b Nov. 8,
1934   CHILD:

    a   Patrick Wayne b Aug. 3, 1957

2   Carroll Gene b July 16, 1935 m
Mar. 1, 1957 Sarah Lou Ray b May
17, 1937   CHILDREN:

a   Mickell Ray b Dec. 29, 1957
d Dec. 29, 1957

b   Frederick Allen b Mar. 13,
1959

c   Carroll David b June   1960
d June   1960

d   Anthony b Sept.   1961 d
Sept.   1961

e   Renee b Nov. 14, 1961
(adopted)

3   Donna Louise b March 10, 1937 m
May 7, 1954 James Thomas Parsley
b Feb. 3, 1933   CHILDREN:

a   Jeffery b Feb. 21, 1958

b   Kathy Louise b Aug. 27, 1962

V   Albert b Apr. 20, 1875 d   Buried in
Clay, Ky., m   Sallie Freer b Feb.
7, 1878 d March 20, 1949   NO ISSUE

VI   Infant b

VII   Infant b

VIII   Daisy Dean b   1890 UNMARRIED
Lives Paducah, Kentucky

IX   Rose b   1893 d   1893

X   Elizabeth Leech (Bessie) b   1895
UNMARRIED. Lives Paducah, Kentucky

369

Descendants of William Washington Dorroh and Mary Avery Easly *

I   Bobby b   ca 1859, Ky., m   Charles
    Guess b   CHILDREN:

    A   Bertie b   m   Logan
        Lowery b   CHILDREN:

        1   Reginald b 1917 m Robbie Lou Hopgood
        2   Kimbrell b 1920 UNMARRIED

        3   Mary Ruth b 1926 m John Eison

        4   Logan Il b 1928 m Edna Oliver

        5

    B   Ruth b   d   UNMARRIED

    C   Mary b   d   UNMARRIED

    D   Herman b   d   m   NO ISSUE

    E   Charles Lee b   m   NO ISSUE

II   Frances (Frankie) Morgan b ca 1862 m
    John Rorer b   CHILDREN:

    A   Earl b   m   Margaret
        Allen b   CHILD:

        1   John Allen b

    B   Eckles Glenn b July 9, 1894 Crittenden Co.Ky. m April 10, 1920 Carrie Marie Muir b Jan. 17, 1894 CHILDREN:

        1   Frances Marie b May 16, 1921 m Oct. 23, 1944 Bryant Westley Beasley b NO ISSUE

        2   Maudie Eloise b Dec. 3, 1922 m Oct. 20, 1941 William Alonzo Lewis I b CHILDREN:

We are indebted to Dr. Glenn U. Dorroh and Miss Thelma Lee Dorroh for material here.

    a   William Alonzo II b July 24, 1942

    b   Barry Glenn b Feb. 13, 1951

    c   Susan Marie b July 10, 1957

3   Eckles Glenn II b April 2, 1928 m May 3, 1958 Betty Lou Lawson b
    CHILDREN:

    a   Deborah Ann b Jan. 15, 1959

    b   David Glenn b May 14, 1960

    c   Daniel Stephen b June 21, 1962

C   Lee Dorroh b Sept. 7, 1896 Crittenden Co.Ky. m FIRST Dec. 26, 1919 Mittie Willoughby b April 30, 1898, Illinois, d Oct. 20, 1924   CHILDREN:

1   Harold D.   b Dec. 26, 1920 Crittenden Co.Ky. d Aug. 21, 1922

2   Lee Roy b Mar. 11, 1923 Crittenden Co.,Ky. , m   Evelyn Bond b

m   SECOND Aug. 24, 1927 Leeta Elnora Guess b Feb. 24, 1907 Marion, Kentucky CHILDREN:

3   Charles D.   b March 26, 1928 Crittenden Co.Ky. m Joyce Cole b Dec. 17, 1930 CHILDREN:

    a   Charles D.II   b July 18, 1952 McCracken Co.

    b   Ronnie C. b May 6, 1955 McCracken Co.

4   Della M.   b Dec. 26, 1929, Crittenden Co.Ky. m   Garland B. Willis b Sept. 17, 1929 Lyon Co. Ky.   CHILDREN:

     a   Brenda Lee b July 4, 1952
             Santiago, Calif.

     b   Susan b Mar. 3, 1960, Long
             Beach, Calif.

D   Henry Leonard b Mar. 28, 1899 Critten-
      den Co., Ky., m   Anna Ruth
      Gilliland b Mar. 16, 1912 CHILDREN:[1]

     1   Douglas Leonard b June 24, 1940

     2   Thomas Phillip b July 12, 1943
             (twin)

     3   Phyllis Ann b July 12, 1943 (twin)

E   Robin Ray b April 29, 1902 m Oct. 4,1943
      Mary Dee Adams b Sept. 1, 1911 CHILDREN:
      [1]

     1   Robert Dixon b Mar. 2, 1945 (twin)

     2   Fraince Ann (twin) b Mar. 2, 1945

     3   James Thomas b June 2, 1947

     4   Mary Catherine b July 4, 1948

III William Thomas b Mar. 24, 1864 d Nov. 14,
     1943 m Jan. 17, 1900 Eva Mae Campbell b Feb.
     13, 1881 d May 12, 1912 CHILDREN:

A   Glenn Urey, M.D., b March 20, 1901
      Caldwell Co., Ky., m June 26, 1926 Ella
      Pearl Neal b Nov. 10, 1902 CHILDREN:

[1] All children born in Crittenden Co., Ky.

1   Glenn Urey II b June 30, 1934 Lex-
ington, Ky., m Aug. 7, 1955
Patricia Carol Coons b Aug. 28,193-
CHILDREN:

    a   Elizabeth Ann b Nov. 5, 1956

    b   Brooks Glenn b May 18, 1959

2   Wilma Jean b Nov. 9, 1937 m June 8,
1958 William Elliott Ashbrook b
CHILDREN:

    a   Debra Carol b June 15, 1959

    b   Pamela Jean b Aug. 11, 1962

B   Lee Richey b Aug. 22, 1902 m
Helen Brown b   CHILDREN:

1   a boy

2   Sue Anne b   m   Tommy___

C   Luke b Mar. 24, 1904 d July 13, 1920

D   Paul Wilson b Aug. 29, 1905 m July 10,
1926 Jim Ella Spickard b Apr. 28, 1909
CHILDREN:

1   Charles Allen b Apr. 14, 1927 m
          1948 Florence Lewis b
Aug. 16, 1929   CHILDREN:

    a   Tom Lewis b Apr. 20, 1949

    b   Charles Link b July 31, 1950

    c   Paul Allen b May 12, 1952

    d   James William (Bill) b Sept.
11, 1953

2   James Thomas b Jan. 12, 1936 m May
4, 1959 Hilda Jane Vinson b April
23, 1938   CHILD:

    a   Robert Allen b Feb. 4, 1960

E   Bayless b May 19, 1907 d July 30, 1909

IV   Annie Hoskins b Nov. 4, 1867 d May 23, 1951
     m   1893 William Thomas Hurt b
     May 11, 1857 d March 18, 1932   CHILDREN:

A   Mary Katherine (Kate) b Sept. 25, 1894
     Hopkinsville, Ky., m Nov. 29, 1916
     Claude McKinley Anderson b Dec. 21, 1895
     CHILDREN:

     1   Betsy Ann b Apr. 16, 1921 Hopkins-
          ville, Ky., m Nov. 8, 1944 Don E.
          Fuller b Oct. 20, 1921   CHILD:

          a   David Andrew b May 10, 1951

     2   Claude Ray b Feb. 21, 1923 m
          Viva Dale Martin b Jan. 3, 1929
          CHILDREN: [1]

          a   Margaret Jane b Sept. 4, 1949

          b   Louise Catherine b July 6,
               1951

          c   Robert Martin b Sept. 25,
               1955

B   Rodman Thomas b March 3, 1897 m Mar.
     29, 1919 Nellie Gertrude Baggett b
     Dec. 13, 1899   CHILDREN:

     1   Mary Evelyn b May 25, 1920 m Dec.
          13, 1943 C. R. Gustafson b March
          25, 1912

     2   Jean Claire b Feb. 27, 1922 m
          Feb. 4, 1946 Philip Leamon b Oct.
          24, 1925   CHILDREN:

          a   Cynthia Jean b Mar. 4, 1947

          b   Victor Allen b June 7, 1953

     3   Barbara Wilma b Aug. 8, 1929 Ind-
          ianapolis, Ind. m May 2, 1947 Dale
          Dickinson b Dec. 30, 1926 CHILDREN:

1]   All children b in Princeton, Ky.

a   Sandra b May 6, 1953

b   Janice b Apr. 14, 1955

c   Laurie b Apr. 24, 1959

4   Carol Jo b Oct. 2, 1937 Indianapo-
     lis, Ind., m Feb. 9, 1963 Richard
     Strange b

C Nellie Fuqua b July 16, 1899 Hopkins-
   ville, Ky., UNMARRIED

D Virginia Rosington b Feb. 23, 1902 Hop-
   kinsville, Ky., m Feb. 19, 1941 Clendis
   Beverly Wilson b Dec. 24, 1891 d July
   11, 1955

E Robert William I b Apr. 8, 1904 m Apr.
   17, 1928 Naomi L. Gish b Feb. 28, 1909
   CHILDREN:

   1   Robert William II b Aug. 4, 1928 m
        Elna Patrick b July 17, 1928
        CHILDREN: [1]

        a   Daryl Blake b June 22, 1951

        b   Mark Galen b Mar. 31, 1953

        c   Janice Evon b June 9, 1956

   2   Wallace Gale b July 18, 1931 m
        Helene Curtis Tanner b Oct. 11,
        1933   CHILDREN:

        a   Wallace William b Mar. 27,
             1954 Honolulu, Hawaii

        b   Gaylene Catherine b April 20,
             1955 Indianapolis, Ind.

        c   Naomi Lynn b Aug. 24, 1956

        d   Susan Rose b Sept. 8, 1959

        e   Stuart Gregory b Feb. 24,
             1962

[1] All children born in Indianapolis, Ind.

F   Wallace Stone b Nov. 30, 1907 Hopkins-
       ville, Ky., m Oct. 16, 1940 Mary Walker
       Hinchman b Aug. 31, 1915   CHILD:

    1   Johanna Sue b Dec. 9, 1947

V   Henry(M.D),   b   1870 d ca 1938
    m   Edna_____b   CHILD:

A   Edna b   May   1912 (or 1914)

VI   Lee (M.D.) b June   28, 1873 d Nov. 9, 1925 m
       Oct. 7, 1906 Ophelia Alvis b Aug. 26, 1880 d
       April 5, 1951   CHILDREN:

A   Thelma Lee b April 28, 1908 Calaveras
       Co., Calif.

B   Louise Camille [1] b Dec. 14, 1910 m
       April 29, 1957 Frank Pearce b Aug. 29,
       1893 d April 18, 1958

[1]   Louise has three children(and nine grandchild-
       ren)(by Frank Pearce's first wife)to whom she
       is most devoted. They are: Marilyn, Bill and
       Cindy......all married and children of their
       own.

Descendants of Caleb Clark Dorroh and Nancy Dyson (1)

I   William Thomas b July 26, 1848 d June 30, 1933 m   Matilda Haupt b   1854 d Jan. 23, 1894   CHILDREN:

A   Mary Ellen b Feb. 11, 1876 m   Jack Berry b

B   Charles William b March 7, 1879

C   Louis John b Sept. 20, 1883 d Sept. 6, 1944 m Oct. 17, 1906 Alta Lee Fagan b April 6, 1888   CHILD:

     1   Elton William b Sept. 12, 1907 m Aug. 17, 1931 Helen Davis b July 24, 1913   CHILDREN:

         a   Michael William b Sept. 8,1936

         b   Paul Elton b Apr. 11, 1943

         c   Lynn Ellen b Feb. 5, 1950

D   Frank Marion b Sept. 9, 1885

E   Harman Clark b July 8, 1887 d June 5, 1960 m Sept. 18, 1915 Dorothy Louise Maker b May 31, 1889   CHILD:

     1   Donald Clark b Apr. 21, 1917 m Apr. 21, 1940 Edna Gratis b Jan. 16, 1914   CHILDREN:

         a   Allan Clark b Dec. 1, 1940 Glendale, Calif.

         b   Raymond Dean b May 21, 1945

         c   Norman Charles b Jan.27, 1951

F   Richard Clay b Sept. 1, 1888

G   Carlton Carlisle b May 10, 1890

H   Enid Katherine b July 20, 1891 m James Marguart b   d   1960   NO ISSUE

[1]   Some include Clay in name of Caleb Clark D.

II   Mary Jane b   ca 1850 d before 1885 m
John Merry b   CHILDREN:

   A   Fred b   m
         Wakefield b   CHILDREN:
         (2 or 3,   NFI)

   B   Ora b   d   when
         young lady   NFI

III   Frank M. b Oct. 14, 1853 d Nov. 13, 1900 m
Jan. 1, 1878 Nellie J. Green b July 2, 1858
d   1931   CHILDREN:

   A   Sallie b Nov. 21, 1878 d June 12, 1880

   B   Charlie* b May 30, 1880 m Feb. 9, 1926
         Mary Aileen Miller b Aug. 15, 1895
         CHILDREN:

       1   Charles Frank b Jan. 28, 1927 m
            June 14, 1951 Martha Wrenn b
                 CHILDREN:

            a   Martha Diane b July 28, 1953

            b   Frank Mark b Dec. 22, 1956
                 d Dec. 26, 1956
            c   Mary Lynn b Oct. 5, 1958

            d   Linda Lee b June 26, 1961

       2   Margaret Jane b May 26, 1928 m
            June 30, 1948 Paul W. Carmean b
            CHILDREN:

            a   Paul William b May 17, 1950

            b   Catherine Jane b June 24,
                 1953

       3   Lee Miller b Nov. 13, 1930 m June
            1, 1954 Elizabeth (Betty) Largent
            b   CHILDREN:

            a   Charles William b Mar. 7,1955

            b   James Lee b June 13, 1957

*   We are appreciative of his help; he lives at
Caruthersville, Missouri.

        c   Cynthia Marie b Aug. 26, 1959

        d   Lawerence Gerard b July 12, 1962

C   Mark b Aug. 17, 1882 d   1928
      m   Belle Moffatt b

D   Gayle b April 17, 1885 d July 9, 1886

E   Nellie Lee b March 31, 1890 d March 28, 1960   UNMARRIED

IV   James L. b   NFI

V   Ellen Caroline b Sept. 21, 1855 d March 7, 1904 m Samuel Grimmet Clark b Aug. 6, 1847 d Jan. 2, 1899   CHILDREN:

A   Alice Buena b Dec. 2, 1876 d Dec. 8, 1876

B   Ernest Randolph b July 7, 1878 d Nov. 12, 1941

C   Frank Eugene b May 16, 1880 d April 27, 1957 m Feb. 8, 1905 Ruth Lee b CHILDREN:

      1   Infant son b and d Aug. 1, 1906

      2   Eugene Phillip b Oct. 17, 1909 m Juanita Sullivan b   CHILDREN:

           a   Ray (twin) b May 5, 1940 m Peggy_____   NFI

           b   Ralph (twin) b May 5, 1940

      3   Virginia Dell b Aug. 15, 1915 m Apr. 27, 1937 Joseph A. Bell b d Sept. 14, 1963   CHILD:

           a   Nolie Lee b Jan. 21, 1938

      4   Samuel Grimmet   b Nov. 20, 1917 d July 16, 1950 [1] m   1944 Cannes, France, Agnes Elasser b (Army Nurse)   CHILD:

[1] Killed in action in Korea.

a   Stephanie Greer b Sept. 12, 1945

5   David Lee b Aug. 21, 1929 m FIRST Dec. 24,   Anna Dean Baker b

    m SECOND March 20, 19_ Lillian Malone b

D   Clara b Jan. 10, 1882 m Oct. 24, 1905 Benjamin B. Cassell b July 19, 1880 CHILDREN:

1   Helen b July 10, 1906 m Sept. 10, 1930 Beverly Morrison Vennum b d   Dec.   1962 CHILDREN:

    a   Beverly Ann b March 6, 1933 m Laurence Allen b   CHILD:

        i   Laurence II b March 3, 1957

    b   Glenda b Apr. 20, 1936 m Shambo b   CHILDREN:

        i   James Edward b Dec. 15, 1959

        ii   Todd Allen b April 3, 1963

    c   Sharon b Dec. 30, 1945

    d   Keith b Jan. 4, 1946

2   Benjamin B. II b Nov. 21, 1917 m Nov. 21, 1946 Ruth Perry b CHILDREN:

    a   Gary b Aug. 28, 1953

    b   Stephen b Aug. 8, 1955

3   Vernon Lee b Feb. 22, 1920 m Dec. 25, 1946   NFI CHILDREN:

    a   Vernon Lee II b Jan. 6, 1950
We appreciate her help on this line.

      b   Laura Lynn b Oct. 30, 1953

      c   Stella Marie b Oct. 24, 1960

4   Glen Ellen b Dec. 14, 1925 m Dec. 24, 1950 James Darnell (AF) b
CHILDREN:

      a   Byron James b Mar. 1, 1953

      b   Loren Lee b Jan. 6, 1954

      c   Paul Edward b Dec. 16, 1956

      d   Terrell Allen b Mar. 28, 1959

E   Samuel Emmett b Apr. 13, 1883 d Oct. 13, 1884

F   Thomas Tedford b Jan. 9, 1885 m April 20, 1904 Zilpha Dever b   CHILDREN:

1   Vernon D. b Dec. 25, 1905 d Nov. 11, 1914

2   Dorothy C. b July 16, 1908 m 1937 S. S. Shadi b   CHILDREN:

      a   Zilpha b June 1, 1938

      b   Ramona b Aug. 6, 1941

      c   Verna b Feb. 3, 1944

3   Amy b Dec. 6, 1910 m   1936 Frank G. Metcalf b   CHILDREN:

      a   Norman C. b Dec. 16, 1937

      b   Marion b June 18, 1940

3   Daisy A. b Apr. 19, 1913 m 1936 Raymond Hansen b   CHILDREN:

      a   Carol b Oct. 3, 1941

      b   Richard b Feb. 12, 1943

      c   Raymond II b Oct. 3, 1946

5   Verna b Sept. 28, 1915 m   1936
     Clarence Barthel b   CHILD:

     a   Vernella b Aug. 12, 1938

6   Tedford T. b Mar. 2, 1920 m
     1942 Barbara Somersell b   CHILD

     a   Terry A.   b Nov. 18, 1951

G   George Madison b Mar. 15, 1889 m Nov.
     21, 1917 Bessie Noble b   NFI

H   Jacob Dorroh b Nov. 11, 1895 d Dec. 10,
     1898

VI   Edward B. b Oct. 17, 1857 d July 15, 1932 m
     1882 Martha Lavonia Clarke b Feb.   1855
     d Feb. 28, 1910   CHILDREN:

A   Ruth b Sept. 20 , 1882 m   1913
     P. P. Houston b   CHILD:

     1   Hellen Lavonia b July 21, 1914 m
          1933 Doyne Franklin Bateman b Oct.
          28, 1912   CHILDREN:

          a   Doyne Franklin II b Oct. 14,
               1940

          b   Bette Ruth b July 12, 1946

B   William b March 18, 1884 m   1919
     May Holefield b   NFI

C   Hellen b April 23, 1894 m   1925
     Joe Seagraves b   NFI

VII John Richard, M.D., b Jan. 10, 1861 d Nov.
     1911 m Sept. 4, 1890 Katherine Ethel Moran
     b Aug. 10, 1863 d Jan. 26, 1937 CHILDREN:

A   John Scribner b Aug. 14, 1891 d Jan. 12,
     1960 m June 25, 1915 Millie Cuneo b
     CHILDREN:

     1   Jane Katherine b July 9, 1919 m
          June 7, 1942 William Buck b
          CHILDREN:

        a   Jo Anne Kay b Feb. 12, 1945

        b   Diane Elizabeth b Dec. 8, 1951

        c   Kathy Laurie b May 28, 1956

    2   Terese Bette b Feb. 11, 1920 m Apr. 4, 1960 Frank Ross b

    3   John Thomas b Jan. 13, 1925 m June 20, 1960 Meriel Bartko b

    4   Nancy Lee b April 20, 1935 m Aug. 10, 1958 William George Davis b
                CHILDREN:

        a   Roxanne Helen b Feb. 25, 1960

        b   Jocelyn Dorroh b Mar. 14,1962

B   Theresa (Terese) Beatrice b Jan. 28, 1894 m Feb. 14, 1917 Philip Huber b Dec. 26, 1883 d Oct. 27, 1961   CHILDREN:

    1   Richard Philip b Mar. 18, 1918 m Nov. 29, 1944 Majorie Jo Welsh b

    2   Luise Ann b June 30, 1919 m April 25, 1948 Raymond Oliver Laurie b
                        *
    3   Albert John b Sept. 2, 1925 m FIRST March 3, 1945 Barbara Lee Ewy b Aug. 26, 1926 d Dec. 1, 1951 CHILDREN:

        a   John Richard b Sept. 19, 1945

        b   Carla Lee b Jan. 18, 1949

        m SECOND Oct. 2, 1954 Ida Mae Howard (Saxon) b April 24,   CHILD:

        c   Kirt Howard b Sept. 2, 1955

VIII Charles b   d   age 17   NFI

IX   Willis   NFI
* We are grateful to Mr. A. Huber for his help.

Descendants of Martha Dorroh and John Roberson Pumphrey

I   Jesse Newton b Jan. 14, 1827 Tuscaloosa, Ala.
        CSA, d Dec. 18, 1909 Edna, Tex., m Oct. 18,
        1849 Mary Sauls Matthews b Mar. 13, 1832
        Upson Co. Ga., d May 2, 1883 Jackson Co.,Tex.
        CHILDREN:

    A   Pike b Aug. 27, 1850 Union Co., Ark., m
            Oct. 28, 1872 Elsie Burnett [1] CHILDREN

        1   Harley b Aug. 1873 d 188_

        2   Moselle b Nov. 1, 1877 m Sterling
                Ferrell b   CHILDREN:

            a   Harold b   m   NFI

            b   Elizabeth b   m George Hartung
                    CHILDREN:

                i   a son   NFI

                ii   a son   NFI

        3   Inez b Mar. 1870 m Col. Richard
                Herringshaw b   NO ISSUE

    B   Lavonia b [2] Nov. 24, 1852 El Toro, Tex. d
            Sept. 15, 1931 m May 4, 1871 Capt. Will-
            iam Pierson Laughter I b Feb. 7, 1840,
            CSA, d Oct. 26, 1900 Edna Tex. CHILDREN:

        1   Maury b Aug. 5, 1872 d Jan. 6,1895
                m Oct. 26, 1892 Ettie Moore CHILD:

            a   Irwin Moore b July 28, 1893,
                    Jackson Co. Tex. d June 18,
                    1916 [3]

        2   Alma Mary b Dec. 1, 1874 Jackson
                Co., Tex. d July 5, 1955 m Dec. 31,
                1891 Walter M. Manly   CHILD:

[1]   Great niece of James Bowie, hero of Alamo.

[2]   All other children of Jesse Newton Pumphrey
        & Mary Sauls Matthews born in Jackson Co.Tex.
[3]   Shot near Vera Cruz, Mex. on U.S.S.Annapolis.

a   Marion b Dec. 5, 1897 d ca 1960 m July 25, 1925 George Kunz b   NO ISSUE

3   William Pierson II b July 29, 1877 Jackson Co., Tex. d Dec. 24, 1948 m Sept. 11, 1916 Ruby Lee Blalock b NO ISSUE

4   Ray Pumphrey b Jan. 4, 1880 d Sept. 8, 1881

5   Charles Pyron b Apr. 4, 1882 d May 20, 1944 m May 26, 1907 Virda Milby b   CHILDREN:

    a   Infant son, b and d, June 3, 1908

    b   Robert Gordon b May 21, 1909 d July 24, 1916

    c   Dix b Nov. 9, 1910 m Emily___ CHILDREN:

        i   Virginia Laverne b July 15, 1940 m June 6, 1958 David Hainline   CHILD:

            (a)   Julie Lynn b April 30, 1959

        ii   Mary Arnette b Nov. 8, 1942

        iii   Leslie Dix (girl) b Nov. 20, 1945

6   Lois Lee b Mar. 12, 1885 d Oct. 18, 1900

7   John Gordon b Aug. 25, 1887 Jackson Co. Tex. d April 18, 1959 m Dec. 24, 1907 Carrie Fisher b   CHILDREN:

    a   Annalee b Dec. 17, 1909 m Mar. 7, 1930 Hubert Westley Ratliff b   CHILDREN:

i   Carol Ann b Dec. 23, 1930 m Martin Strarup II CHILDREN:

    (a) Sarah Ann b Aug. 28, 1952 New York

    (b) Martin III b Aug.12, 1957

ii   Hubert Westley II b May 11, 1940 Edna, Tex. m 1963 Zara Rayburn Bannister b

b   Mary Isabelle b Dec. 20, 1911 m May 3, 1934 Walter Frels b CHILDREN:

i   Richard b Jan. 26, 1935 d Feb. 26, 1936

ii   Suzanne b Dec. 8, 1936 m Oct. 5, 1957 Paul Brantley b   CHILD:

    (a) John Albert b May 17 1958, Maine

iii Donald b Dec. 11, 1937

iv   Pierce Laughter b Jan.14, 1946

c   John Gordon II b Dec. 18,1919 m FIRST Barbara McClung CHILD:

i   Catherine Frances b Oct. 3, 1946

m SECOND Donna Westmoreland

d   William Pierson III b Aug. 8, 1922 d June 21, 1945, [1]

1] U. S. Marines, Okinawa

8   Jessie b Oct. 24, 1890 Jackson Co.
    Tex. m Apr. 27, 1915 Olin Collier
    NO ISSUE

9   Enid Annie b July 1, 1894 m June 3,
    1914 Thomas Jones Bolling [1]
    CHILDREN:

    a   Enid Jean b Dec. 13, 1915 m
        Oct. 26, 1945 Richard W.
        Weaver   NO ISSUE

    b   Thomas Jones II b May 27,1921
        m FIRST Nov. 12, 1945 Marjorie
        Nell Fenner b   CHILDREN:

        i   La Noe b Dec. 29, 1946

        ii Robert Thomas b Oct. 23,
            1950

        m SECOND   NFI

C   Blake b Feb. 20, 1855 El Toro, Tex. d
    Sept. 17, 1865

D   Ray b Jan. 28, 1857 El Toro, Tex. d Jan.
    8, 1875

E   Jessie Lois (twin) b Oct. 30, 1862 El
    Toro, Tex. d Dec. 16, 1926 m May 18,
    1886 Richard Saunders b   CHILDREN:

    1   Allen Pumphrey b Aug. 7, 1887 d
        May 2, 1888

    2   Mildred b ca 1898 d ca 1939 m
        Thomas Holstein b   CHILD:

        a   Thomas II b   (resides in
            Austin, Tex.)

F   Allen (twin) b Oct. 30, 1862 d Nov. 11,
    1863

[1] Direct descendant of Robert Bolling of Va.
    and his wife Jane Rolfe, daughter of John
    Rolfe and Pocahontas.

G   Lee b Mar. 22, 1866 d July 18, 1951 m
Dec. 31, 1884 Nathaniel T. Gaines b
CHILDREN:

1   Lecil b Dec. 4, 1885 m Georgia
Archer b   CHILDREN:

    a   Lecil II b m   NO ISSUE

    b   William b m   CHILDREN:

       i   Jerry b   NFI

       ii   Brian b   NFI

2   Meade b July 24, 1888 m Dec. 30,
1907 Lewis Wasserman b Feb. 5,1885
CHILDREN:

    a   Gertrude Natalie b Aug. 11,
1910 m June 9, 1935 Richard
Thayer b June 19, 1908 CHILD:

       i   Richard II b Oct. 9,1938

    b   David Lewis b Sept. 2, 1914 m
Sept. 23, 1944 Gretta Burnett
b June 7, 1913 Scotland CHILD:

       i   Judith Louise b Sept. 4,
1945

    c   Jessie Marguerite b May 21,
1917 m July 23, 1939 Garnett
William Hudgins b Oct. 30,
1911   CHILDREN:

       i   Garnett William II b Nov.
27, 1944

       ii   David Eugene b June 21,
1951

       iii   Laura Dell b Aug. 29,
1953

    d   Melvin b Oct. 13, 1923 m Dec.
1944 Marie Henry b   CHILD:

       i   Kenneth b Oct. 3, 1945

H A son b Sept. 18, 1868 d Sept. 25, 1868

I Murus Dennis b Mar. 24, 1875 El Toro, Tex. Jackson Co., m Dec. 8, 1897 Mattie Dibrell Simons [1] b Oct. 18, 1876
CHILDREN:

1 Jessie Lee b Nov. 7, 1898 UNMARRIED

2 Mary Lois b Oct. 16, 1900 m June 24, 1923 Ezra Alexander Williams b Dec. 3, 1895 DeWitt Co. Tex.
CHILDREN:

 a Betty Ray b Jan. 19, 1927 m June 19, 1948 James Richard Duvall b June 4, 1927 Baytown Tex. CHILDREN:

  i Mary Elizabeth b Oct. 12, 1951 Baytown, Tex.

  ii Bryan Richard b May 7, 1953 Baytown, Tex.

  iii Leslie Frank b July 6, 1954 Baytown, Tex.

 b Dixie Lee b May 9, 1932, Baytown, Tex., m Dec. 28, 1952 Lt. Bertram Henry Shoopman III b Nov. 23, 1931 CHILDREN:

  i Mary Sue b Oct. 1, 1953 Corona, Calif.

  ii Gretchen b Nov. 28, 1954 Groton, Conn.

  iii Laurel Ann b Aug. 23, 1956, Groton, Conn.

  iv Bertram Henry IV b Mar. 16, 1959

3 Meadie b July 6, 1903 Edna, Tex. UNMARRIED

[1] Through her grandmother Leeanna Lee Dibrell a cousin of General Robert E. Lee.

4 Cornelia Ray b Nov. 6, 1905 m Jan. 8, 1938 Herbert Victor Plagens b July 18, 1900 Bryan, Tex. CHILDREN:

 a Connie Ruth b Nov. 6, 1938 m Aug. 11, 1962 Lt. Darvin Edgar (Eddie) Bremer b Sept. 25, 1940

 b Charlotte Ray b Jan. 15, 1944 m FIRST Jan. 26, 1961 Maurice Cook b CHILD:

  i Elizabeth Lynn b Dec. 2, 1961 Austin, Tex.

  m SECOND July 3, 1963 Donald Lee Abrams

 c Howard Douglas b Jan. 22,1948

5 Georgie* b Aug. 25, 1908 Edna, Tex. m June 18, 1938 Carl Christopher Moore b Aug. 16, 1903, Jackson Co. Tex. CHILDREN:

 a Marjorie b June 4, 1940 Baytown, Tex.

 b John b May 22, 1945, Baytown, Tex.

6 Murus Dibrell II b July 31, 1913 Edna, Tex. m June 1, 1937 Marguerite Marie Gann b Dec. 2, 1914 CHILD:

 a Murus Dibrell III b Nov. 10, 1938 Baytown, Tex. m Feb. 25, 1961 Ella Adele Floyd b Sept. 21, 1941 Charleston, S. C. CHILD:

  i Murus Dibrell IV b June 11, 1962 Panama City,Fla.

* We are appreciative of the material furnished by Mrs. Georgia P. Moore on this line.

II   Clarissa b ca 1828-30, Tuscaloosa, Ala.
d before 1857

III   Morgan b Tuscaloosa Co. Ala. d before 1841

IV   John Lafayette b ca 1835, Tuscaloosa, Ala.
Pvt., CSA, m Feb. 19, 1862 Josephine Cook
b 1845 CHILD:

     A   John Lawrence b   NFI

V   Mary Ann b ca 1836-7, Tuscaloosa, Ala. m
Stephen D. Sullivant

VI   Lewis b ca 1838, Tuscaloosa, Ala. (slain in
Va. in service, Lt., CSA)

VII   Elizabeth b   Tuscaloosa, Ala., d before
1850

VIII Monroe b after 1841, Saline Co.,Ark. d
before 1850

IX   Dennis b ca 1843 in Saline Co., Ark., enlisted in the Confederate service, but
discharged on account of ill health.

Descendants of Clarissa Dorroh and Dave Cole

I   Infant daughter b Aug. 9, 1831 d Aug. 9, 1831

II   Infant son b Aug. 10, 1838 d Aug. 10, 1838

III   Martha Rebecca b Mar. 8, 1840 d July 5, 1877
Union Parish, La., m Apr. 26, 1864 T. W.Eckles
b Jan. 22, 1845 d Jan. 19, 1910 CHILDREN: [1]

    A   Emma Gertrude b Aug. 15, 1867 d Jan. 20,
1951 Spenser, La., m April 16, 1884
Emmett Parks b   CHILDREN:

        1   Gordon Bennett b Dec. 15, 1885 d Jan
19, 1889, Spenser, La.

        2   Martha (Mattie) Juliette b July 7,
1887 m Jan. 3, 1919 Henry Haacks b
                CHILDREN:

            a   Fanny Gertrude b

            b   H. E. b

            c   Joe Ollie

        3   John Reeves b May 15, 1889 m Dec.
24, 1913 Emma Nolan Stokes b
                CHILDREN:

            a   Mildred b

            b   Jack

            c   Robbin

            d   Nellie

            e   Sonny b   d early

        4   Emma Pervie b Sept. 14, 1890 d Sept.
2, 1956 Monroe, La. m Dec. 20, 1914
James M. Nale b   CHILDREN:

            a   Laura Bell b

            b   Ruth

[1]   All children born Union Parish, La., Spenser.

c   James

d   Inez

e   Roy

f   Christine

g   Jean

5   George Brice b Feb. 1, 1892 m Sept. 5, 1917 Amye Barnett b
CHILDREN:

a   George Brice II b

b   William Barnett b

6   Henry Emmett b July 22, 1893 m Feb. 22, 1917 Estelle Jinks b
CHILDREN:

a   Mary b

b   Ruby

c   William Harold

d   Oliver Wendell b

7   William Levi b June 23, 1895 d Sept.18 1895

8   Ernest Reginald b Sept. 26, 1896 m Dec. 24, 1922 Celest Hay b
CHILDREN:

a   Ernestine

b   Preston

9   Sedley Louis b Oct. 18, 1899 m FIRST Aug. 22, 1920 Faye Burford b
CHILDREN:

a   Sedley Louis II b

b   Lolia Zane b

m SECOND   Mardge Mulligan
b

10   Jule Walter b Jan. 31, 1902 d Dec.
      23, 1956 m Oct. 5, 1922 Verda Hay
      b   CHILDREN:

      a   Julian Keith b

      b   William Barnes
      c   Kathleen
11   Eli Percy b Jan. 23, 1904 m June 18,
      1935 Belva Howard b   CHILDREN

      a   Preasley Eugene

      b   Ralph

12   Warford Scott b Dec. 27, 1906 m Mar.
      22, 1933 Hazel Boatright b
      CHILD:

      a   Warford Wayne b

13   Annie Mae b Sept. 17, 1908 m Dec. 24,
      1933 Philip Boughton b
      CHILDREN:

      a   Philip Douglas b

      b   Phyllis Ann b

14   Ollie Whitfield b May 13, 1910 m July
      24, 1935 Offie Catherine Roberson b
                CHILD:

      a   Patsy Jean

B   John Walter b Jan. 26, 1874 Union Parish,
      La., d June 9, 1953   UNMARRIED

C   Mary Ellen b Aug. 5, 1876 Union Par., La.,
      d Nov. 1, 1938 m   John
      Daniel Halley b April 19, 1874 d Oct. 7,
      1928   CHILDREN: [1]

      1   Anna Ruth b Nov. 9, 1901 m Jan. 9,
           1951 Oscar Baker b Oct. 27, 1905

      2   James Daniel b Sept. 19, 1904 m Aug.
           5, 1934 Grey Booth b

[1] All children born in Spenser, La., Union Par.

3 Claude Eckles b Nov. 19, 1905 m Feb. 28, 1938 Claudie Booth b

4 Mattie Mae b May 13, 1907 m Dec. 12, 1928 Doss Williamson b

5 Jessie b Sept. 28, 1909 m 1927 Jasper Snell b

6 Mollie Alvia b Oct. 1911 m Dec. 19, 1930 Charlie Rugg b

IV Nancy b Nov. 30, 1842 Tuscaloosa Co., Ala. d May 23, 1858 Tuscaloosa Co., Ala., (aged 15)

V William Meek b March 10, 1845 Tuscaloosa Co., Ala., d Jan. 28, 1937 Marion, La., m Webb Morris b d Nov. 22, 1908 CHILDREN:

A Willie b m Mattie Albbritton b

B Bertha b m Alex Kyle b

C Ambros b m Minnie Scarbough b

D Mary b m Ed Johnson b

E Mattie b m Allbritton b

F Minnie b

VI Infant son, b and d Mar. 20, 1847, Tuscaloosa Co., Ala.

Descendants of James Dorroh II and Sarah Ross

I   Sarah b   d young   NFI

II   Margaret b   d   m James
      (Enoree) Anderson b   d   NFI

III   Nancy b Jan. 19, 1811 d July 5, 1861 m
Thomas Blakeley b May 31, 1800 d Sept. 4,
1859 Buried Laurens Co., S. C. CHILDREN:

A   Sarah Ann b   d Dec. 9, 1855,
aged 13 yrs. 8 mos. 15 days.

B   John

C   Agnes C.

D   Martha A.

E   George A.

IV   David Ross b Aug. 19, 1812 d June 4, 1860 m
Susan B. Lewers b Jan. 19, 1820 d June 13,
1902 [1]   CHILDREN: SEE SEPARATE LISTING
under DESCENDANTS OF DAVID ROSS DORROH AND
SUSAN B. LEWERS

V   Martha b Aug. 12, 1814 d Mar. 21, 1857 m
Charles Blakeley b Jan. 15, 1798 d Mar. 17,
1857   CHILDREN:

A   Margaret A. b Feb. 12, 1839 d June 28,
1856

B   Martha Ann b   m   David
Clark Templeton b   CHILDREN:

1   Thaddeus McDuffie b Dec. ;20,1834 d
Dec. 19, 1861

2   John Pulaski b May 11, 1836 d

3   James Ludy b Apr. 3, 1837 d May 30,
1863

4   John P. b June 29, 1839

5   M. J. (girl) b July 19, 1845

396

    C   Sarah J.

    D   Pinkney L.

    E   Theodore W.

VI   John Francis, M.D., b July 27, 1816 d May 26, 1893 m May 22, 1845 Mary Elizabeth Saxon b June 19, 1827 d Mar. 8, 1907 Both buried Greenville, S. C. CHILDREN: SEE SEPARATE LISTING under DESCENDANTS OF DR. JOHN FRANCIS DORROH AND MARY ELIZABETH SAXON

VII   William McDavid, M.D., b Oct. 25, 1818 d Dec. 10, 1897 m Lucretia Williams b Nov. 7, 1828 d Feb. 10, 1888 CHILDREN: SEE SEPARATE LIST-ING UNDER DESCENDANTS OF WILLIAM McDAVID DOR-ROH AND LUCRETIA WILLIAMS

VIII   Mary b Nov. 28, 1821 d Apr. 26, 1845 UNMARR-IED (Tombstone shows 24 yrs. 9 mos. 2 days.)

IX   Lewis Cunningham b Jan. 26, 1823 d May 12, 1872 m Jan. 27, 1859 Frances Elizabeth Dick-son b Feb. 14, 1837 d May 4, 1919. Moved to Miss. and both buried in Hinds Co. CHILDREN: SEE SEPARATE LISTING under DESCENDANTS OF LEWIS CUNNINGHAM DORROH AND FRANCES ELIZABETH DICKSON.

[1] She was daughter of Samuel B. Lewers, a Pres-byterian Minister who later, I am told, moved to Miss. following some of his parishoners. Her mother was Sophia Allen. It is not known if she had other brothers or sisters.

Descendants of David Ross Dorroh and Susan B. Levers

I   Samuel L. b   1822 d 1870, Capt. CSA [1] m
    Dec. 1865 Margaret (Maggie) McHugh b   d
    CHILDREN:

    A   David Laurens (Larry) b Oct. 19, 1867 d
        m Kate Fuller b   d   CHILDREN:

        1   Ralph

        2   Dymple

        3   Sulane b   1906 m____ Medlin.
            Lives Sugar Valley, Ga.

    B   James Austen b Sept. 8, 1869 d Aug. 23,
        1933 m Jan. 6, 1904 Bertie Bradford b
        CHILDREN:

        1   Carrie Neal b Sept. 13, 1905 NFI

        2   Jamie Bradford b March 14, 1907

        3   Mary Eugenia b Oct. 29, 1909 m Oct.
            10, 1933 John William Vaughn b
            CHILDREN:

            a   Wilma Jean b Aug. 17, 1934 m
                Oct.   1952 William Eugene
                Rampley II b   CHILD:

                i   Billie Carol b Jan. 24,
                    1954

II James Ross   [2]

III John Allen   [2]

IV William Thomas b Feb. 27, 1844 d Sept. 8,
    1910 m Dec. 10, 1868 Sarah Sims Shell b Feb.
    14, 1851 d July 7, 1924   CHILDREN:

[1] Moved to Mississippi in 1866

[2] Killed in Battle of Fredericksburg Dec. 13,
    1862.

A   Mary (Minnie) Susan b Jan. 17, 1870 d
Dec. 10, 1937   UNMARRIED

B   James Ross b Aug. 17, 1871 d April 14,
1911 m Feb.   1899 Etta Owings b Feb.
15, 1875   NO ISSUE

C   Maggie b Aug. 12, 1873 d Dec. 5, 1873

D   Bessie Florence b Sept. 19, 1874 d
1955 m Oct. 24, 1900 Sam M. Wright b
CHILDREN:

    1   Frank Dorroh b Aug. 8, 1901   NFI

    2   William Thomas b Feb. 13, 1905 m
        June 10, 1930 Kathleen Holland b
        d Nov. 4, 1938   CHILD:

        a   Donald Jerome I b April 21,
            1931 m Sept. 25, 1951
            Patricia Ann Dodson b
            CHILDREN:

            i   Donald Jerome II

            ii   Kathleen Elizabeth b
                1958

            iii Lelia

E   Samuel Ripley b Aug. 26, 1877 d Sept.22,
1942 m Aug. 10, 1911 Ada Leister b Sept.
23, 1886   CHIODREN:

    1   Sarah Susan b Nov. 8, 1912 d Jan.
        10, 1946 m May 10, 1941 John Erwin
        Brock b Sept. 20, 1901 d Feb. 16,
        1956

    2   Elizabeth Ross b Sept. 18, 1918 m
        Jan. 4, 1941 William N. Chandler b
        Nov. 2, 1913   CHILDREN:

        a   Malcolm Ross b Feb. 18, 1943

        b   Patricia b Sept. 12, 1947

F   Nannie Lewers b Nov. 18, 1879 d March
     23, 1955 m Dec. 4, 1912 Thomas Montgom-
     ery Divver b Aug. 1, 1885 d Feb. 1, 1960
     CHILDREN:

     1   Nancy Dorroh b Nov. 14, 1913 *

     2   William Thomas b June 17, 1917 m
          June 15, 1941 Annie M. Camak b Aug.
          7, 1919 CHILDREN:

          a   William Thomas II b Jan. 19,
               1944

          b   Susan Banks b Aug. 13, 1947 d
               July 17, 1948

G   Carrie Lou b March 3, 1882 d Feb. 10,
     1916 m Feb. 19, 1908 Carl Atkins Foster
     b   d   1934 CHILDREN:

     1   Charles Cantzon b Feb. 4, 1909 m
          July 19, 1935 Isabel Witherspoon
          CHILDREN:

          a   Ann Witherspoon b Oct. 12,
               1938 m Robert LeGette Alexan-
               der

          b   Carl McDonald b Nov. 19, 1942

          c   John Witherspoon b Nov. 6, 1948

     2   Henry Dorroh b Aug. 14, 1912 m
          Doris Maddox b   CHILDREN:

          a   Eloise Cantzon b Mar. 28, 1943

          b   Henry Dorroh II b Dec. 8, 1944

          c   Emily Spear b Sept. 4, 1947

          d   Franklin Maddos b Sept. 24,
               1948

          e   Carl Cantzon b Sept. 12, 1950

          f   Charles McDonald b Sept. 3,
               1956

* We are indebted to her for help on this line.

H   Sarah Cornelia b Dec. 6, 1884 m Jan. 20, 1925 Samuel M. Wilkes b d Jan. 12, 1927 NO ISSUE

I   Emma Allen b Nov. 24, 1887 m May 24, 1911 Lawrence G. Roff b d Aug. 1956 CHILDREN:

    1   William Dorroh b July 2, 1912 m Mar. 2, 1941 Jeanne Wilson b May 17, 1917 CHILDREN:

        a   Lucile Shaw b Nov. 18, 1941 m Steven Watters CHILDREN:

            i   Steven

            ii   Jeanne

        b   Elizabeth Allen b Dec. 6, 1942

        c   Sarah Roberta b May 27, 1946

        d   William Dorroh II b Sept. 7, 1948

        e   Marion Bayard b Aug. 26, 1951

        f   Harold L. b 1955

    2   Laurence Grant b Sept. 19, 1919 m Feb. 7, 1946 Mary Wooten b July 17, 1924 CHILDREN:

        a   Lawrence Grant II b Mar. 1, 1947

        b   Mary Irene b May 29, 1959

J   Willie East b Oct. 14, 1889 m June 12, 1917 Robert W. Gilliland b CHILDREN:

    1   Jean Ross b Mar. 17, 1918 m Dec. 24, 1944 Zearl Pierce b CHILDREN:

        a   Jean Ross b Nov. 27, 1945

        b   Mary Susan b Mar. 25, 1947

        c   Harriet Ann b July 21, 1952

2   Mary Shell b April 24, 1920 m July
     10, 1950 Maurice C. Hedin CHILDREN:

     a   Peter Jay b July 10, 1951

     b   Carl Maurice b June 4, 1953

3   Jack Dorroh b Sept. 12, 1923 m
     Carolyn Campbell b   CHILDREN:

     a   Rebecca Carolyn b Jan. 11,
          1955

     b   Nancy Jane b Mar. 6, 1958

4   Nancy b April 14, 1926

K   Laura Roberta b Dec. 4, 1891 d July 23,
     1962 m Aug. 30, 1919 Joe F. Smith CHILD:

1   Joe F. II b July 7, 1921 m June 12,
     1943 Betty Marie Wood b   CHILDREN:

     a   Donna Marie b Jan. 11, 1948

     b   Barbara Wood b May 15, 1951

     c   Deborah (Debby) Roberta b Dec.
          31, 1958

V David Lewers b Aug. 11, 1845 d Jan. 12, 1927
   m Feb. 24, 1870 Mattie Elizabeth Martin b
   April 29, 1850 d Feb. 18, 1957.[1]CHILDREN:

A   Kate b Feb. 4, 1874 d Aug. 10, 1958 m
     Aug. 9, 1892 Laurel Fenton Hall b June
     29, 1866 d Aug. 14, 1931   CHILDREN:[2]

1   Joe Elmo b April 18, 1893 d Sept.
     18, 1962 m June 20, 1915 Fannie
     Hester b Nov. 8, 1894   CHILDREN:

     a   Earlene b Oct. 25, 1919 m May
          29,1937 Haskel S. McNair b Aug
          20, 1915   CHILDREN:

[1] Moved to Martindale, Tex. in 1870. Both died
Williamson county, Texas.

[2] All children born in Hayes County, Texas.

        i   Joe Neal b Aug. 18, 1938
           UNMARRIED

        ii   Sherry b Mar. 1, 1948

    b   Betty Jo b Sept. 10, 1931 m
        Jan. 21, 1949 Rev. H. S. San-
        son II b March 19, 1928
        CHILDREN:

        i   Daniel Wayne b June 13,
           1950

        ii   Dennis b July 31, 1951

        iii   Terrell Lynn b July 2,
           1953

2   David Clarence b Sept. 3, 1895
    UNMARRIED

3   Irene b July 13, 1898 m May 3,1919
    Dave W. Crenshaw b Apr. 18, 1893
    CHILDREN:

    a   David Laurel b Feb. 10, 1920
        m Sept. 21, 1945 Doris Baker
        b Apr. 2, 1923 CHILDREN:

        i   Mary Lynn b Sept. 14,
           1950

        ii   Barbara b Jan. 16, 1952

        iii   Teresa Jane b Dec. 6,
           1956

    b   Katherine b May 14, 1922 d Apr
        14, 1958 Harris, Tex., m Dec.
        19, 1945 Dolly Walker b April
        28, 1922

    c   Eleanor Jane b Sept.9, 1940
        UNMARRIED

4   James Andrew b Nov. 17, 1900 m
    FIRST Jan. 2, 1930 Alice Elizabeth
    Kennerly b Dec. 9, 1906 CHILDREN:

a   Alice Kennerly b May 1, 1932
m June 2, 1951 William Coleman White b Jan. 27, 1930
CHILDREN:

    i   Cindy b Sept. 26, 1952

    ii   Julie Kennerly b Sept.25,
    1953

    iii Karen Elaine b Apr. 23,
    1957

b   Joan b Nov. 20, 1936 m Dec.
22, 1959 Rev. James Warner
Best b July 22, 1934 CHILD:

    i   John Mark b Feb. 5,1962

m SECOND Aug. 16, 1959 Louise
Holcomb Davis b Aug. 13, 1916

5   Albert Frank b Nov. 27, 1904 d Aug.
1963 m Dec. 17, 1928 Clara Williamson b Nov. 19, 1909 CHILDREN:

a   Ronald Beverly b Nov. 8, 1935
m April 17, 1960 Judy Rife b
Aug. 16, 1938 CHILD:

    i   Connie Lynn b June 30,
    1962

6   Laurel Fenton II b April 9, 1909 d
Feb. 14, 1958 Hayes Co.,Tex., m
1936 Louella Watson b Dec. 31,1915
CHILDREN:

a   Laurel Fenton III b July 20,
1938

b   Argie Lou b Mar. 6, 1941 m Mar.
1958 Frank Reiger b CHILDREN:

    i   Kimberley b Dec. 9,1958

    ii   Karen   NFI

7   Mattie Louisa b Mar. 9, 1914 m Dec. 18, 1933 Arnold W. Bryant b Jan. 17, 1913 CHILDREN:

    a   Everett b July 3, 1935 m Nov. 3, 1956 Nancy Smith b Sept.12, CHILD:

        i   Randall b Apr. 12, 1961

    b   David b Mar. 9, 1941 m Nov. 5, 1960 Dorothy Warren b Dec. 10, 1942 CHILD:

        i   Teri Leigh b Nov.7, 1962

    c   Eugene b Aug. 23, 1943

8   Sidney b Apr. 15, 1916 m Nov. 8, 1941 Louise Woods b Aug. 12,1923 CHILDREN:

    a   Sidney Dorroh b Aug. 20,1944

    b   Clifford b Feb. 11, 1947

B   Nannie b Oct. 21, 1875 Laurel, Miss. m April 24, 1904 Albert S. Odom b July 21, 1878 d June 13, 1937 CHILDREN:

    1   Lucille b Nov. 21, 1906 d Apr. 18, 1941 m Nov. 11, 1923 Raymond Reed b Sept. 24, 1906 CHILDREN:

        a   Berta Rae b May 31, 1925 m Jim Bill Clark b Mar. 26,1919 CHILDREN:

            i   Susan Kaye b Apr. 14, 1950

            ii   Stephen Randolph b Mar. 7, 1954

        b   Albert Sidney b Apr. 20,1932 m Nov. 20, 1954 Janice Ruby Hippe b Sept. 3, 1934 CHILDREN:

    i Albert Sidney II b Sept. 18, 1955

    ii Sharon Rae b Mar.3, 1957

    iii David Ward b Jan. 13, 1959

 2 Allyne b Aug. 14, 1910 m Aug. 9, 1934 Robert Gray b Aug. 6, 1908 d May 8, 1957 CHILDREN:

   a Robert Odom b June 9, 1937 UNMARRIED

   b Jane b Sept. 8, 1945 UNMARRIED

 3 Lorena Dorroh b Nov. 23, 1915 m Feb. 13, 1937 Kenneth Davis b Sept. 30, 1915 CHILDREN:

   a Dorroh Nan b May 19, 1940 m Dec. 20, 1961 Laurie Daniels b Sept. 25, 1939 CHILD:

    i Deborah Nan b Dec. 14, 1962

   b William Kenneth b Nov. 12, 1943

   c David b April 11, 1949

C Maggie b 1879 Hayes, Tex. d 1929 m 1903 William Moon b CHILDREN:

 1 Barbara b m   Williams CHILD:

   a Joan   NFI

 2 William   NFI

D Ella b Sept. 15, 1881 Hayes, Tex., d m Nov. 25, 1902 Ike D. Roberts b Jan. 2, 1872 d May 7, 1962 CHILDREN:

 1 Vivian b May 26, 1904 m FIRST Nov. 1, 1934 Elzie Johnson b Dec. 23, 1902 CHILDREN:

a   Elzie Lee b May 21, 1935 m
Jan. 20, 1961 Rhona Beseler b
Sept. 8, 1941 CHILD:

    i   Jennifer Leigh b April
        25, 1963

b   Carolyn b July 24, 1936 m
June 12, 1954 Walter Leonard
b Mar. 30, 1933 CHILDREN:

    i   Randall b Apr. 30, 1955

    ii   Sherrill b Aug. 10,1960

    iii Kelly b Dec. 19, 1961

m SECOND Feb. 17, 1955 David
Brandon b May 15, 1888

2   Dayton b June 18, 1906 Hayes, Tex.
m Mar. 27, 1932 Ruth Perry b July
9, 1912 CHILDREN:

a   Perry Dayton b Aug. 30, 1935
m Aug. 15, 1953 Martha Jo
Maul b June 10, 1935 CHILDREN:

    i   Tommy Gene b June 23,
        1954

    ii   Marty b Mar. 10, 1957

b   Jerry b Dec. 3, 1939 d Dec. 8,
1939

3   Leroy b Aug. 10, 1908 d April 17,
1952 Hayes, Tex. m Katherine King
b Aug. 20, 1915 CHILDREN:

a   Patricia Ann b, d in infancy

b   Kay b Jan. 1, 1946 m Marvin
Hohman b   NFI

c   Bobby Lee b Dec. 19, 1948

4   Blanche b Dec. 8, 1910 m July 21,
1933 Hunter Smith b Aug. 19, 1907
CHILDREN:

a Nancy b Feb. 19, 1936 m July 29, 1956 Marvin Brittian b July 21, 1935 CHILDREN:

 i Eileen b May 24, 1957

 ii Scott b July 20, 1960

 iii Brian b May 23, 1962

b Hunter b Dec. 11, 1938 d Jan. 12, 1940

c Gordon b May 20, 1942 UNMARR_IED

c Gary b Sept. 10, 1951

5 Oliver Ross b Mar. 13, 1918 Hayes, Tex. m April 4, 1942 Lily Fell b Aug. 3, 1919 CHILDREN:

a Bryan b June 13, 1946

b Richard b Mar. 29, 1950

6 Katie Marie b Oct. 30, 1921 m Sept. 1944 Robert Shrader b May 16, 1920 CHILDREN:

a Connie b Dec. 24, 1947

b Carol b Sept. 25, 1950

E Larry R. b July 20, 1883 Hayes, Tex. d Oct. 18, 1951 m Dec. 24, 1907 Lonnie Mason b Nov. 28, 1888 CHILDREN:

1 Alpha b Sept. 24, 1912 m Dec. 16, 1935 Jack West b Jan. 27, 1913 CHILDREN:

a Lani Max b Dec. 12, 1943 m May 20, 1960 Robert Conant King b Jan. 20, 1942 CHILD:

 i Jacqueline West b Dec. 2, 1961

b Judy Rae b Mar. 28, 1947

2 Minna Rae b March 3, 1919 m May 1947 Merrill J. Mitchell CHILD:

a Rebecca Ann b Sept. 1, 1950

F Mary Ethel b April 4, 1885 Hayes, Tex. d Feb. 20, 1920 Travis, Tex. m Apr. 12, 1903 Otis Fenton Eckols b Nov. 4, 1879 d Sept. 26, 1960 Harris, Tex.CHILDREN:

1 Mayme Eleanor b Aug. 17, 1909 m May 12, 1939 Harold Jules Meynier I CHILDREN:

a Harold Jules II b Sept. 3, 1942 d Nov. 11, 1942

b Robert Otis b Mar. 11, 1943 UNMARRIED

c Julie Eleanor b Dec. 28, 1943 m June 16, 1962 W. Carlton Harriman b CHILD:

i Tandi Sue b Mar. 18, 1963

2 Ansyl David I b Sept. 6, 1911 m Jan. 12, 1939 Graciela Felce b CHILDREN:

a Ansyl David II b Feb. 17,1940 UNMARRIED

b Graciela b Nov. 18, 1941 UN-MARRIED

c Marilen Gayle b Sept. 21,1944 UNMARRIED

d Elaine Marie b Aug. 16, 1947

G Lula b May 30, 1887 Hayes, TEx. m Oct. 27, 1907 Ernest T. Hamilton b April 6, 1881 CHILDREN:

1 Nina Marie b Jan. 16, 1910 m Aug. 22, 1936 Wilbur Yancy b Dec. 24,

1908   CHILD:

a   James Douglas b Feb. 25, 1947

2   Nello b July 5, 1912 Williamson, Tex. m Jan. 2, 1934 Stafford Davis b Aug. 11, 1912 CHILDREN:

a   Gale b Nov. 28, 1935 m Dec. 27, 1959 Patsy Smith b Feb. 18, 1937 CHILD:

i   Haston Scott b June 14, 1962

b   Linda b June 4, 1940 UNMARRIED

3   Dorroh Theodore b April 16, 1915 d June 21, 1934 Williamson Tex.

H   Fannie b June 21, 1889 Hayes, Tex. m Dec. 1, 1912 Ernest Mason b Feb. 19, 1888 Williamson, Tex. CHILDREN:

1   Charlie Bess b Sept. 20, 1913 m Sept. 6, 1945 Monroe Davis b Oct. 25, 1908 CHILDREN:

a   Carolyn b Aug. 5, 1946

b   Margaret b Aug. 5, 1949

2   Christine b Feb. 10, 1916 UNMARRIED

I   George Ross b Nov. 15, 1891 Hayes, Tex. d July 8, 1949 Williamson, Tex. m June 23, 1920 Bessie Bragg b June 23, 1896 CHILDREN:

1   George Bragg b July 12, 1921 m Apr. 19, 1953 Carolyn Friday b Mar. 15, 1920 CHILDREN:

a   Lawrence (Larry) Edward b Dec. 23, 1956

2   Bonnie Jean b June 21, 1925 m June 21, 1945 Carson H. Hoge b Aug. 2, 1924 CHILDREN:

We are indebted to her for help on this line.,

        a   James Dorroh b May 27, 1947

        b   Cynthia Marie b Sept. 29,1950

        c   Kenneth b Dec. 12, 1954

        d   Philip b Nov. 16, 1956

  3   Marjorie b Dec. 9, 1931 m Nov. 21, 1953 Robert G. Allen b March 7, 1931 CHILDREN:

        a   David Scott b Oct. 25, 1955 d Feb. 28, 1958

        b   Jean Marie b July 24, 1958

        c   George Dorroh b Apr. 6, 1960

VI   Emma b   m Charles   Brooks b   CHILDREN:

A   Lutie b   m C. C. Whiteside [1]CHILDREN:

    1   Charlie   NFI

    2   Nell   NFI

    3   William   NFI

    4   Emma Lee   NFI

    5   Dorroh   NFI

    6   Jack   NFI

    7   Robert   NFI

B   Bartlett b   m   Carrie Killett   CHILD:

    1   John Charles   NFI

C   Mamie, b   d as a young lady.

D   David Larry b   m Josephine Tull NO ISSUE

VII Sarah Margaret b Nov. 11, 1848 d June 19, 1929   NFI

[1] He is brother of Beulah Whiteside.See XII

VIII Mary b Nov. 4, 1850 d Dec. 31, 1929 m John
Thomas Peden b Jan. 25, 1853 d Jan. 28, 1921.
Both buried Dorroh Presbyterian Church,Gray
Court, S. C.   CHILDREN:

A   David Dorroh b Apr. 1, 1876 d Mar. 23,
        1938 m Louise M. Meredith b Oct. 30,
        1875 d Feb. 14, 1933 [1] CHILDREN:

        1   James b Oct. 2, 1904 d May 10,1907

        2   Flora Meredith b Aug. 20, 1907 d
             Dec. 5, 1921

        3   David Dorroh II b Nov.20, 1913 d
             Nov. 23, 1913

B   Charles b m Cathie Stewart b CHILD:

        1   a girl   NFI

C   Carrie b m David Weymer b CHILDREN:

        Five: NFI

D   Lewers b m Nora Wilson b NO ISSUE

E   Eugene b d Killed in France   NFI

F   Lucy b Feb. 19, 1892 m William F.
        Stewart b Apr. 27, 1877 d Dec. 15,
        1956 [2] CHILDREN: FOUR   NFI

IX Nannie b May 2, 1852 d Oct. 1, 1920 m James
    Henry Garrison b Mar. 30, 1851 d July 9,
    1936 [1]   CHILDREN:

A   Susan b Mar. 26, 1879 d Aug. 9, 1949 m
        1898 W. Des Franks b 1870 d 1934
        CHILDREN:

        1   Henry b 1900 Greenville, S. C.

        2   Nannie b 1904 m Robert Dixon,
             Blackstock, S. C.

[1]   Both, with their children, buried Dorroh
      Presbyterian Cemetery, Gray Court, S. C.
[2]   Both buried Harmony Church, Fountain Inn.
      S. C.

3   Emily b 1906 m Joe Dominick,
     Clinton, S. C.

4   Martha b 1910 m Carter Miller,
     Clinton, S. C.

5   Mary b 1912 m Lewis Bond, Roebuck,
     S. C.

6   NFI

B   Mary b May 2, 1884 d May 22, 1959
     UNMARRIED [1]

C   Samuel Dorroh b Dec. 22, 1881 d Aug. 19,
     1951 Lula Rhoades b 1892 d   CHILDREN:

1   J. Roy b Sept. 25, 1913

2   David Dorroh b July 22, 1915

3   William Henry b   1919

4   Charles b Apr. 15, 1921

D   Fannie Britt b Sept. 21, 1886 d Jan. 26,
     1954   UNMARRIED

E   George B. b Sept. 5, 1889 d Dec. 6,1950
     m Pearl Roper b 1884 Living Miami,Fla.
     NO ISSUE

F   Charles H. b Jan. 17, 1893 m Oct. 17,
     1925 Jean Cunningham b Jan. 3, 1895
     CHILD:

1   Jean Elizabeth b May 28, 1928 m
     Sept. 30, 1950 William A. Wier II
     b   1927 CHILDREN:

     a   William A. III, b Dec. 12,
          1952

     b   Jean Elizabeth b May 3, 1955

     c   Charles Garrison b June 20,
          1960

[1] Buried Dorroh Presbyterian Church, Gray
     Court, S. C.

X   Charles b   d as young man   NFI

XI   George Francis b Dec. 9, 1856 d Jan. 18,
        1927 UNMARRIED

XII   Laurens G. b March 24, 1859 d May 19, 1918
        m Beulah Whiteside b [1] CHILDREN:

      A   Charlie, b   d young

      B   Frank b m Margaret Blakeley CHILD:

           1   NFI

      C   Henry b 1890

      D   David b June 1, 1892   UNMARRIED

      E   Esther b 1894 m Eugene Woodside b
        CHILDREN:

           1   Eugene II   NFI

           2   Dorroh   NFI

*   We are grateful to Mr. Charles H. Garrison
     for material furnished on this line.

[1]   She is sister to C. C. Whiteside who married
      Lutie Brooks.   See VI A.

Descendants of John Francis Dorroh, M.D. and Mary Elizabeth Saxon *

I   Elizabeth Eugenia b Sept. 20, 1847 d Dec. 10
     1884 m April 28, 1868 Robert Creswell Davis
     b June 26, 1846 Clinton, S. C. d July 23,
     1911   CHILDREN:

     A   James William b April 25, 1870   NFI

     B   John Dorroh b Sept. 30, 1871   NFI

     C   George McDonald b June 16, 1874   NFI

II   Sarah Louisa b Aug. 20, 1849 d July 8, 1893

III Mary Cornelia b March 11, 1851 d Oct. 22,
     1853

IV   Elizabeth Louis b Feb. 24, 1853 d Dec. 29,
     1922 m May 25, 1881 John D. Sheldon b
     d   NFI

V   Amelia Jane b Jan. 7, 1855   NFI

VI   Charles Francis b April 8, 1857 d Feb. 17,
     1897

VII William Chalmers b Oct. 24, 1859 d May 27,
     1897   NFI

VIII John Frederick b Nov. 18, 1861 d   NFI

IX   James Thornwell b July 13, 1864 d July 8,
     1883

X   Samuel Joshua b Jan. 7, 1867 d Jan. 9, 1882

XI   Alfred Ross b Dec. 9, 1868 d   1959
     NFI

XII Julia Saxon b Mar. 30, 1871 d Sept. 8, 1873

XIII Louis David b Jan. 22, 1874 d May 29, 1915
     NFI

*   We are indebted to Mrs. Wade Boggs (Louise
     Sheldon, grandaughter)for this information.

Descendants of Dr. William McDavid Dorroh and Lucretia Williams *

[1]

I James William b Aug. 27, 1842 d July 4, 1864

II William Pinckney b May 27, 1846 d July 27, 1864 [2]

III Rose b   d   m Frank Wilson
  b   d   CHILDREN:

 A Lucile NFI

 B (believe there were other children,NFI)

IV Mary b   d   m John Ferguson
  b   d   CHILDREN:

 A George b NFI

 B Dorroh b NFI

 C probably other children NFI

V Sally b   d   m Joseph (Joe)
  Burton b   d   CHILDREN:

 A
 B (daughters, but NFI)
 C

VI Phoebe b   d   m John Pitts
  (Baptist minister) b   d
  CHILDREN:

 A Rouben, also a minister

VII John Henry b   d   m FIRST
  Dora Reeder b   d   CHILDREN:

 A James b died young

[1] Served in Co. G, 3rd Regiment, S.C. Vols., CSA Died in service. Monument erected in old Bush Cemetery in their honor & memory.

[2] Killed in action at Deep Bottom, Va. Co. E, Hampton Legion.

* Thanks go to Mr. Charlie Senn of Silverstreet S.C. for this information.

416

B   William McDavid II b Feb. 8, 1883 d
     Sept. 5, 1930 m Dec. 26, 1909 Annie May
     Chappell b Oct. 27, 1891 d June 17,
     1960   CHILDREN:

   1   John Henry II b Jan. 15, 1911 m
        Dec. 24, 1937 Rita Moore b
        CHILDREN:

      a   Mary Dianne b Nov. 1, 1942

      b   Rita Jon b May 18, 1946

      c   William McDavid III b Sept.
           18, 1951

   2   Eugene Blease b July 30, 1913 m
        FIRST Feb. 21, 1943 Isabelle Allen
        McCoa b Dec. 9, 1916 d Nov. 13,
        1958   NO ISSUE

        m SECOND May 24, 1963 Mrs. Gwen-
        dolyn Koennecke Hennies b
        NO ISSUE   [1]

   3   James Maxwell b April 8, 1922 d
        Jan. 23, 1923

   4   William McDavid III b Jan. 1, 1927
        m Nov. 17, 1952 Mrs. Carolyn Haynes
        McDonald [2] b March 26, 1926
        CHILDREN:

      a   Elizabeth Lillian b June 6,
           1957

      b   Carolyn Eugenia b June 6,
           1959

C   Griffin (Griff) b   d young

[1]   Sandra Hennies and George Daniel Hennies
       were children of Mrs. Gwendolyn Koennecke
       Hennies by a previous marriage.

[2]   Charles Thomas McDonald b Oct. 9, 1945 and
       Gerry Ann McDonald b Mar. 6, 1948 were child-
       ren by a former marriage of Mrs. McDonald.

D   Elizabeth b   m William Laval[1] b
    CHILDREN:

    1   Dora Alice b   m James
       Wilson b   CHILDREN:

        a   June b   NFI

        b   Judy b   NFI

    2   William Henry (Buddy) b   m
       Corinne Cunningham b   CHILDREN:

        a   Billie (daughter) b

        b   William Henry II b

    3   Henry (Harry) b   m
       Margaret Duncan b   CHILDREN:

        a   NFI

        b   NFI

E   Alfred (Alf) Reeder b Sept. 8, 1878 d
    Sept. 17, 1925 m   Mary E. Senn
    b Aug. 7, 1888   CHILDREN:

    1   Henry b Dec. 15, 1907 d Mar. 27,
       1961 m   Veda Pitts b Sept. 29,
       1914   CHILDREN:

        a   Mary b Mar. 21, 1931 m Henry
           Traylor b Apr. 23, 1931
           CHILDREN:

           i   William Eddy b Oct. 21,
              1950

           ii   Mary Ann b June 20, 1954

        b   Alfred M. b Aug. 30, 1936 m
           Susie Sharpe b Jan. 15, 1936
           CHILDREN:

           i   Cassandra (Cassie) Beth
              b Sept. 29, 1958

[1]   Coached at Newberry College & Univ. of S.C.

   ii Douglas Alfred b Oct. 9, 1960

   iii Henry David b May 31, 1963

  c Elizabeth (Beth) b Aug. 30, 1936 m James Osborne Haltiwanger b July 7, 1934 CHILDREN:

   i Brenda Kay b June 1,1960

   ii David Osborne b Oct. 21, 1961

2 Dora Emma b Jan. 13, 1910 m Thomas Boozer b Sept. 25, 1911 CHILDREN:

  a Sylvia b June 26, 1935 m William (Billy) Gibson b June 5, 1936 CHILD:

   i Deborah Lynn b Jan. 24, 1961

   ii Lisa Ann b Aug. 23, 1963

3 James (Pete) b Nov. 7, 1911 [1] UNMARRIED

4 Griffin (Griff) Olin b Sept. 15, 1912 d Mar. 6, 1957 m Elizabeth (Betty) Martin [2] b May 8, 1927 CHILDREN:

  a Griffin Olin II (twin) b Jan. 27, 1946 m Kathy Booknight b

  b Barbara Elizabeth (twin) b Jan. 27, 1946.

  c David Martin b May 23, 1953

[1] Served in Airborne Infantry during World War II

[2] She m SECOND James Connolly.

5   Gladys Frances b Oct. 21, 1915 d
    June 28, 1916

6   William Crocker (Croaker) b Oct.
    11, 1917 [1] m Mar. 7, 1942 Lalla
    Elizabeth Johnston [2] b Mar. 1,
    1917   CHILDREN:

    a   Rebecca Elizabeth b April 21,
        1946

    b   William Crocker II (Bill) b
        Oct. 12, 1950

7   Elizabeth Laval b Aug. 21, 1922 d
    March 18, 1930

8   Mary Louise b Dec. 30, 1919 m Mar.
    17, 1946 Gilder Martin Neel b Nov.
    10, 1906   [3]   CHILDREN:

    a   Gilder Martin II b June 11,
        1947

    b   James Robert b Oct. 21, 1950

    c   William Alfred b Apr. 4, 1954

[1]   In Co. D, 332nd Engineers, World War II

[2]   Daughter of Arthur Middleton Johnston and
      Alma Teague. Mr. Johnston is believed to be
      the descendant of John Johnston and Jean
      Johnston of Orange Co. N. C. John Johnston
      moved from the Hawfields of Carolina to the
      Enoree River Basin before the Revolution;
      and shows to be living there in the 1790
      Census. The Will of Genet McCown, dated
      July 9, 1785, mentions her daughter Jean
      Johnston and "my son-in-law John Johnston;
      also grandsons James, Thomas, John, Charles;
      and Jean."

[3]   Served in Co. E, 321st Reg. 81st (Wildcat)
      Division, World War II.

9 Robert (Bob) Lee b March 7, 1925[1]
m June 27, 1958 Sallie Shirley b
March 22, 1936 CHILDREN:

a Sallie Dianne b April 6, 1960

b Dell Louise b May 6,1961

c Robert Lee II b May 23, 1962

VII m SECOND   Trannie Pitts b NFI

[1] Served in Seventh Fleet during World War II.

Descendants of Lewis Cunningham Dorroh and Frances Elizabeth Dickson *

I   Joseph Dickson (Dixie) b Feb. 5, 1861 Hinds
Co., Miss. d Sept. 28, 1937 m FIRST Margie
Holliday b Jan. 15, 1862 d July 10, 1886
Buried Chapel Hill, Miss.   CHILD:

A   Fannie Minette b Oct. 6, 1885 d Apr. 1,
1950 Buried Crystal Springs, Miss. m
Dec. 30, 1913 Joseph Wilmot Thomson b
Living Jackson, Miss.   CHILDREN:

1   Joseph Wilmot II b Aug. 15, 1921[1] m
Dec. 16, 1950 Peggy Neal Morrison
b June 25, 1929   CHILDREN:

a   Joseph Wilmot III b Sept. 7,
1952

b   Frances Minette b June 10,
1954

c   James Porter b April 27,1957

2   Mary Frances b Sept. 10, 1924 d
Sept. 22, 1924

m SECOND   Mrs. Susie Dorris Hall b
Sept. 29, 1862 d Dec. 10, 1899 [2] CHILDREN:

B   Joseph Dickson II b Nov. 28, 1891 d
Sept. 1, 1958 m   Mary Griffin
b   CHILDREN:

1   Joseph Dickson III b Aug. 3, 1927
m FIRST April 18, 1951 Marian
Gayle Sebasta b   CHILDREN:

[1]   Graduated Miss. State University 1942.Served
in World War II. Presently in Law Firm,
Walker & Thomson and serving as Mayor of
Starkville, Miss.

[2]   Charles Fremont Hall Jr. was her son by first
marriage and he married Lulie Margie Liddell
whose mother was Sallie Ross Dorroh Liddell
and sister of Joseph Dickson Dorroh-- or
Sallie Ross Dorroh & Joseph Dickson were
children of Lewis Cunningham Dorroh.

        a   Charlotte Ann b Jan. 22, 1953

        b   Doris Sue b Sept. 8, 1955

        m SECOND June 4, 1961 Mrs. Ruth
        Brown Beaty b   NO ISSUE

2   William Edgar (Capt. U.S. Air Force)
     b Dec. 22, 1928 m   Mrs.
     Mary Louise Outterside b
     Living California   CHILDREN:

        a   Steve Outterside b Aug. 16,
               1949   [1]

        b   Scott William b Aug. 10, 1955

        c   Dave Keven b April 18, 1957

C   Bonnie Lee b Jan. 13, 1894 d Aug. 24,
     1895

D   James Lewis b Mar. 15, 1896 [2]
              [3]
E   George Dorris b Dec. 6, 1899 m Sept. 27,
     1922 Lesley Nabers b Jan. 22, 1902 d
     March 4, 1952 CHILDREN:

     1   George Dorris II b Mar. 11, 1924 d
         Jan. 19, 1945 Lexington, Ky. [4]

     2   Martha Ann b Jan. 25, 1929 m June
         6, 1948 William Thomas Survant b
         Sept. 16, 1921 Live 126 Shady Lane
         Lexington, Ky.   CHILDREN:

[1]   Step-son, now adopted.

[2]   James Lewis Dorroh wrote back that his wife
      preferred not to be listed in this genealogy.
      Her wish is respected. They have no children.

[3]   Retired Army Officer, lives Lexington, Ky.

[4]   Died while in service.
  *   James T. Liddell helped with this line and
      we are grateful.

a   George Dorroh b Oct. 25, 1950

b   John Kelley b June 6, 1952

c   Thomas Gregory (Greg) b April 22, 1955

II   Sallie Ross b Dec. 15, 1862 d March 30, 1932 m Feb. 12, 1880 Arthur Hamilton Liddell b Dec 8, 1855 d Jan. 8, 1944   CHILDREN:

A   Bessie Ross b Nov. 20, 1881 d April 2, 1963 m Nov. 17, 1907 George Martin Harris b Sept. 27, 1879 d Oct. 13, 1951 CHILDREN:

    1   Edith b Oct. 22, 1908 UNMARRIED NFI

    2   Louise b June 2, 1910 UNMARRIED NFI

    3   Sarah Hamilton b Dec. 15, 1911 UNMARRIED   NFI

    4   George Armond b Dec. 9, 1914 d May 25, 1946   UNMARRIED

    5   William Conrad b April 18, 1919 m Aug. 23, 1958 Eva Lois Beard b Sept. 22, 1926   CHILDREN:

      a   William Conrad II b Sept. 19, 1959

      b   Elizabeth (Beth) Marie b Jan. 6, 1961

B   Lewis Dorroh b Sept. 16, 1884 d May 13, 1901   NFI

C   Lulie Margie b Oct. 6, 1886 d Dec. 17, 1959 m June 20, 1912 Charles Fremont Hall b July 30, 1886   CHILDREN:

    1   Charles Fremont II b Dec. 6, 1914 m Jan. 26, 1946 Gertrude Crabtree b Oct. 17, 1918 Living Leland, Miss.   CHILD:

      a   Charles Allen b July 26, 1955

2   Sarah Frances b Dec. 17, 1917 m
        June 23, 1943 Eli Nichols Lauder-
        dale b Feb. 9, 1913 Living Hernando
        Miss.   CHILDREN:

    a   Eli Nichols II b May 8, 1944

    b   Charles Cobb b Mar. 19, 1949

3   Dickson Liddell [1] b Sept. 27,
        1919 m Aug. 21, 1945 Neanne Marilyn
        Koch b Nov. 6, 1922 Manilla, Phil-
        ippines   CHILD:

    a   Marilyn Liddell b July 21,1948

4   William Thompson b May 7, 1921 m
        June 7, 1959 Hilda Marie Frazier b
        May 15, 1935   Live Hollandale,
        Miss.   NO ISSUE

5   James Dorris b Mar. 21, 1923 d Oct.
        30, 1934

6   Otto Wassman b Sept. 7, 1924 m
        Sept. 6, 1954 Daisy Alberta Hodges
        b Jan. 4, 1926   CHILDREN:

    a   Sarah Alice b April 16, 1957

    b   Otto Wassman II b July 5,
            1963

7   Lulie Margie b Jan. 9, 1929 m June
        1, 1952 Lamar Cornelius Dorris b
        Aug. 26, 1930. Living Hollandale
        Miss.   CHILD:

    a   Margie Liddell b June 29, 1956

D   Arthur Thompson b Dec. 23, 1888 d Jan. 1
    1953 m April 28, 1924 Annie Vernon
    Austin b Mar. 28, 1902 [2]   CHILDREN:

[1]   Postmaster Hollandale, Miss.

[2]   He was Postmaster of Adams, Miss.   She is
      presently a matron in a girls dormitory at
      Hinds Jr. College, Raymond, Miss.

1   Ava Lynn b Mar. 31, 1927 m Feb. 6,
     1949 Elzie Byron Seale b June 16,
     1927 Living Hobbs, New Mexico,
     CHILDREN:

     a   Rebecca Lynn b Nov. 9, 1952

     b   Ava Carol b Dec. 27, 1956

     c   Maribeth b June 10, 1959

2   Dickson Ross b Sept. 3, 1931 m Dec.
     23, 1953 Marlene Love b Nov. 27,
     1933 Living Adams, Miss. CHILDREN:

     a   Hal Thompson b Oct. 7, 1955

     b   Lisa Ann b May 7,

     c   Roy Hamilton b Oct. 1, 1960

E   Mary Dorroh b Feb. 7, 1891 m July 15,
     1929 J. Percer Scott b   d
     Buried Hernando, Miss.   NO ISSUE

F   William Ramsay b May 22, 1893 m May 30,
     1942 Creula Corley b Aug. 12, 1906 CHILD:

     1   William Ramsay II b Feb. 6, 1947 d
          Nov. 24, 1947

G   Frances (Fannie) Lee b Dec. 13, 1895
     UNMARRIED

H   James Hartgrove b Feb. 17, 1899 d May 5,
     1906

I   Roy Hamilton b Feb. 6, 1902 d July 13,
     1920

J   Hattie Rose b Sept. 27, 1904

III James (Jim) Lewis b Sept. 23 , 1865 d Mar.
     20, 1898 (b & d Hinds Co., Miss.)

IV   Mary b Jan. 21,   Lived Jackson, Miss.
     UNMARRIED d Jan. 30, 1964

V   Lucinda b June 15, 1869 d Oct. 2, 1876
VI   Infant son (no name or date on tombstone)

ADDENDUM

to

Little Acorns from The Mighty Oak

by

Henry Poellnitz Johnston

copyrighted 1962

MARRIAGES:

Page 144, Bright Williamson Crosswell married Feb. 1963 Nancy Laird

BIRTHS:

Page 84, Clifton Kirkpatrick Meador III,M.D. (now with University of Ala. Medical Staff) has a daughter, Anna Kirkpatrick, born May 27, 1962.

DEATHS:

Page 176, Nora McDuffey Carter died Oct. 18, 1963

Page 57, Rose Gunter Lawson died March 27, 1963

Page 104, Frank MacMiller Kitchell, Jr. died June 17, 1963

Page 223, James Preston Rogers died May 17, 1963

Page 215, Henry James Rogers died Jan. 24, 1963

Page 188, William Ellerbe Rogers died Aug.16, 1963

CORRECTIONS

Page 62: Mary Farley Alston born Feb. 1 rather than Feb. 21

Page 62: Robert Withers Poellnitz II born June 29 rather than June 19

Farley Alston Poellnitz omitted from INDEX

Page 234: William Walton born Nov. 28, 1877 died Aug. 12, 1951 married June 21, 1905 Lillian Stinson born Dec. 16, 1882 Living in Louisiana.

Katherine Brandenburg (not Brandenbury)

We give thanks to Mr. J. Russell Cross, of Cross, S. C. for the following data:

ROGERS ---------SHAKELFORD-----WICKHAM---MARRIAGES:

MEMORANDA OF MARRIAGE LICENSES ENTERED IN A MINUTE BOOK OF THE PROBATE COURT, MARION COUNTY, 1800-1823:

1804, Sept. 4th. License to the Revd. Mr. Thos. Humphries to marry Benjamin Rogers of Marlborough District and Ann Wickham, Widow.

MEMORANDA OF MARRIAGE LICENSES ISSUED BY THE COURT OF ORDINARY, MARION COUNTY, ENTERED IN WILL BOOK, 1800-1829:

1800, Oct. 15th. License to the Rev. Thomas Humphries to marry Thomas T. Wickham of Catfish and Ann Shakelford of Brittons Neck.

CORRECTION

Having to depend to a great degree upon information from interested parties for present day
dates and the fact that sometimes information goes
through one person to another, being copied several times before it finally reaches the printer,
errors in dates and even the "dropping" of a name
becomes a bit more than just a possibility.

In *Little Acorns From the Mighty Oak* a very
serious error was committed, for which we express
our sincere apology. In this case a willing help-
er wrote numerous letters to people trying to
bring all information together, and somewhere
along the line the name of Edith Lydia Stebbins
was omitted. Her sister, Hazel Louise Stebbins,
was substituted.

We are happy to bring to the attention of our
readers that under DESCENDANTS OF CALEB REMBERT
AND MARY MAGDALINE MICHAU their ninth child was
Elizabeth Amanda Rembert. She married James Richard Bryan II. Their oldest child was Magdalin Mary
who married Clinton Whitfield. In turn, their
third child was Willie Cheney Whitfield, who married Jesse Frank Stebbins. Their fourth child was
Hazel Louise, born Jan. 1, 1907 died March 4, 1907.
Their next child was *Edith Lydia* born June 4, 1911
and it was *Edith Lydia Stebbins* who married FIRST
April 21, 1931 George Williams Blair and married
SECOND April 15, 1955 Charles Mertens. Please refer to pages 252-3 of *Little Acorns From The
Mighty Oak*........To Edith Lydia Stebbins Mertens,
we send our regrets.

WILL OF DANIEL WHITE

Westmorld.ss   At a Court held for the County the
28th. day of August 1700

Psent   Francis Wright Alexr.Spence)
        Lewis Markham Charles Ashton) Gentl.
        Caleb Butler   Jno.Sturman   )Justices,&c.
        Gerrard Hutt   Geo. Weedon   )
              John   Elliott

  The last Will and Testament of Danll. White
decd. was proved by the Oath of Thomas Weedon (Wm.
Plott the other witness thereto being dead) a Pro-
bat thereof granted to John White Executor therein
named and Ordered to be Recorded. It is also Ordered that the sd. Jno. White Doe return a full & perfect Inventory and account of the sd. Estate to the
next Court (haveing already took his Corporall oath
for the performance thereof.) And it is further
Ordered that Capt.Thomas Gilson, Robert Redman,
John Brown, David Brown & Thomas Weedon or any
three of them being first Sworn before some of his
Majties. Justices for the County Doe sometyme before the next Court value and appraise the sd.
Estate and return their sd. Valueacon to the sd.
next Court.

   A COPY TESTE:

   Lucille S. Hutt, Deputy Clerk,
   Westmoreland County Circuit Court.

Orders 1698 - 1705, Page 90,
Westmoreland County Records.

[The order book concerning Daniel White only shows
that there was a will ordered to be recorded and
also appraisement, but neither were evidently recorded. I do not understand why the will was not
recorded after having been ordered to be by the
Court. I know of another case of the same thing.
I find a land patent for Daniel White, William
Baltrop, and William Brown for seven (700) hundred
and some acres in 1664. Following it is a deed
from Daniel White granting his interest to William
Brown. Signed: *Lucille S. Hutt*, **Deputy Clerk, The**
Circuit Court of Westmoreland County, Montross,
Virginia.]

WILL OF JOHN WHITE

In the Name of God Amen I John White aged sixty
three years old or thereabout do make constitute and
appoint this to be my last Will and Testament in
manner & form following & first give & bequeath my
soul into the hands of God that gave it to me hope-
ing and trusting to have pardon of all my sins there
meritted of my Blessed Lord & Savior Jesus Christ &
my Body to be Buryed in a Descent manner att the Discretion of my Executors hereafter named, & for that
Estate that I have I give and bequeath in manner &
form following. Item I give bequeath to my *son
George White* all my land and plantation & my Mill,
& all belonging to it provided he doth not sell it
and if he should that Brother & Sisters should have
an equal parte. I also give to my *son George White*
my Pistols & Holsters & Ketush Box my cart & Wheels
and Collar & plough & Traces one Bed and Bedstead &
furniture that he youeasly lyes on One Brandy Still
wth. tubb & worm one Dozen of tite Casks & one Negro
girl named Sarah & if she should die without heir to
return back. I also give to my *Son George* one Ing-
lish Chest with lock and key & one iron Pot and hooks
& all my carpenters & coopers tools & a set of Shoe
Makers tools & a cutting knife. Item I give and bequeath unto my *Daughter Mary White* One feather Bed
& Bedstead & Furniture, & one large looking glass
One Cubbeard & one pot and hooks & two Pewter Dishes
two pewter porringers & two pewter Basons four Pewter Plates two flagg chairs & one Negro Girl named
Hannah & all her increase & if she should die without heir to return back again. I also give my *Daughter Mary* One half oval table one Brass cittle one
Chest with a Dutch Lock & Key, One Box Iron & heat-
ers. Item I give and bequeath unto my *daughter Ann
Walker* one Negro girl Named Nanny two flagg chairs,
two Pewter Dishes two pewter Plates one Pewter Bason
one Iron pott two pewter porringers.

Item I give and bequeath unto my *Son Willm.
White* One Negro Woman Named Jeaney & if he should
die without heirs of his Body to return back again.

Item. I give and bequeath unto my *Daughter
Sarah Russel* twenty shillings Currt. Money of Virga.
Item I give and bequeath unto my *Grandson John White
& Elizabth. his sister* each of them five pounds
Currt. Money of Virginia to be paid them when they
come of age. Item I give and bequeath unto my Be-
loved *Wife Mary White* One negro man Named Jack and
a Negro boy named Joe & all the rest of my Estate

During her natural life & then that negro Jack may return to my *son George White* & for the rest to be at her own Disposal, & to see the true performance of this my Last Will & Testament. I make constitute & appoint my *wife Mary* and my *son George White* to be my Exors. for to see this my will truly performed.

In Witness Whereof I hereunto set my hand & fix my seals this Eighteenth day of February one thousand seven hundred and forty six seven.

John White   (Seal)

Assigned, sealed & delivered in presents of us

Wm. Rochester, Jun.
Wm. Porter, Junr.
William Baker

Westmoreland: Sc. At a Court held for the said County the 29th. day of January 1750/1

This last Will and Testament of *John White* decd. was presented into Court by *George White* one of the Exors. therein named, (the other Exor. having refused to take the burthen of the Execution) who made oath thereto, and being proved by the oaths of Willm. Rochester & Willm. Porter two of the witnesses thereto is admitted to record, And upon the motion of the said Executor & his performing what the law in such cases require, Certificate is granted him for obtaining a probate thereof in due form.

Test George Lee   C.C.W.

Recorded the 4th. day of February 1750/1
per G.L.   C.C.W.

A COPY TESTE: *Lucille S. Hutt*, Deputy Clerk, Westmoreland County Circuit Court

Deeds & Wills
No. 11, Page 267,
Westmoreland Co. Records.

WILL OF GEORGE WHITE

In the name of God Amen, I George White of the County of Granville and State of No.Carolina, being infirm in Body, but of Sound mind and Memory, do make and Ordain this my last Will and Testament, in manner and form following, Vizt.

First I recommend my Soul to Almighty God who gave it, trusting in and through the merrits of my dear redeamer for full remission of all my Sins, for a resurrection to eternal life, and my Body to the ground to be interd at the discrestion of my Executors hereafter named.

Item. I leave to my beloved *wife Susannah White* the use of my Plantation whereon I now live, & two Hundred Acres of Land & Four negroes by name James, Judah, Charles and Sarah and the household furniture & Stock not given heretofore, to enjoy during her natural life.

Item. I give and bequeath to my *Daughter Mary Meginess* one negro woman nam'd Graul her increase which she has in possession to her and her Heirs for ever-

Item. I give and bequeath to my *Son William White* one negro Boy named Daniel to his and his Heirs for ever-

Item. I give and bequeath to my *Daughter Ruth Read Carter* **one** Hundred Acres of Land, beginning at the mouth of his Spring branch, Including his House and Orchard, to be laid of as near Square as it will allow, also one negro Girl named Milley to her and her Heirs for ever-

Item. I give and bequeath to my *Son John White* one negro boy named David to him for ever -

Item. I give to my *Son Coleman Read White* one Hundred & fifty Acres of Land leaving out the Mill Seat, with fifty Acres and for his land to adjoin it, one negro boy named Jacob.

Item. I give and bequeath to my *Son Phillip White* two Hundred Acres of Land after the death of his Mother, it being the place whereon I now live, one negro boy named James, one Girl

named Selvia, one Feather Bed to him and his
Heirs for ever -

Item. I give and bequeath to my *Daughter Ann Read
White* one negro Girl named Bettey and her increase also a negro Child named Winney one
bed and Furniture one horse and saddle one
Desk after the Death of her Mother, to her
for ever -

Item. I give to my *Son Garrot White* two Hundred
Acres of Land, beginning at Lewis Taylor's
Corner runing to homsbey's Corner from thence
a Strait line to the River one negro boy
named Sam, one negro woman named Sarah, one
horse and Saddle, one Feather bed and furniture to him for ever -

Item. I give to my *Son Joshua White* and to my *Son
Joseph White* Four Hundred Acres of Land to
be equally Devided, also to my *Son Joshua*,
one boy named Ben, one negro man named
Charles, one horse and Saddle, one bed and
furniture.

Item. I give to my Four *Sons Coley, Phillip, Garrot
and Joshua* my Mill Seat and fifty Acres of
Land to them and their Heirs for ever.

I give my Bible to my *Daughter Ruthey Read
Carter*
I give to my *son Garrot* at the Division of
my Estate ten pounds more than the rest of
my Children I do Appoint my *Son Phillip
White* and Jessee Carter the Executors of
this my last Will and Testament, hearunto
I Set my hand and Seal this Eighth day Octo.
in the year of our Lord one thousand Seven
Hundred and Ninety

George White (Seal)

in presence of
    Lewis Taylor
    Elias Jinkins
    Josiah Rucks

Granville County, ss. May Session A.D. 1792

This last Will and Testament was duly proven
in open Court by the Oath of Lewis Taylor
and Elias Jenkins, and J. R. then Came

Jessee Carter & Phillip White and Qualifi'd
as Execrs.

Test

A. Henderson C.C.

North Carolina,

Granville County.

I, *Charlotte Easton*, Assistant Clerk of the
Superior Court of Granville County, North Carolina,
do hereby certify that the foregoing two and a
fraction pages of typewriting are and contain a
true, perfect and correct copy of the last will and
testament of George White, deceased, as the same is
taken from and carefully compared with the original
record of said will in the office of the Clerk of
the Superior Court in the Record of Wills of Granville County, Book 2, page 297.

In witness whereof, I have hereunto set my
hand and affixed the seal of said court in the
courthouse of Granville County in the City of
Oxford, North Carolina, this 14th day of December,
1960.

Charlotte Easton
_____

Assistant Clerk Superior Court

Granville County,

North Carolina

WILL OF JOSHUA WHITE

In the name of God Amen I Joshua White of the County of Granville and State of North Carolina, being perfect memry and mind do make this my last will and Testament first Command my Soal to God hoping in time to find forgiveness for all my Sins, and as for werly goods, I perses I will as follows

First   My will is that all dets be paid.

2   I lend to my *wife Rachel* the hole of my estate both real and personal during of her life if she shood dey befor Philip comes to be 18 Years old at that time my will is that my land in this track split the old Spring Branch the line and sold in Separate trax and the proced of said land to b equally divid a moung my Six Children, and the hole of my negros Sock houshoal and chicke furniture to be equally divided without a sale between my Six Children - I my debts cant be paid without my Maifield land to be Sold for that purpos if they can that to be sold at the same time of the other and the money arise therefrom to be divid as the other, My will is *Joshua A. White* has my case of Bottles, *Phillip W. White* have my pint botel more tha Rest -

Everthing els equel amoung the *Six Deremy R. White, George M. White, Mary B. White, Nancy A. White, Joshua A. White, Phillip D. White.* If any of my Children Shood leave my wife, and she can spar them any thing some a Count be taken of the worth of these artickels.

I further apoint my *Sun George* Extr. to this my last will tho he is not of lawful age.

Given under my hand & Seal this third day of Febury 1826 -

Joshua White (Seal)

Test

Mathew Wilson
State of North Carolina
Granville County   ) May Court A. D. 1826

The execution of the foregoing paper writing purporting to be the last will and Testament of *Joshua White* deceased was proven on oath by Mathew Wilson the subscribing witness thereto, so as to pass the personal property, and it being also proven by the oath of Robert Jeter to have been found among his valuable papers and it being also proven by the oaths of Nathaniel Robards, Claiborn Cooke Senr. and Robert Snipes that the signature and the whole of the body of the foregoing paper writing is in proper hand writing of *Joshua White*. It is ordered by the Court that the same is duly proven to pass the real Estate and that it be recorded. At the same time came forward *George White* named as the Executor in said will and duly qualified as such

Witness

Step K. Sneed Clk

North Carolina,

Granville County.

I, *Charlotte Easton*, Assistant Clerk of the Superior Court of Granville County, North Carolina, do hereby certify that the foregoing page and a fraction of typewriting is and contains a true, perfect and correct copy of the last will and testament of *Joshua White*, as the same appears of record in Record of Wills, Book 10, page 181.

Witness my hand and the seal of said court, this 14th day of December, 1960.

Charlotte Easton

Asst. Clerk Superior Court, Granville County, N. C.

WILL OF COLEMAN R. WHITE

In the name of God, Amen, I, *Coleman R. White*
of Granville County & State of North Carolina being
of Sound mind & disposing memory do hereby make &
publish this my last Will and Testament in manner
& form following -

1st. I give and bequeath my slaves Jacob, Sam &
Beck to my *son John White* & my *daughters Elizabeth
Allison, Mary Vincent, Susan McGehee* & to the children of my *daughter Ruthy Crook* to be equally divided between my said son, three daughters & the
children of sd. Ruthy Crook (the Children to have
their mothers equal share to them & their heirs
forever---

2nd. I give to my Exects. (hereafter to be named)
for the benefit of my *daughter Ruthy Crook* for and
during the term of her natural life, one bay mare
and colt & the following Slaves Davy Willy & Hagar
all of which are now in her possession. The sd.
Mare & colt & slaves to remain in her possession
or not at the discretion of my sd. Executors. If
they should see fit to remove them from her possession they are to hire them out & pay the hire
annually in such a manner as may most conduce to
her comfort & the support of her & her children &
to their education during the term of her natural
life. At the death of my sd. *daughter Ruthy
Crooke* I give & bequeath the sd. mare & colt &
slaves together with their future increase (if
any) to the children of sd. Ruthy Crook which may
be then living and to the descendants if any of
such as may be dead the Children to take their
decd. parents equal share to them & their heirs
forever---

3rd. I give & bequeath to my *daughter Haskey Ann
Nelson Jenkins* the slaves Gracy, Isham & Wesley &
the future increase of the female, together with
one fourth of my tract of land lying on Tar River
& one woman's saddle to her and her heirs forever-

4th I give & bequeath to my *son William George
Vaughan White* one bed and furniture, three bed
quilts one checked & four white counterpanes, One
Corner Cupboard, one Walnut Table, & slaves Anderson, Ned, & Alfred & that part of my tract of land
called Caleb's & one horse bridle & saddle to him
& his heirs forever---

5th   I give & bequeath to my *son Thomas Person White* one horse bridle ⁜ saddle, one bed & furniture three bed quilts, one checked & five white counterpanes, one walnut desk, & slaves Howel, Mary, & John & the future increase of the female & that part of my tract of land called Brassfields old tract together with one fourth part of my tract of land lying on Tar River to him & his heirs forever --

6th   I give and bequeath to my *daughters Frances Lany Jane White* and *Ceely Coleman White* one half of my tract of land lying on Tarriver and Slaves Gilbert, Moses, Winney, Chaney, Burrel, & Mathew to be equally divided between them when either marries or arrives to the age of twenty one years to them & their heirs forever---

7th   I give & bequeath to my *daughter Frances Lany Jane White* one horse bridle & saddle, one side board, one bed & furniture three bed quilts, one checked & five white counterpanes to her & her heirs forever---

8th   I give & bequeath to my *daughter Ceely Coleman White* One horse bridle & saddle, one chest of drawers, one press, one bed & furniture, three bed quilts, one checked & five White counterpanes to her & her heirs forever---

9th   I give and bequeath to my *son John White* all the property of every kind now in his possession. to my *daughter Mary Vincent* all the property of every kind now in her possession. To my *daughter Susan McGehee* all the property of every kind now in her possession. To my *daughter Elizabeth Allison* all the property of every kind now in her possession - To my *daughter Haskey Ann Nelson Jenkins* all the property of every kind now in her possession - To my *daughter Ruthy Crook* all the property of every kind now in her possession except the Mare & colt & slaves Davy, Willie & Hagar mentioned in a preceeding part of thie Will. I have from time to time delivered to each of my sd. children mentioned in this clause barious slaves & other Chattels without executing a legal conveyance therefor, this clause is designed merely to confirm to each one & to their heirs forever all such Slaves & other Chattels except the mare & colt & the slaves Davy, Willie & Hagar delivered to Ruthy Crook which are otherwise disposed of in a preceeding part of this Will---

10th   All the residue of my personal Estate to be
sold by my Exrs. in such manner & on such terms
as they may think best & out of the proceeds pay
all my just debts & funeral expenses & the residue
to be equally divided between all my children----

11th   I do hereby constitute & appoint my *Son John
White* and my *nephew William R. White* Executors of
this my last Will & Testament, hereby revoking all
other Will or Wills by me heretofore made or published. In testimony whereof I have hereunto Set
my hand & affixed my Seal this 27th day of August
1831.

                    Coleman R. White   (Seal)

Signed & acknowledged
as his last Will & Testament
before us

              Anderson H. Walker
              A. Laurence

State   of North Carolina)
) August Court. A.D 1837
Granville County   )

       The execution of the foregoing last Will and
Testament of *Coleman R. White* decd. was duly
proven on oath in open Court by Anderson H. Walker
and Abraham Laurence the Subscribing Witnesses
thereto, and ordered to be recorded - At the same
time came forward *John White and William R. White*
named as Executors in said Will and renounced their
right to qualify as Such - During the said term,
Administration on the Estate of *Coleman R. White*
deceased was granted to James Wyche, with the Will
annexed, who entered into bond in the sum of $8,000
with Jonathan Jenkins and Pleasant Floyd Securities
and qualified as such----

                    WITNESS

              Jas. M. Wiggins ,   Clk.

440

North Carolina

Granville County.

I, Charlotte Easton, Assistant Clerk of the
Superior Court of Granville County, North Carolina
the same being a court of record and having a seal
do hereby certify that the foregoing and attached
three pages of typewriting are and contain a true,
perfect and correct copy of the last will and testament of *Coleman R. White*, deceased, as the same
appears of record in the office of the Clerk of
the Superior Court in Record of Wills, etc. Book
14, page 16.

Witness my hand and the seal of said court,
this 30th day of July, 1963

Charlotte Easton

Asst. Clerk Superior Court
Granville County,
North Carolina

WILL OF JOSEPH WHITE

In the name of God Amen, I, *Joseph White* of
Granville County * State of North Carolina being
of sound mind & disposing memory do hereby make
and constitute this my last Will & Testament in
manner and form following to wit:

1st I give & bequeath to my *daughter Hixy Winston*
one female Negroe Slave, named Patsey, and one
Ditto named Mary, to her & her heirs forever.
Also, one Horse Bridle and Saddle and one Bed &
furniture which have been already delivered to
her and her children.----

2nd. I give & bequeath to my *son Eaton J. White*
one male Negroe Slave named Anthony now in his
possession one Horse Bridle & Saddle, & one Bed
& furniture which have already been delivered to
him, I have already given to him a deed for the
tract of land whereon he now lives, which land,
I hereby give and Confirm to him and his heirs
forever.----

3rd. I give & bequeath to my *daughter Tyson M.
White* one female Negroe Slave named Haley and one
male Negro Slave Billey One Bed and furniture,
one Horse Bridle & Saddle, to be delivered to her
when she leaves her mother To her & her heirs
forever.---

4th I give to my *daughter Ann Moss* one female
Negroe Slave named Milley one Horse Bridle and
Saddle & one Bed & furniture and one Tract of
land containing three hundred and twenty five
acres or thereabouts. It being the whole of the
tract of land which I purchased of Peter Man with
all its appurtenances to her & her heirs forever.

5th I give & bequeath to my *daughter Fanny A.
White* one female negro Slave named Viney, & one
male Negro Slave named Jordan, one Horse Bridle
and Saddle, & one Bed & furniture to her and her
heirs forever.---

6th I give & bequeath to my *son John F. White* one
male Negroe Slave named Dave, one Horse Bridle &
Saddle & one Bed & furniture to him & his heirs
forever. Also after the death of his Mother all
the tract of land on which I now live with all its
appurtenances to him & his heirs forever.-----

442

7th   The ballance of my property including the
land whereon I now live I lend to my beloved wife
for and during the term of her natural life. At
her death my will and desire is that all my estate
not disposed of above be appraised and divided
equally among all my children and the descendants
of such as may be dead. Should such be the Case
to draw the descendants present Share.

8th   Should any Slave devised above to either
of my Children die before Such child receives
possession my will & desire is that at the death
of my beloved wife such Child shall receive another negro as near the value of the dead one as
Can be before the appraisement and division as
directed in the 7th clause above.----

9th   I have above devised a Horse Bridle & Saddle
and Bed & furniture to each of my Children. The
older ones have already received theirs & my will
and desire is that the younger children have a
Horse Bridle and Saddle and Bed & furniture as
near the value of such as have been delivered to
the elder children.----

10th   LASTLY, I do hereby constitute and appoint
my *son Eaton J. White* and my friend James Wyche
executors of this my Will and Testament and my
will and desire is that such part of my property
as Can be spared by my wife be sold to pay my just
debts. Should a Sale be necessary--

        IN TESTIMONY WHEREOF & of all the above, I
do hereby sign seal and publish this as my last
Will & Testament hereby revoking all will or wills
by me heretofore made this the 8th day of June
1827

                        Joseph White (SEAL)

Signed Sealed acknowledged
published as his last Will
& Testament before us.

        Jno. White

        John Smith
                Interlined by me   *Joseph White*

State of North Carolina   )
)May Court A D 1829.
Granville County   )

The execution of the foregoing last Will and Testament of *Joseph White* deceased was duly proven on oath in open Court by John White and John Smith the two subscribing witnesses thereto and ordered to be recorded. At the same time came forward *Eaton J. White* who is named as one of the Executors in said Will and duly qualified as such

WITNESS

Step Sneed,   Clk.

North Carolina,

Granville County.

I, *Charlotte Easton*, Assistant Clerk of the Superior Court of Granville County, North Carolina, the same being a court of record and having a seal, do hereby certify that the foregoing and attached two pages of typewriting are and contain true, perfect and correct copy of the last will and testament of *Joseph White,* deceased, as the same appears of record in the office of the Clerk of the Superior Court in Record of Wills, Book 11, page 150.

Witness my hand and the seal of said court, this 29th day of July, 1963.

Charlotte Easton
_____

Asst. Clerk Superior Court, Granville County, North
                    Carolina

This Joseph White is the son of George White whose will was probated in the May Court, 1792, Granville County, North Carolina

WILL OF PHILIP WHITE

In the name of God, Amen, I, Philip White of the County of Granville, State of North Carolina, being in sound mind and body and disposing memory do make this my last will and testament in the following manner (to wit):

ITEM 1   I give to my beloved *wife Ann* one bed and furniture, one chest, and one family Bible during her life and then to dispose of as she may think fit.

ITEM 2   I give to my *daughter Holly Mitchell* the following negro slaves (to wit) Charles and Nutty and their increase forever.

ITEM 3   I give to my son *William R. White* the following negro slaves (to wit) James and Charlott and their increase forever.

ITEM 4   I give to my *daughter Jaccey Sims* the following negro slaves (to wit) Silvy and Read, and the tract of land whereon I now live with all the ways, privaledges and appertennances thereunto with the increase of said slaves forever with a request to take particular care of her mother during her life.

ITEM 5   I wish my executors as soon as convenient after my death to advertise and sell all the property not devised and otherwise appropriated on the usual credit and the proceeds thereof after paying my just debts if any when they are collected to put out on Int. and out of that amount I wish sixty dollars to be applied annually for the support of my wife, and at her death the balance, if any, to be equally divided between my three children before named.

ITEM 6   And last I nominate my *son William R. White* and my friend Pleasant Floyd Executors to this, my last will and testament. Given under my hand and seal this 28 day of January A.D. 1838

Philip White   (seal)

TEST.
E. I. (J.) White

Jordan D. Moss

NORTH CAROLINA
Granville County   August Court A.D. 1845

The execution of the last Will and Testament
of *Philip White*, deceased, was proved on oath in
open court by Jordan D. Moss, one of the subscribing witnesses thereto and ordered to be recorded
at the same time came forward *Wm. R. White* named
Executor in said will and duly qualified as such.

WITNESS:

Jas. M. Wiggins   , Clerk

*This Philip White was the son of George White
whose will was probated in the May 1792 Court of
Granville County, North Carolina*

WILL OF JOHN WHITE

In the name of God, Amen, I, *John White*, of the County of Granville and State of North Carolina of sound and perfect mind and memory, blessed be God, do this 18 day of June in the year of our Lord one thousand eight hundred and sixty-four make and publish this my last Will and Testament in manner following, that is to say:

FIRST: I will that my just debts be paid and funeral expenses.

SECONDLY: I lend to my *wife Hixey White* during her life time the tract of land I live on, 450 acres, five Negroes Jame, Bobb, Joseph, Cap, and Amye two horses, wagon, buggy, four cows and yearlings, hogs to kill, and enough to raise from household and kitchen furniture (after gaven off *Doctor* two beds and furniture) Plantation tools such as she needs, six sheep.

THIRDLY: I gave unto my *son Doctor C. White* the following Negroes: Charles valued at eight hundred dollars, Sendy and child $800 now has four children: Nancy, John, Franky and Charles, Cate another woman 4 children Dick, Haywood, Siller and Roling valued at $2800 Negro man Pleasant nothing, also 2 bead steads and furniture $58 also sheep and 850 acres of land in Nash $2545.80 which you can see from Shop Book, 174 page, which statement I have made out for *Doctor C. White, my son,* the way I have valued them seven thousand one hundred twenty-eight dollars, 80 cents.

FOURTHLY: I gave to my *daughter Caroline Hunt Roling* valued at $800 Mariah 4 children: Matilda, Samuel, Liew and Henry and her increase since valued at $1400 sence I have given her a bill of sale to Negro woman Selah 4 children: Daniel, Mimma, Betty and Liner, Cate child valued at $2500, also old man James the Black Smith valued at nothing and after my wife's death James Floyd pay you twelve hundred fifty dollars out of the proceeds I shall gave Mary Susannah his wife the land I gave her valued at $2500 below the above with articles in Shop Book, page 172 making

the amount six thousand five hundred ninety
seven dollars 35 cents, also 1 heffer yearl-
ing for his that died.

FIFTH: I gave to *Mary Susanah Floyd Ander-
     son* valued at $800 woman Nancy and three child-
     ren Jane, Viney and Ruffin valued at $1000
     146 acres of land $730 Negro woman Mack 4
     children: Hawkins, Milly, Mary and William,
     old man Sprigg $400, his wife Venea nothing
     and the land I live on 430 acres after my wife's
     death valued at $2500 Dollars James Floyd pay
     to C. Hunt after my wife's decease $1250 twelve
     hundred fifty dollars the accounts in Shop Book
     page 170 and 171 making seven thousand sixty
     four dollars 12 cents the above Negroes I have
     given with their increase Caroline and Mary to
     be paid up to *D. C. White* amount and the bal-
     ance equally divided, if any, after a full
     support for *Hixey my wife* during her stay on
     earth with her mother and *Susanah Megehe, my
     sister,* I lend her one bed and furniture $50
     Dollars in old money what she has put in here
     pay her back in wheat and corn to live on pro-
     vided she leaves my wife.

Gaven under my hand and seal this 18 June,
1864, 5 Barrels corn, 8 1/2 Bushels wheat.

I appoint my *son Docter C. White,* my Execter.

                         Jno White

B. F. Bullock
B. B. Hester
Book 22, page 381
North Carolina)
Granville County)   November Court 1865

     The execution of the foregoing last Will and
Testament of Jno. White deceased was proved on oath
in open court by B. F. Bullock & B. B. Hester, the
subscribing witnesses thereto, and ordered to be
recorded and filed. At the same time came forward
Docter C. White named as Executor in said will and
duly qualified as such.
                 WITNESS: A. *Landis,*Clerk

*This John White is the son of Coleman Read White
whose will was probated in the August Court, 1837
Granville County, North Carolina*

WILL OF SAMUEL ALLEN

It is my will that my *son James* shall have the tract of land on which I now live containing 300 acres, more or less, for which he shall pay to my estate four hundred dollars. But, in case he should not think proper to take the land at that price it shall be sold to the highest bidder on a suitable credit, in either case it is to be divided as below directed:

I will that my stock of all kinds, excepting what I have heretofore given to my children, my household and kitchen furniture, negroes and all other species of Property be sold on a suitable credit and the moneys arising therefrom to be equally divided among my children hereafter mentioned, viz: *Susanna, Zachariah, Garland, Rachel, Nancy, Winnefred,* and *James,* my son Samuel's two children by the names of *Thomas* and *Elizabeth* to have their father's part, but to remain in the hands of my Executors hereafter mentioned until they marry or come of age. My *daughter Mary's* six children to have their mother's equal share to remain in the hands of my Executors till they marry or come of age.

I ordain my three *sons, Zachariah, Garland,* and *James Allen* my Executors of this my last will and testament.

Will made: 29th day of November 1812

WITNESSES: D. Jones
               John Thompson
               I. Boyce
               Moses Winston

Will probated in August Court 1813 by oaths of Daniel Jones, Isham Boyce and Moses Winston and ordered recorded.

Garland Allen qualified as Executor at the same time.

Book 7, page 326, Granville County, North Carolina

WILL OF GERRARD HUTT

In the name of God, Amen, I *Gerrard Hutt,* of Copley Parish in the County of Westmoreland, being weak in body but sound in mind and memory, praised be Almighty God for the same. Do make, constitute appoint and ordain this my last Will and Testament in manner and form following Viz:

PRIMISES: First and principally: I commend my soul into the hands of God who gave it hoping through the meritorious death of Jesus Christ, my Saviour, to receive full pardon of all my sins, and my body to be buried at the discretion of my Executors hereafter nominated.

ITEM: I give and bequeath unto my loving *wife Mary Hutt* all my Estate Viz; Land, Negroes, stock of all kinds and household furniture during her life and after her death to be divided as followeth:

ITEM: I give and bequeath to my *grandson William Hutt* my large case, my young Bay mare, saddle and bridle, housing and clothes to him and his heirs.

ITEM: I give and bequeath to my *grandson Gerrard Hutt,* son of John Hutt, Negro girl Rose to him and his heirs forever.

ITEM: I give and bequeath to my *grandson Joseph Read,* son of Andrew Read, two Negro girls, Let and Bet, to him and his heirs lawfully begotten together with one bed and furniture, in case my *grandson Joseph Read* is under age without such heirs then to go to the next surviving son of my *daughter Mary Ann Read,* and for want of such heirs to be equally divided amongst the several children that shall be born of the body of my *daughter Mary Ann Read.* It is my will and desire that the two Negroes, Let and Bet, shall remain in the hands of my Executors until my *grandson Joseph Read* arrive to the age of twenty-one years.

ITEM: I give and bequeath to my *son Gerrard Hutt* four young cattle, one Negro boy, James, and his father, Davy, to him and his heirs forever.

ITEM: I give and bequeath to my *grandson Gerrard Hutt,* son of Gerrard, four heads of young cattle to him and his heirs.

ITEM: I give and bequeath to my *grandson* *John Brown*, son of William Brown, five Negroes named: Jenny, Charles, Hannah, Nancy, and Silvia, to him and his heirs lawfully begotten and for want of such heirs to return and be equally divided amongst all my children and grandchildren. It is my will and desire that these five Negroes: Jenny, Charles, Hannah, Nancy, Silvia, shall remain in the hands of my Executors until my *grandson John Brown* shall arrive to the age of twenty-one years.

ITEM: I give and bequeath to my *son Gerrard Hutt* all that land that he now lives on to him and his heirs forever, together with three hundred pounds current money to be paid out of my **Estate** that is not already bequeathed.

ITEM: I give and bequeath to my *grandson* *Joseph Read* all that tract of land I purchased of John Crabb, formerly the property of *Coleman Read*, to him and his heirs, lawfully begotten male heirs of his body. For want of such heirs to fall to the next heir male born of my *daughter Mary Ann Read*, and for want of such heir to fall to my *son Gerrard Hutt* and his heirs forever.

ITEM: I give and bequeath to my *grandson* *John Brown* all that tract of land I purchased of John Robinson to him and his heirs lawfully begotten of his body, and for want of such heirs to fall to my *son Gerrard Hutt* and his heirs forever.

ITEM: It is my will and desire that the remainder of my Estate that is not already bequeathed shall be equally divided between all my children and grandchildren after the death of my loving *wife, Mary Hutt*.

ITEM: I leave my *sons John Hutt* and *Gerrard Hutt* Executors of this, my last Will and Testament revoking and making void all other Wills and Testaments before made.

In WITNESS whereof, I have hereunto set my hand and seal this fourth day of May, one thousand seven hundred and seventy.

(signed) *Gerrard Hutt*

TEST: Traviss McGuire
   Thomas Blumdell
   Thos. Edwards

At a Court held for Westmoreland County the 25th day of Sept. 1770, this Will was proved according to law by the oaths of Thomas Edwards, Traviss McGuire and Thomas Blumdell, the WITNESSES thereto and ordered it be recorded and on the motion of John Hutt and Gerrard Hutt, the Exec. therein named who made oath thereto according to law, and together with Alexander Spark and Thomas Edwards, their Securities, entered into and acknowledged Bond with condition as the law directs, Certificate is granted them for obtaining a probate thereof in due form.

TEST:

James Davenport, Clerk

Westmoreland County, Virginia

Deeds, Wills No. 15, 1768-1773

WILL OF MARY READ

In the name of God, Amen, I *Mary Read* of the County of Westmoreland, spinster, being sick and weak but of sound and disposing mind and memory, thanks be to God, do make this my last Will and Testament in manner and form following:

FIRST: I give and devise to my *sister,* Ann Asbury, the four following slaves to wit: Will, Lucy, Dinnah and Nan; and also the bed and furniture that is at her house.

ITEM: I give and bequeath to my *niece, Barbary Hutt,* my wearing apparel.

ITEM: I give the five following slaves to wit: Peter, Dick, Darius, Judy and Dinah and all the rest and residue of my Estate, both real and personal of what nature kind or quality whatsoever, to my *nephew Andrew Read* for and during his natural life, and after his decease to my *godson, Joseph Read,* son of the said Andrew Read and to his heirs forever, and I do hereby charge the said Estate so given to the *said Andrew* with five pounds annually to be laid out in the purchase of clothes for my *brother, Richard Read,* during his natural life a hat only to be purchased this present year he being in every other respect clothed, and I do charge the said **Estate** with the education of my said *godson Joseph Read.*

LASTLY: I do constitute my said *sister,* Ann Asbury and my *nephew, Andrew Read,* Executors of this, my last Will and Testament.

IN TESTIMONY WHEREOF I have hereunto set my hand and seal the twenty-first day of January 1772

Mary Read

Signed, sealed & acknowledged to be the last Will & Testament of the above named *Mary Read* in the presence of us who have hereunto set our names as WITNESSES in her presence and at her request.
Richard Parker   Thomas Asbury

Westmoreland County, Virginia

Deeds, Wills 15, 1768-1773, page 180

At a court held for Westmoreland County the 21st day of March 1772, this Will was proved according to law by the oath of Richard Parker and Thomas Asbury, the WITNESSES thereto and ordered to be recorded and on the motion of *Ann Asbury* and *Andrew Read,* the Executors therein named who made oath thereto according to law; and together with John Lawson their Security, entered into and acknowledged Bond with Condition as the law directs, Certificate is granted them for obtaining a probate thereof in due form.

TESTE: *James Davenport*

Clerk

WILL OF ANDREW READ

In the name of God, Amen, I *Andrew Read* of the Parish of Cople and County of Westmoreland, being very sick and weak of Body, but of perfect and sound memory, and considering the frailty of man's life do make this my last Will and Testament in manner and form following:

Imprimis: I give and bequeath my soul to God that gave it me, and my body to the earth from whence it came to be decently buried as my Exec. hereafter named shall think it fit; and as for such worthy goods as God of His Mercy hath been pleased to lend me, I give and bequeath as follows:

ITEM: I give and bequeath unto my *son Coleman Read* and to his heirs lawfully begotten a parcel of land, beginning at a white oak in a valley by the River Side, and so to run along the line that divideth George Brown and me, to the corner tree of George Brown's land, it being a red oak and from thence to a line southwest, or thereabouts to the land that was formerly Anne Hutts and to northwest down the said line.

ITEM: I give unto my *son Andrew Read* the remainder of the said land that I now live upon; also I give unto my *son Andrew Read* two hundred acres of land which I formerly bought of George Brown as it doth appear by the said George Bworn's Bill of Sale bearing date the 9th day of March 1660 or 1670.

N.B.   This will is so much injured that I cannot proceed to transcribe accurately, which may be found on page 250 of the original book. *(These remarks made by person copying above will to permanent Will Book.)*

Westmoreland County, Virginia

Deeds, Wills No. 2, 1691-1699

WILL OF COLEMAN READ

In the name of God Amen I, *Coleman Read,* of the Parish of Cople and County of Westmoreland being sick and weak of body but of perfect sense and memory, thanks be to Almighty God for the same, and knowing the uncertainty of this mortal life and willing to settle my temporal affairs in order to more ready resignation of my Immortal Soul, when it shall please God to call, do make this my last Will and Testament in the manner form following. Resigning my soul to Almighty God who gave it me, trusting in the merits of my Blessed Redeemer Jesus Christ to obtain mercy and forgiveness of all my sins and of a joyful resurrection at the last.

IMPRIMIS: It is **my will** and desire that all my just debts be paid by my Executors hereafter named as soon as conveniently may be after my death.

ITEM: I give and bequeath to my *son, Joseph Read,* that part of my land on which Sarah Pew lived, containing about one hundred acres beginning at the Eastermost corner tree of Gerrard Hutt, thence up the river to a white oak which divides the said land, and that which I bought of Thomas Brown, thence from the said white oak along Brown's line on the west and by west to a corner red oak of the said Brown's, thence from......by west to the line of Gerrard Hutt from thence down Hutts.....I give to my *son, Joseph Read,* him and his heirs forever........

And a small white oak standing on the north side of Smith's Spring Branch, running from thence North West by West to the.........the said land I give to him and his heirs forever. I also give unto my said.........*Read,* a Negro girl named Cate, and one Negro girl named Doll.

ITEM   I give and bequeath unto my *son, Richard Read,* to him and his heirs forever the remainder of my land which is not already given, being the land on which I now live, to have it after the decease of my loving *wife, Ruth,* as also one Negro woman called Alice, a man named Sam and a Negro boy called David.

I also give to my said *son Richard Read....* all my stock, household goods and chattels, not otherways disposed of to be equally divided between....after the death of my loving *wife Ruth.*

I give unto my said *daughter Mary Susannah* two Negroes viz: a boy named....and a boy named Daniel.

It is also my desire that my said daughters live with my *son Richard* during the time they remain single.

ITEM: I give unto my *grandson Coleman Brown* a Negro named Billy, to be delivered to my said grandson when he shall attain the age of one-twenty years.

ITEM: I give and bequeath to my *grandson Coleman Dunkin* a Negro boy named.....to be delivered to my said grandson when he becomes of age.

ITEM: I give unto my *grandson Hutt* a Negro boy named Guy to be delivered to my said grandson when he comes of age.

ITEM: I give and bequeath to my *granddaughter Ruth Asbury* a Negro Bess to be delivered when she comes of age or marry.

ITEM: I give and bequeath unto my *granddaughter Elizabeth Read* a Negro girl named Ruth to be delivered when my said granddaughter comes of age or marry.

ITEM: It is my will and desire that my loving *wife Ruth* have the use of all my Estate, both real and personal, during her natural life, except the land given to my *sons, Richard and Joseph Read,* and that after the decease of my said wife, my Estate be divided and distributed to the several parts of my will.

ITEM: It is my will that if any law suit should happen....any of my lands, that the charges be paid out of the crops to be made by my slaves during the life of my loving *wife Ruth;* of if the suit should happen after the death of my wife, then the expenses shall be paid by my *sons Joseph and Richard* each one equally.

LASTLY: I nominate and appoint my loving *wife Ruth* and my *son Richard Read,* Executors of this, my last Will and Testament, making void and null all other will or wills heretofore made either by word, writing or any other method whatsoever and do acknowledge this to be my last Will and Testament.

IN WITNESS WHEREOF I have hereunto set my hand and affixed my seal, this first day of March 1768/9

Coleman Read (SEAL)

In presence of William Fitzhugh, William Spencer, Sam, Andrew Thompson.

Westmoreland Ct.: At a court held for the said county, the 26th day of April 1768. This last Will and Testament of *Coleman Read*, deceased was presented into court by *Ruth Read and Richard Read*, Executors in the said will named (who made oath thereto & being proved by.....of the Exec. and their performing what is.....usually in such cases Certificate is granted them for obtaining a Probate thereof in due form.

TESTE: *George See*, CCW.

GS   CCW.

Recorded the 6th day of May 1748

Westmoreland County, Virginia
Deeds, Wills 11, 1747-1753

JOHN WHITE'S ADMINISTRATIVE BOND

North Carolina
Warren County

Know all men by these present that we, Nancy
white, Daniel Fain and Joel Fain are held and firmly bound unto his Excellency Benjamen Williams Esq.
Captain General and Commander in Chief in and over
the said in the sum of two hundred pounds current
money to be paid to the said Govenor his successor
or assigns to the which payment will and truly to
be made, we bind ourselves, our heirs Executor and
Admr. to witt severally, firmly by these presents
sealed with our seals and dated this the 26th day
of May A. D. 1801.

The condition of the above obligation is such
that if the above bounder Nancy White, Administrat-
rix of all and singular the goods and chattels,
rights and credits of John White, Gent. deceased,
do make or cause to be made a true and perfect inventory of all and singular the goods and chattels,
rights and credits of the deceased which have or
shall come to the hands, knowledge or possession of
the said Nancy White or into the hands or possession
of any persons for her and the same to make do exhibit or cause, to be exhibited to the Court of the
County aforesaid within ninety days from the date
of these presents and, the same goods, chattels,and
credits and all other goods, chattels and credits
of the decd. at the time of his death which at any
time hereafter shall come into the hands or possession of Nancy White, or into the hands or possession
of any person for her do well and truly administer
according to law, and further do make or cause to
be made a true and just amount of her said administration within ninety days after the date of these
presents and all the rest and residue of the said
goods, chattels and credits which shall be found remaining upon the said administrators accounts, the
same being first examined and allowed by the Court
of the said County shall deliver and pay unto such
person or persons respectively to which the same
shall be due pursuant to the true and interest and
meaning of the act in that case made and provided
and if it shall appear that any will or testimony
was made by the deceased, and the executor or executors therein named to exhibit the same in to Court
making request to have the same allowed and approved

of accordingly; if the said Nancy White, above
bounder, being thereunto required do render the
said letter of Administration approbation of such
testament being first had and made in the said
Court then obligation to be void, otherwise to
remain in full force and virtue.

X (her mark)
Nancy White   (Seal)
X (his mark)
Daniel Fain   (Seal)
X (his mark)
Joe Fain   (Seal)

Signed and sealed in the
presence of
William R. Johnson

WARREN COUNTY MAY COURT 1801

This Bond was executed in open Court and ordered
to be recorded.

TEST;

M. Duke Johnson   Ct.

WILL OF MARY WHITE

In the name of God, Amen. I, *Mary White*, of Westmoreland County, being sick and weak of body but of sound mind and memory praised be to God for the same and knowing the certainty of death and the uncertainty of the time hereof, do make and ordain this to be my last Will and Testament in manner and form followin g:

Item - I give and bequeath my soul in the hands of Almighty God that gave it me and my body to be decently buried at the discretion of my executor hereafter named and as touching such worldly estate as hath pleased God to bestow upon me I give and bequeath unto my *grand daughter Anne Porter* One seal skin trunk and a bible;

Item - I give and bequeath unto my *daughter Sarah Rupel* One negro boy named Joe during her life and after to return to my *grand daughter Mary White*, daughter of Phillip White;

Item - I give and bequeath unto my *son George White* one negro woman named Alice;

Item - I give and bequeath unto my *grand daughter, Mary White*, daughter of Phillip White, fourteen pounds current money to be raised out of my monable estate;

Item - I appoint and constitute my friend, Griffin Garland, my executor, I also give Griffin Garland six pounds current money. I desire that the rest of my estate if there be any, be divided between my *daughter Anne Walker* and my *grand daughter, Elizabeth Reynolds;*

Item - I appoint my friend Griffin Garland my executor of this my last will and Testament. Given under my hand and seal this twentieth day of October, One Thousand Seven Hundred and Sixty-Four.

Teste;

	Her			Her	
Anne	x	*Davis*	*Mary*	x	*White* (SEAL)
	Mark			Mark	

	Her	
Joane	x	*Davis*
	Mark	

AT A COURT HELD FOR WESTMORELAND COUNTY THE 26th DAY
OF FEBRUARY, 1765.

This Will was proved according to law by the
oaths of William Rochester and Anne Davis, witnesses
thereto and ordered to be recorded, and on the
motion of Griffin Garland the executor therein named
who made oath according to law and together with
Richard Parker and John Rust his securities entered
into and acknowledged bond with condition as the law
directs, certificate is granted him for obtaining a
probate thereof in due form.

Teste: *James Davenport*

A COPY

TESTE: *Betty G. Johnson*
                Deputy Clerk

Westmoreland County, Virginia

Will Book No. 14, page 303, recorded Feb. 26, 1765.

WILL OF AGNES WHITE

North Carolina
Warren County

In the name of God, Amen, I, Agnes White of the County of Warren and State of North Carolina, being of sound mind and memory, do make this my last Will and Testament, in manner and form following to WIT:

ITEM 1st.   I lend to my *daughter Lucy Tucker* one negro girl by the name of Susan and which she now has in possession to have during her natural life; I also lend to my said *daughter Lucy Tucker* one sixth part of the balance of my Negroes, or the money that may arise from the sale of them as the case may be to hold during her natural life, and if the said *Lucy* should have no child or die before her daughter Sally Tucker, then my wish is that the said Negro, Susan, as also the balance of the Negroes to return to the rest of my surviving children and their heirs forever.

ITEM 2nd.   I give to my *daughter Lucy Tucker* one bed and furniture.

ITEM 3rd.   I give to my *son Edmund White* three choices of the cows and calves and all my stock of hogs.

ITEM 4th.   I give to *daughter Ailcy Cole* one bed and furniture and one suite of curtains.

ITEM 5th.   I give to *Martha White* one bed.

ITEM 6th.   I give to *Mary N. White* one bed. I give to *Martha* and *Mary N. White* my two horses to be sold by my Executor and the money to be equally divided between them.

ITEM 7th.   My will is that the tract of land whereon I now live together with my Negroes and all the balance of my property of every description be sold or divided by my Executor as he may think best and the money arising therefrom to be first applied to the payment of my just debts and the overplus to be equally divided between *Edmund White* the heirs of my *daughter Nancey Rooker* (? *hard to read*), *Martha White*, *Ailcy* and *Mary N. White*.

And, I do nominate and appoint my *son*
Edmund White my Executor to this, my last Will
and TEstament this 2nd Day of April, 1830.

Agnes White   (SEAL)
X (her mark)

In the presence of: Jas. O. K. Mayfield
Nancy Robins

WARREN COUNTY, November Session, 1830:

This last Will and Testament of *Agnes White*
being exhibited in open Court for probate and
execution thereof being proved by the oath of
Jas. O.K. Mayfield, one of the subscribing witnesses thereto and on motion, it is ordered to be
recorded.

TEST: *C. Drake*,   C. Ct.

WILL OF JOSHUA ASBURY WHITE

Weakley County, Tennessee
Will Book 1866, page 186

To G. A. (Garland A.) White - one walking cane and
pair of gold spectacles   Also, $250.00

To C. D. (Cullen Debrough) White - 40 acres of
land valued at $650. Also, the case and bottles
from my father's estate.

To Julia A. (Julia Ann) White - 36 acres of land
known as the Houston Finch place valued at $700.00
A writing desk and bookcase valued at $10.00.

To H. L. (Henry Logan) White - 57 acres of land on
which he now lives, valued at $600.00

To Robert, Alice, George and Lizzy Fuller, children of S. C. (Sarah C.) Fuller, decd., - 84 acres
of land where they now live, where Gus Fuller now
lives reserving one-half acre of land for a graveyard.

To my wife Priscilla, as long as she remains a
widow all the remaining property after her death
to go to M.F. (Millard Filmore) the 60 acres known
as the Knight property valued at $1000.00

To C. D. (Cullen Debrough) White $250.00

To the following: E. R. (Elizabeth R.)Hornbeck,
A. B. (Arthur) White, S. C. (Sarah) Fuller, H. L.
(Henry Logan) White, J. N. (Josephine) Jones, Julia
A. (Julia Ann) Jeter $700

To C. D. (Cullen Debrough) White - $1045.00

To all the above named: one bed and bedstead and
furniture.

I appoint A.W. (Alpheus) Jones the guardian for the
children of S. C. (Sarah) Fuller.

All the rest of the property to be sold E. D.
(Elliott Dean) Hornbeck a share; the three children
of A. B. (Arthur) White to have a share and the
four children of S. C. (Sarah) Fuller.

Page 2:   WILL OF JOSHUA ASBURY WHITE:

I appoint no one to execute this will as I
can see no use for one, and nothing for one to do
as long as my wife lives, and when she dies the
heirs can appoint one.

J.A. White   (SEAL)
(Joshua Asbury White)

February--------1883

ADDITION:

In the event that Jacksey Fuller should sue,
I want them to have enough to make up the loss.

WILL OF JOHN HENRY WHITE

Uniontown, Ala.
Feb. 15, 1901

To my Beloved Wife,

Ella S. White

I have heretofore devised and bequeathed to
you all the property which I may own and or be
entitled to at the time of my death. I do this,
in order that you may be fully provided for during
the remainder of your life, and that my bounty for
others may pass through your hands.

I advise and desire you to dispose of my estate
as follows: TO WIT:

As soon as practicable after my disease, you will
give, in,:

1st, To my *Sister Helen* $500.00

2nd, To my *Sister Alice* *$500.00*

3rd. To my *Sister M. J. Brown $250.00*

4th. To the *Presbyterian Church of Uniontown, Ala.,*
the sum of $1250.00. This last named sum you will
pay over to the Elders of said Church, and they will
be expected to invest the same in any safe manner
that they might think proper; except that no part
of said amount shall be loaned to nor used by any
member of said Church. The income from said amount
shall be applied by the said Elders, in their discretion, to the various uses for which collections
are usually made in said Church.

5th. You will give the sum of $500.00 to the *Orphans
Home, in Talladega, Ala.* You will also pay this
amount to the Elders of the Presbyterian Church of
Uniontown, Ala., and the same shall always be held
by them in trust for said Orphans home. They will
be expected to invest this amount in any safe manner
they may desire; except that no part of the sum
shall be loaned to nor used by any member of said
Church. The income from said amount shall be paid
by said Elders to the proper Officers of said
Orphans Home, for the benefit of the children there.

6th. You will lay aside the sum of $1000.00, and use the same, for the purpose of completing the education of our youngest *daughter Eloise*, and the amount so used by her in this, shall not be charged to her in the division of my estate.

7th. You will also lay aside the sum of $500.00 for *Belle*, and $500.00 for *Eloise*,-for the purpose of buying a trousseau for each, when they shall marry and this amount shall not be charged to them in the division of my estate.

8th. As soon as practicable after my disease, you will transfer and deliver my Uniontown City bonds to our *Son, J. Harry White*, in trust for our *Grand-daughter Frances*.

9th. As soon as practicable after my disease you will deliver and turn over to our *daughter Weenona Hanson*, as a part of her distributive share in my estate, the debt due me by W. W. Screws and the securities therefor, of $7500.00.

10th. I have advanced to our *Son J. Harry White* the sum of $7500.00 for which he should account in the division of the estate.

11th. I have advanced to our *daughter Annie Spessard* the sum of $4500.00 for which she should account in the division of the estate.

12th. As soon as practicable after my disease I want you to give to our *daughter Weenona Hanson* $2500.00 in addition to the Screws debt above men-tioned, and to our *daughter Annie Spessard* the sum of $5500.00, in addition to the $4500.00 mentioned above.

13th. You will then give to each of our adult daughters, except to *Weenona and Annie* the sum of 10,000.00; and then to each of our minor daughters the sum of $10,000.00 as soon as she or they may become of age or shall marry. And this amount to be given to our minor daughters is to be held by you or them until she or they may become of age, or shall marry, as above stated.

The purpose of these two last sections, 12 and 13, is to give each one of our daughters, $10,000.00 as soon as practicable or as provided for above to be disposed of by her, in any manner that she might see fit.

14th. My advice to you, is, to keep for yourself
all the real estate that I may own at the time of
my death. And addition thereto you will have the
income from the part of my estate that our minor
daughters will own, as provided for hereinafter.

15th. As soon after my disease as you can do so,
you will make up a full and complete inventory of
my property of every kind and description, and take
the same into your possession at once. And first,
you will pay any and all my debts that I may owe
and next, all bequests that I have mentioned in
paragraphs 1, 2, 3, 4, 5, 6, 7, and 8 hereof, and
after this is done, you will at once allow and turn
over to our *Son J. Harry White*, his full share of
my estate then left, meaning 1/6 of same, less the
amount already advanced him. And in making up
Harry's share, I do not want it all to come out of
any particular or specific branch or kind of my
property but I want you to arrange it so that you
can divide all the stock that I have in each Corpo-
ration, equally, if possible, between him and his
Sisters, I do this so that Harry will look after his
Sisters' interest in these matters, and I want him
to do this free of charge to them and this is one
reason why I have directed that he shall have his
share at once.

16th. Should I make any further advances to any of
my children, such advances must be accounted for in
the final division of my estate, by the party to
whom it was made.

17th. As full division is hereinbefore made for our
Son J. Harry White, my advice is that you give him
no interest in the amount you may reserve or accumu-
late, but that you will the same at your death, to
our daughters share and share alike, or to their
descendants, who may then be living.

18th. As to your household furniture, piano, sil-
verware and jewelry, I have no suggestions to make,
but you may dispose of it all among our children as
you may see proper, but I want you to arrange a division of it so that there will be no dissatisfac-
tion among them.

19th. Now as a final summing up: after you have
paid all the bequests herein made, and have given
Harry his full share, and each adult daughter
$10,000.00 or the amount necessary to make this with
what they have received as mentioned, and have re-
served or for yourself all the real estate and for

each minor daughter $10,000.00 and the several other
amounts herein specified, there will then be on hand
a balance of my estate, which you will call the surplus, and which I want my Daughters jointly to enjoy
share and share alike, for the present, and I want
it so arranged for the future, that it cannot be
disposed of by them, but will always remain as a
protection to them and their heirs against the mis-
fortunes of life that will sometimes overtake us.
And as this surplus, to be enjoyed by our daughters
will consist largely of stocks and securities, the
management of which they may not fully understand
and not wishing to encumber you with the burden
thereof, I suggest that you immediately place it in
the hands of J. Harry White, Walter J. White, G. B.
Johnston and W. H. Tayloe as Trustees, who shall
have control of the same for the present, and the
income from the same shall be paid to our said
daughters in equal proportions, except that the por-
tions of our minor daughters shall be paid to you,
until they may become of age or marry, then it shall
be paid to them, and you shall have and use the
amount so paid to you, for your own use and support,
in addition to your income from the real estate as
mentioned in paragraph 14 hereof. And I desire said
Trustees to dispose of all stocks and securities belonging to said surplus, as soon as they can do so
to the best advantage, and convert it all into money
and turn over all of said surplus to you in money.
Then I want you to invest the whole of said surplus
in real estate as soon as you can do so, and have
all the deed made to yourself. In this I want the
trustees to advise you, and I request that they will
make no charges for their services and advice in any
of the above matters. Then, all the real estate, so
purchased and conveyed to you, I want you to settle
upon our daughters in equal shares and have the
deeds to them so prepared that the said real estate
may vest in the Daughters for their life, with the
remainder in fee, to such children as she may have
in existence at the time of her death, and in de-
fault of such children so living as aforesaid, with
the remainder to my right heirs in fee.

Signed: J. H. White.

70 Erota Street
New Orleans, La
July 11th, 1883

Mrs. George M. White
Uniontown, Alabama

Dear Aunt,

You will I have no doubt be somewhat surprised
in receiving a letter from one whom you have not
seen for years. But never the less not forgotten b
me. In September 1849, I came to your house and I
made that my home, and your kindness I never can
forget. Your husband and my father were brothers.

Father is no more, he departed this life on th
10th of last June at 6 o'clock P.M. Sunday. He was
one of the last of the White family of Granville
County, North Carolina. He was born December 25th
1811, which made him a good old age, leaving a family all grown up and I hope able to provide for
themselves. (George M. White was born April 17,
1807.)

You will excuse me if I have any way been pre-
sumptious. Thinking perhaps you had not heard of
Father's death and the family is not much in habit
of writing is what has called this letter.

Should you feel disposed, I would be glad to
hear from you and also your family.

Yours truly,

Signed: *Garland A. White*

70 Erota Street
New Orleans, La.
Jan. 6th, 1891

Mrs. George M. White
Uniontown, Alabama

Dear Aunt,

I know you will be surprised on receiving a few
lines from your old friend and relative, but I hope
you will take it in good part and excuse my long neglect. I have been thinking for a long time I would
write you a few lines to let you know I am in the
land of the living and have good health. I have
never been down with the rheumatism since I was confined in my bed at your house, and that has been
many years. And your kindness to me I never can
forget as long as God spares my life.

Well Aunt Nancy, I am living at the same place
when I wrote you a long time ago. I have the same
family all living, 6 children. Some of them are
grown. And I have nothing to complain of so far.
We are making a good living, I live in my own house
and I am at work every day at modest wages. Laura,
that is my oldest girl, has a good situation at the
miliners dress and hat making. I send you her card.
William Garland, that is my oldest goy, he is doing
fine at the store of A. Runkel. The rest of the
children are going to school.

Well I would like the best in the world if I
could see you once more but I doubt if I ever shall.
Sometimes I think of making a trip to see you but I
can't get the time to come. I saw a notice of
Dr. Thomas White's death of Uniontown that has been
a long time ago. He belonged to the Knights of
Honor. I have been a member for the last 10 years.
I would not be without it. It gives me satisfaction
to know I will leave something for my family. This
leaves me and family in the best of health. Wishing
you and yours the same, I hope you will excuse me
for writing with pencil and my bad spelling.

Inclosed I send you 2 of William's cards. He says to give them to some of the boys. Perhaps when they are passing they might stop in and buy something. I hope you will drop me a few lines when convenient.

Yours truly,

Signed: *Garland* A. *White*

EARLY TRACT RECORDS

from

PERRY COUNTY TRACT BOOK

PERRY COUNTY, ALA.

NAME	DATE	T	R	SECT.
John Cunningham	Oct.12, 1835	18	7	22
William Cunningham	Jan. 4, 1836	18	7	22
John Dorroh	Dec. __,1828	19	8	19
William Dorroh	Nov. 25,1833	18	7	28

474

Friendship Presbyterian Cemetery

It was a typical gloomy winter day.

Not one bit of blue sky could be seen, and the wind was blowing across Bogue Chitto Creek from the northwest. There was just enough moisture in the chilling air to fog one's glasses.

I was standing in the spot where once stood the old Friendship Presbyterian Church, four miles south of Marion on Alabama State Highway 5.

For fifty odd years I had passed this old burying grounds of my ancestors without stopping. But since I was writing *Pioneers In Their Own Rights*, I wanted to pay my respects.

There had been rain before I arrived and the ground afoot was soaking. Some of the graves in the outer section, now used by negroes, had caved in and water was standing.

As I walked towards the back of the cemetery the going became rougher and tougher. The sagebrush grew thicker and taller and the briars more dense, the cool, damp air more penetrating.

Finally my passage was stopped by the thickness of the growth.

I stood there in humble silence, my hands were pulling back the sage bushes and the briars from my eyes. There were piercing thorns in my legs......I could go no further, but my thoughts did pierce through all the underbrush for just a few feet away the remains of those early settlers rested in the cold winter ground of Perry County......there rested the remains of those who had been truly *Pioneers In Their Own Rights* in the early days of Perry County ......forgotten by many of their descendants.

Just a few feet from where I stood are the graves of:

Martha Dorroh, wife of William Cunningham, who died Oct. 28, 1855, age 80 years.

Margaret Cunningham, wife of William Morgan, died June 16, 1853, age 55 years.

William Morgan* born Laurens District, S. C., died July 19, 1860, age 61 years 1 month 16 days.

John Morgan* born Laurens District, S. C., June 18, 1811, died Oct. 30, 1844.

A. J. Morgan* born Laurens District, S. C., April 10, 1815, died Sept. 24, 1840.

William Morgan** born Laurens District, S. C., Nov. 2, 1825, died Oct. 20, 1845.

James T. Morgan** born Laurens District, S. C., Dec. 14, 1927, died Dec. 19, 1867.

Samuel C. L. Morgan** born Laurens District, S. C., July 6, 1835, died Danville, Va., in connection with Confederate C.S.A. 4th Alabama Reg., June 27, 1862.

Joseph Pitts born Laurens District, S. C., died Aug. 14, 1865, age 63 (though we do not know this for sure, it is likely that he was the father of Lizzie Pitts, who married John Frank Morgan** and later moved to Texas)

May we express our hope that this little article will arouse enough interest that descendants of Martha Dorroh Cunningham will wish to clean this burial ground and show their proper respects to this brave *Pioneer*, born in County Antrim, moved to the pioneering section of old District 96 in South Carolina and then to be among the pioneers of Perry County, Alabama?

*Son of Mary Hopkins and Henry Morgan.

**Son of Margaret Cunningham and William Morgan.

MARRIAGE BOOK 1832-1839

STATE OF ALABAMA, PERRY COUNTY

To any Licensed Minister of the Gospel, Judge of the State or Justice of the Peace of Said County:

You are hereby authorised to celebrate the rites of matrimony between *James J. Simms* and *Nancy A. Phillips* and join them together in the bonds of matrimony and for so doing this, shall be your sufficient authority.

Given under my hand as officer this, the 11th day of October, 1839.

J. B. Nave   , Clerk

No return made.

ESTATE OF SOLOMON S. PHILLIPS
(deceased)

BOOK F : 25, April 1, 1850

Hilliard J. Smith appointed administrator of the estate of Solomon S. Phillips, deceased. Bonded for $12000.00 with Wilson Ethridge, and L. N. Walthall as sureties.

Appraisers appointed by Court: John N. Walthal, Thos. Walthall, George M. White, Thos. Bondurant, and Lincas G. Drake.

BOOK G., page 434-5

July 9, 1855: Final settlement of estate of Solomon S. Phillips by H. J. Smith. Porter King, guardian ad litem of minor heirs. Banance for distribution: $2225.47 distributed to:

1. Elizabeth Phillips, widow
2. E. A. Phillips, a daughter
3. William T. Phillips, a son
4. James M. Phillips, a son
5. Solomon F. Phillips, a son

BOOK G, page 465, Sept. 10, 1855

H. J. Smith applied to be appointed the administrator of the estate of Solomon S. Phillips, deceased. He gave bond for $10000.00 with Elizabeth Phillips and S. D. Petty as securities.

Page 464, Sept. 10, 1855

Elizabeth Phillips made guardian of William T., Elizabeth A., Solomon F., and James M. Phillips, deceased. Bond for $10000.00 with H. J. Smith and S. F. Smith, sureties.

PHILLIPS DEED RECORDS

DEED BOOK H, page 472:   PERRY CO.,ALA.

On the 16th of October, 1847, SOLOMON S.
PHILLIPS and Elizabeth, his wife, sold to Samuel
Dorroh, for $800.00:

W ½ of NE ¼ and E½ of N W ¼ of Sec. 31, T18, R 7,
160 A.

Solomon S. and Elizabeth Phillips acknowledged their signatures to this deed, before John
Cunningham, Clerk of County Court, same date.

DEED BOOK C, page 73:

*Ann C. Smith, for $3000.00 paid by Phillips
and Lockhart, sell them a lot in Marion fronting
72 feet on Washington Street, running parallel
with Lafayette Street, to the first cross street,
thence North to lot lately occupied by Edwin
Reese and General E. D. King with a carriage
makers' shop and blacksmith shop---Jan.12, 1836.

DEED BOOK Q, page 71-2 :

ELIZABETH PHILLIPS to Hilliard J. Smith, for
$1650.00 in Alabama money on Bank of Mobile and
Southern Bank of Alabama, sell him:

W ½ of SE ¼ and SE ¼ of SW ¼ of Sec. 28, T 18,
R 6, 120 acres, and a right of way to the Marion
and Arcola road, February 19, 1864.

* I think she is ancestor of Marius Smith.

WHITE LAND RECORDS - PERRY COUNTY, ALABAMA

GEORGE M. WHITE BOUGHT:

From Whom Bought:	Book	Page	Date	Location
				T	R
F. M. Phillips & Wife	E	442	Sept.2,1840	17,	6
Wm. G. Phillips	E	443	" 3,1840	18	6
Reddick S. Boothe	I	59	Nov.27,1848	18	6
Henry D. Morrison & Wife	I	60	" 27,1848	18	6
Joseph Scott & wife	J	362	Dec.28,1849	18	6
Mary C. Powers, Adm.	K	654	Oct.21,1852	18	6
W. B. Powers Estate	K	654	Oct. 21,1852	18	6
R. V. Montague	K	782	Jan.31, 1853	18	6
W.J.McKerall,Adm.	M	113	Jan.26, 1855	18	6
Thos. Bondurant	N	231	Mar. 9,1857	18	6
Thos. M.Walthall & Wife	O	525	Sept.23,1859	18	6

NANCY M. WHITE BOUGHT:

A.P.,V.G., L.G.,& W.M.	X	500	Aug.16, 1872	Lot in Un.town
Weaver (For $225 Lots #3, 4, 5, 6, & ½ of 7 on Sept. 19, 1870.)				
C.W.Butts & Wm. Flash	X	502	Aug.16, 1872	18	6
Thos. T.A.Lyon & Wife	X	504	Aug. 16,1872	18	6

GEORGE P. WHITE BOUGHT:

Nancy M. White   X   504 Aug. 16, 1872 18 6

The Perry County, Alabama Tax Assessment for the year 1856 was as below:

G. M. White - T 18, R 6, 1000 Acres Total Value $15,000, Amt. of tax $30.00

Dallas Co., Ala. Records also show the same transactions made in DEED BOOK H, pages 195-6, as on June 24, 1840.

PERRY COUNTY, ALABAMA

DEED BOOK E. page 442: Dated 24th June, 1840:

Francis M. Phillips and Martha C. Phillips, his wife sold to George M. White for $4,000 the following land:

SW¼ Sec. 11; NW¼ Sec. 14; E½ NE¼ Sec. 15; E½ SE¼ Sec. 10; & NW¼ SE¼ Sec. 10, all in T 17, R 6, cont. 520 acres.

Signed:FRANCIS M. PHILLIPS
MARTHA C. PHILLIPS

Witnessed: THOS. H. WILEY
Wm. G. PHILLIPS

DEED BOOK E, Page 443: Dated 9th July, 1836

William G. Phillips sold to George M. White for $157 the following tract of land:

E½ of NW¼ Sec. 23, T 18, R 6, cont. 80 acres.

(William G. Phillips was of Dallas County; also were Francis M. and Martha C. Phillips.)

DEED BOOK B, Page 138: Dated July 20, 1831

Archibald Porter & Susannah Porter of Perry Co. sold to George Phillips of Dallas Co. for $200 the following land:

SW¼ Sec. 11, T 11, R 6. (160 A)

DEED BOOK X, page 504, Aug. 16, 1872:

"I Nancy M. White - - - for $3500 in "Gold Coin" sold to Geo. P. White - July 28, 1871"

SETTLEMENT OF ESTATE OF <u>GEORGE W. BROWDER</u>, DECD.

MINUTES OF PROBATE COURT:

<u>BOOK I</u>, page 650, May 12, 1862 Term of Court:

Samuel Dorroh (brother of John) appointed administrator with sureties, $30,000 bond
John A. Craig
Wm. W. Craig
Statement included: "more than forty days has elapsed since death of said GEORGE W. BROWDER has been publicly known."

<u>BOOK P</u>, page 490:

Special Term Probate Court, Aug. 23, 1875:

Samuel Dorroh (brother of John) having deceased without having settled estate.
A. C. Howze, having been administrator of Samuel Dorroh's estate.
L. S. Jones was this day appointed guardian ad litem, to represent and protect the interests of:
George W. Browder
James D.   "
Frank L.   "
Minnie L.   "   the only minors concerned.

It appears to satisfaction of Court that said Samuel Dorroh, had, before and at time of death had received of the assets of the estate of Geo. W. Browder, decd.; and since his last partial settlement $397.40 that Sam'l Dorrough justly expended for and on account of estate of Geo. W. Browder, decd.

PERRY COUNTY, ALABAMA

ESTATE OF JOHN DORROH

Perry County Minute Book G, Page 281 -
Date: November 1, 1854

Jane and Samuel Dorroh apply for letters of administration on estate of John Dorroh, decd.

(Page 298 verifies Jane Dorroh as the widow of
John Dorroh)

(She was the daughter of William and Martha
Dorroh Cunningham)

Min. Book H, Page 310 - Date Aug. 10, 1857

This day came administrators - Jane Dorroh and
Samuel J. Dorroh - who formerly filed accounts and
vouchers - etc. etc.

    Total Amt. $104,526.35
    Credits   9,481.76
    Balance $ 95,044.59 against adms. to be
distributed to following heirs:

    Jane Dorroh, Widow - $12,887.31
    John Bates (Nancy J. Bates) 17,280.95
      previous advancements -   900.00 - paid u
    B. H. Gilliam (Margaret W.
                    Gilliam) 17,280.95
    Donaldson Huff (Malinda L.
                    Huff)   17,280.95
    James Didlake (Dorcas Did-
                    lake)   17,280.95
    Samuel J. Dorroh (for self) 17,280.95

    All had received previous and varied sums and
all had paid in for even settlement.

ESTATE OF WILLIAM DORROH

Box 19, package 10   1808
Laurens Co., S. C.

James Dorroh, Sr., Administrator

Recorded Adm. Book CC, pages 355-356-357 by David Anderson, Ordinary

Administration Bond signed 29 Nov., 1808 by James Dorrough, James Dorroh, and James Dunlap

Appraisers of the Estate were: Joseph Downs, Esq., Wm. Arnold, Esq., and Lewis Saxon, Henery Burroughs

Samuel Cunningham was the Justice of the Peace who certified that the appraisers were qualified 8 Dec., 1808.

Inventory $1755.45

SAMUEL DORROH, deceased

This paper was entered as the will of Samuel Dorroh. It was contested and the contest of this was upheld:

> PERRY CO., ALA. Probate Minutes,
> Book P., Page 506
>
> Special Term of Court, Date: Oct. 2, 1875

A. C. Howze, adm. applied for permission to withdraw above petition, which was accepted and permission given.

A. C. Howze, adm., presented his settlement. Again, Caroline Rogers, sole legatee contested each and every item in settlement and judge ordered it audited.

THE HEIRS OF SAMUEL DORROH:

Left no widow.

Next of Kin:

> Dorcas Didlake)
> Mary J. Bates) widows over 21 yrs of age and
> M. L. Huff   ) reside in Perry Co., Ala.
>
> Cora Gilliam - under 21 yrs - Birmingham,Ala.
> Josephine Gilliam - under 21 -Calhoun Co.Ala.
> Samuel Gilliam)
> Robert Gilliam)
> Caroline Gilliam)
> Julia H. Long, wife of J.W. Long -over 21 yrs.
>   Clarke Co., Ala.
> Mary Dorroh) under 21 yrs. - Perry Co., Ala.

Who are all children and grandchildren of John Dorroh, decd., a brother of decedent.

Also, following children and grandchildren of James Dorroh, decd., brother of decedent:

> John Dorroh, over 21 yrs & resides Brandon,Mis
> Gayle Dorroh, over 21 yrs, - Greene Co., Ala.
> (Ida Rogers, wife of James P. Rogers)
> (Inez Mayfield, wife of Thomas Mayfield)
>   all over 21 yrs. & reside in Hale Co.Ala.
> Timothy T. Tallman - over 21 yrs. - Selma,
>   Dallas Co., Ala.
> Hattie Tallman - over 21 yrs. Etowah Co.Ala.

Page 2:   SAMUEL DORROH, deceased:

Also:

    Nancy Owens - widow, sister of decedent -
over 21 yrs. & resides in Laurens Dist. S. C.

Also: the children and grandchildren of William
Dorroh, decd., brother of decedent:

```
L. L. Jones  ) over 21 yrs  - children of
Sallie Jones ) Frances P. Dorroh Jones
William A. Dorroh ) over 21 yrs. children of
Henry Dorroh        ) William A. Dorroh,deceased
                      and reside in Texas
```

Sarah J. Atkinson, wife of S. M. Atkinson, over
    21 yrs - Lincoln Co., Arkansas
James M. Dorroh - age 30 yrs.
Zachary T. Dorroh - age 28

Chastine B. Dorroh - age 14
Ellen Dorroh   - age 12
Orlanda M. Dorroh - age 10
Eliza A. Dorroh   - age 8

John A. Dorroh - over 21 yrs. Jeff. Co., Ark.

    "It is therefore ordered that the 30th day of
Aug. 1875 be, and it is hereby appointed a day for
hearing the said application, and the proofs which
may be submitted in support of the same. It is
further ordered that due notice of the nature of
said application, and of the time above set for
the hearing thereof be given at least 40 days before the said day bearing the publication .....

    "It is further ordered that said M. L. Huff,
Mary J. Bates, Dorcas Didlake, Mary Dorroh, Samuel
Gilliam, Josephine Gilliam, Robert Gilliam, Caroline Gilliam, Cora Gilliam, Gayle Dorroh, Ida Rogers, James P. Rogers, Inez Mayfield, Thomas Mayfield
T. T. Tallman, and Hattie Tallman, have notice of
this proceeding and of the day set for hearing the
same by citation to be personally served on them
ten days before said day of hearing. It is further
ordered that the said administrator pay the costs
of this proceeding to be allowed to him against estate for which execution may issue."

WILL OF SAMUEL DORROH

Know all men by these present that I SAMUEL DORROH of County and State aforesaid for and in consideration of the sum of Five Dollars per acre the receipt whereof is hereby acknowledged hereby grant, bargain sell and convey unto *Mrs. Ann Caroline Rogers* wife of George Rogers, and unto her bodily heirs, for and further in consideration of being a *daughter* do convey all of my landed estate (viz: Around 537 Acres in Perry Co. T 18, R 7, also lands said Dorroh purchased from Woodson Cocke estate on Dec. 7, 1868; also all lands owned by him in Shelby Co.)

To have and hold the above described lands or with title deeds with her bodily heirs forever, one minute after my death. My debts to be paid by my *daughter, Mrs. Ann Caroline Rogers,* and Mr. Jno. True of my personal property, also my personal property. Notes, papers, deeds, mortgages to be respect or and all other property of any and all descriptions whatever not otherwise disposed of.

Witness my hand and seal this 26th day of Cecember 1868

$$Sam'l \; Dorroh$$

Attest:

    W.A,D , Ramsey

    E. B. Thompson

Probated Nov. 12, 1875
PERRY COUNTY, ALA.
Will Book C, page 37.

WILL OF DAVID R. DORROH

Dated: June 1, 1860
Proven: 26 Sept., 1860
Laurens Co., S. C.
EXECS.: William and John A. Dorroh

Wife: Susan

Sons: Samuel L. Dorroh
       James R. Dorroh
       John F. Dorroh, or John A.
       William T. Dorroh

                    WITNESSES: J. H. Shell
                                Wm. Curry
                                Nat/l Austin

APPRAISERS: Samuel Barksdale
             Nathaniel Barksdale
             James H. Shell

SALE BILL $8959.60

WILL OF JAMES DORROH, SR.

Box 21, pkg., # 13
(Bk not given)
Laurens Co., S. C.
EXEC. James Dorroh

Wife: Jane Dorroh

Son: James Dorroh, Jr.

ITEM: 150 acres whereon I now live to my son,
       James Dorroh, Jr.; also 4 Negroes

DATED 23 April, 1810

INVENTORY dated: 19 Oct., 1820

WITNESSES: John Taylor
            W. Downs
            George Grace

WILL OF JAMES DORROH, JR.

Box 91, # 8
Recorded in Record Book A, pages 11 and 12
Laurens Co., S. C.

EXECUTOR: David R. Dorroh

To his son, Wm. M. Dorroh, he willed "all the land that I now hold on south side of the south Fork of Rabun Creek above and below Mahaffey's Bridge, number of acres not precisely known, perhaps 300 Acres, bounded by Hosea Mahaffey's land and creek on one side and woods, and Crumbie's (Abercrombie's), William Mahon, Asa Garrett, and others. "

Other sons were: David, John, and Lewis C. Dorroh

Wife: Sarah, whom he wished to peaceably enjoy and possess all the land that lies joining here that is, the plantation willed to me by my father whereon we now live, with the Pugh and Tyner tracts

Daughters: Margaret, Nancy, Martha and Mary Dorroh

WITNESSES: John B. Simson
                Jane M. Todd
                Sam R. Todd   Proven 5 Mar. 1842
SETTLEMENT OF ESTATE SHOWS THE FOLLOWING:

To the children of James Anderson and wife
$266.43
To children of Charles Blakely and
wife   "
    To Thomas Blakely   "
    To D. R. Dorroh   "
    To W. M. Dorroh   "
    To J. F. Dorroh   "

5 July 1859

ADMINISTRATION OF THE ESTATE OF SAMUEL DUNLAP
Deceased

Box 21, package 10 - Laurens County, North Carolina

Recorded in Administration Book DD, page 129 by me
this 6th day of October, 1813.
David Anderson, Ordinary

Appraisal of the Estate made by Wm. Owen,
Gideon Thomason, David Stoddard, and Wm. Hill.
Appraised at $1017.65.

Elizabeth Dunlap granted administration on the
goods and chattels of Samuel Dunlap dec'd. She
asked for an order of sale as most of the property
of said deceased was perishable. Oct., 1813.

Administration Bond signed by

Elizabeth Dunlap
Thomas Goodwin
Thomas Mathis
6 Sept. 1813.

Amount of net balance of the Estate of Samuel
Dunlap deceased in the hands of the Executor of said
Estate as per return rendered $528.18 1/4.

Deduct payment to Susanna Dunlap, one of the
legatees of the Estate $18.25.

Deduct payment made to Mary Dunlap, one of the
legatees of the said Estate $16.00.

Balance still in hands of the Executrix, 19 Oct..
1815. $493.95 1/4.

No other Legatees given.

There was no will.

WILL OF SAMUEL DUNLAP

Wife: Nancy

Sons: John, James, Samuel

Daughters: Catheryn, Susanna

Three younger daughters: Sarah, Manicy, Mary

Execs: Martin Dial, John Dunlap, Wm. Hillams

Proven date not recorded.

Laurens County, North Carolina, 1791.

CUNNINGHAM:

BOOK 20, Part II, page 7, January 1853 Term of Court:

DAVE VERSUS THE STATE:

This was an incident against a slave named Dave for an assault upon a white person with intent to kill. The State introduced a witness, John B. Cunningham, and proved by him the following facts: That John Cunningham, the witness's father, hired from Mrs. Sarah Underwood, the defendant Dave for the present year, and that on the morning of the 26th of January he found Dave not at work, that Dave replied that his Master, Franklin Morgan, had sent him word that one of his dogs had run mad and wished Dave to help kill him. A fight ensued. Dave cut him in twenty-six places and he was confined to his room for some six weeks. Dr. Browder testified as to the wounds. Mrs. Underwood testified that Dave was raised by her father--that she knew him well, and had owned him since 1845.

The following is an advertisement which
appeared in "WEEKLY MARION AMERICAN".

T. S. Caswell, Editor

Date: Nov. 28, 1860

S.C.L. MORGAN and JNO. F. MORGAN, Admr's of
WM. MORGAN, decd.:

To sell lands of this estate: 18th Dec., 1860.

Description of land:.......

Personal Property:........

MEMORANDUM OF WILLIAM DORROH

Memorandum, that on the 18th day of August, 1834, William Dorroh of the County Caldwell being sick of the sickness whereof he died on the same day at his dwelling house in said county did make and declare his last Will and Testament nuncupative in these or word of the like substance, that is to say, I give and bequeath unto my *wife Polly Dorroh* all my property to raise my children upon, or do as she thinks best with it these words or to like effect the said William Dorroh declared in the presence of the subscribers with intention that the same should be his last Will and Testament which were reduced to writing this 23rd day of August, 1834.

(signed) *Stevenson Carrick*

Jno. Rorer

Caldwell County, Princeton, Kentucky
Will Book A, Page 452

(This paper furnished by Glenn U. Dorroh, M. D.)
Dr. Dorroh has made an interesting observation,
"My great grandfather died on Aug. 18, 1834; one
child, Mary, died two days later, Aug. 20, we
might assume they died of some epidemic disease
(probably typhoid), and this type of will would
tend to bear this, and since a nun cupative
will is one made when the patient is in extremis,
or dying and in presence of witnesses as this one
was."

WILL OF J. R. PUMPHREY

Union County, State of Arkansas
April 15 Anno Domini 1853

IN THE NAME OF GOD AMEN

JOHN ROBERSON PUMPHREY of Union County, Arkansas
states being in health of body and in sound mind
and memory but knowing it appointed to all men to
die, being blessed with a portion of goods, chattles,
lands and appurtanances, and having the following
natural heirs to wit: Jesse N.,John L, Mary Ann,
Lewis and Dennis D. Pumphrey do make this my last
will and testament, as follows: I will to my beloved wife Martha Pumphrey, all my Estate both real
personal and mixed, during her natural life or
widowhood and in case of her being married a second
time, my will is that she have one third of all I
possess or am entitled to, and I will that she have
my daughter Mary Ann, be paid out of my estate five
Dollars, United States Coin, and the ballance of my
estate at the death or marriage of my above named
wife, my estate be equally divided between my children except Mary Ann. And I do appoint my beloved
wife Martha Pumphrey with one or more others, who
may administer on my will my sole executrixs or executors, to bxecute this my last will, signed in
presence of day and date above written

                              John R. Pumphrey

WITNESS: John Meek
         Eliza J. Meek
         John A. Meek

STATE OF ARKANSAS)
SOUNTY OF UNION   )

I, Mrs. Pansy Bryant, County and Probate Clerk
within and for the county and state aforesaid, do
hereby certify that the foregoing is a true and correct copy of

WILL OF J. R. PUMPHREY

as herein set forth and as the same appears on file
and of record in this office.

Witness my hand and official seal on this 23rd
day of October, 1961

                    Mrs. Pansy Bryant, CLERK

(SEAL)   By Madelyn Rucks, D. C.

WILL OF DAVID R. DORROH

SOUTH CAROLINA   Box 137, pkg. 1
LAURENS DISTRICT   Laurens, S.C.

In the name of God, Amen, I, *David R. Dorroh*, being in feeble health, but of sound and disposing mind, do make this my last WILL AND TESTAMENT:

1st: I give and bequeath unto my beloved wife *Susan Dorroh* during her natural life and at her death to be equally divided amongst her children, the following Negroes, viz; old Patty Young, Patty and her children (Henry), Tom, Hester, Rhody, Dan and Sam, together with all her future increase, and Jane and her future increase.

2nd: It is my will that my Negroes, Toby and Sylvia, be sold by my executors, hereinafter named, privately, if in their opinion a fair price is offered; and that all the remainder of my estate both Real and Personal, be sold by my executors after giving legal notice, and out of the sale of the two last named Negroes and the Real and Personal property they are to pay all my debts including One Hundred Dollars to my *son Samuel L. Dorroh* for his services this year.

3rd: It is my will that my *Sons, Samuel L. Dorroh, James R. Dorroh, John A. Dorroh* and *Tom L. Dorroh* each receive one hundred dollars to be accounted for by them at a final settlement of my estate, without interest, and the balance of my estate to be paid over to my *wife, Susan Dorroh* to be used by her for the general benefit of herself and my children.

4th: I do hereby appoint *John F. Dorroh* and *Wm. M. Dorroh* Executors of this, my last WILL and TESTAMENT, Witness my hand and Seal

This June 1st, 1860

                /s/ *David R. Dorroh*

Signed & Sealed in
the presence of:
J. H. Shell
William Percy
Nathaniel Austin

Article on: *THE JEFFERSON DAVIS DORROH FAMILY:*

(copied from torn page of old family Bible exactly as it was written therein.)

Holy Matrimony between H. J. Dorroh and F. A. Mathis on Nov. 17, 1874

H.J. Dorroh was born Dec. 1, 1850
F. A. Mathis Dorroh was born Oct. 17, 1850
J. D. Dorroh was born Mar. 17, 1889
Marion W. Mathis was born May 21, 1894
William Henry Dorroh was born Apr. 19, 1900
Thomas Franklin Gunn was born July 26, 1901
Eugenia Ileen Sullivan, Deeember 9, 1919.

W. N. Mathis departed this life Nov. 7, A.D.,1873
Mary Elizabeth Mathis departed this life July 30, 1875
Wm. Wells Dorroh died January 1925.
Jimmie Robert Dorroh died June 8, 1926.
Mrs. Fannie Abigail Dorroh departed this life Aug. 28, 1926.
John Washburn Dorroh departed this life Sept. 11, 1928
Henry Jethro Dorroh departed this life Jan. 17, 1929

(Note: These must have been Mathis' before Fanny married Dorroh)
Thomas Nickless was born July 14, A.D., 1870
Mary Elizabeth was born May 7, A.D., 1873
John Washburn Dorroh was born Mar. 8, A.D., 1876
Wm. Wells Dorroh was born Feb. 13, A.D., 1879
A. Eugenia was born Sept. 13,A.D., 1881
Jimmie R. Dorroh was born July 26, A.D., 1884
Mattie Roberta Dorroh was born Feb. 27, 1887

Thomas N. Mathis and Flora E. Manning were married Aug. 14, 1892

The following letter is from Lucy A. Phillips when she was attending Mecklenburg Female College, N. C., to her cousin, Ella A. Simms.

> Mecklenburg Female College,
> Charlotte, N. C.,
> Feb. 27, 1868

My dear Cousin Ella:

No doubt you will be surprised when you receive this letter to hear that I am (120) one hundred and twenty miles away from old Hillsboro' and my dear home, at Mecklenburg Female College, Charlotte, N. C.

I am trying very hard to improve my imperfect store of knowledge, and I also try to appreciate the kindness of my devoted, and very dear Brother, who is sending me to school in order to take some of the hardship off of my precious Father whose once black hair is now streaked with gray, which I do not like to see, for it reminds me that our time, which we are allotted to spend on this beautiful, but sometimes unhappy earth, is drawing near to a close. I write to you on this sheet of paper, so that you can have some idea what kind of looking place my present abiding place is. I will make a cross mark across my window, to let you know what room I occupy, though I don't suppose you care to know! I love all of my schoolmates, especially my roommates.

I received your welcome letter yesterday morning and no one can tell with what pleasure I perused its interesting contents.

I am sorry to hear that you have moved, as you are so displeased with your new house.

We had some very pretty weather last week, no cloud obscured the beautiful blue sky to prevent the sun from shedding its brilliant rays on this continent. But, we have been praying for it this week, for we have had rain in plenty.

I am in the Sophomore Class. I will send you a catalogue of the school so that you know what I study without my naming them. It is the second session.

I would like so much to see you and Katie (*Kate Hunter Simms Wheeler*), but will have to be deprived of that pleasure till a more convenient season; for, as you say, times are so hard that I must wait. Tell Kate to write to me, and send me both of your photographs; also Cousin Louis (*Ludolphus A. Simms*) and as many of the rest as you can. I will send you mine as soon as I have it taken.

You may still direct to Hillsboro, so that Ma can read it.

Well, I must stop. Don't you think this is a very badly written, short, and uninteresting epistle to send as far as Alabama? I feel so bad!

Pa is going to start out on a long journey again in about two weeks.

Goodbye. Write to me soon (a great long letter, for I assure you it will meet with a happy or I should say, a warm reception.)

My love to all.

Your affectionate Cousin,

/s/ *Lucie A. Phillips*

*The following letter is from D. D. Phillips
to Ella Simms White upon the death of her brother
J. D. Simms who died Aug. 29, 1870 and is buried
in Uniontown Cemetery.*

Atlanta, Georgia
Sept. 11, 1870

My Own Dear Precious, surely bereaved, Niece:

Yours of the 1st just received. My heart had
been made sad by the announcement of the sad news
yesterday morning in a letter from Frank Phillips.
And, my heart has not ceased to bleed as it never
does when the wound is opened afresh by the reception of those heart-felt lines, from my almost
heartbroken niece, in consequence of the sudden
death of a beloved Brother.

Would to God, my Dear Niece, that I could restore to you your brother, all cheerful and affectionate, as was his nature and to his, almost
heart-broken Ma and Pa, their beloved boy; and to
the other little sister, her grown-up brother; to
the dear brothers, both older and younger than he;
their brothers and companion for a few brief years,
but alas.....my arm is too short.

I, too, in common with you all....have to bow
in humble submission to the will of Him, before
whom, we all must sooner or later stand. We all
must die. Let me, my Niece, commend you all to the
mercy of that God who is too wise to err, too good
to be unkind to his children, those who love and
serve him.

I inclose Frank's letter to Hollywood.

I thank you for the remembrance you had of
me in dropping me a line. Say to my Precious Sister and her Husband that "Tamesia and I know how
to sympathize with them having lost two dear boys
ourselves, and laid their precious heads under the
sod, out of sight forever, so far as this life is
concerned. Nothing but the grace of God can console parents and friends under such trying circumstances.....and, oh, may that Grace be given to
you all in rich abundance is my prayer."

My dear Niece, I wish I could tell you where
to direct a letter to me with a hope of getting
it, but I cannot. I expect to leave this place
in a few days for the northern portion of the
state, and then perhaps for West Virginia, and
to Richmond, and then sometime between this and
Christmas for Hollywood.

Much love and affectionate regards to all
the loved ones, and of course you are included
in that number.

Your loving Uncle,

/s/ D. D. Phillips

(We are not certain where the "Hollywood" he
mentions in the letter is located. However,
we do have in our possession a letter written
from Tamesia Phillips, his wife, to him on July
9, 1870 from Hollywood, but she fails to give
the state in which Hollywood is located.)

The following is a letter from Lucy Ann Phillips, who married Rev. Hiram Pearson Cole, to her cousin, Ella A. Simms.

Artesia, Mississippi
March 24, 1871

My own sweet Cousin:

Yours received a few days since met with the usual hearty welcome and I cannot acknowledge myself incapable of applying as your letter deserves. You are so sweet and so good, that it serves my whole being to get a letter from you.I do love you so much, and would be so glad to spend even a short time, but cruel fate forbids....deprives me of this pleasure after taking so much more from me.

Yes, it's impossible for me to come. I hope 'twill not be much of a disappointment to you, I know it won't hurt you near as bad to have me not come as it does me; so, if you do feel a momentary pain at my not coming, let sympathy for your lonely cousin over-balance it. I know though how we could do so as to be together once more. You come here at Cousin Oscar's....I feel perfectly fair to ask you, for he was wishing last night for you, and Cousin Donie came out here on the gallery where I am writing and when I told her who this was to, she expressed such a strong desire to have you come and requested me to extend a pressing initation from Cousin Oscar, herself and myself.

Now, do come but let us know when to look for you, and we'll meet you at the Depot. Beg Auntie and Uncle to let you come. Tell them if they knew how bad we wanted to see each other, they wouldn't refuse. Get all the boys to beg for you.

We can go to see Auntie too when you come. I am now at Cousin Oscar's as you have before observed. Emma is with me. The rest are still at Auntie's.

We came over tomorrow will be two weeks ago. Cousin Cad came with us. Poor Cousin Alice, I feel almost lost without her, and I know she misses me. We are strongly attached to each other. I imagine we love like you and Sister did. I wish

I did not care so much for her as I can't be with her. Do you like to love anyone and be deprived of them? I don't. I prefer never loving them. I wrote to her and Cousin Cad and sent your messages. I think they will both write to you. I correspond with both.

Cousin Donie has a nice piano. It is the Grand piano Cousin Add had at Macon. Have you given up music? When you write, tell me if you practice much and what all you play.

I have not seen Ma Harriet to ask her what to tell you for her, but I know she would send you some kind message for she loves you dearly.

Don't fool me any more about that "particular friend" (I don't know what else to call him). In your next, tell me from the first to the last about him. Don't pass me off by saying you'll tell me when you come, for I want to know before. I shall expect a letter in a very short time telling me all about him, and also telling me to meet you at the Depot in a few days. I promise you when I have anything of the sort to communicate, you shall be one of the first to know it and if you'll come, I'll tell you everything I know.

We are not certain when we will go to Louisville or whether we will go at all. When it's settled when and where we'll go, I'll tell you.

I am so glad Cousin Lou is so well and do hope he may stay so. I'll try to write to him and send it in this. I may not have time though for Cousin Oscar is quite sick and I must help Cousin Donie nurse him and attend to all I can for her.

We got a letter from Cousin Lizzie Phillips the day I came over here. Uncle Hilliard is dead. He had not heard of Pa's death. He died a good Christian, looked forward to his death as a release from all suffering. His wife did not cease to torment him though she knew he would die. *(Uncle Hilliard refers to Hilliard J. Smith, the brother of Elizabeth Phillips.)*
Auntie was in better health when I left her than she has been since last August.

I am so glad Aunt Ann's health is tolerably good.

My poor Ma, though.....I do not think she
will live long if she don't get settled soon.
Oh, if she should die! 'Tis too dreadful to
anticipate.

Renan, Cousin Oscar's little boy, is as
sweet as any baby you ever saw, and is certainly
the largest. To be only twelve (12) months old,
he can run all about, but can't talk.

I must quit for Cousin Donie wants me. I
could write a long time yet if I had time.

Give my love to my Cousin Fannie and Annie
Millhouse and ask them to write to me. I'm looking for a letter from Miss Jennie. I received
one from Cousin Frank Phillips, a nice long sweet
letter and appreciated it so much....I will write
to him very soon.

Ask Cousin Bard has he forgotten me?

Tell Kate that Emma will write to her as soon
as she gets to a home. She can't settle herself
sufficiently to write now.Kate ought to write
first.

Give my love to all, everyone, also remember
with kisses---Cousin Donnie, Cousin Oscar and
Emma send love too.

Come soon, but write sooner to

                    Your own

                    /s/ Lucy

P.S. Don't forget, do give love to "particular
friend"

(Artesia, Miss. is in Lowndes County,Miss.)

The following letter is one from Thomas Jefferson White who was attending Medical School in New Orleans, La. to his brother, John Henry White.

New Orleans, La.
Nov. 12, 1871

Dear Henry:

Yours of the 9th came safely to hand and contents noted. You will please hand George the receipt for the $10. It came in good time.

I have paid my board for this month which is always required in advance but as this month is about half out, tell George to send me $50 or $75 by the 1st of Dec. I have made an estimate and I think my expenses will be about $400.00 with considerable economy. "Pretty digging!"

The regular lectures commence tomorrow, Monday 13th. We visit the patients in Hospital from 8 until 10 and the rest of the day until 6 are lectures except 1 hour for dinner. We then dissect from 7 until 10 o'clock at night leaving from 10 to 1 or 2 for reading. If I follow the programme, which I hope to do, I shall be very busy during the time I stay here. Sundays will be my only days for writing letters and looking round the city.

If I knew where Cousin Garland (White) lived, I would take dinner with him some Sunday.

I went to the Presbyterian Church today and heard the renowned Dr. Palmer preach and it was the best sermon and better delivered than any I ever heard. He has a very fine church and a congregation of about 800 or 1000.....I reckon he gets well paid for it. The only objection I have to it is, it is so far to walk.....about 1 1/2 miles.

I went to the Catholic Church tonight and, undoubtedly, it had the best music I ever listened to, one female voice especially.

Well Henry, I expect you are beginning to feel "sorter queer" about now, but put on a bold face! Let me congratulate you now for you will be a married man by the time this reaches you.

You must kiss <u>Sis Ella</u> <u>once</u> for me. I would give anything to be <u>there.</u>

I hope all you young married folks will do well, prosper, multiply and replenish the earth, and give me some work to do when I get back.

As it is getting late for Sunday night I will close. Hoping when your scare is over, you will write me a long letter describing the whole affair with a P. S. from Sis Ella.

My love to all.

Your affectionate Bro.

/s/*Tom*

This letter is from John Henry White when he was employed at HIRSH BROS. & CO. to his wife, Ella when she was in Mobile, Ala.

Uniontown, Ala
Feb. 10, 1880

Mrs. J. H. White
c/o Dr. E. Shackelford,
76 Dauphin St.,
Mobile, Alabama

My Dearest Ella:

I wrote you very hurriedly by Warren Pollard yesterday morning. At dark I received the very gratifying dispatch that no operation was necessary and am truly thankful, both on Anne's account and your own, as no doubt you will have a chance now to enjoy yourself, which I hope you will do. As we are doing finely up here and don't need you, only miss you and little Anne, and if you are having a good time, I can put up with all inconveniences until you get back.

The children are doing very well.

If you need any money, call on Tom for what you wish.

A letter from Kate came for you Sunday night: had sent her dress---but was having chills. She was looking for Lonnis.

I expect a letter from you today, giving full particulars of your trip, Anne's care, etc. I am very much afraid the cars at Meridian were terribly crowded, but hope you got a seat.

Be certain to go to see your kinfolks at Artesia and telegraph your Cousin Addie the day before you leave Mobile to meet you there.

Don't run away with the Theatrical Troupe!

Think of your "old man and chillens" at
home and the consequences!

My regards to Dr. and Mrs. Shackelford,
with much love and a kiss for yourself and
Anne, I am as ever always,

Your

/s/ Henry

The following is a letter from John Henry White to his wife Ella written from the Steamer J. M. White when she remained to visit at Skiss-mith's Landing, Miss.

ON BOARD THE STEAMER J. M. WHITE

1 o'clock, May 17, 1880

My own Darling Ella,

I am not yet over my mad fit and will not be unless we reach Vicksburg in time for the train, which at this time, I am very fearful we will not do, but I am assurred by the Capt. that he will reach there by 5 o'clock. We are now 40 miles off and if I do have to lay over there 24 hours, my patience will become threadbare.

I wrote you a note from Duncausby and gave it to the Agent to send it out, which he promised to do. In that, I stated to you that I had to set up all night and fight mosquitoes(and just to think of it, only 4 miles from my loved ones)However, that note explains what I thought and how I felt on the subject and hope you will get it today.

I got on at 5, breakfasted at 7 (and a good one at that), best steak you ever saw, juicy and tender; went to bed at 8:30 o'clock, slept in a good large stateroom on a first-rate wide bed until 12 N. when I got up, dressed, washed my face and hands, put on a clean collar and cravat, lo and behold! I had no comb and brush to complete my toilet. But, I soon got over this dilemna for on going to the water closet, I discovered an elegant Barber Shop, kept by white barbers and as I needed a shave I went in at once and was fixed up in style for the sum of 25¢, which is pretty high for a shave but!!!they had me where the hair was short, and I had to stand it.

Directly after leaving the Barber, I sought the writing desk and could only find this one sheet of paper to write on to my darling Ella, and I am now telling her, that I am thinking of her and our dear children all the time.

I am going to get a lemonade directly and will drink to your "good health and to your family," and wish you could be with me to enjoy it.

This is indeed an elegant and what may be called a perfect Steamboat, a floating palace, and I trust you will by all means come back on it, but God forbid that you and the children should have to lay over all night at that den of mosquitoes at Duncausby, where there is no accommodation at all.

I trust you didn't wear yourself out listening for the WHITE to blow last night. I know I was. This, I am told, is the first time they have been so far behind for a long while and I hope they will be on time when you are ready to leave. And, after that, it will be immaterial with me whether they are, or not, again.

Well, dinner is ready and I will go and refresh the inner-man....am going to eat just as much as I can hold and come back and finish... that is, if I can find any more paper! I found a little better pen, but you know it is very poorly written on the hard desk with only one sheet.

3 o'clock P.M.

Still finds me on board the WHITE and 25 miles yet to Vicksburg. Have found plenty of paper on which to finish my letter and express my love and affection for my dear wife and children.

Dinner has been over some time. I have enjoyed a good cigar but am "most too full for utterance". I had a splendid birthday dinner (you know this is the 17th May and my 31st year) I can't begin to tell you of the nice things to eat I had, but enclose you the Bill of Fare and you can see for yourself. Only wish I could have had you with me to partake of it...particularly, the elegant and delicious ice cream. Nothing on the Bill of Fare is in the least exaggerated.

We have a great many passengers on Board. Several ladies and children....and wouldn't I be happy to have my wife and children here too! We would walk around and see all the sights.

If Bud comes to Vicksburg with you, let him take Harry and Weenona, and you too, if you will go up to the Pilot House; they will perhaps remember it in after years.

There is an elegant large mirror and piano in the Parlor and a gentleman is now playing and it is so far to the other end of the Boat, you can hardly hear it.

I am very much afraid you will make yourself miserable here trying to keep up with the children. It will be a very easy matter for them to get out of your sight and a hard one for you to keep up with them. Nevertheless, I hope you will not let the Bell and Whistle of the Boat trouble you too much, you may have a good night's rest.

When you leave, it may be best to get to the Landing by Dark....bring enough home folks with you to keep you company, put your shawl down on the floor in the office, let the children go to sleep and keep off the mosquitoes and wait patiently for the Boat which I trust won't be long. This season of the year they usually get there between 8 and 10.

I hope little Annie is not sick today. Please write me often. I will love to hear from you. I think it would be well to give the children Quinine every morning any way, and if you need a Dr. you must have one. I think you will have money enough to pay one if necessary, and get home too.

I will not attempt any further description of the WHITE, but let you see for yourself.

With much love for yourself, and children, and all the family, I remain

Yours devotedly, and only Yours,

/s/ Henry

The following is a letter from John Henry White to his wife, Ella, when he was employed at the general mercantile store HIRSH BROS. & CO, under Sam HIrsh, Samson Fried, and Leo Hirsh. It was sent to: Mrs. J. H. White, Skissmith's Landing, Mississippi

                                        Uniontown, Alabama
                                        May 18, 1880

My own Dearest Ella:

I reached home this morning at 9 o'clock and found everybody well and surprised to see me. My office was all torn up, having it calcimined and painted...which they promised to do the next day after I left, but kept putting it off. However, I didn't expect to move today anyway, for I don't feel like it, but will commence in the morning.

No one had heard a word from us. Your letter came to me on the same train I did and I gave it to her. The people here were very uneasy about me as the report had gotten out that I was seriously sick in Vicksburg, caused perhaps by Dick Hudson's wife writing him about my being sick on the train, and by not hearing from us. The firm would have telegraphed to know about it, but did not know where any office was.

Our garden is looking awful bad, nearly burnt up, have had no rain since we left and no prospects for any soon.

Everything at home looks quite natural. Aunt Mary was digging a few potatoes to sell, said it was the first call she had and was only offered 25¢ per peck.

Your goslins are looking very fine, so the grass in the front yard. Just did take a peep in the house, but was too dark and lonesome and left.

Brown has traded for Jim Ware's house and Matt has already moved in. Saw her at Ma's to dinner. Bradley Brown has bought Ware's Drug Store and he (Ware) speaks of going to Chattanooga.

I met the Bridal Party at Faunsdale this morning--viz; Joe Brown and Lady, just married this morning and going off to Nashville.

The convention which I wanted to attend meets this evening, so I am in good time.

I wrote you a letter from Duncrusty and one on board the White which I mailed on the Cheeck, which was going right back and I hope you have received them both.

I think I am doing pretty well in the letter line, but don't know how it will be when I get to work for I have a sight of it to do, and I know you will excuse me and write often yourself.

I enclose your ticket in this, my first letter, for fear it will not reach you in time if I wait any longer as the mails are very uncertain and irregular. Conductor Harrison only punched out 78 miles and make him do the same for you as you will strike his train by coming on the White.

When you get off the White at Vicksburg coming home, take a cab and drive direct to the V & M ticket office, where you will find a sitting room to stay until the train leaves at 6. It will save you Hotel bill and other expenses.

If Bud comes with you, he can see you there and go right back on the Cheek and not lose any time. The conductor will check your baggage.

It is most mail time and I will cease.

Will write again as soon as I have a chance to look around and hear some news.

Truly your own,

/s/Henry

This letter is from John Henry White to his wife Ella Simms White when she was in Skissmith's Landing, Miss. and he was employed by HIRSH BROS. & CO., Uniontown, Ala.

Uniontown, Alabama
May 24, 1880

My own Dear Ella:

I am as mad as an old setting hen this morning. I ought by all means to have had a letter from you by now, but not a word, except the letter written by you the evening I left. I wouldn't live in any such a country, for I know you have written and the fault must be with those Boats and Postmasters on the River.

I wrote you down at home yesterday evening and expected to take it down to the train and mail it myself, but my watch was behind and the first thing I knew, the train blew and I was too late, so it goes off in same mail with this.

If I can hear from you regularly I would be much better satisfied and would be willing for you to stay another week if you want to. If you conclude to stay, I cheerfully give my consent, but you must write me. I don't expect to write any more after this unless you stay. I wrote you all the news in my letter of yesterday.

Love to all and I hope you are enjoying yourself.

Yours only,

/s/ *Henry*

514

The following letter is from John Henry White to his wife Ella when she was in Skissmith's Landing, Miss. and he was employed at HIRSH BROS. & CO. in Uniontown.

Uniontown, Alabama
May 20, 1880

My dearest Ella,

I only have time to drop you a few lines..
...am very busy and will be for several days, and hope to have everything in order by the time you get back so I can see you and the children as much as possible, as we shut up now at 7 o'clock and can go home soon.

My office is about finished and have gone regularly to work. Find my books a long ways behind and out of order.

I was too late to telegraph you Tuesday night, but did so last night.

I attended the Convention here Tuesday evening, but can't tell how George's chances are. I am going to Marion next Tuesday 25th in his interest and cannot tell how it will be until after that time.

The house looks and feels very dark and lonesome when I go there every night. but I lost so much sleep on the way, that I soon "pile in " and forget I don't have you to put my arms around and feel....

I wrote you on my arrival Tuesday evening, about all the news, have had no chance to hear anything since.

Our garden is about burnt up, needing rain badly. I made Aunt Mary fill up your Bl. around the cucumbers, says you never told her to keep water in it. She has kept the tree in front yard watered. I told her this morning to water your vines every evening.

Don't bother yourself about me. I will get
along all right and I am getting very anxious to
hear from you and the children and to know if Anne
has been sick any more.

Am going out to Matts to dinner today. Dined
at Ma's yesterday. Called on Mrs. P. and Miss
Mary: she has not reeeived your letter yet. Says
she will write you today.

Give my love to all the children and kiss
them for me. As for you....you know that I love
you better than anybody in the world.

If no one will come with you, let me know.
Mr. Evans told me that he would meet you at the
Boat and see you on the train. I saw him as I
came through.

Has Lou's family come, or did you hear from
them?

Regards to all the family and write often to

Yours only & affectionately,

/s/ *Henry*

516

Following is a correspondence from John Henry White to his wife Elgiva Simms who was known to me as Ella when she was visiting her father in Mississippi. This letter was sent to Skissmiths Landing, Mississippi.

Uniontown, Ala.
Saturday Evening
May 28th 1881

My Darling Ella,

I was somewhat disappointed today in not getting a letter from you, but I know it was no fault of yours. Harry & Weenona didn't have their letter ready yesterday, so I enclose them in this. I mailed you a long letter yesterday & promised to mail you another one tomorrow (Sunday) & I commence this now, as I am not busy at present & will send it off as promised.

Lewis & Lottie are both better & think they are all right now. Mrs. Phillips staid with us last night, but is spending the day with Cousin Bettie & Mrs. Temple is in charge & will also stay tomorrow & has learnt the children their Sunday School lessons perfectly. Uncle Lewis didn't come & suppose he will not be here for several days yet. We have had no rain yet, but it looks a little like it this evening. Several farmers have had enough, but it has been very spotted.

Had a letter from Mr. Evans today apologizing for not meeting you as he promised, but said he didn't receive my postal in time. Went in in same that you did, which was just as I expected. Bob Houston didn't send it off Sunday--

Matts baby is right sick & sent for Ma to go & stay with her last night. Havnt heard from them today. Won't I miss you tomorrow? No preaching at our church & I believe I will stay at home with the children. I understand Mrs. Baird & Celia have given up the singing altogether. The former in the plea of bad health & the latter on ac/of some throat complaint. Cousin Bettie vows not to have anything more to do with it, so I reckon we will do without hereafter, unless Mr. Russell & myself take charge of it. I hope you will help us out, wont you?

Dr. Bradfried showed me a letter from Mrs. Pettius today. Asking what she must do. If wife

Mary could get a school if they came back. That she had not been able to get a situation there, but was offered a small school out in the country, & to see what rent Mrs. Turner would pay, And, wanted to know what I thought about it. Of course I couldn't tell him much about it now, but was satisfied Mrs. Turner would get her share of the scholars & it was too small a school to divide.

I hope you found your Pa in a better fix than you expected & that your stay will be more pleasant on that account. Ann had the baby at Janes when I was dined & didnt see her. She is as good and sweet as can be & no trouble. In fact all the children are good & getting along splendidly & hope they will not get sick until you get back anyway & most not then even.

Well- it is 10 o'clock Saturday night & I am just through & will proceed to finish writing to my precious wife, though I dont expect to add much more & dont know that I will write again until Monday night, so that it will go off by Tuesdays mail, as this leaves tomorrow (Sunday). Uncle Lewis walked in today & surprised them all. Havnt seen him yet. Their children are all right again. Matts baby is better, so Brown says. Seems to be affected same way as Lewis & Lottie - Ann brought the baby by to see me this evening. Something mighty sweet & good. Dont trouble yourself about them - They are doing well - What is Jim doing & is he coming home with you? No letters have come for you since you left - Well as they are closing up I must quit for tonight & go home to my bed with nobody to kiss & hug, so goodnight my darling & write often to --

Yours Devotedly

Henry

(*Modern day maps do not show Skissmith's Landing, Mississippi, but the author believes it must have been in Claiborne County on the Mississippi River, between Vicksburg and Natchez. No doubt when visiting relatives in Claiborne County, Skissmith's Landing was the closest boat landing for the people to go from there to Vicksburg, catch a train, or trains, to Jackson, Meridian, and thence eastward to Uniontown, Alabama.*)

This letter is from John Henry White to his wife Ella Simms White when she was at Skissmith's Landing, Miss., and written at the time he was employed by HIRSH BROS. & CO. in Uniontown, Ala.

Tuesday Eve.
May 31, 1881

My Darling Ella:

Tomorrow is 1st and won't have time to write you much of a letter then. I have been busy all day making out monthly bills and feel a little tired, so I will commence you a short letter this evening, as I will be the last one I will write you, for I expect now you will leave before this reaches its destination.

Your letter written Thursday 26th was just received today and was mighty glad to get it, as I was getting real anxious to hear from you. Your other letter left you at the Landing and didn't know how you had been getting along since then.

Am glad your Pa is better than you expected to find him and trust you will be able to have a more pleasant visit on that a/c .

Annie don't cry for you at all and they are all very good and well except colds and coughs. Pearl, Annie and Belle coughing a good deal, but as yet have been no trouble. Mrs. P. tries to keep them in all she can. The baby's head is mostly stopped up and coughs a good deal, but has no fever, vis very good and rests pretty well at night.

Don't think your Aunt B. has lost much sleep on a/c of any of the children.

I mailed a letter for you from Miss Belle today. She sent it to me. I haven't seen her for several days. We are getting another little shower now, but am afraid it will stop before we get enough to do any good.

Matt's baby was right sick again last night.
Lonis and Lottie are well again. Haven't seen
Uncle Lewis since yesterday, don't know what day
he will go back. Tom has been right sick in bed
since Friday, something like Jaundice. I believe he is better....will go and see him this
evening.

I will finish this in the morning and let
you know how the children rested. So I kiss you
good evening.....

Wednesday Morning, June 1

When I went home last night Mrs. P. and Mrs.
Temple were right uneasy about the baby, thought
she had fever, but afterwards concluded she
didn't. She is stopped up with cold and coughs
a good deal, but rested very well last night,
only woke up once and think she is much better
this morning.

Annie coughed pretty hard during the night
too, but nothing serious. If any of them get
sick much will telegraph you.

Mrs. Temple says you must not "sit up at
night thinking about her" and is much obliged
for all the kind messages you send in your letters.....it seems you forgot to mention her in
any of them.

Have just had a fine rain. I will not
write any more and will look for you next Tuesday, 7th.

Yours devotedly,

/s/ Henry

Uniontown, Ala.
May 27, 1871

My Dearest Miss Ella:

I have just received your note by Jimmie Phillips and he promised me to call by tomorrow for this. You may know I was very agreeably surprised to hear from you, for I thought you would do as you said, and only answer mine. That's right Miss Ella, and I hope you will not always wait for me, for you know I am a right "bashful" boy.

To come at once to the point, Miss Ella, I was very much surprised at the "something in the Box". I meant for Joe H. to know the contents. I pledge you my word, I was perfectly ignorant of the contents. I asked Joe to put me up a box of nice things for you, and he brought it to me, tied up so soundly, that I didn't have time to undo it, nor did I think to ask him what he put in it. When I received your letter and saw him about it, he says he put some candy, nuts, figs, and 2 bunches of fire crackers in it. Is it these you allude to? Well, I wanted to know what he meant by putting fire crackers in it and he says they were for George and Johnnie. Are you satisfied? A thoughtful chap, isn't he?

Miss Ella, I got home safe, but had a miserable long, lonesome ride and you know I couldn't enjoy it as much as going down with you. I believe you think I was troubled by carrying you home. Miss Ella, I love you too much to even think it was anything but the greatest pleasure and I hope you will always think that I don't care for the trouble, so I can add in anyway to your happiness or enjoyment.

Tell your Pa am much obliged to him for holding my horse. I was too "excited" to think of it when I left. Write soon to
Your own sweetheart,
/s/ · Henry

The following letter is one from John Henry White's son (Harry) which he wrote to his mother when he was 9 years old.

Uniontown, Perry Co., Ala.
May 26, 1881

My dear Mother:

I have been wanting to write to you for a long time but have not had time.

Ann says we have been very good children since you have been gone. Lewis was worse last night but is better this morning.

Dr. Coleman had to burn out Lotty's throat last night.

How is Grandpa? I hope he is better.

Father tells me that he had a letter from you today. Sister and I got a letter from Uncle Lewis yesterday.

Aunt Bettie says she tryed to make us behave while you was gone.

Your affectionate Son

/s/Harry White.

The following letter is one from John Henry White's daughter (Weenona) which she wrote to her mother when she was 7 years old.

Uniontown, Perry Co. Ala.
May 26th, 1881

My Dear Mamma,

I have been trying to write to you for a long time. How is grandpa, I hope he is better.

I have not answered Cousin Addie's letter yet.

Budie and myself got a answer from Uncle Lewis letter we wrote. Little Sister has been eating this morning. You must exuce bad mistakes. Buddie has finished his letter; I will finish this morning.

I have not missed since you have been gone. Little Lotty has been very sick. I was up to see them yesterday eving, had some fever but they were better than they were day before. Aunt Bettie has gone up there now to see them.

Grandma staid with us Thirsday night, she had to go to Aunt   as her baby was sick.

Grandma says she was glad to hear little sister was so glad good. I hope you will have a good time when you come back.

Your Dauter,

/s/Weenona

The following letter is from Kate Hunter Simms to her sister Ella Simms White. It is written from Percy, Miss.

Percy, Miss.
Jan. 16, 1896

Dear Sister:

I received your long looked for letter a few days ago and was so glad to hear from you once more. But, you did not say anything about when you were comming to see me. I certainly would, if I was able, come to see you rite away and spend a month for I am so very anxious to see you all.

Tell Annie I <u>know</u> she had some pictures taken in her graduating suit and I certainly want one. Weenona would not send me one of hers and Pearl <u>never</u> has given me one of hers , and I want some of Annie's paintings tell her. She must not forget her old Auntie.

Does Annie play by ear yet, or does she take music lessons? I so often wish I could step in and have Weenona play some for me. I am real hungry to hear some good music. A Negro passed by yesterday with an accordian and I had him stop and play some for me and he played real well and passed his missionary glass around for a <u>nickle.</u> I wish I was able to give Annie and Emma music lessons.

You asked me about Charlie and Buddie. I don't know where Buddie is, he never writes to me. And Charlie is here with us, has no work, works whenever he can get a job. His lady (Abe) is in Claiborne spending the summer with her sister Annie. Say, ask Weeze why she does not answer her letter.

You spoke of sending me a box and asked me not to get offended, and what you would send. If you only knew.....how I appreciate what you send me, you would not think I would be offended, for I can use anything that you would send me.

Sister, you don't know how bad I want to see you. I feel like I could sit and talk with you a week without stopping.

My health is not good ever since I had the grippe last winter. My throat and lungs hurt me nearly all the time. I suffer also with my head and a bad circulation of glood generally. Tho I try to hold up and have to do my work ex-cept my washings that I can't do any more. I think I will try to go to Greenville soon and consult Dr. Shackelford.

I will have to say goodbye for this time. Now, please don't wait so long before you write. Give my love to Harry, Fannie and the little darling Babe...I would give anything to see her.

Tell Harry and Fannie the first photos they have taken, not to forget me.

With a heart full of love and kisses for each and all of you, from your devoted sister,

Kate
(Kate Simms Wheeler)

Love to Cousin Betie and family and tell her I am going to write to her before long. How is Belle Anderson and Babe, and what is it named? Love to her.

This is a letter from John Henry White to his wife Ella when she was in New York.

OFFICE of J. H. WHITE & CO.
General Merchants,

Uniontown, Alabama
April 2, 1896

Mrs. J. H. White
220 E 17th St.,
New York, N. Y.

My dearest girl:

I wired you last night as soon as I could. Both operators were at supper when I got through with hand shaking all around and had to wait til I got supper and came back before I could get a telegram off.

I found all doing very well at home. Eloise has been suffering for two days with tooth ache and her jaw is all swollen. I wanted to take her to Dr. Guen this morning but she said it was too sore and it did not hurt now. I concluded to let her wait a day or two.

The baby was sick yesterday, but rested well last night and is better this morning.

Renan is here, came yesterday. They are looking for Weenona today, but are not sure as she wrote she wanted to wait til you got back. Had a big rain here and is quite cool this morning, but they say it has been very warm since Sunday.

The garden is looking tolerable well, nothing was killed. The Blue Grass needs mowing, which I will have done. Madeira vines are coming up, strawberries are blooming nicely. I see some of your pansies are blooming too.

Nora Carr and Dr. Connor will marry next week.

Azzie is improving.

Had to lay over four hours in Washington, but after leaving came right on through, stopping in Selma 1 1/2 hours, but didnn't go up town at all.

Harry has traded with Joe for his house at $1,700.00

Our goods are coming in very slow....not half are here yet. Need them badly.

Florence Hudson died last night, just heard it.

Eloise slept with me last night, but it was not like having you, and I wondered how you and Sister DuBose got along....what kind of substitute she made for me! I was awful lonesome travelling without you.

Hope Dr. Pack treated you nicely yesterday. Write me all about it.

I saw a nice criticism on "Chimmie Fadden". Suppose you go...

Love to Ola. Remember me to all in the house, with much love for yourself.

Yours truly,

/s/Henry

This letter is from W. C. Simms when he was in Holland, Tex. written to his sister, Ella Simms White

Holland, Texas
July 6, 1896

Dear Sister:

I thought I would write you a few lines to let you know how I am getting along. Sis, I am just getting along by the toughest. I have no one to wash for me and no money to get any done, have to try and do it for myself.

I tryed to get some money from Bob Underwood but failed to get it. If ever I can get money enough to get away from here will leave Texas never to return any more. I never saw such times in my life before. I never was at a place before that I could not get my washing done. I tell you it is enough to dishearten any one to be in my fix.

I am not as well as I was when I first got here. I am not as heavy by 15 or 20 lbs. When I lie down, I never feel like getting up.

If I live to see the day that I can get $10 or $12 I will leave this country. I cannot get work enough to board me, if I was not with the man I am with I don't know what I would do. I feel like sometime I would like to die and be out of everybody's way and would not have to be dependent on anyone. I could have done a great deal better with Bill. Think I can see no chance for any work here and don't think there will be enough cotton made to hire any picked. So, I don't know what I will do. Oh, if I was away from here, I never would see this country any more.

I am not able to buy my Tab (tobacco?). I never saw such times before.

Well, I have said enough.

Give my love to all, and if you can give me enough to pay a Mrs. Kelly for two months washing . I don't like to ask you. Do you ever see anything about Charlie?

Love to all

Your Brother
/s/ W. C. Simms

P.S. I have not much to wash for I am about out of clothes anyhow.

Brother, W. C. Simms

The following is a letter from J.B.K. Spain,
a Methodist minister once in Uniontown and Marion,
written to my grandmother, Ella A. Simms White,
concerning the illness of her daughter, Eloise.
He was the father of Frank E. Spain of Birmingham
who now lives across the street from the author.

Marion, Alabama
July 10, 1896

Mrs. J. H. White,
Uniontown, Alabama

Dear Mrs. White:

Your letter bearing the news of the serious
sickness of Eloise and requesting prayers in her
behalf came promptly to hand, and we took the
matter to Him who careth for us, and twice we
have brought the matter before the church for
prayers, besides daily we have remembered you in
our private devotions.

I have waited to hear something more from
her before writing you. I could hear nothing
definite till this morning, and to our delight,
we heard that she is better.

I am glad to see your faith in prayer. Time
and again I have seen the sick raised again to
health through the prayers of God's people.

My wife and I have felt a deep sympathy for
you all in your distress. We trust God will
spare her to you. Just put the whole matter
in His hands and leave it with Him. That is
the highest expression of faith when we commit
all our interests to him and leave the results
to Him.

We often think of you and your family and
of the many expressions of kindness that you all
have shown us. Always feeling a deep interest
in your entire family.

Truly your friend,

/s/J. B. K. Spain

The following note is one written to Mr. and Mrs. John Henry White on the eve of their Silver Wedding Anniversary from Mr. and Mrs. J. B. K. Spain.

Marion, Alabama
November 17, 1896

Dear Friends:

We so much regretted that we were unable to attend your "Silver Wedding". If it hadn't been such a busy season with us, we would certainly have been there.

We send our congratulations and wish that the next twenty-five may be crowned with every blessing and that the golden may find you as happy and prosperous as the present.

With much love, we are

Yours sincerely,

Mr. & Mrs. J.B.K. Spain

This is a letter to Ella Simms White from her cousin Weenona Poindexter who was over fifty years head of the Music Dept. at Mississippi State College for Women, Columbus, Mississippi

Ashville, N. C.
Friday,
July 10, 1896

My darling Cousin Ella:

I was so happy to have Budy's letter this morning bringing good news from our dear little Elouise. I was just about to telegraph, but I decided to wait to get the eleven o'clock mail first.

All day yesterday, and the day before, I could think of nothing else, and thought it was hard for me to be so far away.

Miss Bynum has been in bed 4 days now, but will be up this afternoon. She has been sick all week but Wednesday had a chill and considerable fever.

I was never better in my life. Ashville suits me.

Darling, I have been so uneasy lest you overtax your strength during Elouise's illness and felt so relieved to know you had a nurse from Montgomery. Remember, dear, you cannot stand all you have in days past when you used to nurse us night and day. The anxiety, of course, no one can take from you, but the constant nursing is too much.

Now, darling, write me as soon as you can, but I would not have you take the time when you need to be resting or taking fresh air.

A whole heart full of love,

Yours,

/s/ Nona

(Weenona Poindexter)

The following is a letter from A. M. Spessard to Ella Simms White when her daughter, Eloise, was very ill of typhoid fever. The letter was mailed from Cavetown, Md.

A. M. SPESSARD
Superintendent of City Schools,

Uniontown, Ala.
July 12, 1896

My dear Mrs. White:

I appreciate your extreme kindness in advising me as to dear Little Eloise's condition. I am truly sorry she has been so ill and I have been extremely solicitous as to the outcome. Each day finds me watching for a letter from some member of the household, informing me as to her condition.

If prayers of friends are of any avail, the Dear Child will recover. I have known her so well and having thought more of her than any other child I have ever known, you can readily understand how much concerned I have been and I pray that she may be saved to you many, many years.

The thought that the very good die young has come to my mind dozens of times since her illness and knowing what a good child she is, I have felt more alarmed than I would have under other circumstances.

I think she is the best child I have ever known...honest to a fault and without the slightest semblance of deception. In fact, her innate honesty forbids the cultivation of deception. I am so glad she is thus constituted, for we rarely ever find a true friendship. You know this to be true. You know how often your confidence has been misplaced. You know the natural disposition of mankind. Experience has taught us to confide in very few and even then, errors will be made in our selection of friends.

I would trust Eloise in anything. She will always be loyal to her professions and could not be otherwise if she could.

I have so frequently wished I could call in and see her. Tell her she must save for her sweetheart a lock of her hair so that he can carry it in his watch. Do you know of anything she could eat or would like to have that is beyond your reach? It will be such a pleasure to send her anything you can suggest....possibly something sent her would for a brief time take her mind from sickness and make her more cheerful.

The doctors seem to be at variance. I have confidence in Whitfield and am inclined to risk his judgment though Dr. Sadler is a splendid physician. I am sorry for the two that prove to be in error. They will forever lose your confidence.

Tell Miss Pearl the promised letter is slow coming.

My pen failed to give out ink and upon investigation found it empty.

I am having a very pleasant and quiet rest. Have remained at home and will not take any trips as heretofore. I find it more restful. I expect to go to Hancock soon to see a friend of mine who is quite ill, Dr. Perkins. He was such a warm friend of mine when I taught there and though a Republican, gave me earnest support when I was a candidate for the Legislature. He asked for me last Sunday and in response to a letter from his wife, I advised her I would go whenever called.

Sister Edna and brother are enjoying their honeymoon with us. They go off on little jaunts for a day and we like her so much. I think it is mutual. An Iowa cousin came in to see them and will be with us 3 or 4 weeks.

Tell Henry he has never sent me the bill for my suit. I asked him the eve before I left what it was and he did not know. Cannot pay for it unless he send me bill or fills up and signs check for amt. in my name. Tell him either will be agreeable.

I went hunting this morning at 3:15 and got four fox squirrels. I deserved better success for such early rising.

You must write me when you are at leisure.

I appreciate your kindness in advising me of Eloise's condition and I trust your present anxiety has been dissipated by a great change for the better. I will always be delighted to hear from you.

Mother and Sister have asked me daily as to her condition and they join me in prayers with you for her recovery.

All send you love and in this, I surely join them.

With much love to Dear, little Sweetheart,

I am,

Your sincere friend,

/s/ A. M. Spessard

The following is a letter from Fannie Tamesia Phillips Spring to Ella A. Simms White written from Baltimore, Md.

1513 Linden Ave
Baltimore, Md.
Nov. 13, 1896

Mrs. Henry White,
Uniontown, Ala.

Congratulations and many many good wishes for my dear Cousins. May your golden wedding be spent on earth, your diamond one in heaven.

Of course, I know you knew it would be impossible for me to be present, but don't I wish I could slip in and surprise you. How I would love to see you on Monday evening. I just know you both will look splendidly. Quite a handsome couple, I imagine, I hear the guests say.

How I wish it was in my power to send you something as a souvenir of this occasion and as a slight token of my love for you, but as usual, I have to plead an empty purse, for that is the normal condition of mine.

It has been such a long time since I have heard from you except through Cousin Frank Phillips. He always tells me something of your dear family, but that is not quite as nice as it would be to hear from you direct. I certainly would enjoy a long letter, and do hope you will write and tell me something of each one of the family.

I suppose Weenona, Pearl and Annie are handsome young women by now, and that even your baby is getting too large to be called a baby any longer. My little charge, Grace, of whom I have written you, is nearly twelve and is quite a little woman. She is a very sweet interesting child.

Have had letters this week from Mama and

Emma and from Lucy last week and all were about as usual, but Emma, poor dear child, is never well. Mama weighs 147 lbs. and looks so well. She writes that she misses me very much, but she bears the separation very well. It is hard for us both to be separated, and at times, I get right homesick.

Now, I will say goodnight and wish you much, yes, very much, happiness, and many returns of Nov. 16th. Much love for you each one, and a sweet kiss for your dear self.

As ever,

Your devoted cousin,

/s/Fannie T. Phillips

The following is a letter from Lizzie Lee Smith (Vaiden) to Ella Simms White. Lizzie was the daughter of Permelia Stevenson and James Acton Smith. Permelia was daughter of William Craig and Sarah Woods.

Keatchie, La.
Sept.27, 1898

My Precious Muddee,

I feel like it is my duty, as well as a pleasure to write to my dear, sweet, Muddee. Little did I think last Sunday I would be writing to you from this place today.

I am very much pleased with the place so far, only wish my **Art** class was larger which I am in hopes it will be.

One good thing, I don't have to pay any board. Any 5 percent of what I make goes to the agent. My expenses here were nearly $16. My only objection is the fare. Tell the girls I know now what school girls have to eat. What we have is prepared real nice but we have the same thing three times a day. Muddee, I wish for some of your good cooking. Tell Tena I miss her nice cake and rolls.

Tell Annie I did not get the cake she sent me by Pearl last Sunday. Tell her to send me a slice in a letter.

Mary Hurt, from home, is teaching here also. She was in my room this morning wishing she had something **good** to eat. She said she was going to write home for a box.

I send a picture of the main building. There are two others not in the picture. The young men occupy them. This school is the largest in La.

All of the teachers are real nice to me, but I get terribly homesick sometime. I have had one good big cry since ⊥ have been here. I thought about you and your dear girls, if I could only have one of them with me I would feel all right.

Tell Annie I am going to write to her soon.
I am going to try to be satisfied here and see if
I can't make some money so I can help my poor father. he says he is afraid he won't get through
this winter. I only hope I will keep well so I
can work.

The water here is lime. I am in hopes it will
fatten me. Once a month I have a week to look
after the girls, I keep study hour at night two
hours, and take the girls to walk in the afternoon. I am afraid I will turn Babtis while I am
here as I am the only Presbyterian in the house.
There is no Presbyterian minister here. The
President of the school is a Babtis minister.

Tell Weenona when she finishes my frame to
please send it to me here. I want to put it in
my room.

How is my raffle getting along? Tell Mr.
Kenody to please get all the chances he can as I
will need every cent of it this winter. I wish
you would see the following parties for me and
ask them to take a chance: Cousin Burke, Miss
Sallie, Prof. Bachman, Val Taylor, Lee and B. Harwood, Phil Hudson. Tell Weenona to make Phil take
one for her. I wish you would see Mr. Kenody and
find out how many chances have been taken that are
not paid for and let me know. I know I collected
about $10 and something before I left. I wish I
could get up all my no. as I need the money.

I hope you are better, if not well, I only
wish I could be with you this winter. I know I
am going to miss you more than ever being so far
away. Please write to me often and tell the girls
to write. I always enjoy a letter from my dear
Muddee.

It has been raining all day and has turned
so cold.

Give my love to Fan. Kiss the dear baby for
me. Give my love to Grandma's family. Regards to
Mr. Walter.

Ask Miss Alice what will she charge to em-
broidry me a simple design for a picture frame

forget me not, or some small flower. I want it
for my room. All the teachers here have fixed
up their rooms so nicely I want to make mine look
as nice as I can without too much expense. I
thought if she didn't charge too much, I would
get one.

Now, I have written you a long letter, so
you must answer like wise.

Remember me to Tena. Tell her I wish she
would come out here and cook for this school.

Goodby my precious Muddee. Love to all the
family, much for your own sweet self.

Lovingly,

/s/ Lizzie
(Lizzie Lee Smith Vaiden)
% Prof. C. W. Tomkies,
Keatchie, La.

The following is a letter from Ella Lee Didlake Roden to her cousin, Eloise Simms White (Johnston) before her marriage.

Birmingham, Ala.
Jan. 30, 1901

Miss Eloise White
c/o Mr. Henry White

Uniontown, Ala.

My dearest Eloise:

Do forgive Cousin Ella for not writing and telling you how much she appreciated your Christmas remembrance before now. You'll excuse everything I know when I tell you that my precious babies left me on Thursday after Christmas. Though I had Ola and the other children, I felt so lonesome without them.

Charlie took a sudden notion to go to Cincinnati and we were all in a whirl helping Florrie to get ready. I don't think he intended to live there for long, but any time seems long without Dorothy and Eleanor.

It was very sweet of you to remember me.

Did you get the book I sent you? I left the selection to Ola and Lillian as thought possibly they might please you better than I could.

Now, dear, tell me something of your dear father and mother. How are they? If I were well I'd certainly come to see them for I love them both dearly. Kiss them both for me and tell them I think of them, and pray God to restore them to perfect health.

Little darling, take time from your girlish pleasures to comfort and cheer them. The love and tender care of our children is more to mother and father than all else.

Why don't my little girl send me her picture?
I'd love to have pictures of your mother's entire
family. Can't you see that I get them?

Aren't you glad to have Pearl home with you?
It is so bad to have our loved ones so far away
from us.

Tell Mother she owes me a letter, and has,
for a long time.

Give my best love to dear father, mother and
the entire family.

You write me dear, and let me know how all
are. With a heart full of love, I am your

Loving Cousin,

/s/ Ella L. Roden

(Ella Lee Didlake Roden)

*The following is a note from Mrs. M. S.
Temple, a teacher and friend, written to
Ella Simms White upon the death of her husband,
John Henry White.*

March 6, 1901

Mrs. Ella White
    At   Home

My dear Friend,

With a sad heart I fain would say or
do something to comfort you.

You and the <u>dear</u> <u>one</u> have so often
bound my wounds that I pity my own inability
to console you. Only God has the power to sustain my poor dear Ella. You know that you have
the love, prayers, and sympathy of

Your friend,

/s/ M. S. Temple

The following is a letter written by
the Rev. J. L. Arbuthnot, the pastor who married
John Henry White and Ella Simms. He wrote this
at the time of Mr. White's death.

Nashville, Tenn.
March 9, 1901

Dear Mrs. White:

I read in the Marion paper on last evening
of the sudden death of my friend and your devoted
husband. I shall never forget the eventful evening when I pronounced the holy bonds that united
you and him in the most sacred of earthly re-
lations. And, now as I think of your mutual love
and helpfulness through so many years, it seems
hard that such congenial and tender ties should
be severed.

I know that your loss is beyond reach of all
human sympathy and that God alone in his love and
grace can sustain you.

There is one consolation in the midst of your
sore bereavement; that is, you appreciated your
noble husband's worth in life and can now look
forward with increasing faith to a blessed reunion in another and brighter world, where pain,
suffering and death are forever excluded, and
where the faithful shall receive a crown unfad-
ing and a life unending amid scenes of joy and
glory forever more.

I always looked forward to my annual visits
to Ala. knowing that I would meet with many of my
old friends and, especially with your dear husband whose kindly greeting and generous hospital-
ity it was my good fortune to share.

It is said that we live in deeds, not years.
Judging by this standard, our friend has lived
long as he accomplished much for his church and
community.

I remember when Henry first joined the church
We were a feeble flock but from the first, he was
a source of strength as he was always steadfast
and liberal and one upon whom we could rely with
confidence.

Our friendship has continued through the years and if I had been present at the funeral, I would have felt more like taking my seat with the bereaved family rather than to have pronounced a public tribute of respect.

But why should we lament the death of one who was so well prepared to go, who through faith has conquered Death and entered into eternal rest?

Give my kindest regards to all the dear children and tell them that their Father has left them in his deeds and life a legacy beyond all price.

May his mantle fall on his only son, and may he have a son worthy of such a noble Father. God grant that his richest blessings may rest upon you and yours, and may you realize God's promise to be a husband to the widow and a Father to the Fatherless.

My wife joins me in love and sympathy to you and yours.

Your friend and former pastor,

/s/ J. L. Arbuthnot

NANCY DORROH & WILLIAM McDAVID RECORD

The following information was copied from the Madison County Court Records by Mesdames Jones and Gandrud:

Family graveyard in NE 1/4 Sec. 13, T 1, R 1, W. This graveyard is in bad shape, needing much repair. What could be read reveals:

In memory of *Nancy (Dorroh) McDavid*, born in Ireland 1766, died 26th Oct. 1845.

In memory of *James McDavid*, born in South Carolina Oct. 10, 1795 Died 21 Sept. 1842.

In memory of *Nancy McDavid* born in North Carolina May 18, 1801 Departed this life Sept. 23, 1852.

....of......*Davie*.....3, 1849 (this is believed to be the marker for *Brancie Ann McDavid*, wife of Gabriel S. Davie.)

Richard Taylor McDavid born Oct. 1, 1824 Died Oct. 1834 buried Plainview Church in south part of Sec. 36, T 1, R 1, W.

Vol. 197 p 41: James McDavid (son of William and Nancy Dorroh McDavid) was a Justice of the Peace in Lincoln Co., Tenn. in 1826. He moved to Madison Co., Ala. and had a large tavern several miles north of Hazel Green, Ala.

Vol. 12, p 72 June 27, 1840-Democratic Meeting. At a meeting of the citizens of New Market and its vicinity on the 19th instant, James McDavid was appointed to a committee to meet with such other committees as might be appointed in this county, to be styled Madison Democratic Committee. Paint Rock Valley (Jackson County) Trenton, 2 July 1840 at Democratic Meeting Col. James McDavid elected one of vice-presidents.

Probate Records 10, p 32 Non cupative will of James McDavid, whose decease took place on the 24th of Sept. 1842. He requested his property to be man. aged by his wife Nancy (last name not given),Gabriel L. Davie (husband of Branchie Ann), and Joseph Taylor....it (his property) should be kept together for the benefit of the family. His wife, Nancy, to have one slave over her distributive share. The children, as they come of age or married to receive, each portion equal to what his daughter Branchie Ann had at her marriage (to Gabriel S. Davie). Oldest son, after becoming of age, to assist in managing affairs and youngest children to be educated as the oldest have been. Slaves in possession of Dr. Gabriel L. Davie 16 Oct. 1842. Letters of administration granted Nancy McDavid, et al.

Probate Mins. 3, p 293 Jan. 1, 1855 James L. McDavid applied for letters of guardianship for Stephen P. McDavid, infant, with Joseph Taylor and G.L. Davie, securities. He is also appointed guardian of Nancy A. and Wilson S. McDavid minors. (His mother, Nancy McDavid, had died Sept. 23, 1852.)

Probate Min. 3, p 577 L.B. McDavid applied for letters of administration on the estate of James L. McDavid, deceased, and on the same day (Oct. 29th, 1855) L. B. McDavid applied for letters of guardianship for Stephen P. McDavid with Joseph Taylor and W. McDavid Taylor securities in both cases.

Probate Min. 2, p 152 Sept. 8, 1853. Gabriel S. Davie applied for letters of administration on the estate of William C. McDavid with Joseph Taylor and James L. McDavid, securities. At the same time he applied for letters of guardianship for his daughter, Brancy A. J. Davie, a granddaughter of James McDavid.

Vol. 12, on various pages, we find that on Oct. 7, 1835 Samuel McDavid served on a Committee of Vigilance from Jackson Co., Ala. On July 25, 1837 Col. Samuel McDavid was candidate for House of Representatives from Jackson Co. On Nov. 7, 1840 the Jackson Co., Sheriff ordered to sell the property of Samuel McDavid (supposedly had died).

Probate Record 21, p 164 Final settlement of Lunsford B. McDavid, adm. of James L. McDavid, Nov 1857. Heirs at-law are the said Lunsford B. McDavid adm. and brother; Martha, wife of William M. Connor, a sister; John J. McDavid, a brother; Wilson P. McDavid, a brother, all of age; Stephen P.

McDavid, a brother; and Nancy A. McDavid, a sister, infants, and Brancie Ann Davie, infant, only child of Brancie Ann Davie, deceased, formerly Brancie Ann McDavid, who was in her lifetime a sister. Gabriel S. Davie is guardian.

From the above we thus conclude that James McDavid was the father (and thus Nancy Dorroh and William McDavid were grandparents) of: Brancie Ann, who married Gabriel S. Davie, and was deceased by 1857 leaving only the child Brancie Ann; Stephen P; John J.; Lunsford B.; Wilson (whose middle initial sometimes is shown as P., sometimes as N., and sometimes as S.V.); James L.; Martha Jane, wife of William M. Connor.....who were living in Noxubee Co., Miss. by 1859; and Nancy A., who was living with her sister, Martha Jane Connor, by 1859 and is spoken of as more than 14 years of age (though she was still a minor.).

We found in Probate Book 4 B, p 280, that Wilson S. McDavid married Nancy A. Thompson Aug. 26, 1858 in Noxubee Co., Miss. (She was daughter of Wiley); and Vol. 197, p 100 of the Jones-Gandrud Works shows that he died May 2, 1888.

We found that Lunsford B. McDavid married Margaret A. Garner, daughter of Samuel F. Garner. His only other child was Ellen, sometimes referred to as Ellenor, and she married a Mayhew. The Lunsford B. McDavids moved to Noxubee Co., Miss.

There was a William C. McDavid, also a son of James McDavid who died single between 1844-46. Richard Taylor McDavid,(whom we mentioned on page 1), as dying in 1834 could also have been a son of James McDavid.

John J. McDavid is better known to the Alabama McDavids. He married Mary Jane Patton, daughter of Robert Miller Patton. She is buried in the Maple Hill Cemetery, Huntsville and her grave marker reads: Marie Patton McDavid born March 20, 1840 died March 15, 1908.

Vol. 161, p 28 carried a notice in the *Independent*, published in Huntsville, in 1886 that John J. McDavid will become a citizen of Birmingham and has sold his home on Randolph Street.
Their son was Robert Patton McDavid.

INDEX

Brantley,
    Paul, 385
    Suzanne Frels, 385
Branyon,
    Docia L. Howard, 313
    Glenda Gail, 313
    Lucile, 313
    Martha Ellon, 313
    Pearl Richardson, 313
    Royce Roy, 313
    Tollie H., 313
Brasfield,
    Alba Swaim, 35
    Caleb, 23, 34
    Caleb Samuel, 34
    Elizabeth Jeter, 34
    E. Tansil, 35
    George Jeter, 35
    K. A. Overton, 34
    Kate McKenzie, 34
    Len Brock, 35
    Leonard, 34
    Lyndell, 35
    Mamie, 35
    Minnie, 35
    Nancy White, 23, 34
    Nannie Ward, 34
    Ola Womble, 35
    Oscar, 35
    Stella May 35
    William Dennis, 34
Brasher,
    Caroline (Cad), 363, 365
    Kirk, 366
    May Dorroh, 366
Brawley,
    Edward Dorroh, 285
    Jack Tyson, 285
    Jane Eloise Dorroh, 285
Breedlove,
    Oscar, 52,
    Sally Harris, 52
Bremer, Connie Ruth Plagens, 389
    Darvin,Edgar, 389
Brett, Elizabeth Jones, 276
Brice, Thomas, 12
Britt, Jeannine, 306
Brittian,
    Brian, 407
    Eileen, 407
    Marvin, 407
    Nancy Smith, 407

Brittian,
    Scott, 407
Britton,
    Bettie Tutt, 122
    Elizabeth, 264
    Mabel Levy, 122
    Margaret Inda, 122
    Nancy Morgan, 122
    Richard Henry, 122
    Richard Morgan, 122
    William Henry, 122
Brock,
    Evelyn, 171
    John Erwin, 398
    Sarah Susan Dorroh, 398
Brooks, Bari Renée, 211
    Bartlett, 410
    Carrie Killett, 410
    Charles, 410
    David Larry, 410
    Emma Dorroh, 410
    Grace, 355
    Helen Foster, 211
    John Charles, 410
    Josephine Tull, 410
    Lutie, 410, 413
    Mamie, 410
    Nancy Williams, 252
    Rebecca Elizabeth, 274
    Robert Fay, 211
Browder,
    Dr. 491
    Frank L., 173, 481
    George W., 173, 481
    James D., 173, 481
    Minnie L., 173, 481
    Rebecca Cunningham, 173
    Tommy, 173
Brown,
    Alice, 78
    Albert Walter, 78
    Benjamin Roden, 180
    Bradley, 511
    Carol Lee Roden, 180
    Coleman, 16, 456
    Falks, 233, 234
    George, 77
    Helen, 77, 372
    James, 22
    James Joyner, 75, 77
    Jane, 231, 233, 234, 236, 242,
    244, 248

Dorroh,
James, 110, 231, 232, 233, 234,
235, 236, 237, 239, 240, 241,
242, 243, 244, 245, 248, 274,
352, 484, 487, 488
James Elton, 351
James F. 249, 254, 266, 267,
335, 488
James Franklin, 359
James Grady, 352
James Hyler, 258
James J. 359, 361
James Jacob, 349
James L. 364, 377, 378, 422, 425
James Madison, 281, 282
James Maxwell, 416
James R. 266, 276, 279, 487, 495
James Robert, 359
James Stanley, 351
James Thomas, 363, 364, 372
James Thornwell, 414
James Tinsley, 360
James Willard, 347
James William, 328, 372, 415
James Zachary, 287
Jamie Bradford, 397
Jane 243, 300, 301, 481, 487
Jane Brown, 231, 233, 234, 236,
162, 163, 242, 244
Jane Cunningham, 143, 162, 169,
245, 249
Jane Elizabeth, 322
Jane Eloise, 285
Jane Gordon Baird, 249, 274
Jane Gordon Beard, 249
Jane Katherine, 381
Janie F. 366
Janie Sue Pratt, 325
Janie West, 350
Jarusha, 349
Jasie Smith, 274
Jean Jennings, 336
Jean Marie 280
Jean Stout, 280
Jeanette Harkins, 284
Jeanette House, 352
Jefferson Davis, 280, 496
Jennie Stokes, 336
Jerald, 277
Jerusha Pearl, 349
Jesse Robert, 276
Jesse Stephen, 351
Jewel Richards, 335

Dorroh,
Jim Ella Spickard, 372
Jimmie Bell, 352
Jochael Ruth, 367
Joe Barber, 276
Joe Cooper, 325
Joe Earl, 336
Joe Frank, 325, 326
Joe Lee, 276
Joel, 301, 349, 350, 322, 348
Joel Langston, 352
Joel Young, 334
Joetta Adams, 280
John, 110, 163, 169, 177, 232,
234, 237, 241, 244, 245, 248, 249
300, 306, 308, 482, 484, 488
John A. 281, 287, 397, 485,
487, 495
John Bunyan, 349
John F. 396, 414, 495
John Hazard, 267, 268
John Henry, 415, 416, 420
John Hunter, 259
John Hyle, 255
John Marion, 325
John Olive, 277
John Quinn, 325
John Richard, 367, 381
John Scribner, 381
John Thomas, 382
John Washburn, 277
John Wayne, 325
John Wesley, 363, 366
John William Stephen, 353
Jonathan Wesley, 359
Joseph Bell, 353
Joseph Dickson (Dixie) 421
Joseph Marshall, 330
Jaunita, 363
Jaunita J. Johnson, 330
Julia Ann, 254
Julia Elizabeth, 257
Julia H. 192
Julia Saxon, 414
June O. 326
Kate, 401
Kate Fuller, 397
Katherine, 287
Katherine Elizabeth, 335
Katherine Ethel Moran, 381
Kathleen, 349
Kathryne Glasscock, 278

Foster,
  Lutrola Levert, 254
  Marcus Lucillus, 254
  Silvia Lucile, 210
  Willie Sample, 254
Fowler,
  Cynthia Lynne, 136
  Eldie Toxie Dorroh, 328
  Mary Virginia, 328
  Myrtle, 132
Fox,
  Angeline, 348
  Dorcas Ann, 300, 313, 348
  Edna Opal, 357
  Elizabeth, 298
  Elizabeth Clayton Daniel, 298
  Emma Camilla, 357
  Fannie E. Pryor, 357
  Fred Tillman, 298
  Jacob, 348
  John Edward, 298
  John M., 348
  Joseph Spencer, 298
  Lillian Estelle, 358
  Martha, 348
  Mary Helen Tillman, 298
  Mary Lynne, 276
  Mary Melissa, 298
  Sarah, 307
  Sarah Temperance Atkinson, 298
  Susan Elizabeth, 298
  Thomas Sidney, 357
  Vera Sue Puckett, 298
  William Harris, 298
  William Spencer, 298
Franklin, 216
Franks,
  Emily, 412
  Gwendylon, 126
  Henry, 411
  Martha, 412
  Mary, 412
  Nannie, 411
  Susan Garrison 411
  W. Des, 411
Frazier,
  Eveline Elliott, 61
  Frank Norman, 61
  Hilda Marie, 424
  L. Frank, 61
  Lila Johnson, 61
  Mary Norman, 61

Frederick, Marilyn, 279
Free,
  Emma, 304
  Icie Willie Parker, 304
  Robert Earl, 304
Freel, Mary, 280
Freeman,
  Donna Jean, 189
  Elizabeth Dorroh, 361
  Hilma Jane, 189
  Jane Elizabeth England, 189
  Janet Ann, 189
  Jim, 361, 362
  M. S., 361
  Mollie Bice, 361, 362
  Rodney George, 189
  Sarah, 361
Freer, Sallie, 368
Frels,
  Donald, 385
  Mary Isabelle Laughter, 385
  Pierce Laughter, 385
  Richard, 385
  Suzanne, 385
  Walter, 385
Frentz, Georgine W., 255
Fretwell,
  Kenyon B., 325
  Minnie Florence Dorroh, 325
Friday, Carolyn, 409
Frost,
  Arthur Dickinson, 141
  Burl Bryan, 141
  Clara Morgan, 141
  Marion Morgan, 141
  Rachel, 361
  Vernice Louise, 141
Fulcher,
  Sudie Fuller, 57
  W. D., 57
Fulford, Eleanor, 181
Fuller,
  Alice, 102, 464
  David Andrew, 373
  Don E., 373
  Edwin, 57
  George, 102, 464
  Ida, 57
  Jacksey, 465
  James, 57
  June Johnson, 57
  Kate, 397

Manness, Maggie May Hulse, 317
Manning, Mary Frances, 324
Mannsdale, Miss., 260
Manring, Stephen, 7, 9, 10, 11
Maples,
    Mabel DuBose, 124
    Mary Lee, 124
    Parkie, 124
Marchese,
    Michael Watson, 260
    Robert Anthony, 260
    Sara Jane Law, 260.
Marchioness of Titchfield, 151
Marengo Co., 257
Marguart,
    Enid Katherine Dorroh, 376
    James, 376
Marion, Ala., 22, 40, 80, 120,
        132, 141, 164, 244, 474,
        514, 529, 530
Markham, Lewis, 429
Marks, Alice, 142
Marshall Co., Miss, 118
Martian,
    Capt. Nicholas, 11
    Elizabeth, 11
Martin, Tenn., 60, 61, 70
Martin,
    Betty Elizabeth, 401
    Charlotte, 229
    Elizabeth (Betty), 418
    Frank, 360
    Hattie Floyd, 56
    Henry, 359
    Jimmie, 360
    Julian F., 256
    Mary, 360
    Monica Jeanette, 256
    Nancy, 229
    Ollie, 360
    Press, 360
    Ras, 360
    Rebecca Dorroh, 359, 360
    Thomas, 359
    Tobie Roxanne, 256
    Vina Dale, 373
    William C., 359
    Willie, 360
Mary, Queen of Scots, 149, 150
Mary, Queen Regent, 149
Mashulaville, Miss., 285, 287
Mason, Annie Cunningham, 171

Mason,
    Charlie Bess, 409
    Christine, 409
    DeWitt King, 171
    Ernest, 409
    Evelyn Brock, 171
    Fannie Dorroh, 409
    Harriet Jane Meyers, 171
    John Dew, 171
    Lonnie, 407
    Mary Dew, 171
    Mary Jane, 171
    Nicholas Boddie, 171
Massey,
    Betty Jean, 132
    Julia Eloise (Judy) England, 189
    Robert Lee, 189
    Susan Michelle, 189
Masters, Juanita Moody, 84
Mathis,
    Clarence K., 328
    Fannie, 277
    Frances Abigail Shaw, 277
    Lellon Dorroh, 328
    Rufe, 328
    Thomas, 489
    Vera Mae, 328
Matlock,
    John, 366
    Lillian Dorroh, 366
    Phillip, 366
Matthews,
    B. W., 201
    Mary Sauls, 383
    Nancy Smith, 201
Mattoon, Ill., 180
Maul, Martha Jo, 406
Maverick, Tex., 183
Mayfield,
    Agnes, 19, 27
    Aimee, 262
    Alma, 262
    Alma Eaton Kimball, 39
    Andrew Middleton, 261
    Annie Clifton, 265
    Barbara Ann, 264
    Carolyn Inez, 264
    David Glen, 39
    Deborah Frances, 39
    Diana, 39
    Dorris Oneal, 262
    Elizabeth Britton, 264

Parker,
    Anna Sue, 316
    Beatrice, 304
    Bird, 302
    Cheryl, 316
    Clersie Thornton, 303
    Della Gordon, 304
    Dessie Beulah, 304
    Dolly Ardell, 305
    Eva Lois, 304
    George, 73
    George Belton, 304
    Helen Ruth, 306
    Herman, 304
    Honnie Kaye, 316
    Honnie O'Neal, 316
    Icie Willie, 304
    Inez, 304
    James Henry, 301
    James Hugh, 306
    Jeannine Britt, 306
    Jennie, 306
    Jesse, 316
    Jessie Mae, 321
    Joel Stephen, 306
    John Bascom, 305
    Kari Sue, 316
    Louis, 305
    Lucy Hannan, 306
    Margaret M., 302
    Marion Pearl, 316
    Martha Dorroh, 283
    Martha Melvina, 302
    Mary, 306
    Mary Jeter, 73
    Mary Orzula, 305
    Matilda, 302
    Mellie, 306
    Minnie Cork, 306
    Nancy Emily, 301
    Nancy White, 27
    Opal, 304
    Otis, 304
    Rebecca, 306
    Rebecca Dorroh, 301
    Rebecca Eliza, 304
    Richard, 452, 461
    Robert Hunt, 29
    Romulus Bragg, 28
    Ruby, 304
    Sarah Ann, 301
    Sidney Ethel, 316

Parker,
    Stephen Decatur, 302
    Velma Gordon, 305
    Victor, 283
    Victoria Hunt, 28
    William A., 301, 304
    Willie, 306
    Zelda Ann, 302
Parkerson and/or Parkinson,
    Matilda, 301
    Tom, 301
Parks,
    Amye Barnett, 392
    Annie Mae, 393
    Belva Howard, 393
    Catherine Roberson, 393
    Celest Hay, 392
    Eli Percy, 393
    Emma Pervie, 391
    Emma Gertrude Eckles, 391
    Emmett, 391
    Ernest Reginald, 392
    Ernestine, 392
    Estelle Jinks, 392
    Faye Burford, 392
    George Brice, 392
    Hazel Boatright, 393
    Henry Emmett, 392
    Jack, 391
    John Reeves, 391
    Jule Walter, 393
    Julian Keith, 393
    Kathleen, 393
    Lolia Zane, 392
    Mardge Mulligan, 392
    Martha Juliette, 391
    Mary, 392
    Mildred, 391
    Nellie, 391
    Ollie Whitfield, 393
    Oliver Wendell, 392
    Patsy Jean, 393
    Preasley Eugene, 393
    Preston, 392
    Ralph, 393
    Robbin, 391
    Ruby, 392
    Sedley Louis, 392
    Sonny, 391
    Verda Hay, 393
    Warford Scott, 393
    Warford Wayne, 393